TEXTBOOK

Equity and Trusts

CONSULTANT EDITOR: LORD TEMPLEMAN
EDITOR: MARGARET HALLIWELL
AIPM, LLB, Lecturer in Law, University of Manchester

OLD BAILEY PRESS

OLD BAILEY PRESS
200 Greyhound Road, London W14 9RY

1st edition 1997
Reprinted 1999

© Old Bailey Press Ltd 1997

Previous editions published under The
HLT Group Ltd.

ISBN 1 85836 213 X

British Library Cataloguing-in-Publication.
A CIP Catalogue record for this book is
available from the British Library.

Acknowledgement
The publishers and author would
like to thank the Incorporated
Council of Law Reporting for
England and Wales for kind
permission to reproduce extracts
from the Weekly Law Reports, and
Butterworths for their kind
permission to reproduce extracts
from the All England Law Reports.

Printed and bound in Great Britain

Contents

Preface

Old Bailey Press textbooks are written specifically for students. Whatever their course they will find our books clear and concise, providing comprehensive and up-to-date coverage. Written by specialists in their field, our textbooks are reviewed and updated on a regular basis. A companion Casebook, Revision WorkBook and Statutes are also published.

In addition to the updating that we undertake, we have included a chapter called 'Recent Cases' which includes the most significant new cases relating to the subject area. In order to assist the student extracts from the judgments and commentary, where appropriate, have been included. In many instances these cases highlight new interpretations of particular facets of existing law.

Knowledge of recent cases is extremely important for those studying for their examinations. It demonstrates not only an active interest in the law as it develops, but also the dynamic nature of the law which is constantly adapting to changing social and economic trends.

This *Equity and Trusts* textbook is designed for use by both LLB and CPE/LLDip students. While the bulk of the material it contains is relevant to both courses, there are several chapters, for example, those dealing with equitable doctrines, which are outside the parameters of some syllabuses. Each student should refer to his or her own syllabus to confirm which chapters need to be covered. The book will also be of use to those studying Equity and Trusts for another course.

The most important and interesting case arising recently was, undoubtedly, the decision of the House of Lords in *Westdeutsche-Landesbank Girozentrale* v *Islington Borough Council* [1996] 2 All ER 961. Statutory developments have also been incorporated.

The Trustee Investments (Division of Trust Fund) Order 1996 (SI 1996/845) came into force on 11 May 1996 and the Trusts of Land and Appointment of Trustees Act 1996 came into force on 1 January 1997.

The law is stated as at 1 January 1997.

Table of Cases

Table of Statutes

1

Introduction to Trusts

1.1 Definition of a trust

1.2 Classification of trusts

1.3 Trusts distinguished from other relationships

1.4 Powers of appointment

1.5 Relevance of trusts today

1.1 Definition of a trust

Many attempts have been made to define a trust but no definition is entirely satisfactory. The variety of trusts, as seen from their classification in section 1.2, leads to definitions which omit some of the types, or are vague and unhelpful. Therefore no definition is proposed here, merely an explanation of what a trust can be.

The trust is probably the most important invention made by equity and it calls for distinction between the legal interest or estate and the equitable interest in property. Under the trust the legal title will be vested in the trustees and the equitable title in the beneficiaries under the trust. This might arise where S (settlor) transfers land to T1 and T2 (trustees) to hold the land on trust for the benefit of A, B and C (beneficiaries). Diagramatically the position will be:

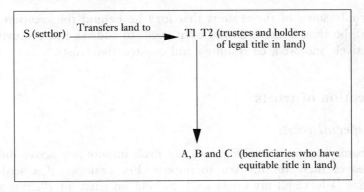

S (settlor) —— Transfers land to ——▶ T1 T2 (trustees and holders of legal title in land)

A, B and C (beneficiaries who have equitable title in land)

The trust does not interfere with the legal position of title to the land; at law the title is in T1 and T2, since it was conveyed to them by S. However, equity recognises that the title was not conveyed to T1 and T2 for their own use or benefit, but to be held for the benefit of A, B & C as the settlor intended. The trustees are considered as having a bare legal title only, and the benefits of the land will accrue to the beneficiaries. By this device the courts are able to uphold essential doctrines of common law but give effect to the true intention of S.

This example deals with land but a trust may also comprise personal property or equitable interests in property (this being a sub-trust). If it is a trust of an equitable interest then there is no legal title in the trustees as in the diagram, but they will hold the equitable title on trust. The complications that may arise in such instances are considered in Chapter 3. In certain cases such as charitable or discretionary trusts, the beneficiaries have no equitable title in the sense that they can enforce them, although the trustees have no more than legal title as usual.

Many reasons may lie behind the creation of a trust, including the following:

1. Settlor may wish to provide for his spouse and family after death. This might arise where the settlor makes a will appointing, say, his solicitor and accountant as trustees, to hold his assets on trust for the benefit of his wife for life, remainder to his children. The trust may be imposed if the settlor feels his wife and children lack experience and expertise to deal with the property themselves. The trustees will be able to avoid unnecessary losses or dissipation of the property.
2. Settlor wishes to provide for his children in a particular manner. For example, a trust may be created to provide a handicapped child with financial security, or to provide funds for the education of the settlor's children, or on their marriage.
3. Settlor wishes to pass funds to members of his family who are financially irresponsible, such as a spendthrift son. A trust, especially a protective trust, can be used to prevent the funds being wasted by the beneficiary.
4. Settlor wishes to take advantage of tax concessions which are granted to trusts created for certain purposes or objects.

These are only some of the reasons that may lie behind the creation of a trust. Further, as will be shown, these do not even begin to address those situations where a trust is effectively imposed, eg resulting and constructive trusts.

1.2 Classification of trusts

Simple and special trusts

A simple, or bare, trust is one which does not itself impose any active duties on the trustees but leaves these for the law to impose. For example, if a settlor made a short will stating 'I leave all my estate to T to hold on trust for B', this would be a simple trust. The trustees' duties here are not stated, whereas with a special trust its nature is made clear. For example, '£20,000 to T on trust to pay the income to B or C at his discretion' would be a special trust, as the trustee's duties are defined in the trust deed. The position is similar where the trust is 'Blackacre to T upon trust for sale for B': see *Re Cunningham and Frayling* [1891] 2 Ch 567.

Statutory trusts prior to 1 January 1997

These are created or implied by statute and the following are the most important examples:

1. *Section 33 Administration of Estates Act 1925* – the property of a person who dies intestate, that is, without making a will, vests in his personal representatives on trust for sale.
2. *Section 34 Law of Property Act (LPA) 1925* – where land is conveyed to persons in undivided shares, it will vest in the first four named in the conveyance upon trust for sale.
3. *Section 36 LPA 1925* – where a legal estate is held by two or more persons as joint tenants, it is held on a trust for sale.
4. *Section 19 LPA 1925* – where there is a conveyance of a legal estate to an infant, the estate is held on statutory trusts for him until he comes of age.

The Trusts of Land and Appointment of Trustees Act 1996

The effect of this statute, which came into force on 1 January 1997, is that any trust of property which consists of or includes land now becomes a trust of land. According to s1(2)(b), all trusts for sale in existence at the commencement of the Act are converted into trusts of land. The circumstances when a trust is imposed by statute remain as above but, following the recommendation of the Law Commission in its report on *Transfer of Land: Trusts of Land* Law Com no 181, the Act replaces the dual systems of settled land and trusts for sale.

Express trusts

An express trust arises where a settlor makes a declaration that certain property is to be held upon trust for certain persons or objects. The term is commonly used to refer to cases where the trust is created for the benefit of private individuals. The requirements for such trusts are dealt with in Chapters 2 and 3. An example would be where S executes a trust deed declaring that T1 and T2 are to hold Blackacre upon trust for the benefit of A, B and C. Express trusts may be divided into further categories.

Executed and executory trusts
These terms refer to the creation of the trust, not to whether it has or has not been

carried out. A trust is merely executory if the settlor declares an intention to create a trust of property but has not set out in detail the precise interests of the beneficiaries. A trust may be created in this way but the precise terms must be outlined in a further document. A trust is said to be executed when all its terms have been set out so that no further documents are necessary, nor is the court required to make out from general expressions what the settlor's intentions were: see *Egerton* v *Earl Brownlow* (1853) 4 HLC 1. For a recent example of the distinction between executed and executory trusts see the decision in *Davis* v *Richards & Wallington Industries* [1990] 1 WLR 1511.

Completely and incompletely constituted trusts

A trust is completely constituted when the settlor, having made his declaration of trust, either declares himself trustee or conveys the property concerned to the trustees in accordance with the formalities laid down by law for the transfer of that type of property: see *Milroy* v *Lord* (1862) 4 De GF & J 264. A trust into which the property has not been transferred in this way is said to be incompletely constituted. In strict terms there is no such thing as an incompletely constituted trust, because equity will not, as a general rule, recognise or enforce such trusts: see *Richards* v *Delbridge* (1874) LR 18 Eq 11. This general rule, and the established exceptions, are dealt with in Chapter 4.

Private and public trusts

Express trusts may be private, that is, they are created for the benefit of an individual or a class. As will be seen in Chapter 2 there are strict rules as to the ascertaining of beneficiaries under such trusts.

A public trust is one which is intended to promote the public benefit or welfare in some way. Such trusts are often referred to as charitable trusts and are dealt with in Chapter 10.

Discretionary and fixed trusts

A discretionary trust is one where the trustees are given a discretion as to the payment of income or capital or both, to certain beneficiaries or all the beneficiaries under the trust. The beneficiaries under such a trust will only receive those benefits over which the trustees have a discretion, if the discretion is exercised in their favour. A fixed trust provides for fixed interests for the beneficiaries, and the trustees have no powers to alter or withhold these unless the law permits them to do so. An example of a discretionary trust is: '£20,000 to T1 and T2 to pay any or all of the capital and income to such of my children as they shall in their absolute discretion select'. An example of a fixed trust is: '£20,000 to T1 and T2 to hold the capital and income for my children in equal shares'. See Chapter 2.

Protective trusts

These are trusts set up to prevent a beneficiary disposing of all or any of his beneficial interests so long as the trust subsists. Such trusts are designed to ensure that, for example, a spendthrift beneficiary does not dissipate the trust fund. For example, a trust in terms: '£50,000 to T1 and T2 to hold upon protective trusts for X' would be sufficient, and would invoke the provisions of s33 Trustee Act 1925. These trusts are considered further in Chapter 2.

Secret trusts
A secret trust usually arises under a will and is intended to enable provision to be made for an object or purpose without this being revealed on the face of the will. Such trusts divide into fully secret and half secret trusts. The former appear as an absolute gift on the face of the will and the beneficiary under the will is informed of the trust outside the will: see *Wallgrave* v *Tebbs* (1855) 2 K & J 313. The latter appear as a trust on the face of the will but the details of the trust are revealed outside the will, for example, '£10,000 to X upon trust for the purposes I have communicated to him': see *Blackwell* v *Blackwell* [1929] AC 318. There is still some dispute as to the proper classification of secret trusts. These matters are considered further in Chapter 5.

Charitable trusts
These are public trusts designed to promote some object recognised by the courts as being of benefit to the community in a way the court regards as charitable. They are intended to confer benefits on the community at large rather than a few private individuals. Their position is considered in detail in Chapter 10.

Purpose trusts
These are private trusts intended to benefit purposes rather than beneficiaries, and are sometimes referred to as trusts of imperfect obligation. As a general rule they are void. The law of private trusts is based on the concept of trusts being created for persons rather than purposes, so that a trust to promote sport or to promote capitalism is void. There are a number of exceptions: see *Re Endacott* [1960] Ch 232. Many trusts which fall to be treated as purpose trusts and are therefore void, arise because they are failed attempts to create a charitable trust. See Chapter 9.

Resulting trusts

Some writers distinguish between implied and resulting trusts, but it seems that they are different labels for the same kind of trust. They arise out of the presumed intention of the settlor where he has failed to express his intentions adequately or at all. An implied or resulting trust would arise if a settlor created a trust of £100,000 'for A for life'. This does not indicate what is to happen to the money on A's death, and equity steps in by presuming he intended that the money should result to himself or his estate on A's death: see *Re Abbot* [1900] 2 Ch 326. A resulting trust may arise where two or more persons have purchased property in the name of one or jointly, and have contributed in various proportions and ways to the purchase price. Equity will presume that there is a resulting trust in favour of all who have contributed to the extent of their respective contributions: see *Gissing* v *Gissing* [1971] AC 886, and Chapter 6.

Constructive trusts

Constructive trusts are imposed by the court where the conduct of a party makes it unjust that he should retain the whole or part of the beneficial interest in certain property for himself. The intentions of the parties are irrelevant to the imposition of a constructive trust because it arises by operation of law. For example, a constructive trust will be imposed on a fiduciary who tries to make a secret profit from his fiduciary position; it is imposed whether or not he realises this: see *Keech* v *Sandford* (1726) 2 Eq Cas 741.

1.3 Trusts distinguished from other relationships

Bailments

Bailments and trusts differ in important respects, even though they appear to have some similar characteristics. Bailments were recognised at common law, though trusts were not. Bailments could only be made of chattels, while trusts could be made of all forms of property. Bailments do not pass the legal title in the property bailed to the bailee; the legal title remains in the bailor. But the bailee acquires mere possession, and this gives him certain possessory rights in the chattels bailed and he can apply these rights for his own benefit. In a trust the legal title is in the trustee. Generally it is a bare legal title with the trustee having no rights in the trust property, merely duties and obligations in dealing with it for the benefit of the beneficiaries. For example, if X lends a book to Y, the legal title in the book remains in X; Y merely acquires possession of the book for the purpose for which it was lent, presumably to be read. As title does not pass to Y then, as a general rule, if Y sold the book to Z, Z would not acquire title in it as Y had no title to give him. But, if X gave the book to Y to hold on trust for his daughter A, Y has only a bare legal title. However, if Y sold the book to Z he would pass a title to him. The book could only be recovered from Z if he was not a bona fide purchaser for value without notice.

Agency

A principal/agent relationship has one major similarity to a trustee/beneficiary relationship, but there are also important differences. Both relationships are fiduciary in the sense that the agent and the trustee must not make secret profits, and have a duty of good faith. The important difference is that a trust relationship is proprietary while an agency relationship is personal. Usually the beneficiary under a trust has equitable ownership in the trust property while the trustee has only a bare legal title. An agent does not have his principal's property vested in him but only has possession of it. This stems from the fact that the agency relationship was recognised at law: see *Cave* v *MacKenzie* (1877) 46 LJ Ch 564. The distinction between a trust relationship and an agency relationship is best illustrated by the consequences to a beneficiary or principal if the trustee or agent is insolvent. If a trustee holds £10,000 upon trust, his insolvency will not affect that £10,000 and his creditors cannot have it to satisfy their claims. If the trustee has applied the money in breach of trust the beneficiary may 'trace' in equity to recover it: see *Chase Manhattan Bank* v *Israel–British Bank* [1981] Ch 105 and he may also recover any profits on it. Thus, a beneficiary's claim to recover the trust property will not be affected by the trustee's insolvency. But, whether the insolvency of an agent will affect the rights of the principal to recover money in the agent's hands is more complex. If the agent is bound to apply money he has received in a particular way or is bound to keep it separate, he will be regarded as a trustee of it: see *Burdick* v *Garrick* (1870) LR 5 Ch App 233. But, if the agent is entitled to mix the money he has received with his own, he will be a debtor to his principal, who will only have a personal claim against him. The distinction between the proprietary nature of a trust relationship and the personal nature of an agency relationship was brought out in the Court of Appeal decision in *Lister & Co* v *Stubbs* (1890) 45 Ch D 1. In that case Stubbs was a foreman of the Listers employed to buy materials for their silk spinning business. Stubbs corruptly received large commissions from those whom he dealt with on behalf of Listers, and much of this money was invested in land and shares. Listers sought to restrain Stubbs by an injunction from dealing with the investments, basing their claim on the assumption that Stubbs was a trustee for Listers. This was rejected; there was only a personal relationship which at most gave rise to a debtor/creditor obligation at this stage of the case, and until a final decree was made. As Cotton LJ said:

> '... in my opinion this is not the money of the Plaintiffs, so as to make the Defendant a trustee of it for them, but it is money acquired in such a way that, according to all the rules applicable to such a case, the Plaintiffs when they bring the action to a hearing, can get an order against the Defendant for the payment of that money to them. That is to say there is a debt due from the Defendant to the Plaintiffs in consequence of the corrupt bargain which he entered into; but the money which he has received under that bargain cannot, in the view which I take, be treated as being money of the Plaintiffs ... '

See also *Re Attorney-General's Reference (No 1 of 1985)* [1986] 2 All ER 219 where it was claimed that an employer had proprietary rights in secret profits made by an employee using the employer's premises and facilities. The claim was rejected; there were personal rights only.

However, this apparently illogical distinction has been disapproved of by the Privy Council in the recent decision in *Attorney-General for Hong Kong* v *Reid and Others* [1993] 3 WLR 1143. The facts, in brief, involved Reid accepting (admitted by

Reid) various bribes in breach of his fiduciary duty as a Crown servant in Hong Kong. The Crown sought to pursue that money by way of actions against houses purchased with it in New Zealand. The houses were in the names of Reid's wife and his solicitor. After a detailed analysis of the caselaw the Privy Council ruled that (per Lord Templeman):

> 'The decision in *Lister & Co* v *Stubbs* is not consistent with the principles that a fiduciary must not be allowed to benefit from his own breach of duty, that the fiduciary should account for the bribe as soon as he receives it and that equity regards as done that which ought to be done. From these principles it would appear to follow that the bribe and the property from time to time representing the bribe are held on a constructive trust for the person injured. A fiduciary remains personally liable for the amount of the bribe [on a debtor-creditor basis] if, in the event, the value of the property then recovered by the injured person proved to be less than that amount.'

Whilst the decision is only that of the Privy Council and, theoretically, not binding in England and Wales it will almost certainly be followed in the future. Hence, whilst the debtor-creditor remedy remains available the decision opens up the more far reaching opportunity of imposing a constructive trust and, for example, the ability to trace the trust property (ie an action in rem and not solely in personam).

Contract

A contract gives rise to personal obligations which are enforceable at law or in equity, while a trust gives rise to a proprietary relationship. The two concepts are quite different. A contract will not be enforceable unless there is consideration, or under seal, but a trust may be enforced by a volunteer (someone who has not given consideration) provided it is completely constituted. The trust and contract may often come into close relationship with each other because a contract may be made to create a trust. This can occur where S covenants with T1 and T2 to settle Blackacre upon trust for the benefit of B. The problems that arise if S refuses to fulfil the covenant are considered in Chapter 4.

Interests under a will or intestacy

If a testator dies leaving a will under which he appoints A and B his executors and leaves C a legacy of £10,000, the issues arise whether A and B are trustees for C, and whether C's interest is to be treated in the same way as a beneficial interest under a trust. There are many similarities between this relationship and the trust relationship but their origins are different. The trust was developed by the Court of Equity, while the administration of wills and distribution on intestacy were developed by the Ecclesiastical Court. The work of the Ecclesiastical Court in this respect was taken over by the Court of Chancery at a later period. The administration of estates and trusts by the same court has led to much assimilation. The following points should be noted on the example above:

Are A and B trustees for C?

A clear answer cannot be given because in some respects they are while in other respects they are not, and much will depend upon the circumstances of each case. The similarities between trustees and executors are that both are under almost identical fiduciary duties, and executors are for most purposes treated as trustees under the Trustee Act 1925. The main differences between these positions are:

1. An executor holds office for life and may not retire; he can only relinquish office with leave of the court. A trustee may retire under either ss36 or 39 Trustee Act 1925.
2. The statutory power to appoint new trustees under s40 Trustee Act 1925 do not apply to executors.
3. Trustees are only trustees of the trust to which they were appointed; an executor may find himself involved in the administration of several estates by reason of the chain of representation under s7 Administration of Estates Act 1925.
4. One of several executors has greater power to dispose of property than trustees. A single executor can pass title to a chattel but trustees must act jointly in such instances: see *Attenborough* v *Solomon* [1913] AC 76.
5. There are different limitation periods for executors and trustees. Actions for breach of trust have a six-year limitation period, whereas there is a 12-year limitation period for claims against executors in respect of personal estate: see Limitation Act 1980.

What is the nature of C's interest under the will?

An executor is not a trustee of the benefits conferred by a will, and the beneficiaries do not acquire equitable or beneficial interests in the legacies and bequests made to them at the moment of the testator's death. Instead, the executor takes both the legal and equitable title to the property, subject to his fiduciary duties to the beneficiaries and also the creditors of the testator, for whose benefit he will administer the estate: see *Commissioner of Stamp Duties* v *Livingston* [1965] AC 694. The nature of the interest of a beneficiary under a will is a right to require the estate to be duly administered. This right is a chose in action which is transmissible: see *Re Leigh's WT* [1970] Ch 277.

Powers

A power is an authority given to a person either by instrument or by statute to deal with or dispose of property in which he may have no beneficial interest. Powers come in two main forms, those which give a power of disposition over property, such as powers of appointment, and those which give a power to deal with property in a particular manner. Under a power of appointment the owner of certain property (the donor of the power) may give another (the donee of the power) power to appoint the property to some third parties. The donee of the power is sometimes referred to as 'the appointor' and the beneficiary under the power as 'the appointee'. An example of a power of appointment would be '£50,000 to A for life with remainder to whomsoever he shall appoint'. Powers of appointment are frequently given in trusts or settlements to enable the trustees to provide funds for the beneficiaries in circumstances unforseeable when the trusts were set up. For example, trustees may have a power under a trust to appoint to the settlor's children or grandchildren, which might be used when family changes occur through births, marriages and deaths. Powers to deal with property in a particular manner are frequently encountered in trust instruments. They include powers of sale, investment, maintenance and advancement, and may also be found outside a trust, for example, a power of attorney.

A power, whether it be a power of appointment or otherwise, differs from a trust in a number of important ways including:

1. A trust is imperative while a power is discretionary. This means that if a trust directs that the trustees do something, they are bound to do it. The holder of a power is under no such obligation. This is illustrated by the distinction between a trust for sale and a power of sale. If shares are left to executors upon trust for sale, the trustees must sell. The fact that the executors may have a power to postpone sale does not alter matters as it only gives a discretion as to when they should sell and not as to whether they should sell at all. But if shares were held upon trust and the trustees given a power of sale, they could decide whether they should sell, and no obligation to sell would fall upon them.
2. A trust is always equitable whereas a power may in some cases be legal, such as a power of attorney to convey land on behalf of a vendor. However, the majority of powers are equitable. Since 1925 powers of appointment may only subsist behind a trust or settlement, as they operate in equity only: see s1(7) Law of Property Act 1925.
3. A trustee is always under a fiduciary duty, while the holder of a power may or may not be under a fiduciary duty in relation to the power.
4. A power may be released by the holder but a trustee may not release his trust.

1.4 Powers of appointment

Powers of appointment which were referred to in *Powers* above fall into three main categories:

1. *General powers*. The donee of the power is not subject to any restrictions as to who he shall exercise the power in favour of. For example, a will or trust may contain a devise 'to A for life with remainder to whomsoever he shall appoint'. A may appoint to anyone, including himself, so that a general power may be regarded as tantamount to absolute ownership.
2. *Special powers*. The donee of the power is restricted to exercising it among a class

or description of persons designated by the terms of the power. For example, '£10,000 to such of A's children as he (A) shall appoint'. The donee of the power may himself be a member of a class in whose favour the power may be exercised.

3. *Hybrid powers.* These are powers under which the donee may appoint to anyone except a certain class or certain description of person, for example, '£50,000 to X to whomsoever he shall appoint except my brothers and sisters and their descendants '. Hybrid powers are so called because they do not fit into the first two categories; the class is restricted by exclusion so they cannot be general, and it is not sufficiently confined by definition to be regarded as special: see *Re Hay's Settlement* [1982] 1 WLR 202.

When a power of appointment is given to a trustee under the terms of a trust instrument two issues may arise:

1. Whether what appears to be a power also involves a trust, ie a power in the nature of a trust.
2. What criteria the trustee should apply in deciding who are the objects of the power in whose favour it may be exercised, ie certainty of objects. It is worth noting that trustees who hold a power of appointment or any other power are under a fiduciary duty to consider whether it is appropriate to exercise it even though they are under no obligation to do so. In *Re Gulbenkian* [1970] AC 508 Lord Reid said:

'It may be true that when a mere power is given to an individual he is under no duty to exercise it or even to consider whether he should exercise it. But, when a power is given to trustees as such, it appears to me that the situation must be different. A settlor or testator who entrusts a power to his trustees must be relying on them in their fiduciary capacity so they cannot simply push aside the power and refuse to consider whether it ought in their judgment to be exercised.'

The reference to 'mere power' is one that covers a power given to the donee which need not be exercised; indeed there is in fact no obligation or fiduciary duty on the donee to exercise the power at all. An example would be a general power of appointment: see *Re Combe* [1925] Ch 210.

The problem of deciding if a power involves a trust is really a matter of construction of the words used. Sometimes a provision in a will or settlement may be referred to as a power when on construction it is in fact a trust – a power in the nature of a trust. This difficulty has frequently arisen in cases where there is a fund to such members of a class as A shall select. As already stated, A would have no obligation to make a selection and the objects of the power could not force him to do so. But if A fails to make a selection, the issue arises whether the objects are entitled to the fund in any event in equal shares on the basis that there is a trust. The leading case on this point is *Burrough* v *Philcox* (1840) 5 My & Cr 72 where a testator gave his surviving child a power 'to dispose of all my real and personal estates amongst my nephews and nieces or their children, either all to one of them, or to as many of them as my surviving child shall think proper'. The surviving child failed to make any appointment but it was held that the fund should be divided equally among the objects because there was in fact a trust in favour of them subject to the power of appointment. On this Lord Cottenham said:

> 'When there appears a general intention in favour of a class, and a particular intention in favour of individuals of a class to be selected by another person, and the particular intention fails, from that selection not being made, the Court will carry into effect the general intention in favour of the class.'

In other words the rule of construction to be applied is whether the settlor intended the objects to benefit in any event, and merely gave a power of appointment to enable the beneficial interests to be altered if circumstances required this. Much will depend on the words used in the instrument. Cases in which the courts refused to construe a power in the nature of a trust arising include: *Re Weekes' Settlement* [1897] 1 Ch 289 where a testatrix gave her husband 'power to dispose of all such property by will amongst our children'; *Re Combe* [1925] Ch 210 'in trust for such person or persons as my said son ... shall by will appoint', and *Re Perowne* [1951] Ch 785 in which a testatrix left all her estate to her husband for life and added: 'Knowing that he will make arrangements for the disposal of my estate, according to my wishes, for the benefit of my family.' Another way of looking at these cases is whether there is a gift over in default of appointment: see *Re Wills's Trust Deed* [1964] Ch 219. If there is a gift over in default of appointment then no trust on the failure of the exercise of the power can be inferred; for example '£10,000 to A to appoint among such of my children as he shall select and in default of appointment to X': see *Re Sprague* (1880) 43 LT 236. The reasoning is that the donor of the power has anticipated its possible failure, or non–use, and provided for an alternative.

In dealing with the problem of what test is applied in determining who are the objects of the power, a distinction has to be drawn between cases where the power is given to trustees 'as such' so that they must exercise it in a fiduciary capacity, and cases where the power is given to a person who is not in a fiduciary position in exercising it. It appears that in the former case the power will be valid only if 'you can with certainty say whether any given individual is or is not a member of the class' per Lord Upjohn in *Re Gulbenkian* [1970] AC 508. This is known as the 'individual ascertainability' rule. In the case of other powers it seems that no such tests are applicable and the width of the power will not always affect its validity. The court will ensure that the holder of the power exercises it in accordance with the provisions of the instrument creating it. These principles were summarised by Megarry V-C in *Re Hay's Settlement* [1982] 1 WLR 202:

> 'First, it is plain that if a power of appointment is given to a person who is not in a fiduciary position, there is nothing in the width of the power which invalidates it per se. The power may be a special power with a large class of persons as objects. The power

may be what is called a "hybrid" power or an "intermediate" power, authorising appointment to anyone save a specified number or class of persons; or the power may be a general power. Whichever it is, there is nothing in the number of persons to whom the appointment may be made which will invalidate it. The difficulty comes when the power is given to trustees as such, in that the number of objects may interact with the fiduciary duties of the trustees and their control by the court ...

... second ... the extent of the fiduciary obligations of trustees who have a mere power vested in them, and how far the court exercises control over them in relation to that power. In the case of a trust, of course, the trustee is bound to execute it, and if he does not the court will see to its execution. A mere power is very different. Normally, the trustee is not bound to exercise it, and the court will not compel him to do so. That, however, does not mean that he can ... ignore it, for normally he must from time to time consider whether or not to exercise the power, and the court may direct him to do this.

When he does exercise the power, he must of course (as in the case of all trusts and powers) confine himself to what is authorised, and not go beyond it. But that is not the only restriction. Whereas a person who is not in a fiduciary position is free to exercise the power in any way that he wishes, unhampered by any fiduciary duties, a trustee to whom, as such, a power is given is bound by the duties of his office in exercising that power to do so in a responsible manner according to its purpose. It is not enough for him to refrain from acting capriciously; he must do more. He must 'make such a survey of the range of objects or possible beneficiaries' as will enable him to carry out his fiduciary duty. He must find out the permissible area of selection and then consider responsibly, in individual cases, whether a contemplated beneficiary was within the power and whether in relation to the possible claimants, a particular grant was appropriate, per Lord Wilberforce in *Re Baden (No 1)* [1971] AC 424 ...

The last proposition, relating to the survey and consideration, at first sight gives rise to some difficulty. It is now well settled that no mere power is invalidated by it being impossible to ascertain every object of the power; provided the language is clear enough to make it possible to say whether any given individual is an object of the power, it need not be possible to compile a complete list of every object ... '

A power of appointment must be exercised within the limits laid down by the donor of the power; any exercise of it beyond those limits is void. If the power is exercised in favour of several objects some of which are outside its limits, the court will, if possible, sever the invalid excess: see *Churchill* v *Churchill* (1887) LR 5 Eq 44. For example, if A was given a special power of appointment over a fund in favour of his children and exercised the power in favour of his son and his nephew, the latter part is void and would be severed. Apart from the rule that the power must be exercised within its limits, it is also necessary that it should be exercised bona fide; any fraudulent exercise of the power will be void. This may arise in the following ways:

1. Where the appointment is made in a manner which is primarily intended to benefit the appointor. In *Hinchinbroke* v *Seymour* (1789) 1 Bro CC 395, a father who had a special power over property in favour of his children exercised it in favour of an infant child who was ailing and likely to die. The exercise was void as it was made with the purpose of benefiting the father as next of kin on the child's death intestate.
2. Where the appointment is made to an object of the power but the intent behind

it is to benefit non-objects. In *Re Dick* [1953] Ch 343 an appointment was made to the appointor's sister coupled with a moral obligation that the sister should pay an annuity to a family caring for the appointor. This was regarded as fraudulent as the sister was unlikely in the circumstances to resist the moral obligation.

3. Where the appointment is made in pursuance to a prior agreement with the appointee as to what he shall do with the proceed: see *Vatcher* v *Paull* [1915] AC 372.

The distinction between powers of appointment and discretionary trusts is often very fine and difficult to draw; this is especially so given the all too common mistake of the terms trust, fiduciary powers and powers being seen as one and the same. However, the distinction lies in the main difference between trusts and powers – the former are imperative while the latter are not. These matters are considered in the section on discretionary trusts in Chapter 2.

1.5 Relevance of trusts today

Trusts are perhaps more important today than they have been at any time in the past. However, their functions, and uses, have been modified by legislation. Tax laws have made some trusts less popular and disadvantageous, for example, inheritance tax has been particularly severe on discretionary trusts while income tax relief for charitable trusts has encouraged a growth in their use.

Private trusts are used in relation to large settlements of land and in providing for the settlor's family:

1. By virtue of s27 Settled Land Act 1925 a conveyance in favour of a minor (regardless as to whether or not it is for value) does not convey a legal estate to the minor; rather it will operate as an agreement for valuable consideration for a settlement in favour of the minor, with the land being held in trust for him.

2. A settlor may impose a private trust either during the lifetime or in his will to provide for his wife for the remainder of her life and for his children.

3. A trust may be imposed by a settlor to prevent property being dissipated by wastrels, especially where his children are irresponsible or where persons concerned are bankrupt.

Many commercial organisations use trusts to invest money to provide pensions for present and past employees or to provide benefits if the employees should suffer illness or disability leading to premature retirement: see *McPhail* v *Doulton* and *Dingle* v *Turner* (below). The funds of trade unions and unincorporated associations may also be held on trust for members.

In business trusts are used in investment, for example, unit trusts, which invest in stocks and shares to provide a return on deposits made to them by persons with small savings.

Where a husband and wife or an unmarried couple wish to purchase a house in their joint names, then a trust is necessary, as a joint tenancy can only exist behind a statutory trust.

Many people set up trusts in their wills in order to provide for members of their family and others to whom they have a moral obligation, after their death, for example, a secret or half-secret trust to provide for the mistress and illegitimate child of the testator, or a trust to provide an income for his wife and/or children after his death.

When a person dies intestate, under the Administration of Estates Act 1925 a trust is automatically imposed, comprising all the intestate's property. This is done for convenience to enable the estate to be administered properly and smoothly.

Charitable trusts provide for various objects which are generally recognised as being for the good of society as a whole, such as education, religion and the relief of poverty. Such trusts obtain relief from taxes provided they apply their income and capital for charitable purposes.

Where a trust is not expressly set up, the law may often presume one. These are constructive trusts capable of arising, for example, where a person in a fiduciary position abuses that position to his personal gain. The gain will in such circumstances be held on trust by that person for the proper objects concerned. These types of trust are becoming increasingly important in today's business and commercial climate.

2

The Three Certainties

2.1 Introduction

2.2 Certainty of words or intention

2.3 Certainty of subject-matter

2.4 Certainty of objects

2.5 Nature of discretionary and protective trusts

2.1 Introduction

The creation of an express private trust involves three main stages: satisfying the three certainties; fulfilling any formal requirements laid down by statute for the creation of the trust; and transferring the subject-matter of the trust to the trustees by the appropriate formal method laid down by law. The second and third of these stages are considered in Chapters 3 and 4.

The court will not recognise a transaction as involving the creation of an express private trust unless the three certainties are satisfied. These are rules which are intended to ensure that there is certainty about intention to create a trust, that there is certainty about what the trust is to include in the way of property, and that there is certainty about who the trust was intended to benefit. All three certainties must be fulfilled. The need for these three certainties has been stated in several cases but the dictum of Lord Langdale MR in *Knight* v *Knight* (1840) 3 Beav 148 is frequently cited. He said:

> 'As a general rule, it has been laid down, that when property is given absolutely to any person, and the same person is, by the giver who has the power to command, recommended, or entreated or wished, to dispose of that property in favour of another, the recommendation, entreaty or wish shall be held to create a trust. First, if the words were so used, that upon the whole, they ought to be construed as imperative; secondly, if the subject of the recommendation or wish be certain; and thirdly, if the objects or persons intended to have the benefit of the recommendation or wish also be certain.'

2.2 Certainty of words or intention

The settlor must be shown to have intended a trust before the court will hold that one has been created. In most cases this will be a matter of looking at words used in a trust deed or a will to see if they can be construed as a trust. No particular form of words need be used and it is not necessary to use the word 'trust'. The court will look at the words used to see if the obligation on the alleged trustee is sufficiently imperative as to amount to a trust. The use of the word 'trust' although unnecessary is advisable as it will leave little room for doubt as to the settlor's intentions.

In the 18th century and the early part of the 19th century the Court of Chancery quite readily construed precatory words as creating a trust. Words in a will or deed accompanying a gift which expressed the donor's wish, hope, desire or confidence that the donee should deal with the property in a particular way were upheld as creating a trust. The attitude of the court changed in 1871 with the Court of Appeal decision in *Lambe* v *Eames* (1871) 6 Ch App 597. In that case a testator left his estate to his widow 'to be at her disposal in any way she may think best, for the benefit of herself and her family'. The court refused to treat the gift as one upon trust to the widow; it was an absolute gift to her. In giving judgment James LJ observed on the older cases cited to him supporting the contention of a trust: 'I could not help feeling that the officious kindness of the Court of Chancery in interposing trusts where in many cases the father of the family never meant to create trusts, must have been a cruel kindness indeed'.

A leading case in the courts' approach to precatory words is *Re Adams and The Kensington Vestry* (1884) 27 Ch D 394 in which a testator left all his estate 'unto and to the absolute use of my wife ... in full confidence that she will do what is right as to the disposal thereof between my children, either in her lifetime or by will after her decease'. The Court of Appeal held the gift to be absolute. Cotton LJ added:

> 'It seems to me to be perfectly clear what the testator intended. He leaves his wife his property absolutely, but what was in his mind was this: I am the head of the family – my children: my widow will succeed me when I die and I wish to put her in the position I occupied as the person who is to provide for my children ... '

On the issue of whether precatory words could create a trust he said:

> 'I have no hesitation in saying myself, that I think some of the older authorities went a great deal too far in holding that some particular words appearing in a will were sufficient to create a trust. Undoubtedly, confidence, if the rest of the context shows that a trust is intended, may make a trust, but what we have to look at is the whole of the will which we have to construe, and if the confidence is that she will do what is right as regards the disposal of the property, I cannot say that that is, on the true construction of the will, a trust imposed upon her. Having regard to the later decisions, we must not extend the old cases in any way ... '

The words used to create a trust must, in the light of *Re Adams and The Kensington Vestry*, make it plain that a trust is intended. Precatory words are unlikely to be sufficent to establish this intention in the majority of cases, as the following cases show. In all of them it was held that no trust was created by the precatory words used:

1. *Re Diggles* (1888) 39 Ch D 253 'it is my desire that she allows (X) an annuity of £25 during her life'.
2. *Re Williams* [1897] 2 Ch 12 'in the fullest trust and confidence that she will carry out my wishes in the following particulars'.
3. *Re Hamilton* [1895] 2 Ch 370. 'I wish them to bequeath the same between the families of (X) and (Y)'.
4. *Re Conolly* [1910] 1 Ch 219. 'I specially desire that the sums herewith bequeathed shall ... be specifically left by the legatees to such charitable institutions ... as my sisters may select, and in such proportions as they may determine ... '.
5. *Re Hill* [1923] 2 Ch 259 'for the benefit of themselves and their respective families'.

It should be noted that in these cases the words were held not to create a trust in the particular context. As Cotton LJ's judgment indicates, context is all-important. In *Comiskey* v *Bowring-Hanbury* [1905] AC 84, a trust was construed because the whole context indicated this as being the testator's true intention. In that case the testator left his estate to his wife 'in full confidence that she will make such use of it as I should have made myself and that at her death she will devise it to such one or more of my nieces as she may think fit and in default of any disposition by her thereof in her will ... I hereby direct that all my estate and property acquired by her under this my will shall at her death be equally divided among the surviving said nieces'.

There is some authority that if a modern will or other document uses precatory words indentical to such words as were held in the older cases to create a trust, then these will still be held to create a trust. In *Re Steele's WT* [1948] Ch 603 the testator used precatory words identical to those upheld as a trust in *Shelley* v *Shelley* (1868) LR 6 Eq 540. Wynn-Parry J held there was a trust despite his doubts that the same conclusion would have been reached on the basis of the trend in modern decisions. The decision has been criticised as it implies that the courts look to previous case law on a precedent basis. This conflicts with the effect of the *Re Adams and The Kensington Vestry* decision which implies that each case should be decided on its individual merits.

In some cases there may be no documents evidencing the alleged trust. Instead, it may be argued that certain words spoken and certain conduct show that a trust was intended. This arose in *Re Kayford* [1975] 1 WLR 279 in which a mail order company in financial difficulties sought professional advice on how to protect customers' monies sent to it for goods, the aim being to avoid them falling into the hands of the liquidator. A special account was opened at a bank and called a 'Customers' Trust Deposit Account' into which customers' monies were paid pending fulfilment of orders. When the company went into liquidation there was some money in the account and the question arose whether this was held upon trust. Megarry J held that there was a trust since the whole purpose was to ensure that the beneficial interest in the money remained with the customers until their orders were despatched.

Finally it is stressed that if there is insufficient certainty of intention then the gift takes effect as an absolute gift: see *Lassence* v *Tierney* (1849) 1 Mac & Cr 551.

2.3 Certainty of subject-matter

There are two aspects to this requirement:

1. There must be certainty as to what property is to be held upon trust.
2. There must be certainty as to the extent of the beneficial interest of each beneficiary.

Certainty as to what is the trust property is essential since the trustees must know exactly what is and what is not included in the trust. A failure by them to deal with property which belongs to the trust could lead to breach of trust. For example, if a trust is declared of 'Blackacre' or '£10,000' the requirement is satisfied. If there were doubts as to the extent of Blackacre or what the settlor meant when he referred to Blackacre, these would be matters of construction to be solved by the admission of evidence. But, if the settlor declares a trust of the 'bulk of my estate' as happened in *Palmer* v *Simmonds* (1854) 2 Drew 221, this will fail. The trustees will have no way of determining what does or does not come within the trust. A similar problem arose in *Sprange* v *Barnard* (1789) 2 Bro CC 585 where a testatrix left £300 to her husband for his sole use 'and at his death, the remaining part of what is left, and he does not want for his own wants and use, to be divided between my brother ... and my sister ... equally'. Arden MR held this was not a trust for the husband with remainders over but rather an absolute gift. There could be no certainty as to what would be left for the brother and sister on the husband's death; he was entitled to dissipate the entire fund.

The beneficial interest of each beneficiary must be certain so that the trustees know exactly what or how much each beneficiary will be entitled to on distribution of the trust property and prior to that, what income should be accumulated for or paid to the beneficiary. In *Boyce* v *Boyce* (1849) 16 Sim 476 a trust failed for uncertainty as to beneficial interest where a testator left several houses on trust for his wife for life and on her death to convey any one house to his daughter A, as she might choose, and the remaining houses to his daughter B. A died before she could make a choice; this left uncertainty as to what particular houses B should receive, so the trust for B was void. This case may be contrasted with *Re Golay* [1965] 1 WLR 1969 where a testator created a trust for his daughter under which she was to receive 'a reasonable income' from certain properties. Ungoed-Thomas J held that as the courts were constantly making objective assessments of what was reasonable, it could determine what the daughter was to receive in income. Support for the court's decision is found in the early decisions in *Broad* v *Bevan* (1823) 1 Russ 511n and *Minshull* v *Minshull* (1737) 1 Atk 411. In the latter, Lord Hardwicke LC at p412 commented that 'a court never construes a devise void, unless it is so absolutely dark, that they cannot find out the testator's meaning'.

There will be no uncertainty in the following cases:

1. Where the trustees have a discretion as to what each beneficiary should receive, as in the case of a discretionary trust: see section 2.5.
2. Where a trust does not refer to the beneficial interests of the beneficiaries and it is possible to apply the maxim 'equity is equality' and divide the trust property equally between the beneficiaries. For example, '£10,000 upon trust for my children' would, prima facie, be regarded as for the children in equal shares: see *McPhail* v *Doulton* [1971] AC 424.
3. Where a settlor declares a trust in respect of an identified bank account which, unknown to the settlor, is subsequently changed in form (ie to a higher interest bearing account): *Smith* v *National Children's Home and Orphanage (Re Dorman)* [1994] 1 WLR 282.
4. Where a settlor declares a trust of five per cent of company X's shares, of which the settlor holds 950 out of the 1,000 shares issued. So long as there was trust property available, even if intangible, the court could step in and subsequently enforce the trust and, if necessary, identify the 50 shares on trust: *Hunter* v *Moss* [1994] 1 WLR 452.

If there is uncertainty about subject-matter of the whole trust this may raise doubt as to whether the settlor intended a trust at all – see, for example, *Sprange* v *Barnard* (above) – so an absolute gift to the donee will be upheld. If there is a clear intention to create a trust but only uncertainty as to the beneficial interests, as in *Boyce* v *Boyce* (above), a resulting trust to the donor's estate will take effect.

2.4 Certainty of objects

It is essential that the beneficiaries under a trust should be clearly defined or that a formula is put into the trust which enables the trustees to ascertain them. A trust in which the beneficiaries are not ascertainable is void for uncertainty of objects. The importance of ascertaining the beneficiaries stems from the need on the part of the trustees to execute the trust This they cannot do if those for whom the trust was intended are defined in vague terms, leaving doubt as to who are beneficiaries. Trustees do not want to discover that distributions they make from the trust are subsequently proved to have been made to non-objects, as they could be held personally liable to replace the wrongly distributed funds in a breach of trust action: see Chapters 20 and 21.

There are different rules or tests for certainty of objects in fixed and in discretionary trusts. The position is further complicated by the fact that in the context of both fixed and discretionary trusts certainty of objects may involve four different matters, dealt with separately later.

Fixed trusts

A fixed trust is one under which the settlor has defined the beneficial interests which the beneficiaries are to receive and the trustees have no authority to alter them; for example, '£10,000 to my children in equal shares', or '£10,000 to A for life, remainder as to two-thirds to B and one-third to C'. In the first of these examples the extent of each child's beneficial interest is dependent on the total number of children so that that number when applied to divide the fund will produce the sum each child is to receive. The test of certainty of objects in fixed trusts is that it must be possible to draw up a complete list of all the beneficiaries, and if this is not possible it is void, the 'class ascertainability' rule: see *Re Gulbenkian* [1970] AC 508 per Lord Upjohn and *IRC* v *Broadway Cottages Trust* [1955] Ch 20. In the second of these examples, the objects are named and their shares defined so that listing is not necessary although, of course, possible.

Discretionary trusts

A discretionary trust is one under which the trustees are given a discretion as to who shall receive income and/or capital from the trust, and in some cases what amounts, if any, they shall receive. Certainty of objects is important when the trustees can decide who among the beneficiaries shall receive benefits from the trust. Except in rare cases of a discretionary trust to distribute only, the trustees do not have to exercise their discretion; at most they merely have to consider whether it is appropriate to exercise the discretion from time to time. It seems that there are two kinds of discretionary trust from the point of view of applying a test for certainty of objects:

Burrough v Philcox trusts

A power in the nature of a trust arises where an instrument is drafted to give a person a power of selection among a class, but if the power is not exercised or fails to deal with all the property, there is a trust for equal division among the class: see Chapter 1, section 1.4. The leading case is *Burrough* v *Philcox* (1840) 5 My & Cr 72 where Lord Cottenham said of such trusts:

'When there appears a general intention in favour of a class and a particular intention in favour of individuals of a class to be selected by another person, and the particular intention fails, from that selection not being made, the Court will carry into effect the general intention in favour of the class.'

It would appear that in trusts of this nature a situation could arise where equal division of the trust fund may be necessary as, for example, where the power of selection is not exercised. Equal division could only be made if all the beneficiaries were capable of being listed. The test for this type of discretionary trust must be the complete list test used in fixed trusts.

McPhail v *Doulton* trusts

Discretionary trusts were once frequently created to reap tax advantages – though they are no longer as advantageous as they were previously – or to provide benefits for employees and former employees of a commercial organisation. In such cases equal division of the trust fund is not contemplated by the settlor, but merely the provision of benefits in the most tax efficient manner, or to those who meet specific criteria. An example of the latter case would be a discretionary trust to provide scholarships for the children of employees. The appropriate test for certainty of objects in these cases was at one time the complete list test: see *IRC* v *Broadway Cottages Trust* [1955] Ch 20. The House of Lords overruled the *Broadway Cottages* case, insofar as it applied to discretionary trusts, in *McPhail* v *Doulton* [1971] AC 424 and held that the test was 'whether it can be said with certainty that any given individual is or is not a member of the class'. That is, the court adopted the existing test applied to determine if a fiduciary power was valid: see *Re Gulbenkian* [1970] AC 508. In *McPhail* v *Doulton* a settlor executed a deed in which he declared his wish to establish a fund to provide benefits for the staff of Matthew Hall & Co Ltd and their relatives and dependants. In the deed he directed the trustees of the fund to apply it 'in making at their absolute discretion grants to or for the benefit of any of the officers and employees or ex-officers and ex-employees of the Company or to any relatives or dependants of any such persons'. It was held that this direction amounted to a trust power and, by a majority of three to two, that the test outlined above was the appropriate test of certainty of objects to apply.

The rationale behind this test is that if a settlor never intended equal distribution of a fund among the beneficiaries, then the trustees would not need a list of all the beneficiaries in order to make distribution. If they refused to act, and the court had to execute the trust for them, it too would not contemplate equal distribution. All that is required is that the trustees should when exercising their discretion be able to say of any person who they contemplate bestowing benefits upon, that he is or is not a member of the class for which the discretionary trust was intended. As Lord Wilberforce said in *McPhail* v *Doulton* on the trust power there:

> 'As a matter of reason, to hold that a principle of equal division applies to trusts such as the present is certainly paradoxical. Equal division is surely the last thing the settlor ever intended: equal division among all may, probably would, produce a result beneficial to none. Why suppose that the court would lend itself to a whimsical execution? And as regards authority I do not find that the nature of the trust, and of the court's powers over trusts calls for any such rigid rules. Equal division may be sensible and has been decreed in family trusts, for a limited class; here there is life in the maxim "equality is equity",

but the cases provide numerous examples where this has not been so, and a different kind of execution has been ordered, appropriate to the circumstances ...'

The application of the test of certainty of objects in discretionary trusts as laid down in *McPhail* v *Doulton* gives rise to two important questions:

How do the trustees decide who is to benefit under the trust?

As has been seen, the trustees do not have to make a complete list of all the potential beneficiaries; it is enough if they can say of an individual that he is or is not a member of the class. But the trustees have nevertheless a fiduciary duty to survey the whole class of potential objects and consider whether or not to appoint; albeit that after conducting such a survey they still retain their discretion as to whether or not to appoint. Arguably a complete list is needed in order to carry out this survey, and as this would simply be impossible in a trust like that in the *McPhail* v *Doulton* litigation. The trust fails through impossibility to carry out the survey. This argument was first raised in *Re Gestetner's Settlement* (1953) Ch 672 before Harman J in a case concerning powers of appointment, and rejected by him on the ground that such a task was impossible and must have been known to the settlor to be impossible. The court would not construe the settlement as intending the trustees to do the impossible. This point was accepted by the House of Lords in *McPhail* v *Doulton* who approved the following passage from Harman J's judgment:

'The settlor had good reason, I have no doubt, to trust the persons whom he appointed trustees; but I cannot see here that there is such a duty as makes it essential for these trustees, before parting with any income or capital, to survey the whole field, and to consider whether A is more deserving, than B. That is a task which was and which must have been known to the settlor to be impossible, having regard to the ramification of the persons who might become members of this class. If, therefore, there be no duty, to distribute, but only a duty to consider, it does not seem to me that there is any authority binding on me to say that this whole trust is bad. In fact, there is no difficulty, as has been admitted, in ascertaining whether any given postulant is a member of the specified class. Of course, if that could not be ascertained the matter would be quite different, but of John Doe or Richard Roe, it can be postulated easily enough whether he is or is not eligible to receive the settlor's bounty. There being no uncertainty in that sense, I am reluctant to introduce a notion of uncertainty in the other sense, by saying that the trustees must worry their heads to survey the world from China to Peru, when there are perfectly good objects of the class in England.'

It seems that the trustees merely have to make a survey of the potential class of beneficiaries and in doing this appreciate the width of the field – ie how many beneficiaries are involved. Having done this they may then compare individual cases to see if, in broad terms, one claimant is more deserving than another: see *Re Hay's Settlement* [1982] 1 WLR 202.

What will happen if the trustees refuse to make a selection from the potential class of beneficiaries?

If the trustees fail to carry out their duty to consider their discretion and exercise it in appropriate cases, then it seems that the court will not order equal division in *McPhail* v *Doulton* trusts because, as stated above, this is unlikely to accord with the settlor's intentions. Lord Wilberforce's answer to this in *McPhail* v *Doulton* was:

> '... the court, if called upon to execute the trust ... will do so in the manner best calculated to give effect to the settlor's or testator's intentions. It may do so by appointing new trustees, or by authorising or directing representative persons of the classes of beneficiaries to prepare a scheme of distribution, or even, should the proper basis for distribution appear, by itself directing the trustees so to distribute ... '

An interesting variation on this theme was discussed in the recent decision in *Mettoy Pension Trustees Ltd* v *Evans and Others* [1990] 1 WLR 1587. This involved a company pension scheme, part of which conferred an absolute discretion on the company (employer) to provide certain benefits for company pensioners. The trust fund consisted of surplus funds on the company's winding up. Justice Warner held, on the application by the trustee, that the fund was not a company asset and therefore was not vested in the liquidator. Further as this was a fiduciary power which had to be considered and exercised, the court must step in in the absence of the trustees who had effectively ceased to exist when the company was wound up.

The problem of certainty of objects may arise in both fixed and discretionary trusts in at least four different ways:

Conceptual uncertainty

In *Re Tuck's Settlement* [1978] Ch 49 Lord Denning MR described this as:

> '... when a testator or settlor makes a bequest or gift on a condition in which he has not expressed himself clearly enough. He has used words which are too vague and indistinct for a court to apply.'

Trusts for 'my brothers and sisters' or 'my nephews and nieces' would be conceptually certain since these are terms which are understood as referring to specific relationships with the settlor. Trusts for 'my friends' or 'persons having a moral claim on me' would be conceptually uncertain since the meaning of the term 'friends' or 'moral claim' vary from person to person: see *Re Gulbenkian* [1970] AC 508 per Lord Upjohn. But a settlor may give some special 'dictionary' meaning to these phrases so as to enable the trustees to identify the class, for example, a clause in the trust stating exactly what the settlor means by the terms. Conceptually uncertain phrases may not defeat the trust if the settlor has left a discretion to someone to decide who falls within the term, for example, '£10,000 to my friends as determined by X in his absolute discretion': see *Re Tuck's Settlement*. Cases may arise in which the terms used to describe the class are capable of bearing two or more specific meanings as opposed to meanings which vary from person to person, for example, a trust for 'my relatives'. In these cases the proper approach appears to be to determine from the context in which the term is used which particular meaning the settlor intended. In *Re Baden (No 2)* [1973] Ch 9 the Court of Appeal had to consider whether the trust in the *McPhail* v *Doulton* litigation satisfied the test laid down in the House of Lords. The term 'relative' was considered as passing this test of certainty. The judgment of Sachs LJ suggests that the reason for this is that the term must be applied in a common sense manner, so that relative does not mean 'kinsman' or 'distant relative' but those whom a reasonable and honest person would introduce as a relative. In the construction of wills, the term relative can be restricted to the testator's next of kin by reason of an artificial rule of construction: see *Wilson* v *Duguid* (1883) 24 Ch D 244 and *Re Poulton* [1987] 1 All ER 1068. The problem of conceptual uncertainty is similar in trusts which require a complete list for certainty and those which do not: see *Re Sayer* [1957] Ch 423.

Evidential uncertainty

In *Re Tuck's Settlement* [1978] Ch 49 Lord Denning MR described this as:

'... where the testator or settlor in making the condition has expressed himself clearly enough. The words are sufficiently precise. But, the court has difficulty in applying them in any given situation because of the uncertainty of the facts.'

For example, a trust for the former employees of X Co may be evidentially uncertain if the company was dissolved some years ago and its records of names of former employees lost. There may be problems in proving that certain claimants were former employees. It appears that in the case of fixed trusts and *Burrough* v *Philcox* type trusts it is essential that all evidential uncertainty be overcome, otherwise the principle of equal division cannot be carried out. This can normally be overcome by the admission of extrinsic evidence. If the trust is a *McPhail* v *Doulton* type discretionary trust it will not be defeated by evidential uncertainty. In *Re Baden (No 2)* Sachs LJ said:

'Once the class of person to be benefited is conceptually certain then it becomes a question of fact to be determined on evidence whether any postulant has on inquiry been proved to be within it: if he is not so proved, then he is not in it. That position remains the same whether the class to be benefited happens to be small or large. The suggestion that such trusts could be invalid because it might be impossible to prove of a given individual that he is not in the relevant class is wholly fallacious ... '

In these trusts it appears that it is up to a claimant to prove that he is within the class and his failure to do so will mean he is rejected. This approach has much to recommend it. It does least violence to the settlor's intentions and enables the trustees to obtain a satisfactory degree of certainty in making distribution.

Ascertainment of beneficiaries

This was referred to by Lord Upjohn in *Re Gulbenkian* where he said:

'If the class is sufficiently defined by the donor the fact that it may be difficult to ascertain the whereabouts or continued existence of some of its members at the relevant time matters not. The trustees can apply to the court for directions or pay a share into court.'

This statement refers to cases where there is neither conceptual nor evidential uncertainty but, rather, difficulty in tracking down known beneficiaries. For example, a testator may have made a trust in his will for 'my nephews and nieces'. The names of all nephews and nieces may be known but in, say, the case of nephew X, it may not be clear if he is alive or dead, and in the case of nephew Y, it may not be known where he is at present residing. In a fixed trust these matters have to be resolved if equal division is to be made. Directions may be given by the court on the matter, and these may include advertising for the beneficiaries under s27 of the Trustee Act 1925, or a 'Benjamin' order under *Re Benjamin* [1902] 1 Ch 723: see Chapter 16. In a discretionary trust of the *McPhail* v *Doulton* type it is unlikely that such problems would arise.

Administrative workability

This was referred to by Lord Wilberforce in *McPhail* v *Doulton* where he said:

> 'There may be a ... case where the meaning of the words used is clear but the definition of the benenficiaries is so hopelessly wide as not to form "anything like a class" so that the trust is administratively unworkable or in Lord Eldon's words one that cannot be executed ... I hesitate to give examples for they may prejudice future cases, but perhaps "all the residents of Greater London" will serve.'

The reason for holding a trust such as to 'all the residents of Greater London' to be administratively unworkable is because there is no class of objects as such and the trustees could not, in the case of a discretionary trust, begin to exercise any power of selection. This problem appears to be confined to discretionary trusts of the *McPhail* v *Doulton* type. In *R* v *District Auditor, ex parte West Yorkshire Metropolitan County Council* (1986) 26 RVR 24, a supposed trust of money 'for the benefit' of the residents of a local authority area was struck down for this reason.

In some instances trusts have been created for the benefit of the members of a class with each member's share being defined. This might arise where a settlor leaves '£100 to each of my nephews and nieces'. The amount each beneficiary is to receive is fixed by the settlor so that the total number of beneficiaries cannot affect it. If the class of beneficiaries were defined in a manner which was conceptually uncertain, for example, '£100 to each of my friends' it seems that the trust is not valid. This point arose in *Re Barlow's Will Trusts* [1979] 1 WLR 278 where a testatrix left a collection of paintings directing that they be sold, but giving an option to 'any members of my family or any friends of mine' to purchase the paintings at the lower of either a certain catalogue price or probate value. Browne-Wilkinson J held that had this been a gift to a class, it would have been void for conceptual uncertainty. However, he treated the limitation as creating a series of individual gifts subject to a condition precedent. To meet the condition all the executors had to be satisfied of was that any person who wished to buy a painting was 'family' or 'friend' and it was up to such persons to prove they fell within these categories. See also *Re Allen* [1953] Ch 810.

It is inherent in the test of certainty of objects that there must be some objects for a private trust to be upheld. If the trust has no objects at all, but is merely to achieve a stated purpose, it will be held void; for example, a trust to 'encourage co-operation between nations': see *Re Astor* [1952] Ch 534. In *Morice* v *Bishop of Durham* (1805) 10 Ves 522 Grant MR gave the reason behind this rule, namely, that 'there must be somebody in whose favour the court can decree performance'. The general rule that purpose trusts are void is subject to a number of exceptions, and these are dealt with in Chapter 9. Trusts for the benefit of unincorporated associations frequently give rise to problems as to whether they are valid express private trusts or purpose trusts. This happens because the gift may be construed as either a trust for the members of the association beneficially, or a trust to carry on the purposes for which the association was founded. These problems concern the status of an unincorporated association in law and are considered further in Chapter 9.

2.5 Nature of discretionary and protective trusts

A discretionary trust is one where the trustees have a discretion as to the distribution of income or capital or both among the beneficiaries under the trust, and may be either exhaustive or non-exhaustive. An exhaustive discretionary trust is one under which the trustees have a duty to distribute and only a discretion as to how much, if any, they shall give to each of the objects. A non-exhaustive discretionary trust is one under which the trustees have a discretion as to whether they shall distribute at all and, should they decide to distribute, a discretion as to how much, if any, they shall give to each of the objects. In the latter variety of discretionary trust the trustees will normally accumulate any income which they do not distribute: see *Gartside* v *IRC* [1968] AC 553.

The nature of the interest of a beneficiary under a discretionary trust has been the subject of considerable discussion, particularly in tax cases. In *Gartside* v *IRC* [1968] AC 553 the House of Lords was asked to consider whether a deceased beneficiary under a discretionary trust had an interest ceasing on his death which was liable to tax. In deciding that he had not a sufficient interest liable to tax, Lords Reid and Wilberforce viewed the beneficial interest in the context of various rights given to the beneficiary. According to Lord Reid these included a right to prevent misappropriation of the capital, a right to require the trustees to exercise bona fide their discretion as to whether and if so to whom income should be distributed, and a right to take and enjoy whatever part of the income the trustees choose to give. But it would appear that the rights do not include a power to demand that the trustees hand over income to the beneficiary unless the rule in *Saunders* v *Vautier* (1841) 4 Beav 115 is satisfied. See Chapter 16 on this point.

One object of creating a discretionary trust is to prevent the trust fund from dissipation by beneficiaries who are financially inexperienced or who lack prudence in dealing with money. The trustees can make decisions as to how much, if any, they should give to beneficiaries and may base their decisions on their behaviour. Another reason for creating a discretionary trust is that it can enable trustees to provide such sums as the future circumstances of the beneficiaries require, for example, '£20,000 to A, on trust to pay or apply such capital or income to my children as he shall in his absolute discretion think fit'. In this trust A might provide funds to enable a child to receive further education or, should a child become an invalid, provide money for a house and facilities to enable that child to cope with the disability.

In this context, note the ruling of the Court of Appeal in *Jones* v *Jones and Another* (1989) The Independent 27 January. In this case two children were living with their maternal grandmother who, on the mother's death, had custody and control of them. The children were beneficiaries under their mother's will, the mother having left property on trust for the children with power, at the trustees' discretion, to advance income and capital during the children's minorities until, on coming of full age, they would become absolutely entitled.

The question for the court's ruling was whether, in assessing the amount of maintenance to be paid by the children's father, the court should have regard to the children's interests under the discretionary trust. At first instance, both the registrar and the judge had, on the grandmother's application, declined to order an increase in the father's periodical payments, in view of the fact that the children were beneficiaries under the discretionary trust. On appeal by the grandmother, the Court of Appeal remitted her application to the judge for further consideration since, although he had been correct in concluding that he must have regard to the trust fund as a financial resource, he was incorrect in assuming that the whole income would necessarily be available to the children.

The Court of Appeal pointed out that although the children's interest under the trust was 'a potential source of income' it was necessary for an assessment to be made of 'the realities of the situation and what each might reasonably expect to receive by way of income or capital until attaining the age of eighteen'. The court had thus 'to perform a careful balancing exercise'. The father should not be asked to pay more than he could reasonably afford, but undue pressure should not be placed on the trustees to make them exercise their discretion in a way they would not have otherwise decided to exercise it. The children's rights under the trust should not be regarded as 'something of a windfall' to the father.

Protective trusts are designed to combine the advantages of a beneficiary having a fixed right to the income with those of discretionary trusts to prevent the property being dissipated. This can be done in two ways, expressly by the trust instrument or by taking advantage of the provisions of s33(1) Trustee Act 1925. The use of the s33(1) provisions is the most common way of creating a protective trust.

In *Harrison and Others* v *Tew* [1989] QB 307 the plaintiffs had, by deed, transferred certain property to trustees on protective trusts for themselves and their son, including their interest in certain litigation. The object of this transfer was to prevent the relevant property, including the interest in the litigation, passing on their deaths to the son's trustee in bankruptcy. In upholding the validity of this arrangement, the Court of Appeal rejected the argument that the arrangement amounted to the wrongs of champerty or maintenance.

Section 33(1) provides a shorthand method of establishing a protective trust, where the settlor intends to settle any income including an annuity or other periodical payment, without setting out its terms in detail. The subsection provides:

'Where any income, including an annuity or other periodical income payment, is directed to be held on protective trusts for the benefit of any person (in this section called "the principal beneficiary") for the period of his life or for any less period, then, during that period (in this section called "the trust period") the said income shall without prejudice to any prior interest, be held on the following trusts, namely:

i) Upon trust for the principal beneficiary during the trust period or until he, whether before or after the termination of any prior interest does or attempts to do or suffers any act or thing, or until any event happens, other than an advance under any statutory or express power, whereby, if the said income were payable during that trust period, he would be deprived of the right to receive the same or any part thereof, in any of which cases, as well as on the termination of the trust period, whichever first happens, this trust of the said income shall fail or determine.

ii) If the trust aforesaid fails or determines during the subsistence of the trust period, then, during the residue of that period, the said income shall be held upon trust for the application thereof for the maintenance or support, or otherwise for the benefit, of all or any one or more exclusively of the other or others of the following persons (that is to say): the principal beneficiary and his or her wife or husband, if any, and his or her children or remote issue, if any; or if there is no wife, husband or issue of the principal beneficiary in existence the principal beneficiary and the persons who would, if he were actually dead, be entitled to the trust property or the income thereof or to the annuity fund, if any, or arrears of the annuity, as the case may be as the trustees in their absolute discretion, without being liable to account for the exercise of such discretion, think fit.'

The effect of s33 can be seen from the example: '£100,000 upon protective trusts for A for life remainder to B absolutely'.

So long as the protective trust runs in accordance with s33, A will receive all the income arising from it as if he were a life tenant under a non-protective trust. But, should A attempt to do something which would deprive him of the right to receive some or all of the income in the future – an event within s33(1)(i), for example assigning his right to future income – the protective trust 'element' of the trust (under subs(i)) fails and is replaced by the second 'element' (under subs (ii)), a discretionary trust. The beneficiaries of this discretionary trust will be A, his wife and children or, if he has no wife and children, A and B: see s33(1)(ii). It would appear that the discretionary trust arising is an exhaustive trust. There is only one case where A may certainly avoid destruction of the protective trust by alienating his interest under it, namely by consenting to an advancement. This will normally arise under s32(1)(c) Trustee Act 1925 which is dealt with in Chapter 18. It is also possible that such destruction may arise under the Variation of Trusts Act 1958.

See also *Gibbon* v *Mitchell and Others* [1990] 1 WLR 1304. Here a donor with a protected life interest in a fund attempted, by deed of surrender and the release of powers of appointment, to surrender his interest in favour of his children. However this resulted in his interest being forfeited and the scheme's failure. Millett J held that an application to rectify, for mistake, would succeed irrespective if the mistake were one of law or fact so long as the mistake related to the legal effect of the transaction, not merely its consequences or intended benefits.

3

Formal Requirements for Creating a Trust

3.1 Introduction

3.2 Trusts of land

3.3 Trusts of personalty

3.4 Trusts of equitable interests

3.5 Application of s53(1)(c) LPA 1925

3.1 Introduction

The creation of an express private trust, inter vivos, may require certain formal requirements as to the manner in which the trust is declared. This is principally for the purpose of preventing fraud. The need for such formality originates with the Statute of Frauds 1677, to provide documentary evidence of declarations of trust in respect of certain classes of property. The provisions of the Statute of Frauds are now embodied in s53 Law of Property Act 1925 insofar as they affect inter vivos trusts. The provisions of s9 Wills Act 1837 govern the formalities for the creation of a trust by will. These are referred to in Chapter 5.

3.2 Trusts of land

Section 53(1)(b) Law of Property Act 1925 provides:

'A declaration of trust respecting any land or any interest therein must be manifested and proved by some writing signed by some person who is able to declare such trust or by his will.'

'Land' for the purposes of s53(1)(b) is defined by s205 LPA and it includes not only freehold land but also leaseholds (see *Foster* v *Hale* (1798) 3 Ves 676) and such things as incorporeal hereditaments, that is, intangible rights governed by real property law such as easements, profits à prendre, titles of honour and franchises such as market rights.

To satisfy s53(1)(b) the declaration of trust itself need not be in writing; it can be oral. What is required is that it be 'manifested and proved' by writing. So long as there is some written evidence which shows that a trust exists, this will do. In *Childers* v *Childers* (1857) 1 De G & J 482 a letter which referred to a trust was held sufficient while in *McBlain* v *Cross* (1871) 25 LT 804 a telegram was sufficient. The writing need not be made at the time the trust is declared, but may be made subsequently. However, the trust will take effect from the date of the oral declaration and not from the date of the writing. This is because s53(1)(b) does not require the trust to be created by writing but only to be 'manifested and proved' by writing: see *Foster* v *Hale* (1798) 3 Ves 676.

Whatever form of writing is used to evidence the declaration of trust for the purposes of s53(1)(b), it must be signed by the 'person who is able to declare such trust'. This means the settlor, and if the settlement is created by will then this provision will be automatically satisfied by s9 Wills Act 1837, something which s53(1)(b) recognises by its last words. There is no provision in s53(1)(b) for signature by an agent on behalf of the settlor as in s53(1)(c).

3.3 Trusts of personalty

No formal requirements are necessary for the creation of a trust of personalty as a general rule. So long as there is some evidence showing a clear intention to create a trust, whether oral or written or both, the trust will be upheld. In *Petty* v *Petty* (1853) 22 LJ Ch 1065, it was held that a trust had been created when a payment of money was made into a bank account with an oral declaration to the bank clerk accepting payment that it was for a named child. The need for a clear intention can be seen from cases such as *Re Kayford* [1975] 1 WLR 279 at section 3.2 and *Jones* v *Lock* (1865) 1 Ch App 25 in Chapter 4.

Although a trust of personalty does not need to be declared in writing or evidenced in writing, it is often advisable that it should be, especially if the property is valuable, for example rare paintings or large holdings of stock and shares. One peculiarity which will be apparent on considering the position vis-à-vis formalities in trusts of equitable interests, is that no formalities are necessary to declare a trust of mere personalty, but formalities are essential for the disposition, including a declaration of trust, of an equitable interest in personalty.

3.4 Trusts of equitable interests

Section 53(1)(c) Law of Property Act 1925 provides:

'A disposition of an equitable interest or trust subsisting at the time of the disposition, must be in writing signed by the person disposing of the same or by his agent thereunto lawfully authorised in writing or by will.'

The purpose of this provision seems to be to provide documentary evidence of the movement of equitable interests in property. As these are intangibles, evidence of their movement is essential to prevent hidden transactions which might defraud those who are properly entitled to them, and also to enable those who hold the legal title, for example, trustees, to know exactly where the equitable interests lie at any given moment.

Section 53(1)(c) has a wide application. The term 'disposition' is by s205(1)(ii) of the Act given a wide definition and includes a conveyance, a devise, bequest, or appointment of property. The term 'equitable interest' is defined by s205(1)(x) 1925 Act and includes 'interests and charges in or over land or in the proceeds of sale thereof'. This definition would appear to confine s53(1)(c) to equitable interests in realty, and the fact that s53(1)(a) and (b) are confined to land would seem to support such a conclusion. However, the definitions of 'conveyance' and 'disposition' in s205(1)(ii) appear to contemplate the disposition of equitable interests in personalty, and the House of Lords appeared to assume that equitable interests in personalty were included in *Grey* v *IRC* [1960] AC 1; *Oughtred* v *IRC* [1960] AC 206; and *Vandervell* v *IRC* [1967] AC 291. The Australian High Court, in dealing with a corresponding provision in *Adamson* v *Hayes* (1973) 130 CLR 276, held by a majority that equitable interests in personalty were included.

The provisions of s53(1)(c) should be contrasted with those in s53(1)(b). The former requires a disposition of an equitable interest or declaration of trust of an equitable interest to be in writing, whereas the latter provision merely requires evidence in writing of a declaration of trust of land. The effect of these provisions leads to some curious results. First, a trust of personalty, say, valuable chattels, may be declared orally, but a sub-trust affecting the same property would, it seems, have to be in writing. Second, the declaration of trust of land itself need only satisfy s53(1)(b), but a declaration of trust of an equitable interest in land must satisfy the more stringent requirements of s53(1)(c). The reason for these odd results lies in the policy behind s53(1)(c).

Section 53(1)(c) applies whether the disposition of an equitable interest involves a valuable or a valueless equitable interest. The section is merely concerned to provide evidence of their movement, it is not concerned with their pecuniary value.

The application of s53(1)(c) has given rise to some difficulties in particular situations and in one or two cases there seems to be inconsistency in its application.

The reasoning behind these difficulties is, however, not the section itself, rather the desire of parties to avoid the payment of tax in its various forms. This will be seen in the following scenarios.

If A is beneficially entitled to property under an existing trust it might be necessary to satisfy s53(1)(c). This depends on whether it is determined to be a disposition under s53(1)(c) or a declaration of a new sub-trust: see *Grainge* v *Wilberforce* (1889) 5 TLR 436 (dealt with subsequently).

The importance of this distinction is shown by the decision in *Grey* v *IRC* [1960] AC 1. Mr Hunter (H) established six settlements in favour of each of his grandchildren. He then transferred 18,000 shares to the same trustees under the six settlements. In turn those trustees held the shares on bare trust for H, with the transaction attracting only nominal stamp duty (ie tax) as H had not disposed of any property.

H then orally directed the trustees to hold his beneficial interests in favour of the six grandchildren settlements. He subsequently confirmed this in writing. At this point the Inland Revenue claimed stamp duty on the full value of the shares transferred, claiming that the transaction was effected by the subsequent writing required by s53(1)(c) as he was in truth disposing of his existing equitable interest.

H argued against this, stating that he was not disposing of his equitable interest. Rather he was declaring it to be held in favour of his grandchildren. This was effected by his oral directions, and the subsequent writing attracted only nominal stamp duty as it passed no additional value.

The House of Lords backed the Inland Revenue, stating that the overall effect of the transaction was that of a disposition, not a declaration, hence required writing which in turn attracted ad valorem stamp duty.

3.5 Application of s53(1)(c) LPA 1925

Assignment of equitable interest

Two different situations call for examination here.

First, where the assignor (L) is both the legal owner and the beneficial owner, and he assigns his beneficial interest to E while retaining the legal ownership. In such circumstances it is arguable that L has disposed of the equitable interest because E now has this. The main weakness of this argument, which would make observance of s53(1)(c) essential, is that it rests on the concept of duality of estates, that L had both a legal and an equitable estate in the property. This duality was considered in *Commissioner of Stamp Duties* v *Livingston* [1965] AC 694 and on the basis of what the Privy Council said there it seems incorrect to say L has two estates. It is submitted that s53(1)(c) does not apply here, because L is in fact 'creating' an equitable interest in favour of E. Prior to the disposition there was no equitable interest because, according to Viscount Radcliffe in *Livingston's* case, it is only necessary to call into existence the equitable interest to give effect to equity's doctrines, and that could only have occurred at the moment L gave the beneficial interest to E. At that moment there was creation. In any event, if s53(1)(c) had to be satisfied here then the creation of all trusts would have to be in writing and many existing trusts would be void for want of it. Further it is clear, with reference to the public policy underlying s53(1)(c) ie fraud, that writing is not necessarily required. At this point L, as the previous absolute owner of the property, becomes the trustee knowing exactly the property he holds on trust and who has the beneficial interest.

The second situation is where L possesses only the equitable interest and assigns this to E. In these circumstances there is no question of creation; the equitable interest is being disposed of so s53(1)(c) must be satisfied. If the equitable interest is assigned for consideration in the second situation then, in some cases, it is arguable that s53(1)(c) may not have to be satisfied.

Direction to trustee to transfer trust property to a third party

This situation differs from the foregoing as it envisages both legal and equitable titles moving, and being merged. This is in effect the reverse of a declaration of trust with the settlor naming trustees as here the legal and equitable titles are divided. As was seen in the decision in *Vandervell* v *IRC* [1967] 2 AC 291 this analogy is an important one to remember.

Vandervell, a beneficiary of certain family shares, wanted to fulfil two key roles; firstly to fund a chair at the Royal College of Surgeons (RCS), a charity; and secondly to benefit certain settlements in favour of his children/grandchildren. At the same time he wished to minimise the tax exposure of this transaction. Therefore he transferred 150,000 shares to his trustees, and then directed them to transfer these on to the RCS along with his own equitable interest. This transfer was effected with the proviso of an option to repurchase the shares for £5,000. These were the facts for the first *Vandervell* decision.

As regards s53(1)(c) the House of Lords agreed that as both legal and equitable titles in the shares were merged in the RCS it was not a disposition, hence no writing was required. However, the IRC did succeed in levying tax on Mr Vandervell for the transaction. For the period that the RCS held the shares dividends of up to £250,000 were declared. The RCS, being a registered charity, was exempt from the surtax otherwise payable on this. However, Mr Vandervell was held to have the beneficial interest in the option to repurchase the shares, by way of a resulting trust. Therefore he was liable to pay the surtax as the dividends could be his, albeit that the RCS took them pending the exercise of the option.

Before continuing on to the next phase of the *Vandervell* litigation it is useful to stress that the resulting trust, which attached to the option, also did not require writing per s53(1)(c), being exempt under the provisions of s53(2).

The next step for Mr Vandervell was to direct the trustees to exercise the option and repurchase the shares. This they did with money from the pre-existing children's settlements; then the shares were immediately held on trust for those settlements. By comparing this with *Grey* v *IRC* the courts would be expected to find this to be a disposition, required to be in writing under s53(1)(c), with that instrument attracting ad valorem stamp duty. Unfortunately this was not the case.

The argument put forward by the Court of Appeal, *Re Vandervell's Trusts (No 2)* [1974] Ch 269, rested on the oft-termed 'stop-gap resulting trust'. The initial resulting trust, in favour of Mr Vandervell, only arose in the absence of his true intention being clear. This was rectified when the option was exercised, with the children's settlements recognised as being the rightful beneficiaries under the resulting trust. Therefore the initial resulting trust, a necessary stop-gap, died and was replaced with a newly declared trust in favour of the children. In turn this did not require to comply with the provisions of s53(1)(c).

This rather convenient argument ignored the fact that Mr Vandervell played an active role in the transaction; he had already paid surtax under the old resulting trust; and also assumes that resulting trusts are phantoms that can merely die overnight.

Declaration of trust of subsisting equitable interest

This situation is concerned with cases where the equitable owner of property declares a trust over that property. For example, if A, a beneficiary under a trust, declares a sub-trust over his beneficial interest in favour of B, the question is whether the declaration of sub-trust must be in writing under s53(1)(c). There are no clear authorities on this point and much, it seems, will depend on how the sub-trust actually operates, ie is it a true sub-trust which imposes active duties on the sub-trustee, or is it a mere sham being in essence a disposition to the sub-trust beneficiary?: see *Grainge* v *Wilberforce* (1889) 5 TLR 436.

Examples are:

1. If the sub-trust was in fact nothing more than an assignment of the beneficial interest from A to B, then s53(1)(c) must be complied with.
2. If it is a true sub-trust with A remaining to perform active duties, for example, where he declares a discretionary trust in favour of B of his (A's) interest under a fixed trust, it is arguable that A has created an interest in favour of B but it is also arguable that he disposed of some, but not all, of his subsisting equitable interest to B. The creation argument can be supported by analogy to the position where the legal and beneficial owner of property declares a trust in favour of a third party. The weakness is that the concept of duality of estates does not fit in neatly here, though in the case of *Commissioner of Stamp Duties* v *Livingston* it was pointed out that it is not necessary always to be able to identify separate legal and equitable estates. As for the disposition argument, it would seem to accord with the policy of s53(1)(c) as referred to in *Vandervell* v *IRC* (above). If the position of A is viewed both before and after the transaction he has got rid of some of his rights – equitable rights – while the position of B, if viewed before and after the transaction, is that he has gained equitable rights which he did not previously possess and those could only have come from A.
3. The sub-trust may also be one under which A has declared himself trustee but has no active duties to perform so that he can 'drop out of the picture'. He is nothing more than a bare trustee holding the bare equitable estate for B. It is arguable that s53(1)(c) should be satisfied here because the position is not dissimilar to what happens in assignment. However, it is possible to say that in this situation A has transferred all the benefits of an equitable owner without

actually passing the equitable title, so that he still remains in possession of a bare (and valueless) equitable title. But, in this case it is difficult to see how B's interest could be classified as anything other than equitable. Further viewing the transaction before and afterwards, it is clear that A has got rid of something while B has gained something.

Contract to assign an equitable interest

A written contract to assign an equitable interest, for example, a beneficial interest under a trust, would clearly satisfy s53(1)(c). However, if the contract was oral the issue arises whether the equitable interest would pass to the purchaser despite s53(1)(c). It is arguable that if consideration has passed from the purchaser a constructive trust arises in his favour. This seems to be so in the case of a contract to assign a legal interest: see *Howard* v *Miller* [1915] AC 318. For example, if X contracts to sell Blackacre to Y a constructive trust arises once the contract is signed and is specifically enforceable: see *Lysaght* v *Edwards* (1876) 2 Ch D 499.

But such a constructive trust would not avoid the necessity of complying with s53(1)(c), where the contract is to assign an equitable interest. This problem arose in *Oughtred* v *IRC* [1960] AC 206. Mrs Oughtred and her son Peter agreed to exchange some property in order to mitigate liability to estate duty on Mrs Oughtred's death. Under a trust 200,000 shares in a company were held for Mrs Oughtred for life, remainder to Peter absolutely. Mrs Oughtred also owned some 72,000 shares absolutely in the same company. It was agreed that Mrs Oughtred would transfer the 72,000 shares to Peter and in return he would release his remainder in the trust fund, thus making her the absolute owner of the 200,000 shares. This agreement was made orally and it was followed by a deed which recited what had happened and that Peter had released his interest in the trust in Mrs Oughtred's favour. The Revenue claimed that the deed was liable to ad valorem stamp duty on the basis that it transferred the shares, the earlier oral agreement having been ineffective to do so.

At first instance Upjohn J held that the oral agreement gave rise to a constructive trust which, by reason of s53(2), did not need to be in writing. Section 53(2) provides: 'This section does not affect the creation or operation of resulting, implied or constructive trusts.' The equitable title passed under the constructive trust and the deed was nothing more than a winding up of the trust. This decision was reversed by the Court of Appeal and that reversal was upheld by the House of Lords by a majority. In their view the oral agreement did transfer to Mrs Oughtred the beneficial interest in the shares, but Peter still remained the holder of the bare equitable title to the shares. This title could only be effectively transferred under s53(1)(c) and the deed had made such a transfer. As Lord Jenkins said:

> 'The parties to a transaction of sale and purchase may no doubt choose to let the matter rest in contract. But, if the subject-matter of a sale is such that full title to it can only be transferred by an instrument, then any instrument they execute by way of transfer of the

property sold ranks for stamp duty purposes as a conveyance on sale notwithstanding the constructive trust in favour of the purchaser which arose on the conclusion of the contract.'

The minority view seems to be that the bare equitable title could be ignored since it was one that could not have been asserted to claim the equitable interest in the shares. On this Lord Cohen said:

'Before your Lordships, Mr Wilberforce was prepared to agree that on the making of the oral agreement Peter became a constructive trustee of his equitable reversionary interest in the settled funds for the appellant [Mrs Oughtred] but he submitted that none the less s53(1)(c) applied and, accordingly, Peter could not assign that equitable interest to the appellant except by a disposition in writing. My Lords, with that I agree, but it does not follow that the transfer was a conveyance of that equitable interest on which ad valorem stamp duty was payable under the Stamp Act 1891. It might well be that there was no document transferring the equitable interest. The appellant may have been content to rely on getting in the legal interest by the transfer and on the fact that it would be impossible for Peter to put forward successfully a claim to an equitable interest in the settled shares once the consideration shares had been transferred to him or his nominees by the appellant.'

It appears from the *Oughtred* case that the minority view did not deny the existence of a constructive trust on the facts but considered that it did not avoid the need for a formal conveyance by Peter under s53(1)(c). This uneasy situation in part deflects the otherwise completely contradictory first instance decision in *Re Holt's Settlement* [1969] 1 Ch 100.

In *Re Holt's Settlement* the court faced a difficult position. The earlier enacted Variation of Trusts Act 1958 enabled the courts to vary trusts in certain circumstances. These effectively result in a variation, or disposition, of beneficial interests under the trust. However Megarry J held that this did not in turn require a separate deed, or writing, as per s53(1)(c) for each variation. He held that, when beneficiaries agree, for valuable consideration, to a variation of their interests, their existing equitable interests are varied without any need for writing.

Disclaimer

A disclaimer of property is not within s53(1)(c) according to the Court of Appeal in *Re Paradise Motor Co* [1968] 1 WLR 1125. In that case A owned shares in the company which he registered in the name of B by way of gift, but B orally disclaimed the gift. The company was eventually wound up with a surplus of assets and the question arose as to which of A or B should be placed on the list of contributories to claim a share of the surplus. B argued that as his disclaimer was oral it was ineffective because of s53(1)(c). The court rejected this argument, pointing out that the disclaimer operated by way of avoidance and not by way of disposition. Unfortunately the decision does not explain how the disclaimer actually operates so as to make s53(1)(c) inapplicable. One explanation is that the legal and equitable title vested in B on A making the transfer, but that his disclaimer caused a resulting trust to operate in favour of A. This resulting trust was outside s53(1)(c) by reason of s53(2).

4

Completely and Incompletely Constituted Trusts

4.1 Introduction

Assume S, a settlor, wishes to benefit B, a beneficiary. There are basically three ways in which S can reach this goal, as follows:

1. An outright gift to B.
2. By S declaring himself as trustee of property he holds in favour of B.
3. By S declaring a trust in favour of B, but with T being trustee of the property.

The first of these does not strictly involve trust law. Similarly, as will be seen, the second does not per se involve issues of constitution.

With the above in mind let us now look at the issue of constitution. In essence this involves the transfer of property from one party to another. Depending on the choice being followed, either (1), (2) or (3) above, different considerations apply.

As noted, constitution involves the transfer of property. Exactly how this transfer is to take place depends on the nature of the property being transferred: see *Milroy*

40

v *Lord* (1862) 4 De GF & J 264 which is expanded upon in section 4.4. Further, the importance of constitution is highlighted by the decision in *Re Bowden* [1936] Ch 71, as are the consequences of failure.

In *Re Bowden*, prior to becoming a nun, a settlor decided to settle certain property she was entitled to on her father's death. The property was duly transferred to the trustees. However, some 60 years later she requested the return of the property, claiming it was a voluntary settlement. Bennett J, upholding the trustee's refusal to comply, stated that the property was bound by the trusts. Further, the settlor no longer had beneficial interest in the property and therefore could not demand its return.

This case highlights the importance of transfer of property, constitution, when required. Unless the beneficiary, B, can enforce the means by which S intends to benefit then (as noted above) by alternative methods S will not be bound. In turn S will effectively regain the property. Put differently:

1. A completely constituted trust binds all persons including the settlor, except the bona fide purchaser of a legal estate for value without notice. The beneficiary can therefore take all necessary steps to protect, preserve or recover trust property. This is irrespective of his having given consideration or not: see *Fletcher* v *Fletcher* (1844) 4 Hare 67.
2. An incompletely constituted trust is not a trust per se. However, there are means of enforcing it nevertheless. This is subject to the general maxim of equity that 'Equity will not assist a volunteer'. As will be shown there are also exceptions to this maxim.

This convoluted reasoning leads us on to examine the relationship of consideration, the volunteer and constitution.

4.2 Consideration and the volunteer

Consideration and the volunteer are mutually exclusive concepts. That is, a volunteer is someone who has not given good consideration, money or money's worth. If B has given consideration then he creates a contractual relationship with S and can enforce the settlement either indirectly in a claim for damages or directly via an action for specific performance. Therefore if B has given consideration issues of constitution do not practically concern him. It is therefore important to determine what the courts see as being good consideration.

As noted, consideration is money or money's worth. See: Anson, *Law of Contract* (2nd ed), Chapter 3. However, an important extension of this in equity is that of being 'within the marriage consideration' under a covenant to marry.

It appears that three conditions must be satisfied before the court will recognise a settlement as being a marriage settlement. These were outlined by Goff J in *Re Densham* [1975] 1 WLR 1519:

1. it must be made on the occasion of the marriage, ie before and in consideration of the marriage, or, if made after the marriage, in pursuance of an ante-nuptial agreement;
2. it must be conditioned only to take effect on the marriage taking place; and
3. it must be made for the purpose of or with a view to encouraging or facilitating the marriage.

If a settlement is a marriage settlement then it may be enforced by those persons who are within the marriage consideration. It is irrelevant that they have not given value for the settlement; they stand outside the rule that 'equity will not assist a volunteer' because marriage consideration is deemed to be 'good consideration'. In *Pullan* v *Koe* [1913] 1 Ch 9 the parties to the marriage and their issue – children and grand-children – were held to be within the marriage consideration. In *Attorney-General* v *Jacobs-Smith* [1895] 2 QB 341 it was held that the children of former marriages of either the husband or wife whose interests are so closely intermingled with those of the children of the present marriage as to be inseparable would also be included. The last cited case suggests that children to whom the husband or wife stand in loco parentis, or who are the illegitimate children of either of them, are not included.

Next-of-kin are frequently included in a marriage settlement as ultimate remaindermen in default of issue; they are not within the marriage consideration and thus are only mere volunteers. Consequently, should the settlor refuse to settle property on the marriage settlement they cannot, in general, do anything about it. In *Re Plumptre's Marriage Settlement* [1910] 1 Ch 609 the next-of-kin, under a marriage settlement by which the wife had covenanted to settle all her after-acquired property on the settlement, failed to enforce the settlement of £1,125 of stock which the wife had acquired from her husband. The decision in this case would appear to apply to any beneficiary named in a marriage settlement who is outside the marriage consideration: see also *Re D'Angibau* (1880) 15 Ch D 228.

The Limitation Act does not affect a claim by those within the marriage consideration to obtain property within the terms of the settlement but not yet settled. Thus, if a marriage settlement was made under which the settlor covenanted to settle Blackacre, which he then owned, and all after-acquired property of a value exceeding £50,000, those within the marriage consideration could enforce the covenant 20 or even 30 years later. This point arose in *Pullan* v *Koe* (above) where a wife covenanted in a marriage settlement to settle all after-acquired property of the value of £100 upwards. She received £285 in 1879 which she gave to her husband who invested it in bonds. On the husband's death the trustees claimed the £285 of bonds from his executors. Swinfen Eady J held the trustees could recover them because the moment the £285 came to the wife's hand in 1879 it was bound by the covenant and impressed with a trust. He cited the dicta of Jessel MR in *Collyer* v *Isaacs* (1881) 19 Ch D 342 who said:

'A man can contract to assign property which is to come into existence in the future, and when it has come into existence, equity, looking on as done that which ought to be done, fastens on the property, and the contract to assign then becomes a complete assignment'.

The decision in *Pullan* v *Koe* might be compared with *Re Plumptre* where the next-of-kin sought to enforce the covenant and failed to obtain damages at law since the limitation period had expired. The property was not impressed with a trust the moment the covenantor obtained it so far as they were concerned, because the principle 'equity looks on that as done which ought to be done' applies only in favour of persons entitled to enforce the contract.

Once a marriage settlement is completely constituted those who are outside the marriage consideration obtain rights in that property which they are entitled to protect and which the court will protect. In *Paul* v *Paul* (1882) 20 Ch D 742 a marriage settlement provided for the husband and wife and the survivor of them for life, remainder to their issue and with ultimate remainders in favour of the next-of-kin. There were no children of the marriage and the husband and wife sought to have the settled fund paid to them, on the ground that the next-of-kin were mere volunteers. This was rejected because the trust was completely constituted of this money and thus the next-of-kin had rights in it under the terms of the settlement.

If no consideration is given, and the trust is not constituted, the beneficiary must look to alternative methods of enforcement. These involve the exceptions to the rule 'equity will not assist a volunteer' and also the complex debate surrounding covenants to settle. Both are dealt with in subsequent sections. Before proceeding to these it is appropriate now to consider the situation where S declares himself a trustee and also the mechanics of transferring property.

4.3 Declaration of self as trustee

The problem of transferring trust property to trustees may be avoided if the settlor declares himself to be trustee thereof. Since the settlor will have both legal and equitable title in the trust property already, the only issue here will be if he has manifested his intention to create a trust in terms which are sufficiently clear. The court is not prepared to construe mere theatrical gestures as amounting to a declaration of self as trustee. In *Jones* v *Lock* (1865) 1 Ch App 25 a father was scolded for failing to bring back a gift for his nine-month-old son from a business trip, whereupon he took a cheque for £900 payable to himself from his pocket saying, 'Look you here, I give this to baby ...' The cheque was put in a safe and found there after the father's death a few months later. Lord Cottenham LC refused to treat the words spoken by the father as amounting to a declaration of self as trustee; he said:

> 'I think it would be of very dangerous example if loose conversations of this sort, in important transactions of this kind, should have the effect of declarations of trust.'

Clear words giving an unequivocal demonstration of the settlor's intentions are necessary.

A combination of words and conduct may show that there is a declaration of self as trustee. This occurred in *Paul* v *Constance* [1977] 1 WLR 527 where Mr C said to Mrs P, his cohabitee, that money in his bank account was as much hers as his. He said this on a number of occasions and arranged for her to draw on the account which she did on numerous occasions. On Mr C's death intestate his widow claimed the money left in the account, but the Court of Appeal held there was a trust in Mrs P's favour. Scarman LJ pointed out that the unsophisticated nature of Mr C and Mrs P and the nature of their relationship all went to support the view that the money was as much hers as his. On his death she became the sole owner by right of survivorship under a joint tenancy.

As *Richards* v *Delbridge* (1874) LR 18 Eq 11 clearly indicates, a declaration of self as trustee will not be held to arise where there has been an ineffective attempt at an outright transfer. There must be clear evidence of declaration of self as trustee. This can be seen from another decision of Jessel MR, namely, *Middleton* v *Pollock* (1876) 2 Ch D 104 where a client gave a solicitor money for investment. The solicitor died insolvent having failed to invest the money but after his death there were found among his papers written declarations of trust by him in favour of the client over some of his property. These trusts were upheld.

A point which emerges from decisions such as *Middleton* v *Pollock* and *Richards* v *Delbridge* is that a declaration of trust need not be communicated to the beneficiary. This is because the main issue is whether the beneficial interest has passed, not whether the beneficiary knows it has passed.

4.4 Transfer of property to trustees

The vast majority of settlements are made voluntarily and there is very little the beneficiaries can do in order to obtain the trust property should the settlor refuse to transfer the intended trust property (either to the trustees or beneficiaries) so as to give effect (ie enable the trust to be enforceable) to the settlor's declaration of trust. It is essential to see that the property has not only been transferred but that all the appropriate formalities required by law for that property have been complied with.

This point was made by Turner LJ in the leading case of *Milroy* v *Lord* (1862) 4 De GF & J 264. In this case a man named Medley executed a deed which purported to transfer to Lord 50 shares in the Louisiana Bank, to hold these upon trust for a number of persons, including Milroy. The deed was not a proper transfer of the shares because they could only be effectively transferred in law by the execution of a share transfer and registration in the books of the bank. However, Lord held a power of attorney from Medley as well as the share certificates, and he could have effected the transfer under the power of attorney. But this he failed to do. On Medley's death the power of attorney ceased to have effect and the question arose whether or not the shares belonged to Medley's estate. In holding that the shares were still part of Medley's estate, Turner LJ put forward the following principles:

'I take the law of this court to be well settled, that, in order to render a voluntary settlement valid and effectual, the settlor must have done everything which, according to the nature of the property comprised in the settlement, was necessary to be done in order to transfer the property and render the settlement binding upon him. He may, of course, do this by actually transferring the property to persons for whom he intends to provide, and the provision will then be effectual, and it will be equally effectual if he transfers the property to a trustee for the purposes of the settlement, or declares that he himself holds it in trust for those purposes; and if the property be personal, the trust may, as I apprehend, be declared either in writing or by parol but in order to render the settlement binding, one or other of these modes, must, as I understand the law of this court, be resorted to, for there is no equity to perfect an imperfect gift. The cases, I think, go further to this extent: that if the settlement is intended to be effectuated by one of those modes to which I have referred, the court will not give effect to it by applying another of those modes. If it is intended to take effect by transfer, the court will not hold the intended transfer to operate as a declaration of trust, for then every imperfect instrument would be made effectual by being converted into a perfect trust.'

Analysis of Turner LJ's judgment shows that:

1. The property must be transferred by the appropriate method laid down by law.
2. There may be a transfer in three different ways – by giving the property outright to the beneficiary without the imposition of a trust; by giving the property to trustees upon a declaration of trust; and by the settlor declaring himself trustee of his own property.
3. If the settlor has clearly intended one of these three methods, the court will not hold that another of them applies so as to give effect to the transfer.

The appropriate method of transfer will depend upon the type of property which is the subject-matter of the trust. There is no limitation on the types of property which may be put into a trust. The following are some of the more common types of trust property:

1. Land – this must be conveyed be deed: see s52(1) LPA 1925.
2. Leaseholds – by deed under s52(1) LPA 1925 unless they are for less than three years and come within s54(2) LPA 1925.
3. Chattels – by delivery of the chattels to the trustees. In such cases the act of delivery must be unequivocal, and all the circumstances must make it clear that delivery is being made. In *Re Cole* [1964] Ch 175 the court refused to accept that a husband had given the contents of a house to his wife where he merely showed her the house saying 'It's all yours'. The circumstances in which he said this and his subsequent behaviour in dealings with the chattels were taken into account.

In *Jaffa and Others* v *Taylor Gallery Ltd*; *Jaffa and Others* v *Harris* (1990) The Times 21 March, where the trust property was a painting, it was held that the declaration of trust itself was a sufficient transfer of property. No physical transfer was necessary in this case in that the making of the document, in respect of which each trustee had agreed to act, and had received a copy, constituted the transfer.

4. Shares – a share transfer must be executed and the shares registered in the name of the new holder in the company's share register, as a general rule: see s183 Companies Act 1985.

5. Choses in action – the requirements laid down in s136 LPA 1925 must be satisfied to have an assignment at law, but if these are not satisfied there may be an effective assignment in equity.

An equitable interest may form the subject-matter of a trust. But it is necessary to ensure that any disposition is in writing to satisfy s53(1c). Normally both the disposition, and, depending on the facts, declaration, will be found to arise from the same writing. Thus, for example, in *Kekewich* v *Manning* (1851) 1 De GM & G 176 a remainderman under a trust assigned that remainder in writing to trustees to hold upon certain trusts. There was a completely constituted trust of the equitable interest.

The transfer of shares has its own peculiar difficulties. There would seem to be four distinct phases in the transfer:

1. Execution of share transfer form by S.
2. Delivery of share transfer form and share certificates to donee.
3. Delivery of share transfer form and share certificates to company.
4. Registration of transfer by company.

On a strict interpretation of *Milroy* v *Lord* stage (4) must be reached. That is, the actual transfer must be registered by the company. Anything short of this is insufficient. This view was adopted in *Re Fry* [1946] Ch 312. Here the donor, domiciled abroad, could not comply with the necessary Treasury regulations in force at the time. This was despite the fact that he, personally, had done all that he could.

This is contrasted with the subsequent decision in *Re Rose* [1949] Ch 78. In 1943 the settlor left some shares to B in his will. In 1944 he went one stage further and executed a share transfer form in favour of B and handed it to him with B then failing to register them prior to S's death. The court, nevertheless, held that the inter vivos transfer was effective, as there was nothing else that S could have done.

This more literal interpretation is supported by the more recent decision in *Mascell* v *Mascell* (1984) 81 LS Gaz 2218. A father agreed to sell his house to his son for £9,000. The appropriate documents were duly executed but not stamped and registered as per Land Registry procedure. Before this occurred there was a falling out and the father attempted to recover the deeds prior to registration. The question of consideration aside, it was held that the transfer had been properly constituted. That is, the father had done all that he needed to and was therefore bound by his actions. This was despite the fact that actual registration had not taken place and also despite the provisions of s19 LPA 1925. The latter, albeit only technically, places the onus on the vendor to arrange for this registration and on that basis alone could, or should as per the *Re Fry* (1946) decision, have decided the case in favour of the father.

The emphasis therefore seems to be on whether enough has been done to effect transfer, not whether everything possible has been done.

Both *Milroy* v *Lord* and *Re Rose* [1952] Ch 499 emphasise that if a settlement is intended to be effected by one mode the court will not give effect to it by applying another of those modes. This issue arose directly in *Richards* v *Delbridge* (1874) LR 18 Eq 11, where a grandfather endorsed on the back of the deeds of his leasehold shop: 'This deed and all thereto belonging I give to (my grandson).' He delivered the deed to the child's mother who kept it until his death. The issue arose whether the beneficial interest in the lease had passed to the grandson. Jessel MR held it had not as there was intended to be an outright assignment of the lease which was ineffectual. He rejected an argument that the words used should be construed as a declaration of trust observing: 'However anxious the court may be to carry out a man's intention, it is not at liberty to construe words otherwise than according to their proper meaning.'

The assignment of choses in action to trustees to hold upon trust also requires special attention. A chose in action is a property right which can only be enforced by taking legal action. A classic example is a debt: see *Torkington* v *Magee* [1902] 2 KB 427. Other examples are beneficial interests under trusts and contractual rights. Choses in action may be legal or equitable, and this distinction is based upon whether the chose was recognised by the common law or equity prior to the Judicature Act 1873. A debt is an example of a legal chose, while an interest under a trust is an example of an equitable chose. The assignment may be made under the provisions of s136 LPA 1925 (a statutory assignment) or in equity. A statutory assignment must satisfy the three conditions laid down in s136:

Absolute assignment

The settlor must pass the whole interest he has in the chose in action to the trustees in order that it be absolute. If he retains some interest s136 is not satisfied. An assignment of a £10,000 debt owed to the settlor to trustees would be absolute but if only £5,000 of it was assigned it would not be absolute: see *Harding* v *Harding* (1886) 17 QBD 442.

Written assignment

The provisions of s136 require that the assignment be 'in writing under the hand of the assignor'. No particular form is required: see *Re Westerton* [1919] 2 Ch 104.

Written notice

Notice in writing of the assignment must be given 'to the debtor, trustee or other person from whom the assignor would have been entitled to claim such debt or other thing in action'. Thus, if the settlor assigns a £10,000 debt to trustees, the trustees should give written notice to the debtor of the fact of the assignment. If the provisions in s136 are not satisfied, then it may be that the assignment will be effective in equity. Equity does not require any particular form for the assignment; it is sufficient that there is an intention to assign: see *William Brandt's Sons & Co* v *Dunlop Rubber Co Ltd* [1905] AC 454. For example, an assignment of a debt may be made orally. If the chose in action being assigned is equitable in nature, for example an interest under a trust, then it will be necessary to comply with the provisions in s53(1)(c) LPA 1925 and the assignment would have to be in writing to be effective: see Chapter 3.

Whether an assignment of a chose in action by a settlor to trustees satisfies s136, or is only recognised in equity, is important in the context of the maxim 'equity will not assist a volunteer'. If the assignment complies with the provisions of s136 the chose in action is effectively assigned to the trustees without the need for consideration, regardless of whether the chose in action is legal or equitable in nature: see *Re Westerton* [1919] 2 Ch 104. If the assignment does not meet the requirements of s136 it may not be effective to pass the settlor's interest in the chose in action to the trustees without being supported by consideration. In determining if consideration is necessary, equitable assignments must be looked at on the basis that they do not fulfil one or more of the following requirements in s136:

Assignment not absolute

It seems that such an assignment is an effective transfer of the settlor's interest even though it is voluntary. There are no clear authorities on the point, but some dicta in *Re Macardle* [1951] Ch 699 tend to suggest this.

Assignment oral

If an assignment is oral then it must be ascertained whether it involves a legal or an equitable chose in action. If it involves an equitable chose, then it is void under s53(1)(c) LPA 1925: see Chapter 3. The presence or absence of consideration may be irrelevant, though if the trustees have given consideration the settlor will hold on a constructive trust for them, and they will hold the benefit on trust for the beneficiaries. If the assignment involves a legal chose, it appears that as an oral voluntary assignment it will be ineffective because of the maxim 'equity will not assist a volunteer'. This point was brought out in the Australian case of *Olsson* v *Dyson* (1969) 120 CLR 265 where a husband, who was owed £2,000 by a company, told the company's managing director orally to pay the £2,000 and the future interest on it to his wife. Interest was paid to the wife by the company. On the husband's death the issue arose whether there had been a good assignment to the wife by the husband, or whether the £2,000 should be paid to the executors of his estate. The assignment was held to be ineffective at law and also in equity because, as Kitto J said:

'There is no valid assignment in equity either for property which is assignable at law but is not assigned in the manner which the law requires for a legal assignment of it cannot be held in equity to be assigned unless by reason of some fact or circumstance which a court of equity regards as binding the legal owner in conscience to hold the property on trust for the assignee. A promise for valuable consideration to assign property is enough for this purpose, for equity, regarding that as done which ought to be done for the consideration given, holds the assignee to have an equitable interest commensurate with the legal interest which specific performance of the promise would give him. But, there is no equity to perfect an imperfect gift; because of the absence of consideration a purported assignment, if incomplete as a legal assignment, effects nothing in equity.'

No written notice

It appears that such an assignment is effective in equity even if voluntary. In *Milroy* v *Lord* (above) Turner LJ said:

'... in order to render a voluntary settlement valid and effectual, the settlor must have done everything which, according to the nature of the property comprised in the settlement, was necessary to be done in order to transfer the property ...'

This dictum refers to the settlor doing all that is 'necessary' on his part to make the transfer effective. Thus, if one of the formalities of transfer is not 'necessary' on his part, the transfer is effective in equity if it has not been observed. It is not necessary that the settlor give the written notice required by s136.

In some cases a declaration of trust may at the same time amount to an assignment of property, so completely constituting the trust of a chose in action. This happened in *Re Wale* [1956] 1 WLR 1346 where a settlor covenanted with trustees to transfer certain shares to them. Two shareholdings were involved. One, the 'A investments', were owned absolutely by the settlor; the other, the 'B investments', were part of the settlor's late husband's unadministered estate at the date of the settlement. The settlor forgot about the settlement and on her death the issue arose whether the shares belonged to her estate or to the trust. The position on the 'A investments' was clear; these had not been properly transferred so the trust was incompletely constituted as regards them. As for the 'B investments' the settlor did not have the title to those shares when she made the covenant. At most she had a chose in action to see that her husband's estate was duly administered and to receive them in due course. The covenant was in fact an assignment of the chose in action. This case does not run contrary to the rule that if the settlor has intended one mode of transfer the court will not imply another because the settlor at all times intended a trust and had in fact completely constituted it. Finally, before considering covenants to settle et al it is necessary to expand upon the oft forgotten decision of

Re Ralli's WT [1964] Ch 288. This decision dealt with the situation where a voluntary covenant had been made by a settlor to settle certain property and the property to which the settlement referred had come into the hands of the trustees by some route other than by being handed over by the settlor or his representatives. The question arose whether the trustees could keep the property in the face of a claim for its return by the settlor or his representatives. The answer, in short, seems to be: yes.

In *Re Ralli's WT* a testator who died in 1899 left his residuary estate upon trust for his wife for life, remainder to his two daughters, Helen and Irene, in equal shares absolutely. Helen made a marriage settlement in which she covenanted to settle any property she would receive under her father's will. Helen died in 1956 and the testator's wife died in 1961. Irene's children were entitled to the property under Helen's marriage settlement and Irene's husband was the sole surviving trustee under the testator's will and of Helen's marriage settlement. The question arose whether he held Helen's share of the residuary estate for the benefit of those claiming under Helen's will or whether he held it subject to the trusts of the marriage settlement. Buckley J held that it was subject to the trusts of the marriage settlement. The ratio of the case seems to be that as Irene's husband had obtained the legal title to the property and wished to settle it on the marriage settlement, it was up to those claiming it under Helen's will to assert that they had a better right in equity to it, and this they failed to do:

'In my judgment the circumstance that the plaintiff holds the fund because he was appointed a trustee of the will is irrelevant. He is at law the owner of the fund, and the means by which he became so have no effect upon the quality of his legal ownership. The question is: For whom, if anyone, does he hold the fund in equity? In other words, who can successfully assert an equity against him, disentitling him to stand upon his legal right? It seems to me to be indisputable that Helen, if she were alive, could not do so, for she has solemnly covenanted under seal to assign the fund to the plaintiff, and the defendants can stand in no better position ...'

Buckley J went on to point out that this was not a case of equity assisting a volunteer because the plaintiff was not seeking any assistance from equity; instead, it was the defendants who were looking for equity's assistance:

'As matters stand, however, there is no occasion to invoke the assistance of equity to enforce performance of the covenant. It is for the defendants to invoke the assistance of equity to make good their claim to the fund. To do so successfully they must show that the plaintiff cannot conscientiously withhold it from them. When they seek to do this, he can point to the covenant which, in my judgment, relieves him of any fiduciary obligation he would otherwise owe to the defendants ... In doing so the plaintiff is not seeking to enforce an equitable remedy against the defendants on behalf of persons who could not enforce such a remedy themselves: he is relying upon the combined effect of his legal ownership of the fund and his rights under the covenant.'

4.5 Covenants to settle

If a settlor has covenanted to settle property on certain trusts the issue arises whether the covenant can be enforced against him if he refuses to settle the property. At law a covenant is enforceable as it amounts to a promise under seal, the seal being recognised as an alternative to consideration: see *Hall v Palmer* (1844) 3 Hare 352. But in equity the mere fact that a promise is made under seal makes no difference. In *Jefferys v Jefferys* (1841) Cr & Ph 138 a father covenanted to settle certain copyholds on trust for the benefit of his daughters but failed to do so. On his death the court refused to compel performance of the covenant in equity; in the eyes of equity it was a voluntary promise.

The main remedy for breach of covenant at law is damages, while the main remedy in equity is specific performance. It was the latter remedy which was sought in *Jefferys v Jefferys* and, of course, refused because 'equity will not assist a volunteer'. As James LJ said in *Re D'Angibau* (1880) 15 Ch D 228: 'Volunteers have no right whatever to obtain specific performance of a mere covenant which has remained a covenant and which has never been performed.' This dictum clearly rules out any claim for specific performance whether it is made by the trustees or by the volunteer beneficiaries. However, there remains the matter of suing for damages at law. It would seem that the trustees could get damages by suing at law on the covenant (but see below), because as parties to it they have a right to sue. But, the volunteer beneficiaries could not sue at law, for their equitable rights would not be recognised there and also because they are not parties to the deed.

There is much controversy as to whether substantial, as opposed to nominal damages may be obtained for breach of a covenant to settle property on trust. A strict view would suggest that such damages should be recoverable at law by the trustees provided the subject-matter of the covenant is property recognised at law. For example, if the covenant was to settle Blackacre or £10,000, damages to the value of Blackacre or £10,000 should be recoverable in each case. A covenant to settle future property has been said in a controversial line of cases (*Re Pryce*, *Re Kay* and *Re Cook*) not to be a property right. The decision in *Re Cavendish-Browne's ST* [1916] WN 341 seems to support the view that substantial damages may be recovered but, unfortunately, it is a poorly reported decision. Other authorities suggest that such damages are not recoverable. The leading, and much criticised, decision is *Re Pryce* [1917] 1 Ch 234 in which a wife covenanted to settle all her after-acquired property on the terms of a marriage settlement. After the husband's death the wife held certain property which was subject to the covenant but refused to settle it; the next-of-kin, who were the ultimate remaindermen, wished this to be settled. Thus, the trustees asked the court for directions as to what they should do. Eve J directed them not to sue because the next-of-kin were volunteers. He said:

'... they are volunteers ... volunteers have no right whatever to obtain specific performance of a mere covenant which has remained a covenant and has never been performed ... Nor, could damages be awarded either in this Court, or, I apprehend, at law, where since the Judicature Act 1873, the same defences would be available to the defendant as would be raised in an action brought in this court for specific performance or damages. In these circumstances, seeing that the next-of-kin could neither maintain an action to enforce the covenant nor for damages for breach of it ... ought the Court now for the sole benefit of these volunteers to direct the trustees to take proceedings to enforce the defendant's covenant? I think it ought not; to do so would be to give the next-of-kin by indirect means relief they cannot obtain by means of direct procedure ...'

One important aspect of this case is that it relieves trustees of the need to sue on such covenants, a need which would otherwise arise from their duty to get in the trust property. However, there is the question as to whether it is correct to direct trustees not to take proceedings to enforce what otherwise appear to be enforceable legal rights. The following points on this decision are worth noting:

1. Eve J directed the trustees that they 'ought not' to sue, which appears to be no answer to the proper question put: Were they under a duty to sue? and, perhaps, leaves trustees in a quandary as to what their duty is in relation to such covenants.
2. Eve J considers the right of action for damages and a claim for specific performance of the covenant. There cannot be any dispute that the trustees would not have obtained specific performance but refusal of relief in equity does not prejudice rights to relief at law. This point was made by Lord Eldon LC in *Mortlock* v *Buller* (1804) 10 Ves 292.
3. Eve J referred to the Judicature Act 1873 as giving the same defences in an action for damages in law as were available in claims for equitable relief. This dictum is hard to reconcile with *Re Cavendish-Browne's ST* [1916] WN 341, where the judge did award damages, and also *Re Parkin* [1892] 3 Ch 510 where damages were also awarded. Both these decisions were after the Judicature Act 1873.

The decision in *Re Pryce* might have been justified on another ground, namely, that the covenant to settle after-acquired property was dealing with a species of property which is not recognised at law. In *Re Cook's Settlement Trusts* [1965] Ch 902 a settlor covenanted with trustees that if certain paintings he owned should be sold during his lifetime the proceeds of sale would be settled on the trustees. A painting was sold and the issue arose whether the trustees were obliged to enforce the covenant.

In holding that they were not, Buckley J followed *Re Pryce* and went on to say:

'The covenant with which I am concerned did not, in my opinion, create a debt enforceable at law, that is to say a property right, which, although to bear fruit only in the future and upon a contingency, was capable of being made the subject of an immediate trust, as was held to be the case in *Fletcher* v *Fletcher*. Nor is this covenant associated with property which was the subject of an immediate trust as in *Williamson* v *Codrington*. Nor did the covenant relate to property which then belonged to the covenantor, as in *Re Cavendish-Browne's Settlement Trusts*. In contrast to all of these cases, this covenant upon its true construction is, in my opinion, an executory contract to settle a particular fund or particular funds of money which might never come into existence. It is analogous to a covenant to settle an expectation or to settle after-acquired property.'

This point does not seem to have been raised in *Re Pryce* or in *Re Kay's Settlement* [1939] Ch 329 where Simonds J followed *Re Pryce* and rejected a claim for a direction to the trustees in that case to take proceedings at law to recover damages for breach of covenant. In doing so he said:

'I must say I felt considerable sympathy for the argument ... that there was ... no reason why the trustees should not be directed to take proceedings to recover what damages might be recoverable at law for breach of the agreements entered into by the settlor in her settlement. But on a consideration of *Re Pryce* it seemed to me that so far as this Court was concerned the matter was concluded and that I ought not to give any directions to the trustees to take the suggested proceedings ...'

Two points arise in consideration of *Re Pryce*, *Re Kay*, and *Re Cook*. First, whether the trustees would be refused damages if they went ahead and claimed them without asking the court for directions. In these cases the trustees were merely seeking directions from the court. Second, whether the court should have considered if, in each case, there was already a completely constituted trust of the promise itself to settle, and given directions as to the enforcement of that promise. This is considered at section 4.6.

The decisions in *Re Pryce* and *Re Kay* were considered in *Cannon* v *Hartley* [1949] Ch 213 where Romer J had to consider whether a daughter who was a party to a deed of separation could claim damages from her father who had agreed under the terms of the deed to make certain payments to her. This case differed from *Re Pryce* and *Re Kay* in that the daughter was herself a party to the deed; there were no trustees seeking to make a claim for her benefit. As Romer J said, *Re Pryce* 'is quite clearly no authority for the proposition that a direct covenantee, although a volunteer, cannot sue for damages upon any covenant of this description'. Romer J went on to hold that she could recover damages at law because:

'She does not require the assistance of the court to enforce the covenant for she has a legal right herself to enforce it. She is not asking for equitable relief but for damages at common law for breach of covenant.'

This dictum would suggest that if trustees sued on a covenant for damages they should obtain them. Other dicta of Romer J in this case explain Eve J's judgment in *Re Pryce* as concerning a claim by the next-of-kin for equitable relief or damages at common law:

'I think that what Eve J was pointing out in *Re Pryce* was that the next-of-kin who were seeking to get an indirect benefit had no right to come to a court of equity because they were not parties to the deed and were not within the consideration of the deed and, similarly, they would have no right for damages, as the court of common law would not entertain a suit at the instance of volunteers who were not parties to the deed which was sought to be enforced, any more than the court of equity would entertain such a suit.'

This dictum does not deal with trustees suing on the covenant and, if anything, supports the view that they could do so.

4.6 Trusts of a promise

The case law clearly demonstrates that a trust may have as its subject-matter a chose in action. For example, in *Re Wale* [1956] 1 WLR 1346 the trust included the right to see that the estate of a testator was properly administered. Choses in action include the benefit of a promise and the cases clearly show that a trust can be made of the benefit of a promise. In *Lloyd's* v *Harper* (1880) 16 Ch D 290 the father of a Lloyd's underwriter gave a guarantee to the managing committee of Lloyd's under which he promised to pay all his son's underwriting creditors should the son default. The Court of Appeal held that the managing committee were trustees of the benefit of the father's promise for the son's underwriting creditors. The House of Lords approved the concept in *Les Affreteurs* v *Walford* [1919] AC 801, and in that case a shipowner promised a charterer to pay the broker who negotiated the charter party a commission. It was held that the charterer was a trustee of the shipowner's promise for the benefit of the broker.

The main difficulty in cases where it is alleged there is a trust of a promise is proving that there was an intention to create such a trust. If S covenants with trustees to pay them £10,000 for the benefit of X then it is more likely that he intended the £10,000 to be the subject-matter of the trust and not his mere promise to pay it. The importance of this is that if the promise itself could be regarded as the intended subject-matter of the trust, then from the moment the promise had been given the trust would be completely constituted. Consequently, if the promise were made voluntarily by the settlor, the volunteer beneficiaries could get the trustees to enforce it without in any way offending the rule 'equity will not assist a volunteer'.

The leading case on this problem is *Fletcher* v *Fletcher* (1844) 4 Hare 67 where a father entered into a voluntary covenant with trustees to pay to them £60,000 within 12 months of his death for such of his sons who attained 21 and survived him. One son, Jacob, fulfilled these conditions but the trustees were reluctant to carry out the trust unless the court ordered them to do so. Wigram V-C held that Jacob could enforce the covenant even though he was a volunteer. It has been suggested that the decision was based on there being a trust of the promise to pay the £60,000 and that, the trust being completely constituted of this promise, equity could assist in the enforcement of it. The dicta of Wigram V-C would apply to such a case:

> 'The first proposition relied upon against the claim in equity was, that equity will not interfere in favour of a volunteer. That proposition, though true in many cases, has been too largely stated. A court of equity, for example, will not, in favour of a volunteer, enforce the performance of a contract in specie. That it will, however, act sometimes in favour of a volunteer is proved by the common case of a volunteer on a bond who may

prove his bond against the assets. Again, where the relation of trustee and cestui que trust is constituted, as where property is transferred from the author of the trust into the name of the trustee, so that he has lost all power of disposition over it, and the transaction is complete as regards him, the trustee, having accepted the trust, cannot say he holds it, except for the purposes of the trust; and the Court will enforce the trust at the suit of a volunteer. According to the authorities, I cannot, I admit, do anything to perfect the liability of the author of the trust if it is not already perfect. The covenant, however, is already perfect. The covenantor is liable at law, and the Court is not called upon to do any act to perfect it. One question made in argument has been, whether there can be a trust of a covenant the benefit of which shall belong to a third party; but I cannot think there is any difficulty in that. Suppose, in the case of a personal covenant to pay a certain annual sum for the benefit of a third person, the trustee were to bring an action against the covenantor; would he be afterwards allowed to say he was not a trustee? If he cannot do so after once acknowledging the trust, then there is a case in which there is a trust of a covenant for another.'

This judgment does not clearly state if there was a trust of a covenant in *Fletcher* v *Fletcher* and the facts of the case do not show any clear intention on the part of the settlor to constitute the trust of the promise. At most it seems the case is only positive support for the view that there can be a trust of a promise if that was what was intended. *Fletcher* v *Fletcher* would appear to be really based on the idea that trustees can enforce a voluntary covenant at law, provided it is not concerning future property and that if the trustees do not take action to enforce the covenant, the beneficiary may sue in their name. It seems to add weight to the criticism of the decision in *Re Pryce* and the cases which followed it. As Wigram V-C points out, if the trustees are able to sue at law then there is no need for equity to intervene and the rule 'equity will not assist a volunteer' has no application.

4.7 Trusts of future property

A settlor may covenant to settle upon trust property which he already possesses or property which he expects to receive in the future. There is no difficulty in the enforcement of a covenant to settle property which the settlor already possesses by way of a claim for damages, assuming that the court would allow this contrary to what was said in *Re Pryce* (above). But, if the covenant is to settle property which the settlor expects to receive in the future, for example, a legacy under the will of a person who is still alive, such a covenant could not be the subject-matter of an action at law. The position at law is that it is impossible to own something that does not exist and impossible to make a present gift of such a thing to another. Equity does, however, recognise and enforce a gift of future property where the future property has been the subject of an agreement to assign that property when acquired. But, if the agreement to assign was made voluntarily, equity would afford no assistance as this would be contrary to the rule 'equity will not assist a volunteer'. In *Re Ellenborough* [1903] 1 Ch 697 a settlor made a voluntary settlement in 1893 under which she purported to assign to trustees all property she might receive under the wills of her brother and her sister. The settlor received property under her sister's will which she gave to the trustees, but on her brother's death in 1902 she refused to convey property she received under his will to the trustees. Buckley J held that the trustees could not enforce the covenant against the settlor. He said:

'The question is whether a volunteer can enforce a contract made by deed to dispose of an expectancy. It cannot be and it is not disputed that if the deed had been for value the trustees could have enforced it … An assignment for value binds the conscience of the assignor. A Court of Equity against him will compel him to do that which ex hypothesi he has not effectually done. Future property, possibilities and expectancies are all assignable in equity for value … But, when the assurance is not for value, equity will not assist a volunteer …'

The covenant to assign future property was voluntary in *Re Ellenborough*. But, if it had been for value, it would have been enforceable in equity, as Buckley J pointed out. The mechanism by which equity will enforce the covenant was explained in *Tailby* v *Official Receiver* (1888) 13 App Cas 523, a case which concerned an assignment of future book debts for value. When the assignment is made for value then at the moment property of the description falling within the agreement to assign comes into the hands of the assignor, equity vests that property in the assignee. For example, if the covenant in *Re Ellenborough* had been for value and she had received land under her brother's will, the moment she received this land it would have vested in the trusts in equity – equity regarding that as done which ought to be done. Hence, she could have been compelled by a court of equity to convey the legal title to the trustees.

A major difficulty in considering trusts of future property is in determining whether the trust is concerned with future property at all. As *Re Ellenborough* indicates, an interest under a will which has not yet come into operation is future property. Contrast this with *Re Wale* (above), where the will had come into operation when the covenant was made. Covenants to settle after-acquired property involve future property: see *Re Cook's ST* [1965] Ch 902. Such covenants are only enforceable in equity if consideration has been given. The assignment of beneficial interests under a trust may cause problems. If X is entitled in remainder under a trust he might assign the remainder itself, or he might assign the property he will receive as remainderman when that interest fall into possession. An assignment of the former would be an assignment of existing rights, whereas the latter would involve an expectancy: see *Shephard* v *Commissioner of Taxation* (1965) 113 CLR 385. This problem arose in the New Zealand case of *Williams* v *Commissioner of Inland Revenue* [1965] NZLR 395 in which a life tenant under a trust executed a deed assigning the first £500 he would receive from the trust to a church, in each of four specified years. The court rejected the argument that this was assignment of a portion of the life tenant's existing rights, finding that it was an assignment of future rights. As Turner J said:

'What then was it that the assignor purported to assign? What he had was the life interest of a cestui que trust in a property or partnership adventure vested in or carried on by trustees for his benefit. Such a life interest exists in equity as soon as the deed of trust creating it is executed and delivered. Existing, it is capable of immediate assignment. We do not doubt that where it is possible to assign a right completely it is possible to assign an undivided interest in it ... if here ... the assignor had purported to assign (say) an undivided one-fourth share in his life estate, then he would have assigned an existing right ... But in our view, as soon as he quantified the sum in the way here attempted, the assignment became one not of a share or a part of his right, but of moneys which should arise from it. Whether the sums mentioned were ever to come into existence in whole or in part could not at the date of the assignment be certain. In any or all of the years designated the net income might conceiveably be less than five hundred pounds. ... The first £500 of the net income, then, might or might not ... in fact have any existence. Because of this they are dealt with subsequently on an individual basis.'

4.8 The exceptions

Having detailed why and how property is transferred and the various arguments used to sidestep the necessity for constitution let us now focus on the exceptions. That is the exceptions to the much quoted maxim 'equity will not assist a volunteer'. These exceptions have no common theme; rather they arise out of a series of distinct historical policy decisions and pieces of legislation. Because of this they are dealt with subsequently on an individual basis.

4.9 The rule in *Strong* v *Bird*

This rule takes advantage of the special position of a personal representative. If the personal representative is an executor, appointed by the will of the testator, then all the testator's property will vest in him immediately on the testator's death: see *Woolley* v *Clarke* (1822) 5 B & Ald 744. If the personal representative is an administrator, because there is no executor appointed in the will, or a case of intestacy, then the property of the deceased will vest in him on the court making a grant of representation to him: see *Woolley* v *Clarke*.

In its original form the rule concerned the forgiveness of a debt. In *Strong* v *Bird* (1874) LR 18 Eq 315, B borrowed £1,100 from his stepmother. She lived in B's house as a lodger paying £212.50 a quarter for her board. It was agreed that the debt was to be repaid by the stepmother deducting £100 from each quarterly payment as it fell due. After making two such deductions the stepmother insisted on paying the full rent and did so until her death fours years later. B was appointed sole executor by her will. The next-of-kin claimed that B owed the estate £900. It was held that the debt had been released by the appointment of B as executor because at law he could not sue himself for the debt. Further, the act of appointing him executor together with full payment of the quarterly rent showed a continuing intention up until death to release the debt.

The principle was extended to imperfect gifts of property in *Re Stewart* [1908] 2 Ch 251. The rule can now be stated to apply where there is either:

1. an imperfect gift of real or personal property or an intention of releasing a debt;
2. the intention of giving a property or releasing the debt continues up until the donor's death;
3. the donee is appointed executor in the donor's will or administrator of the donor's estate by the court.

In these circumstances the title to the property which the donor intended to give or the rights to the debt he intended to release, vest in the donee qua executor or administrator, and the gift to him is perfected.

With regard to the intention of giving on the part of the donor, which is vital to the rule, two points should be noted:

1. The intention must be a present intention of giving; a future intention to give will not suffice, nor will a testamentary intention. This is to avoid any conflict with the provisions of s9 Wills Act 1837. In *Re Pink* [1912] 2 Ch 528 Farwell LJ said:

   'Since *Strong* v *Bird* ... It is plain that a mere intention to give not carried out ... will not do ...'

   The point was elaborated upon by Evershed MR in *Re Freeland* [1952] Ch 110, who said:

   '... the words an intention to give may mean either one of two things: they may mean an intention of giving, that is to say, an intention to do that which at the time of doing it was meant to be a gift out and out; or they may mean an intention to make a gift in the future, which is in effect a promise, not enforceable in the eyes of the law, to make a gift thereafter.'

2. The intention of giving must continue unbroken until the donor's death. If the donor should after the intention of giving was evinced, deal with the property in a manner which is inconsistent with this intention, the rule is not applicable. In *Re Freeland* [1952] Ch 110 the rule was not applied because the testatrix, having promised to give the plaintiff, her executrix, a motor car in her garage, subsequently lent the car to a friend who was still using it at her death. The fact that the testatrix had lent the car in this way negatived the intention of giving.

   In *Re Gonin* [1979] Ch 16 the plaintiff was promised her parents' house and its contents in 1944 if she gave up her work and returned home to look after them. When the last of the parents died in 1968 she claimed the house and contents under *Strong* v *Bird*. The court held that the contents passed under the rule but that the house did not because the mother had sold off plots of land from the large garden at the back of the house and this negatived any continuing intention of giving, and evinced an intention on her part to treat the property as her own.

It is irrelevant whether the property vests in the donee qua executor or qua administrator: *Re James* [1935] Ch 449. In *Re Gonin* (above) Walton J criticised the application of the rule to administrators on the basis that their appointment was purely arbitrary, in that who took a grant of administration was dictated by rules 19 or 21 Non-Contentious Probate Rules 1954.

The use of the rule in *Strong* v *Bird* to perfect an imperfect gift appears to take it beyond its original ambit, and to be based on weak foundations. *Strong* v *Bird* itself was based on release of a debt at law because of the procedural obstacle of the executor having to sue himself. There was no reason for equity to interfere, especially as there was an intention to give the same debt to the executor. But *Re Stewart* does not fit within these confines. In that case the testator purchased three bearer bonds a few days before his death. He gave his wife an envelope containing a letter from the brokers plus a bought note for them, saying to her: 'I have bought these bonds for you.' The bonds had not been delivered to the wife at the testator's death and she had neither a legal nor equitable title in them. But the wife, as an executor of the testator's estate, claimed the bonds. Neville J held she was entitled to them under *Strong* v *Bird*. He said:

'Where a testator has expressed the intention of making a gift of personal estate belonging to him to one who upon his death becomes his executor, the intention continuing unchanged, the executor is entitled to hold the property for his own benefit. The reasoning by which the conclusion is reached is of a double character – first, that the vesting of the property in the executor at the testator's death completes the imperfect gift made in the lifetime, and, secondly, that the intention of the testator to give the beneficial interest to the executor is sufficient to countervail the equity of beneficiaries under the will, the testator having vested the legal estate in the executor.'

This reasoning is open to some criticism. First, the wife as executor took the estate in a fiduciary capacity for the purpose of carrying out the administration of the estate and not for her own benefit. Second, the executor is able to prefer himself to the other beneficiaries under the will and to defeat the intention to benefit them in some cases. Third, the appointment of an executor is most unlikely to have been designed to take advantage of the rule so that it gives an unintended windfall to the executor which he could not otherwise obtain.

It is not clearly established whether *Strong* v *Bird* applies to a case where the personal representative was promised a gift of property to hold as trustee rather than for himself beneficially. This point does not appear to have been considered in the English courts. It is arguable that it should not apply here as this would extend the rules to enable a person who was not appointed as executor to claim the property. Neville J's judgment (above) appears to assume that this is necessary. Such an extension would move even further away from the rule as originally laid down by Jessel MR in *Strong* v *Bird*.

4.10 Donatio mortis causa

A donatio mortis causa is the reverse of the imperfect gifts considered so far. Under it the donor passes possession of the subject-matter of the gift to the donee but on condition that it is not to become his (the donee's) absolutely until the donor's death. The gift is conditional on the donor's death. For example, if X was involved in a serious road accident, and fearing imminent death from his injuries, he gave his much prized Rolex watch to his friend Y saying: 'Keep this for yourself if I die', then the gift is conditional on X's death. If X dies then the condition is fulfilled and the watch belongs to Y absolutely. If X recovers then he may recover the watch.

If anything remains to be done to complete the donee's title, he can compel the personal representatives of the donor to carry out the requisite act, since they hold the legal title in the property on trust for the donee, although in most cases the legal title will have passed at the date of the donatio mortis causa. If the donor made a donatio mortis causa of a chose in action by delivering the documents representing it to the donee, and further formal requirements were required by law to vest these in the donee after the donor's death, the court would order the personal representatives to carry out the requirements: see *Birch* v *Treasury Solicitor* [1951] Ch 298.

There are four conditions which must be satisfied for property to pass by a gift donatio mortis causa:

The gift must be intended to be conditional upon death

The donor is making a gift which will only be absolute on his death and is in the meantime revocable. The donor's intentions to make a donatio mortis causa need not be expressed in words; it is sufficient that they can be inferred from the circumstances: see *Gardner* v *Parker* (1818) 3 Madd 184. As the gift is intended to be conditional on death then it follows that it will fail if the donee fails to survive the donor: see *Tate* v *Hilbert* (1793) 2 Ves Jun 111.

The gift must be made in contemplation of death

A donatio mortis causa can only be made if the donee expects to die in the near future, death for some reason pending. Thus, a man about to be hanged could make a donatio mortis causa, and so could a very sick man: see *Re Craven's Estate (No 1)* [1937] Ch 423. It was held in *Agnew* v *Belfast Banking Co* [1896] 2 IR 204, that a donor going on a dangerous mission in which he expects to die is sufficient. The fact that the death does not occur in the manner contemplated is irrelevant, and in *Wilkes* v *Allington* (1931) a donatio mortis causa was upheld when it was made by a donor who believed he was dying of cancer but eventually died through contracting pneumonia by riding on an open-topped bus in the rain. There is some doubt if a donatio mortis causa can be made where death is contemplated by suicide. In *Re*

Dudman [1925] Ch 553 it was held such a donatio mortis causa was not valid. However, matters may have been changed by the Suicide Act 1961.

The donor must part with dominion over the property before his death

There must be delivery of the subject-matter of the gift to the donee during the donor's lifetime and this must be accepted by the donee: see *Bunn* v *Markham* (1816) 7 Taunt 244. The delivery of the property may take place either before or after the intention to make a gift donatio was evince: see *Cain* v *Moon* [1896] 2 QB 283. The handing over of the property must not be subject to any conditions that it shall be returned to the donor for any reason other than if he recovers from his illness: see *Reddel* v *Dobree* (1839) 10 Sim 244. A donatio mortis causa is good if the means of attaining the property are given to the donee, for example the keys of a safe, but if the donor retains one of the keys it becomes insufficient: see *Re Lillingston* [1951] 2 All ER 184.

The property must be capable of passing by way of donatio mortis causa

Generally all pure personalty is capable of passing donatio mortis causa, for example, insurance policies, savings certificates and chattels: see *Birch* v *Treasury Solicitor* [1951] Ch 298. Some particular classes of property have, however, caused doubts and difficulty:

Land

It was long thought, following obiter dicta of Lord Eldon in *Duffield* v *Elwes* (1827) 1 Bli (NS) 497, that land could not be the subject of a donatio mortis causa.

In fact, this issue recently came before the Courts in *Sen* v *Headley* [1991] Ch 425. In this case a man who knew he was dying and who had wished a friend to have his house on his death, had given the friend the key to a steel box in which, as he informed her, the deeds of the house were kept. He then told her that she was to have the house. Shortly afterwards he died intestate. A dispute arose between the deceased's administrator and the friend as to whether there had been a valid donatio mortis causa with regard to the house. At the first instance Mummery J, following dicta of Lord Eldon in *Duffield* v *Elwes* (above), and views expressed by academic writers (see, in particular, *Snell's Principles of Equity*) concluded that a valid donatio mortis causa had not arisen in these circumstances. In particular, the judge held that the requirement that the donor must part with dominion over the property – that he must put beyond himself the power to alter the subject-matter of the gift between the date of the donatio and his death: see *Re Craven's Estate* [1937] Ch 423 at p426 – could not be complied with.

On appeal the Court of Appeal reversed the first instance decision and accepted that land is indeed capable of being the subject of a donatio mortis causa. Nourse LJ, delivering the judgment of the court, observed that: 'It was agreed that the doctrine was anomalous. Anomalies did not justify anomalous exceptions.' As his Lordship also indicated, the point had not actually been decided by the House of Lords and thus was not binding on the Court of Appeal, which '... could not decide a case in 1991 as the House of Lords would have decided it, but did not decide it, in 1827'.

Cheques and promissory notes

If the cheque is drawn on the bank account of the donor it cannot be the subject of a donatio mortis causa as it does not constitute property but merely an order to his bank which is revoked on his death: see *Re Beaumont* [1902] 1 Ch 889. However, if the donee receives payment on the cheque during the donor's lifetime or negotiates it in his lifetime, then the donatio mortis causa will be valid: see *Re White* [1928] WN 182. Similarly a promissory note is a gratuitous promise which fails on death if it has not been acted on: see *Re Leaper* [1916] 1 Ch 579.

Shares

There are conflicting decisions on shares. In *Staniland* v *Willott* (1852) 3 Mac & G 664 it was held there had been a valid donatio mortis causa of shares but this had been revoked by the recovery from illness of the donor. In *Moore* v *Moore* (1874) LR 18 Eq 474 and *Re Weston* [1902] 1 Ch 680, the court held that railway stock and building society shares respectively could not pass donatio. Both are first instance decisions and it is submitted that *Staniland* v *Willott* is the better decision as the other two cases appear to be based on *Ward* v *Turner* (1752) 2 Ves Sen 431, which held that a delivery of the receipts of some shares was insufficient.

Choses in action

These are capable of passing donatio mortis causa. If the delivery of the document is sufficient to transfer the chose in action no problems arise, for instance, as in the case of a banknote. If the title to the chose in action does not pass by mere delivery then delivery of the appropriate documents which are evidence of title will do: see *Birch* v *Treasury Solicitor* [1951] Ch 298.

It should be noted that there can be no donatio mortis causa if the donor intends to make an immediate gift inter vivos or a gift by will. The former is an immediate gift and not conditioned on death, while the latter expresses wishes which are only intended to take effect after death.

For another recent example of this doctrine in operation see the decision in *Woodard* v *Woodard* [1991] Fam Law 470.

5

Secret Trusts

5.1 Introduction

5.2 Fully-secret trusts

5.3 Half-secret trusts

5.4 Basis of secret trusts

5.5 Secret trusts and the Wills Act 1837

5.6 Miscellaneous

5.1 Introduction

If an individual wishes to dispose of his property after his death this can only be done by making a will in accordance with the provisions of s9 Wills Act 1837. The section requires the will to be in writing, signed by the testator and attested by two witnesses. As a general rule any attempt to make testamentary dispositions which do not comply with s9 are ineffective. However, secret trusts are in some respects an exception.

The main object of a secret trust is to keep secret the identity of a person upon whom a testator wishes to confer benefits. If a testator made a will in accordance with s9 and left legacies to his mistress or illegitimate children whose existence he had managed to conceal during his lifetime, then on the will being admitted to probate these matters would become public, as a proven will is available for public inspection at the probate registry. The secret trust avoids such problems; under it the testator leaves a legacy to a trustee, generally a close and trusted friend, either absolutely or upon trust, but not revealing the objects of the trust. The friend is told in confidence who the objects of the trust are and undertakings extracted from him to apply the legacy for their benefit. If the friend carries out the undertakings all is well, but if he refuses or claims the legacy for himself, the question arises whether he can be made by the court to fulfil his undertaking.

Secret trusts are classified into two categories – fully secret and half-secret. The former arise where no trust appears on the face of the will and the gift would otherwise be taken as an absolute gift to the beneficiary named in the will, for

63

example, '£10,000 to X'. A half-secret trust arises where the gift appears as one upon trust to the beneficiary named on the face of the will, but the objects of the trust are not revealed, for example, '£10,000 to X upon trust for the purposes I have communicated to him'. There are differences in some of the rules which apply to each of these types of secret trust.

Problems sometimes arise as to the proper classification of a secret trust as fully secret or half-secret. This may be important where the trust satisfies the tests, as later described, for the former but not the latter. The examples given above are obvious examples of the categories. But, what if the testator made a disposition in the following terms: '£10,000 to X knowing that he will carry out my wishes regarding the same as I have told him' or '£10,000 to X in full confidence that he will apply it as I have communicated to him'? In *Briggs* v *Penny* (1851) 3 Mac & G 546 provisions such as these were accepted as importing a trust. However, this case was decided before the courts' attitude to mere precatory words changed (see Chapter 2). Since the decision in *Re Adams and The Kensington Vestry* (1884) 27 Ch D 394 it is clear that such words would not, in themselves, create a trust and accordingly, they would not satisfy the rule that the trust must appear on the face of the will, necessary in half-secret trusts. Support for this can be found in *Irvine* v *Sullivan* (1869) LR 8 Eq 673, where James V-C refused to consider a disposition to a beneficiary 'trusting that she will carry out my wishes with regard to the same, with which she is fully acquainted' as showing a trust. In these cases the court will look to see if there is any confession by the legatee that there is a trust, or if there is any evidence of a trust having been communicated to the legatee behind the will. These would amount to fully secret trusts: see *Irvine* v *Sullivan* (above), and *Johnson* v *Ball* (1851) 5 De G & Sm 85.

However in one case, *Re Spencer's Will* (1887) 3 TLR 822, the Court of Appeal showed its willingness to go behind words in the will to see if a trust was imposed. In this case the terms were 'relying, but not by way of trust, upon their applying the sum in or towards the objects privately communicated to them'. Despite these words negativing a trust, the court admitted evidence to show that a secret trust had in fact been imposed on the legatees.

A form of secret trust may arise, albeit extremely rarely, in cases of intestacy, as Lord Westbury pointed out in *McCormick* v *Grogan* (1869) LR 4 HL 82:

'And if an individual on his deathbed, or at any other time, is persuaded by his heirs-at-law, or his next-of-kin to abstain from making a will, or if the same individual, having made a will, communicates the disposition to the person on the face of the will benefited by that disposition, but, at the same time, says to that individual that he has a purpose to answer which he has not expressed in the will, but which depends on the disponee to carry into effect, and the disponee assents to it, either expressly, or by any mode of action which the disponee knows must give to the testator the impression and belief that he fully assents to the request, then, undoubtedly the heir-at-law in the one case, and the disponee in the other, will be converted into trustees, simply on the principle that an individual shall not be benefited by his own personal fraud.'

Before considering the policy reasoning behind such trusts it is useful to first detail the distinct requirements imposed before they are enforced by the courts.

5.2 Fully-secret trusts

This is a trust which does not appear on the face of the will, the testator having told the legatee of the purpose of the trust outside the will. Before the court will declare a fully-secret trust to be valid the following conditions must be satisfied:

Communication

The testator must communicate the fact that the property is to be subject to a fully-secret trust to the legatee under his will. If there is no communication the legatee may take the property beneficially even if it is possible to prove that the testator intended him to hold it on a fully-secret trust. This is illustrated by *Wallgrave* v *Tebbs* (1855) 2 K & J 313, where a testator left £12,000 and certain lands to two persons apparently absolutely and as joint tenants. Shortly before his death he asked his executor to write to the two persons informing them of the objects towards which he wished them to apply the money and property. The executor wrote the letter but never sent it. The question arose whether the persons were bound by secret trusts on being informed of the testator's wishes after his death. It was held that there was no secret trust, and the two persons were entitled to the property for their own absolute benefit. In reaching this conclusion Wood V-C said:

> 'Here the devisees knew nothing of the testator's intention until after his death. That the testator desired, and was most anxious to have, his intentions carried out is clear. ... He has abstained from creating, either by his will or otherwise, any trust upon which this court can possibly fix. Upon the face of the will, the parties indisputably take for their own benefit ...'

Time for communication

Communication of a fully-secret trust can be made at any time during the testator's lifetime. It is irrelevant for these purposes whether the fully-secret trust was made known to the legatee before or after the date of the will: see *Wallgrave* v *Tebbs* (above). In that case Wood V-C said:

> 'If I knew perfectly well that a testator in making me a bequest, absolute on the face of the will, intended it to be applied for the benefit of a natural child, of whom he was not known to be the father, provided that intention had not been communicated to me during the testator's lifetime, the validity of the bequest as an absolute bequest to me could not be questioned ...'

All the terms of the trust must be communicated

The testator must make it clear what property is to be held on the secret trusts – this will normally be clear from the will itself – and he must also indicate who the beneficiaries of the secret trust are to be and how much each beneficiary is to receive. In *Re Boyes* (1884) 26 Ch D 531 a testator made a will leaving all his estate to his solicitor and appointing the solicitor as executor. The testator intended to communicate the terms of a fully-secret trust to the solicitor but failed to do this. The solicitor knew of this as he had been told that a secret trust was intended at the time the will was drawn up. After the testator's death his next-of-kin sought a declaration that they were entitled to the estate. The solicitor argued that there was a valid fully-secret trust. Kay J held there was no secret trust. The testator had failed to communicate any of the terms of the trust to the solicitor; the trust was therefore indefinite and the solicitor held the property for the next-of-kin. However this rule is tempered by the possibility of the courts holding that there has been 'constructive communication'.

Constructive communication

Communication need not be express, it can be constructive, for example, in the form of a sealed letter which is handed to the legatee with the instructions that it is not to be opened until after the testator's death. The letter should be handed to the legatee in the testator's lifetime for an effective constructive communication. In *Re Keen* [1937] Ch 236, the Court of Appeal accepted the words of Kay J in *Re Boyes* (above) and that:

> 'It may possibly be that he (the legatee) would be bound if the trust had been put in writing and placed in his hands in a sealed envelope, and he had engaged that he would hold the property given to him by the will upon the trust so declared, although he did not know the actual terms of the trust.'

This form of communication is commonly referred to as 'sailing under sealed orders'.

Communication of a legally binding obligation

The testator must communicate a legally binding obligation, not a mere moral obligation. The court will not enforce moral obligations as secret trusts. In *McCormick* v *Grogan* (1869) LR 4 HL 82 the testator made a will leaving all his property to Grogan. On his deathbed he summoned Grogan and informed him of the contents of his will and said a letter would be found with it. No undertaking was extracted from Grogan and the letter contained the names of various persons but went on: 'I do not wish you to act strictly to the foregoing instructions, but leave it entirely to your own good judgment to do as you think I would if living and as the parties are deserving.' Grogan excluded one of the persons named in the letter from any benefit and that person brought an action claiming there was a secret trust to give effect to the instructions contained in the letter. The House of Lords held there was no secret trust as the testator had imposed no legally binding obligation on Grogan. In giving judgment in the Court of Appeal in Ireland Christian LJ said:

> 'The real question is, what did he intend should be the sanction? Was it to be the authority of a Court of Justice, or the conscience of the devisee? In my opinion, expressly and exclusively the latter.'

This dictum was applied by Megarry V-C in *Re Snowden* [1979] Ch 528. In this case the testatrix could not make up her mind how to leave her estate in her will as she had many relatives. She finally made a will leaving all her substantial residue to her brother and told her solicitor that her brother could 'see to everybody and look after the division for her' and 'would know what to do'. The brother agreed to this but unfortunately he died six days after the testatrix and before he could deal with the residue. By his will all his estate went to his only son. The question arose whether a secret trust had been imposed on the brother. It was held that it was necessary to show that the sanction of the court had been intended to enforce the gift before a secret trust could be imposed. On the evidence only a moral obligation had been imposed on the brother and he took the residue free from any trust.

Acceptance

The legatee must accept the fully-secret trust. This can be either an express acceptance or implied from circumstances or conduct. In *Wallgrave* v *Tebbs* Wood V-C said:

> 'Where a person ... either expressly promises, or by silence implies, that he will carry the testator's intentions into effect, and the property is left to him upon the faith of that promise or undertaking, it is in effect a case of trust.'

The legatee is of course, free either to accept or reject the obligation, once its terms have been communicated to him, and if he does not, he will hold on resulting trust. He will only take beneficially if he did not know the terms of the trust in the testator's lifetime. In that case he may take beneficially even if he knew a trust was intended, but not its terms: see *Wallgrave* v *Tebbs*. There appears to have been implied acceptance in *Ottaway* v *Norman* [1972] Ch 698, where the testator made a will leaving his bungalow and all its contents to his housekeeper, apparently absolutely. Once, when one of T's sons was visiting him, the testator said in the presence of his housekeeper that he had made a will leaving the bungalow to the housekeeper but that after her death she should leave it to the son. The housekeeper said nothing at the time. After the testator's death, the housekeeper made a will leaving the bungalow to the son but subsequently they fell out and she made another will leaving the bungalow to a friend. It was held that there was a secret trust which the housekeeper had accepted by her conduct. She was placed in a position where it was her duty to speak up if she did not wish to be bound by the terms of the trust: see also *Moss* v *Cooper* (1861) 1 J & H 352.

Additions to the secret trust

If the testator, after having established the secret trust, wished to add more property to it or to add the names of other beneficiaries, then each and every addition to the secret trust must be communicated to and accepted by the trustees. That is, whilst they are additions to an existing secret trust they must comply with all of the normal requirements in full. In *Re Colin Cooper* [1939] Ch 811 the testator made a will leaving £5,000 on secret trusts to two persons jointly. The secret trust was communicated to both of them before the will was made. The testator increased the legacy by codicil by another £5,000 to the two persons, adding 'they knowing my wishes regarding that sum'. There was no mention of this increase to the two persons concerned during T's lifetime. The Court of Appeal held that there was a good secret trust of the first £5,000 but not of the second. As Lord Greene MR said:

> 'In order that a secret trust might be made effective with regard to that added sum ... the same factors were necessary as were required to validate the original trusts, namely, communication, acceptance or acquiesence and the making of a will on the faith of such acceptance or acquiescence.'

Presumably, the same principle will apply if the testator seeks to decrease the amount to be held on the secret trusts. However, see the following discussion as to the nature of secret trusts and the interest held by the beneficiary.

Sometimes the testator may make the gift by will to two or more legatees so that they all take as trustees of the secret trust, as was the case in *Wallgrave v Tebbs* and *Re Colin Cooper*. In such a case for all legatees to be bound depends very much on when communication was made to them and whether on the true construction of the will they take as joint tenants or tenants-in-common. The latter is purely a matter of construction, whilst the former is dealt with as follows.

Tenancy-in-common

Where there is a tenancy-in-common then each legatee is entitled to a separate share of the total gift, for example '£10,000 to A and B equally'. Should A in this example accept the secret trust on behalf of himself and B, then A but not B will be bound for the following reasons:
1. Any other conclusion would enable A to deprive B of his benefits by accepting a secret trust on his behalf and without his consent: see *Re Stead* [1900] 1 Ch 237.
2. Both A and B had definite shares and each share should therefore be considered in isolation: see *Tee v Ferris* (1856) 2 K & J 357.

These reasons were considered by the Irish Court of Appeal in *Geddis v Semple* [1903] 1 IR 73 where it was emphasised that the tenant-in-common who was not told of the secret trust could only take free from it if the gift to him could be treated as an independent one, and that he would have got it regardless of the undertaking given by the other tenant-in-common.

One possible exception to this is if his gift was induced by the other tenant-in-common's undertaking, then he too should be bound by the secret trust on the ground that one man should not profit by another's fraud: see *Huguenin* v *Baseley* (1807) 14 Ves 273.

Joint tenancy

If property is given to A and B as joint tenants, two possible situations must be considered where A accepts the secret trust on behalf of himself and B:

1. Where A accepts the secret trust *before* the will is made. In this instance the trust will bind both A and B for two reasons: first to allow B to claim for himself would be to permit him to claim under the fraud of another, see *Russell* v *Jackson* (1852) 10 Hare 204; second, a joint tenancy is convenient where there is a secret trust as it enables the survivor of the secret trustees to carry the purpose of the trust into effect in respect of the whole interest: see *Re Stead* [1900] 1 Ch 237.
2. Where A accepts the secret trust *after* the will is made. In this instance A but not B is bound and B can take his share beneficially. The reason given for this is that the gift is not tainted with any fraud in procuring the execution of the will: see *Moss* v *Cooper* (1861) 1 J & H 352.

This is of course subject to the same argument that B should be bound regardless if A procured the property by fraudulent methods. See: *Huguenin* v *Baseley* (above).

Further this second scenario clearly does not apply to half-secret trusts, as regardless as to the nature of A and B's interest in the property communication must take place before or at the same time as the will. (See later notes on this point.) No satisfactory reasons have been given for this illogical distinction apart from those mentioned above, and even these reasons are far from satisfactory because they overlook the fact that there may have been fraud inducing the testator not to revoke the will. This distinction was not accepted by the Irish Court of Appeal in *Geddis* v *Semple* where Holmes LJ said:

> 'I think it is settled that where a gift is given to two persons as joint tenants, a secret trust imparted to one of them will affect the whole gift; but that this arises from the peculiar nature of a joint estate is shown by repeated decisions that this rule does not apply to tenants-in-common.'

This dictum suggests that the acceptance by one secret trustee in a joint tenancy case binds all the trust property so that the other secret trustee can get nothing as a result. It may be that it carries the nature of joint tenancies too far, leaving no room for cases where the rule that one man should not profit by another man's fraud cannot apply. In *Re Stead* the court did not even find a secret trust so the facts of the case are not a useful illustration. But *Moss* v *Cooper* (1861) 1 J & H 352 supplies this. In that case the testator left his residuary estate to A, B and C absolutely. At the execution of the will a memorandum was prepared by A for the testator in which it was suggested that A, B and C should retain £25 each for themselves and apply the remainder in benefiting a number of named charities. A told B and C of the testator's wishes. B agreed to abide by them but C remained silent. It was held that A was the testator's authorised agent to communicate the trust and B and C knew this. B was bound as he had expressly accepted the trust, C was also bound because his silence led to the belief that he had accepted the trust and to allow him to take beneficially would be a fraud. Wood V-C stated:

> 'If immediately after making his will the testator had invited (the legatees) to his house, and said to them, "Here is my will, made in this form, ... but I want a promise from you to dispose of it in a particular way:" and if they, by their silence, led him to believe that they would so apply it, I apprehend that it is quite clear that a trust would be created ...'

5.3 Half-secret trusts

Half-secret trusts arise where the testator mentions the trust on the face of the will but does not state the purpose of the trust there but, instead, tells the legatee of the trust's purpose. There is much dispute as to the relationship of half-secret trusts and fully-secret trusts. The following conditions must be satisfied in the case of a half-secret trust:

Communication

The testator must communicate the half-secret trust to the legatee before or contemporaneously with the making of the will. This was finally settled by the House of Lords in *Blackwell* v *Blackwell* [1929] AC 318 where the testator gave a legacy of £12,000 to five persons upon trust 'for the purposes indicated by me to them'. He informed one of the legatees, in detail, of the objects of the trust and informed the other four, in outline, before he executed the will. The objects of the trust were the testator's mistress and his natural son by her. His wife brought an action for a declaration that the trust was invalid on the ground that parol evidence was inadmissible to prove the terms of a trust. It was held that as the trust had been communicated before the will was executed it was a good half-secret trust. Viscount Sumner gave reasons for the rule that communication must be before or at the time of the making of the will in half-secret trusts. He said:

> 'A testator cannot reserve to himself a power of making future unwitnessed dispositions by merely naming a trustee and leaving the purpose of the trust to be supplied afterwards, nor can a legatee give testamentary validity to an unexecuted codicil by accepting an indefinite trust, never communicated to him in the testator's lifetime. To hold otherwise would indeed be to enable the testator to "give the go-by" to the requirements of the Wills Act, because he did not choose to comply with them.'

It is difficult to see how this reasoning can be reconciled with that which applies to fully-secret trusts.

All the terms must be communicated

As in fully secret trusts the testator must tell the legatee of all the terms, though of course in the case of a half-secret trust the fact that the property is to be held on trust appears in the will and there is a presumption that the trustee was not intended to take beneficially: see *Re Boyes* (above).

Constructive communication

The rules are the same here as in fully-secret trusts and were considered in *Re Keen* [1937] Ch 236. In that case the constructive communication was ineffective because it contradicted the terms of the will and on the 'best evidence' rule the court was bound to prefer the words of the will to the parol evidence of those claiming there was a secret trust. In *Re Keen* the testator made a will by which he gave £10,000 to his executors 'to be held on trust and disposed of by them among such person, persons or charities as may be notified by me to them or either of them during my lifetime'. The testator had made a previous will in similar terms and at that time handed the executors a sealed envelope containing the terms of the trust directing them not to open it until his death. The question arose whether there was a valid secret trust. The Court of Appeal held that on the facts of the case the delivery of the envelope took place before the second will was executed. Therefore, the communication was not consistent with its terms and parol evidence could not be adduced to contradict the terms of the will. The secret trust was invalid. In giving judgment Lord Wright MR said of the clause referred to above:

> '... in my judgment clause 5 should be considered as contemplating future dispositions and as reserving to the testator the power of making such dispositions without a duly attested codicil by simply notifying them during his lifetime, the principles laid down by Lord Sumner must be fatal to the ... claim [see 'Communication' above] ... but, there is still a further objection which in the present case renders the appellant's claim unenforceable; the trusts which it is sought to establish by parol evidence would be inconsistent with the express terms of the will ... while clause 5 refers solely to a future definition or to future definitions of the trust subsequent to the date of the will, the sealed letter relied on as notifying the trust was communicated before the will ... the notification ... was anterior to the will and hence not within the language of clause 5, and inadmissible simply on that ground as being inconsistent with what the will prescribes.'

Communication must be of a legally binding obligation

The principles are the same in half-secret trusts, as in fully-secret trusts.

Acceptance

The rules are similar to those in fully secret trusts: see *Wallgrave* v *Tebbs* and *Ottaway* v *Norman* (above).

Additions to the secret trust

The rules are the same as in fully-secret trusts: see *Re Colin Cooper* (above).

5.4 Basis of secret trusts

The principle underlying secret trusts is thought to be the prevention of fraud, or, to put it another way, the courts will refuse to permit statute (the requirements of s9 of the Wills Act 1837, amended) to cloak a fraud: see *Rochefoucauld* v *Boustead* [1897] 1 Ch 196. Fraud is of course the basis of many trusts, and is of course the basis of all trusts, and many modern commentators such as Pettit, Hanbury and Maudsley see secret trusts as an enforcement of an inter vivos express trust which takes effect on the death of the settlor. This theory also avoids the difficulty of explaining why the secret trust takes effect outside of the Wills Act. Fraud of course certainly plays a part. This appears from the speech of Lord Westbury in *McCormick* v *Grogan* (1869) LR 4 HL 82 (see section 5.1) and from what was said by Viscount Sumner in *Blackwell* v *Blackwell*. Lord Westbury also said in *McCormick* v *Grogan*:

> 'The jurisdiction which is invoked here is founded altogether on personal fraud. It is a jurisdiction by which a Court of Equity, proceeding on the ground of fraud, converts the party who has committed it into a trustee for the party who is injured by that fraud. Now, being a jurisdiction founded on a personal fraud, it is incumbent on the court to see that a fraud, a malus animus, is proved by the clearest and most indisputable evidence. You are obliged, therefore, to show most clearly and distinctly that the person you wish to convert into a trustee acted malo animo. You must show distinctly that he knew that the testator or intestate was beguiled or deceived by his conduct. If you are not in a condition to affirm that without any misgiving, or possibility of mistake, you are not warranted in affixing on the individual the delictum of fraud, which you must do before you convert him into a trustee ...'

However, Viscount Sumner seems to base the jurisdiction for the enforcement of secret trusts on wider grounds, involving the enforcement of equitable obligations binding on a man's conscience:

> 'A court of conscience finds a man in the position of an absolute legal owner of a sum of money which has been bequeathed to him under a valid will, and it declares that, on proof of certain facts relating to the motives and actions of the testator, it will not allow the legal owner to exercise his legal right to do what he will with his own ... The necessary elements, on which the question turns are intention, communication and acquiescence. The testator intends his absolute gift to be employed as he and not his donee desires; he tells the proposed donee of his intention and, either by express promise or by the tacit promise, which is signified by acquiescence, the proposed donee encourages him to bequeath the money in the faith that his intentions will be carried out ... in its application to a bequest the doctrine must in principle rest on the assumption the the will has first operated according to its terms. It is because there is no one to whom the law can give relief in the premises, that relief, if any, must be sought in equity ... For the

prevention of fraud equity fastens on the conscience of the legatee a trust, a trust that is, which would otherwise be inoperative, in other words it makes him do what the will in itself has nothing to do with; it lets him take what the will gives him and then makes him apply it, as the Court of conscience directs, and it does so in order to give effect to the wishes of the testator which would not otherwise be effectual ...'

This dicta conveniently leads to a split into the fraud theory supporting secret trusts. The first limb rests on preventing the unjust enrichment of the legatee; the second that of preventing a fraud on the testator's intention and/or beneficiary's interest.

The first of these was relied on in the decision in *McCormick* v *Grogan* (above). Yet it clearly cannot support half-secret trusts given that the legatee is actually stated to be a trustee on the face of the will. Hence in a half-secret trust the legatee has nothing to gain; any failure of the trust will lead to a resulting trust being imposed in favour of the testator's residuary beneficiaries, or next-of-kin under partial intestacy. Only if the legatee (failed half-secret trustee) is a beneficiary via this route will he be guaranteed any interest: see *Re Rees WT* [1950] Ch 204. In fact the only additional support that can be found for half-secret trusts under this limb is the now superseded rule that in the instances previously noted the resulting trust would automatically be in favour of the initial legatee: see *Thynn* v *Thynn* (1684) 1 Vera 296. This is tenuous support to say the least.

The second limb of the fraud theory is that of preventing a fraud of the testator's intention and, or of the beneficiary's interest. This was argued extremely persuasively in *Blackwell* v *Blackwell* (above). However, again this theory has a rocky foundation. First it rests on the presumption that a fraud is being perpetrated; hence the courts waive the statutory provisions involved in order that this fraud might be established. Further it implies knowledge on the part of the beneficiary of his interest in the secret trust, not normally required for other trusts: see *Middleton* v *Pollock* (1876) 2 Ch D 104.

Given the uncertain validity of the fraud theory it is not surprising that a champion seems to have replaced it; namely the 'de hors' the will theory. That is that the trust is an inter vivos creature, activated on the testator's death and taking effect outside of the terms of, and provisions governing, the will. This theory further rests on the strict communication requirements which imply that the testator has only created the trust on the mutual understanding that the trustee has agreed to hold the property on trust for the named beneficiary.

The follow-on from what is the theory underlying secret trusts is what type of trusts are they; namely express trusts, constructive trusts and so on? The former finds support in the 'de hors' the will theory, whilst the latter avoids the previously explained difficulties in s53(1)(c). Given the clear conflict it is best to deal with fully-secret and half-secret trusts separately once more.

Fully-secret trusts

These are arguably constructive trusts because they are imposed either to prevent fraud or by equity acting at the conscience of the legatee, though the decision in *Re Young* that they operate outside the will does not support this. They could be claimed to be express trusts, since the testator's wishes are expressed and the trust is imposed to carry these out. If this view is correct then there could not be effective fully-secret trusts of land or equitable interests unless s53(1)(b) and (c) LPA 1925 were satisfied. The decision in *Ottaway* v *Norman* which concerned a secret trust of land did not raise these points, suggesting negative support for the view that they are not express trusts. It is arguable that fully-secret trusts are implied trusts, implied to give effect to the wishes of the testator, but there seems to be little in the way of judicial dicta to support this view. However, it is submitted that they are constructive trusts.

Half-secret trusts

These appear to be express trusts. The existence of the trust is clearly stated on the face of the will and the subject-matter of the trust is referred to there. However, the court has to look behind the will to discover the objects and the nature of their interests. These matters have to be communicated before or at the time of execution of the will. The cases seem to treat communication of these matters on a parallel with the probate doctrine of incorporation by reference. Whether this is justified is questionable. In support of the view that half-secret trusts are express trusts is the fact that there can be no fraud about the existence of the trust and there seems little chance of the secret trustee claiming benefits under it on the present state of the authorities: see section 5.5. Also the trust is expressly set out. These facts negative the imposition of a constructive trust, but as yet the classification of half secret trusts as constructive trusts cannot be ruled out completely because of the problem over communication of the objects.

5.5 Secret trusts and the Wills Act 1837

There are some situations where the rules for secret trusts and the provisions of the Wills Act 1837 come into conflict. Most of the conflicts have been resolved by decided cases but, as will be seen, some matters are still without a clear answer.

Attestation of the will by secret beneficiary

Under s15 Wills Act 1837 a witness to a will, or his spouse, cannot benefit under that will. This is to ensure that if the witnesses are required to testify as to the circumstances in which the will was executed, their evidence will be impartial rather than tainted because they have a pecuniary interest in the will. But what if the beneficiary under the secret trust, or his spouse, witness the will? In *Re Young* [1951] Ch 344 it was held that secret trusts operate outside the will so that a beneficiary under a secret trust who witnessed the will would not be deprived of his benefit. The rule appears to apply to both fully- and half-secret trusts. In *Re Young*, a testator made a bequest to his widow 'leaving such small legacies as she knows I wish to be paid'. T told his wife, before executing the will, that he wished her to give his chauffeur £2,000. The chauffeur was a witness to the will. Danckwerts J held he was not affected by s15. He said:

> 'The whole theory of the formation of a secret trust is that the Wills Act has nothing to do with the matter because the forms required by the Wills Act are entirely disregarded, since the persons do not take by virtue of the gift in the will, but by virtue of the secret trusts imposed upon the beneficiary, who does in fact take under the will ...'

Attestation of the will by the legatee

Whether the legatee can take as a secret trustee if he witnesses the will is not entirely clear. In fully-secret trusts the answer appears to be that he cannot because no trust is revealed on the face of the will so that in deciding whether, under the Wills Act 1837, the legacy should vest in him, s15 must be applied. The legacy then fails and the secret trusts have nothing to operate upon. Such a conclusion is consistent with Viscount Sumner's explanation of the basis of secret trusts in *Blackwell* v *Blackwell* (above), and obiter dicta of Cozens-Hardy LJ in *Re Maddock* [1902] 2 Ch 220 at 251 support this conclusion. In half-secret trusts the trust is revealed on the face of the will. It is well established that attesting witnesses can take as express trustees under the will: see *Cresswell* v *Cresswell* (1868) LR 6 Eq 69. In the Canadian case of *Re Armstrong* (1969) 7 DLR (3d) 36 a half-secret trust was upheld where the legatee witnessed the will. There is no English authority on the point, but there seems no reason why the half-secret trust should be struck down in these circumstances, especially if it is classified as an express trust, since the decision in *Cresswell* v *Cresswell* would apply.

Secret beneficiary predeceases the testator

Under a will a beneficiary must survive the testator in order to benefit by the will: see s25 Wills Act 1837. In *Re Gardner (No 2)* [1923] 2 Ch 330 it was held that a beneficiary under a secret trust received his interest when the trust was created, so it could not be subsequently defeated by his death. This conclusion appears to ignore the fact that a will is ambulatory, that is, of no effect, until the testator's death and that until then the trust is incompletely constituted. In *Re Gardner* the testatrix left all her estate to her husband 'knowing that he will carry out my wishes'. The wishes were that at the husband's death the property was to be divided among three named persons. The husband died five days after the testatrix and it was then discovered that one of the three named beneficiaries had died before the testatrix. The question arose whether that beneficiary's share had lapsed. Romer J held that as the beneficiary's share arose under the trust and not under the will, it was not affected by the doctrine of lapse. This decision seems to treat the legatee as an express trustee, whose death does not affect the trust, as such, and the secret beneficiary as the beneficiary under an express trust whilst at the same time it has been suggested that the corollary argument is that therefore the secret beneficiary has some form of interest even prior to the testator's death. This almost implies that a constructive trust arises as soon as the trust is first communicated.

Legatee predeceases the testator

In fully-secret trusts the position is clear, if the legatee predeceases the testator then the fully-secret trust fails: see *Re Maddock* (1902) (above). This can be supported on the ground that the legacy must be valid under the will before the secret trust operates on it; in a half-secret trust the position may well be different. It is well accepted that equity will not allow a trust to fail for want of a trustee: see *Re Smirthwaite* (1871) LR 11 Eq 251. So long as the purpose of the half-secret trust is known, it should be enforced. This illogical distinction points again to the difficulties in establishing a common overall theme for secret trusts.

A similar reasoning seems to apply to when a trustee disclaims his role. For a half-secret trust equity will simply step in to appoint a new trustee. However, for a fully-secret trust the trust could arguably fail unless fraud can be imputed as a reason behind the actual disclaimer by the fully-secret trustee: see *Bannister* v *Bannister* [1948] 2 All ER 133.

Legatee a beneficiary under secret trust

There is nothing in the Wills Act to prevent a legatee and secret trustee being a beneficiary under a secret trust. However, equity takes a different view of the position. The problem has arisen particularly in cases involving half-secret trusts and here it appears that the general rule is that a secret trustee cannot usually benefit under a half-secret trust, mainly because of problems of proof. But this general rule and the reasons behind it require careful consideration. If the trustee of a half-secret trust claimed to be the sole beneficiary under the trust, it is clearly established that this would be rejected. In *Re Pugh's Will Trusts* [1967] 1 WLR 1262 Pennycuick J said such a claim would raise the suspicion of the court because there would seem no useful purpose in creating such a secret trust. This problem does not appear to have arisen in the context of fully-secret trusts, but if a fully-secret trust were clearly established, then presumably a claim by the secret trustee would meet with the same answer. If the secret trust is that the secret trustee should, for example, keep £100 for himself and apply the remainder for specified charitable purposes, the rationale in *Re Pugh* cannot apply. In such cases it would appear that the courts are more concerned with the nature of the evidence presented to justify the secret trustee's claim.

In *Re Rees* [1950] Ch 204 a testator created a half-secret trust and asked the trustees to apply the money for certain objects and to keep any surplus for themselves. There was a surplus. The Court of Appeal held that this must be returned on resulting trusts to the testator's estate. The judgments in this case do not go so far as laying down an absolute rule that the secret trustee under a half-secret trust cannot benefit. Instead, the court appears to have refused to accept the word of the secret trustees alone that they were intended to keep the surplus, in view of the fact that they were also entitled to receive remuneration under the will for their work. The judgments tend to suggest that if a letter in the testator's hand had been produced then the position would have been different. Indeed, such a letter would in many cases avoid the need to resort to secret trusts, as it might be part of the will under the probate doctrine of incorporation by reference. But on the facts of *Re Rees* there was an unresolved conflict of interest and duty on the part of the trustees and so the court considered that they should not be permitted to benefit.

5.6 Miscellaneous

Onus of proof and standard

It is now established that the onus of establishing a secret trust rests on the secret beneficiary: see *Re Snowden* (above). Further the standard of proof is the normal civil one, as opposed to the slightly higher test imposed when fraud is being alleged: see *Jones* v *Badley* (1868) LR 3 Ch App 362.

Incorporation by reference

Under this doctrine a paper can be read into a will provided three conditions have been satisfied: (1) it is in existence at the date of the will; (2) it is referred to in the will as being in existence; (3) it is clearly identified in the will: see *Singleton* v *Tomlinson* (1878) 3 App Cas 404. This doctrine permits a testator to include a long document as part of his will without having to rewrite it into the will itself. The doctrine has been used in the past as an alternative to half-secret trusts, to save gifts originally intended to be on half-secret trusts. If T left £10,000 to X on half-secret trusts, stating in the will that X could find the terms of the trust in a letter addressed to X and now in T's writing desk, the letter would satisfy the conditions for incorporation by reference. Therefore, should the secret trust fail for some reason, this doctrine could be relied on to save the gift. The main difficulty with incorporation by reference is that the letter would be deemed part of the will and available for all to see. Secrecy would not be preserved.

6

Resulting Trusts

6.1 Introduction

6.2 Presumed resulting trusts based on intention

6.3 Failure to exhaust beneficial interest

6.4 Joint ownership of matrimonial property

6.1 Introduction

Resulting trusts arise where a donor or settlor has made a transfer of property but that transfer does not for some reason divest him completely of his interest in the property. A recent, authorative formulation of the nature of the resulting trust was made by Lord Browne-Wilkinson in *Westdeutsche Landesbank Girozentrale* v *Islington London Borough Council* [1996] 2 All ER 961. Lord Browne-Wilkinson identified two sets of circumstances when a resulting trust arises:

1. Where A makes a voluntary payment to B or pays (wholly or in part) for the purchase of property which is vested either in B alone or in the joint names of A and B, there is a presumption that A did not intend to make a gift to B: the money or property is held on trust for A (if he is a sole provider of the money) or, in the case of a joint purchase by A and B, in shares proportionate to their contributions.
2. Where A transfers property to B on express trusts, but the trusts declared do not exhaust the whole beneficial interest.

He went on to say at 991:

'Megarry J in *Re Vandervell's Trusts (No 2)* [1974] Ch 269 suggests that a resulting trust of type [2] does not depend on intention but operates automatically. I am not convinced that this is right. If the settlor has expressly, or by necessary implication, abandoned any interest in the trust property, there is in my view no resulting trust: the undisposed of equitable interest vests in the Crown as bona vacantia: see *Re West Sussex Constabulary's Widows Children and Benevolent (1930) Fund Trusts* [1970] 1 All ER 544, [1971] Ch 1.'

The resulting trust envisaged by Lord Browne-Wilkinson depends upon express or implied intention. In the absence of such intention, difficulties arise as to what happens when the trusts declared do not exhaust the whole beneficial interest. See Chapter 28, section 28.1, for further details.

6.2 Presumed resulting trusts based on intention

Presumed resulting trusts arise in three main situations described below. But they also arise where matrimonial property is involved and this is considered separately in section 6.4. However, before considering these three main situations it is useful to stress that they are only presumptions. Therefore, on each case's individual facts, that presumption can be rebutted and a full transfer, for example a gift, can be found.

Purchase in the name of another

Where A purchases property with his own money and directs that it be transferred into the name of B there will be a resulting trust in the absence of any legal presumption or evidence to the contrary. B will therefore hold the property in resulting trusts for A. The resulting trust is based on what equity considers to have been the presumed intention of A. The earliest, and leading, decision on this point is *Dyer* v *Dyer* (1788) 2 Cox Eq 92 where Eyre CB said:

> 'The clear result of all the cases, without a single exception, is that the trust of a legal estate, whether freehold or copyhold, or leasehold; whether taken in the names of purchasers jointly, or in the name of others without that of the purchaser; whether in one name or several; whether jointly or successive, results to the man who advances the purchase money.'

As *Dyer* v *Dyer* indicates, the principle applies where A purchases the property and has it conveyed into the names of himself and B. It also includes cases where property is purchased by A and B jointly but is conveyed into the name of A alone: see *Bull* v *Bull* [1955] 1 QB 234. In all cases the presumption in favour of a resulting trust depends upon the facts and circumstances adduced in evidence. In *Fowkes* v *Pascoe* (1875) 10 Ch App 343, a Mrs Baker purchased stock in the joint names of herself and the son of her widowed daughter-in-law. As the son was a stranger in the circumstances he would normally have been regarded as a resulting trustee of the stock in his name, but the Court of Appeal held that on the evidence before it the presumption of a resulting trust was rebutted. The son was entitled to the stock absolutely on Mrs Baker's death as surviving joint tenant. In giving judgment Mellish LJ said:

> '... the presumption must, beyond all question, be of very different weight in different cases. In some cases it would be very strong indeed. If, for instance, a man invested a sum of stock in the name of himself and his solicitor, the inference would be very strong indeed that it was intended solely for the purpose of a trust, and the Court would require very strong evidence on the part of the solicitor to prove that it was intended as a gift;

and certainly his own evidence would not be sufficient. On the other hand a man may make an investment of stock in the name of himself and some other person, although not a child or wife, yet in such a position to him as to make it extremely probable that the investment was intended as a gift. In such a case, although the rule of law, if there was no evidence at all, would compel the Court to say that the presumption of trust must prevail, even if the Court might not believe that the fact was in accordance with the presumption, yet, if there is evidence to rebut the presumption, then, in my opinion, the Court must go into the actual facts ...'

In *Fowkes* v *Pascoe* the son of Mrs Baker's widowed daughter-in-law lived in her house, she provided for him and had no nearer relatives. In addition, she already had a large holding of stock similar to that she purchased in joint names, and this was vested in her sole name. The court concluded that she must have intended the stock as a present for him after her death.

Whether a resulting trust arises from any particular circumstances depends very much on the actual or presumed intention of the parties at the time of acquisition. If there is an agreement, this will be taken into account, but it is not conclusive. In most cases there will be no express agreement; the parties may have made contributions to the purchase of the property or conducted themselves in a manner which can only infer agreement to particular things: see *Cowcher* v *Cowcher* [1972] 1 WLR 425.

There may be purchase in the name of another where A and B pay for property by making contributions and where the property is conveyed into the name of A alone. For example, a husband, A, and a wife, B, buy a house with the assistance of a mortgage which is conveyed into the sole name of A, and the mortgage is subsequently paid off by their joint efforts. In such circumstances A will hold some interest in the property on a resulting trust for B: see *Cowcher* v *Cowcher*. However, the contributions in such cases must have been intended as part of the purchase price and not merely a loan or contributions towards rent or household expenses. In *Savage* v *Dunningham* [1974] Ch 181 one of several flat occupiers who shared under an informal agreement as to the payment of rent and other outgoings, was offered the chance by the landlord to purchase the flat for himself. He bought the flat and shortly afterwards gave the other sharers notice to quit. They argued that he held the property on a resulting trust for all of them. It was held that there was no resulting trust. Contributions to the purchase money did not include rent and household expenses in these circumstances.

See also the recent decision in *Harwood* v *Harwood* [1991] Fam Law 418. This, in part, addressed the ownership of a house purchased in the name of A and B with some of the purchase monies coming from a partnership between A and others. On the facts, and in the absence of any contrary intention, the court found that a resulting trust arose in favour of the partnership in the proportion of their contribution to its purchase price.

Transfer into the name of another

The treatment of the transfer of property into the name of another depends initially on whether the property in question is realty (ie land) or personalty.

Where land is concerned, both freehold and leasehold, there is no presumption of a resulting trust when it is voluntarily conveyed by one party into the name of another. Section 60(3) LPA 1925 negatives a resulting trust here because it states that a resulting trust is not to be implied 'merely by reason that the property is not expressed to be for the use or benefit of the grantee'. The last words are a reference to the Statute of Uses 1535 which was repealed in 1925, by which a resulting trust would arise if there was a voluntary conveyance which did not state that the land was conveyed to the use and benefit of the grantee.

The point was mentioned obiter in *Hodgson* v *Marks* [1971] Ch 892 but nothing was decided on it. However, it should be noted that in *Hodgson* v *Marks* a resulting trust was imposed in any event. In this case Mrs Hodgson, aged 83, had a lodger called Evans who had gained her confidence and looked after her affairs. Mrs Hodgson's relatives were suspicious and pressed her to give him notice to leave but, instead, she conveyed the house they lived in to Evans to protect him. This was done on the basis of an oral agreement that she would remain the beneficial owner. Evans sold the house to Marks and the Court of Appeal held that Evans was a resulting trustee so that Mrs Hodgson was the equitable owner and had an overriding interest under s70(1)(g) Land Registration Act 1925. This case highlights well the effect of s60(3) which effectively reverses the presumption of a resulting trust for the transferor in favour of a use for the transferee. However this too is only a presumption which, on the facts, can itself be rebutted.

In the case of a voluntary transfer of pure personalty into the name of another the weight of opinion favours a resulting trust for the transferor, and so there is no gift to the transferee. In *Re Vinogradoff* [1935] WN 68 a woman transferred stock into the name of herself and her four-year-old granddaughter. A resulting trust was held to exist. Apart from tax reasons it is difficult to see any reason behind such actions other than an intention to benefit the granddaughter.

Presumption of advancement

As noted, these resulting trusts are merely presumptions in the absence of any contrary intention. However, in addition to these presumptions there are contrary presumptions which imply an outright gift in favour of the transferee. These fall under the general term 'advancement'. The presumption of advancement only operates in specific situations which raise an obligation on the part of the donor to provide for the donee. The main cases where it may arise are between husband and wife and father and child, including a person standing in loco parentis to a child. The basis of the presumption was explained by Jessel MR in *Bennet* v *Bennet* (1879) 10 Ch D 474:

'The doctrine of equity as regards the presumption of gifts is this, that where one person stands in such a relation to another that there is an obligation on that person to make a provision for the other, and we find either a purchase or investment in the name of the other, or in the joint names of the person and the other, of an amount which would constitute a provision for the other, the presumption arises of an intention on the part of the person to discharge the obligation to the other; and, therefore, in the absence of evidence to the contrary, that purchase or investment is held to be in itself evidence of a gift.'

However, the recent decision of the Court of Appeal in *McGrath* v *Wallis* (1995) The Times 13 April confirms the recent trend of authorities to the effect that the equitable presumption of advancement should only be considered as a judicial instrument of last resort where properties are acquired for joint occupation but conveyed to a sole name. Arguably, the Court of Appeal's reasoning extends beyond purchases of property and sounds the death knell for the effectiveness of this presumption, save in circumstances where there is absolutely no evidence to contradict the presumption.

Husband and wife

Where a husband makes a voluntary conveyance of his property into the name of his wife, prima facie it is considered as a gift to her: see *Thornley* v *Thornley* [1893] 2 Ch 229. The presumption is very weak today and is easily rebutted: see *Pettitt* v *Pettitt* [1970] AC 777. The presumption does not apply where the reverse occurs, and a wife purchases property and conveys it into the name of her husband. In such a case there is, prima facie, a resulting trust: see *Mercier* v *Mercier* [1903] 2 Ch 98.

Father and legitimate child

Where a father makes a voluntary conveyance of his property into the name of his legitimate child there is a presumption of gift: see *Shephard* v *Cartwright* [1955] AC 431. The same rules apply to the payment of premiums on an insurance policy for the benefit of a legitimate child: see *Re Roberts* [1946] Ch 1. This presumption does not apply to mother and child (*Bennet* v *Bennet* (1879) 10 Ch D 474) nor does it apply between a father and son-in-law or uncle and nephew. The presumption of advancement may, however, apply between a man and a child to whom he stands in loco parentis, where he has assumed the duty of providing for the child. In *Ebrand* v *Dancer* (1860) 2 Ch App 26 it applied to a grandchild and grandfather where the child's father was dead.

The presumption of advancement can be rebutted by evidence which shows that it was not the intention of a husband or father to make gifts to a wife or child. As in the case of a husband and wife, the presumption of advancement between father and legitimate child would appear to be relatively easily rebuttable with the judicial doctrine of advancement being one of last resort (per the Court of Appeal in *McGrath* v *Wallis* (above)). In *Re Emery's Investment Trusts* [1959] Ch 410 a husband purchased American Bonds and registered them in the name of his wife to evade American tax. Wynn-Parry J refused evidence of this illegal purpose to be admitted to rebut the presumption. In *Gascoigne* v *Gascoigne* [1918] 1 KB 223 evidence that a husband put land and a bungalow he built on it into the name of his wife in order to protect the property from his creditors was not admissible to rebut the presumption of advancement. In reversing a county court judge's decision to the contrary Lush LJ said:

> 'He has permitted the plaintiff to rebut the presumption which the law raises by setting up his own illegality and fraud, and to obtain relief in equity because he has succeeded in proving it. The plaintiff cannot do this ...'

Further the courts will hold against a resulting trust in situations where the actual property, albeit notionally transferred to the donee, is retained by the donor. See *Warren* v *Gurney* [1944] 2 All ER 472 where the donor transferred property but retained possession of the deeds and was thereby deemed to have retained control and ownership of it.

Even in the case of evidence not involving an improper purpose there are limitations as to admissibility. In *Shephard* v *Cartwright* [1955] AC 431 a father transferred shares in a number of family companies into the name of his children when they were young. Later, when the companies went public, the father got the children to sign the necessary documents transferring the shares to him again without telling them what they were signing. On the father's death, his executors claimed that the shares belonged to the estate, relying on the way he procured the signatures. The House of Lords held that the presumption of advancement had not been rebutted and affirmed the rules that all acts and declarations made before or at the time of the transfer are admissible either for or against the party whose acts or declarations are in question, but subsequent declarations are only admissible as evidence against the party who made them and not in his favour.

Ineffective declaration of trust

A settlor who makes a declaration of trust which is ineffective because of, for example, uncertainty of objects, failure to satisfy formal requirements or perpetuity, will be entitled to the trust property on resulting trusts, so that the trustees will hold on trust for him. This problem arose in *Re Vandervell's Trusts (No 2)* [1974] Ch 269 which has already been referred to in Chapter 3. Vandervell directed his trustees to transfer shares to the Royal College of Surgeons to endow a chair of pharmacology. The scheme was that £145,000 of dividends would be declared on the shares and an option to repurchase them would be exercised by the trustees for £5,000 giving the Royal College £150,000 in all. The Revenue were successful in assessing Vandervell to surtax on the dividends received by the Royal College. The option was trust property, it was a chose in action, and in the period before its exercise by the trustees it was held on a resulting trust for Vandervell.

6.3 Failure to exhaust beneficial interest

Failure to dispose of entire beneficial interest

If a trust is created which does not deal with all of the beneficial interest in the trust property, then, so much of it as is not dealt with by the trust is held on resulting trusts for the settlor. For example, if a settlor created a trust for A for life but failed to indicate what should happen to the trust property thereafter, a resulting trust would arise immediately to take effect on A's death. In *Re Trusts of the Abbott Fund* [1900] 2 Ch 326 Dr Abbott settled funds, in his will, upon trust for his two daughters, who were deaf and dumb. One of the trustees misappropriated all the trust funds and this was not discovered until after the trustee's death in 1889. A fund was raised by friends to support the two daughters. On the death of the last surviving daughter in 1900 there was a surplus left in the fund. Stirling J held that this money was held on resulting trusts for the subscribers. A resulting trust may arise here whether the beneficial interest is undisposed of once the trust as declared has run its course, or the beneficial interest is undisposed of during the trust. For example, in a trust to A for life, so long as she lives with B, remainder to B for life, remainder to the survivor, when A ceased to live with B there was a resulting trust though both were still alive: see *Re Cochrane* [1955] Ch 309.

Failure of an express trust

An express trust may have made disposal of the entire beneficial interest in the trust property but it may be subject to conditions being fulfilled which are not, in the events which happen, fulfilled. For example, if a settlor sets up a trust for his only son contingent on the son attaining 25, and he dies at 22, there will be a resulting trust. This problem has arisen in the context of marriage settlements. In *Re Ames' Settlement* [1946] Ch 217 a father settled £10,000 on the trusts of a marriage settlement on the marriage of his son. The marriage took place but was held to have been void in court proceedings in 1926. The son continued to receive income from the settlement until his death in 1946. On the son's death the question arose whether the money should go to those who took as ultimate remaindermen under the settlement, or to the estate of the settlor on resulting trusts. Vaisey J held there was a resulting trust as marriage had been void ab initio; the settlement was based on consideration which had failed.

See also the decision in *Re Gillingham Bus Disaster Fund* [1958] Ch 300. This case concerned the disposal of a fund subscribed by the public to relieve the victims of a serious accident. Much of the money had come from street collections and other untraceable sources. The actual fund itself had in effect failed as part of its objects had been covered by various insurance payments, and the other objects terms 'worthy causes' were held to be void for their uncertainty. A resulting trust was imposed because as Harman J said:

'I see no reason myself to suppose that the small giver who is anonymous has any wider intention than the larger giver who can be named. They all give for one object. If they can be found by inquiry the resulting trust can be executed in their favour. If they cannot I do not see how the money could then, with all respect to Jenkins LJ, change its destination and become bona vacantia. It will be merely money held upon a trust for which no beneficiary can be found. Such cases are common and where it is known that there are beneficiaries the fact that they cannot be ascertained does not entitle the Crown to come in and claim. The trustees must pay the money into court like any other trustee who cannot find his beneficiary. I conclude, therefore, that there must be an inquiry for the subscribers to this fund.'

Surplus on trust being fulfilled

It is uncommon for there to be a surplus in a private trust as the settlor usually gives the full benefit of the property to the beneficiaries. For example A transfers property to B for life, remainder to C. However, as previously noted it is possible for only a part benefit to be given to the beneficiaries: see *Re Trusts of the Abbott Fund* (above). In addition it is possible for beneficiaries to have only a limited interest by way of the trust being linked to a purpose which itself might become fulfilled: see *Re Derley's Trust Deed* [1969] 1 Ch 373. In such circumstances a resulting trust in favour of the original donor is usually inferred.

However, this resulting trust can itself be rebutted if the facts permit it. A classic means is that of referring to the precise wording of the donor's initial gift or trust and determining its proper meaning. By so doing it is possible for the surplus to be held either to be that of the trustees or beneficiaries absolutely. That is, if the courts find the trust is actually an absolute gift to the beneficiaries subject to a stated purpose then the beneficiaries will be granted the surplus: see *Re Andrew's Trust* [1905] 2 Ch 48. In contrast if the transfer is held to be an absolute gift in favour of the trustees again subject to a minor purpose in favour of the beneficiaries any surplus will be the trustees': see *Re Foord* [1922] 2 Ch 519. It is a matter of construction as to which scenario prevails.

Unfortunately the concept of a resulting trust does not necessarily represent the most logical or convenient means of distributing such surpluses. This is particularly so when mutual benefit societies, or unincorporated associations, are considered. The best definition of an unincorporated association is found in the dicta in *Conservative and Unionist Central Office* v *Burrell* [1982] 1 WLR 522. In essence they are viewed as organisations of two or more persons bound by a common purpose, effort, usually monetary contributions, and striving towards a definite goal governed by rules. The difficulties with them arise when they cease to exist. Such 'dissolution' can take four possible routes: that of a voluntary member-driven termination; the occurrence of a specified event as per its rules; the loss of the association's purpose or sub-statum and finally via the court's power to wind them up if it is just and equitable to do so: see *Re William Derby Sick and Benevolent Fund* [1971] 1 WLR 973.

The dissolution of such associations and the ultimate distribution of surplus assets requires careful explanation. Two distinct theories for distribution have been proffered. The first, the trust theory, is applied as in the previously mentioned *Re Trusts of the Abbott Fund*; the money reverts via a resulting trust to the original donors. This clearly poses problems when the membership of the association has not remained fixed during its life. Therefore is the surplus divided amongst all previous members or only the current membership? Support for the former is found in *Re Hobourn Aero Components Air Raid Distress Fund* [1946] Ch 194. In contrast, the latter option was adopted in *Re Printers and Transferers Amalgamated Trades Protection Society* [1899] 2 Ch 84. The latter is preferable given its administrative benefits; there being no need to undertake a potentially fruitless task of tracing all of the association's past members.

The main criticism of the trust theory is that it implies a naive and ultimately unworkable intention on the part of the original donor. This dissatisfaction is admirably revealed by the decision in *Cunnack* v *Edwards* [1896] 2 Ch 679 which forms the basis of the second theory, the contract theory. Here a society was formed to provide annuities for widows of deceased members. Funds came from subscriptions, fines and forfeitures. All of the members had died by 1879 and the last widow died in 1892. The problem for the court was what to do with the £1,250 surplus. Holding that a resulting trust should not be applied, L Smith LJ said:

> 'As the member paid his money to the society, so he divested himself of all interest in his money for ever, with this one reservation, that if the member left a widow she was to be provided for during her widowhood. Except as to this he abandoned and gave up the money for ever.'

As there was no longer any beneficiary entitled to the surplus it went bona vacantia to the Crown, the contract having been fulfilled. Attempts to sidestep this perceived unfair result, whilst still harassing the contract theory have confused matters further: see *Re West Sussex Constabulary's Widows, Children and Benevolent (1930) Fund Trusts* [1971] Ch 1 and *Re Buckinghamshire Constabulary Fund (No 2)* [1979] 1 WLR 936. Both essentially concerned themselves with providing benefits to widows and orphans of deceased police officers. Funds for the former came from anonymous donations, entertainment profits (jumble sales, raffles etc), subscriptions and identifiable donations. Funds for the latter came from the last three sources, that is there were no anonymous donations.

In *Re West Sussex* Gough J held a resulting trust arose in respect of the identifiable donations; however the remainder went bona vacantia to the Crown. In contrast in *Re Buckinghamshire Constabulary Fund* Walton J took a different view. He found that the members of the association were bound in a contractual relationship by its rules and regulations. During its lifetime the association held its property for its members subject to those rules. Therefore on its dissolution the funds went to its members subject to those rules, with any former members having been discounted. These members would take equality, subject to any contrary provisions in the rules themselves: see *Re Sick and Funeral Society* [1973] Ch 51. It is difficult to resolve the two lines of reasoning. (See 'Unincorporated Associations and their Dissolution' (1980) CLJ 88, Rickett).

Failure of purpose of loan

In *Barclay's Bank* v *Quistclose Investments* [1970] AC 567 the House of Lords held that a contractual arrangement under which A paid money to B for a specific purpose which had been made known to B, impressed a trust on the moneys. In the *Quistclose* case a public company in financial difficulties borrowed money from Quistclose for the specific purpose of paying a dividend already declared on its shares, so as to avoid a loss of confidence. The money was paid into a special account at Barclay's Bank, who were notified of the limitation placed on the use to which the money could be put. The company went into liquidation before the dividend could be paid and Barclay's claimed it against debts due to them, while Quistclose claimed to recover it under a resulting trust of which Barclay's had notice. It was held that there was a resulting trust for Quistclose. As Lord Wilberforce said:

> 'That arrangements of this character for the payment of a person's creditors by a third person give rise to a relationship of a fiduciary character or trust in favour, as a primary trust, of creditors, and secondly, if the primary trust fails, of the third person, has been recognised in a series of cases of some 150 years.'

The position in this case seems to be that an advance of money for a specific purpose by, say, A to B, gives A an equitable right to see that it is applied for the designated purpose or, alternatively to see that it is not applied for any other purpose. B, it seems, is a trustee of the money and does not acquire a beneficial interest in it so long as the specified purpose can be carried out. When the purpose is carried out the trust comes to an end, but if it cannot be carried out there is a resulting trust for the benefit of A. The resulting trust in favour of A seems clearly established by the *Quistclose* case in the event of the specified purpose being impossible. However, it is far from settled what the true nature of the primary trust referred to by Lord Wilberforce really is.

This problem has been considered in two cases: *Re Northern Developments (Holdings) Ltd,* 6 October 1978 (unreported) and *Carreras Rothman Ltd* v *Freeman Matthews Treasure Ltd* [1985] 3 WLR 1016. If the primary trust, as Lord Wilberforce called it, is an express trust, this could lead to problems because those in whose favour it was made could claim the moneys in it. The decision in the *Quistclose* case is silent on this but on its facts an express trust would, presumably, have enabled the shareholders to claim their dividend unless prevented by legislation to the contrary. In the *Northern Developments* case Megarry V-C seems to treat the trust as a purpose trust, which would have been to be out of line with the court's attitude to such trusts as being void, and the exceptions as not to be extended. In the *Carreras Rothman* case Peter Gibson J seems to treat the primary trust as a constructive trust. It is perhaps arguable that the 'primary trust' is a resulting trust in that if A gives money to B for a specfic purpose there is a resulting trust throughout for A until the purpose is fulfilled. The references to 'primary' and 'secondary' trust merely represent different stages in the life of this resulting trust: see *Millett* (1985) 101 LQR 268. In the *Carreras Rothman* case Carreras Rothman (CR) employed Freeman, Matthews Treasure (FMT) as its advertising agents for cigarettes. FMT got into financial difficulty and CR, in order to protect goodwill with the media, agreed with FMT to set up a special account for the purpose of paying for CR advertisements in the media. FMT went into liquidation and at the time there were substantial funds in the account. CR sought a declaration that the money in the account be used either to pay FMT's media creditors incurred on behalf of CR ('the primary trust') or be repaid to CR ('the secondary, resulting trust'). Peter Gibson J held in favour of the former.

More recent applications of this principle are found in the decisions in *Re Eastern Capital Futures (In liquidation)* [1989] BCLC 371, and *Stanlake Holdings Ltd and Others* v *Tropical Capital Investments Ltd* (1991) The Financial Times 25 June. See also the decision in *Kingscroft Insurance Co Ltd* v *HS Weavers (Underwriting) Agencies Ltd* [1993] 1 Lloyd's Rep 187 in which the court rejected the contention that certain monies were advanced pursuant to a specific purpose and therefore did not have that specific purpose attached to them.

6.4 Joint ownership of matrimonial property

This is concerned with the application of resulting trusts to problems concerning matrimonial and similar property, where the joint owners of such property ask the court to determine their rights therein. Resulting trusts are the one way of ascertaining such rights. In the case of married couples the provisions of the Matrimonial Causes Act 1973 may give additional rights but it is not proposed to consider them here.

The main problem arises where, say, A and B, a couple, whether married or unmarried, acquire a house to live in together. The house may be conveyed into the name of A or B alone or into their names jointly. The funds needed to purchase the house may come from both A and B in various ways, such as cash deposits on purchase, payment of mortgage instalments, or by making some other material sacrifices by contributions to or economy in the family expenditure. If A and B decide to divorce or separate they may ask the court to determine their respective interests in the property. In the House of Lords decisions in *Pettitt* v *Pettitt* [1970] AC 777 and *Gissing* v *Gissing* [1971] AC 886 it is clearly established that the interests of such couples are to be determined under trusts law. It should be noted that these principles apply whether the couple are married or unmarried. The court will determine their interests to be to the extent of their contributions.

Although trusts law is applied in this context it seems that it is subject to a number of qualifications. These include:

Presumption of advancement

In *Re Ekyn's Trusts* (1877) 6 Ch D 115, Malins V-C said:

'... when a husband transfers money or other property into the name of his wife only, then the presumption is, that it is intended as a gift or advancement to the wife absolutely ...'

Presumed resulting trust

If a wife purchases or transfers property and has it conveyed into the sole name of her husband there will be a presumed resulting trust in her favour. In *Mercier* v *Mercier* [1903] 2 Ch 98 a husband purchased a house in his sole name using some of the funds in a joint bank account with his wife which comprised funds belonging to the wife. The house was held by him on resulting trust for the wife.

Express declaration of beneficial interests

If a couple have the foresight on acquiring property to make express declarations as to the extent of their beneficial interests in the property then these will be given effect. As Lord Diplock said in *Gissing* v *Gissing*:

'An express agreement between spouses as to their respective beneficial interests in land conveyed into the name of one of them obviates the need for showing ... that the other spouse so acted with the intention of acquiring that beneficial interest ...'

An express declaration is advisable on the acquisition of property by a couple as it will avoid the possibility of expensive litigation in the future should the relationship end. The effect of an express declaration was considered by the Court of Appeal in *Goodman* v *Gallant* [1986] Fam 106. In this case Mrs Goodman and Mr Gallant purchased a house which was conveyed into their names as joint tenants. Mrs Goodman later served a notice to sever the joint tenancy and issued a claim for three quarters of the proceeds of sale as this represented the amount she had actually contributed to the purchase of the property. Her claim was rejected because the declaration was conclusive of the interests of the parties and the court would not go behind it in the absence of mistake or fraud. As a joint tenant Mrs Goodman was entitled only to a half share of the proceeds of sale. In judgment Slade LJ said:

'In a case where the legal estate in property is conveyed to two or more persons as joint tenants, but neither the conveyance or any other written document contains any express declaration of trust concerning the beneficial interests in the property (as would be required for an express declaration of this nature by virtue of s53(1)(b) of the Law of Property Act 1925), the way is open for persons claiming a beneficial interest in it or its proceeds of sale to rely on the doctrine of "resulting, implied or constructive trusts" ... If, however, the relevant conveyance contains an express declaration of trust which comprehensively declares the beneficial interests in the property or its proceeds of sale, there is no room for the application of the doctrine of resulting, implied or constructive trusts unless and until the conveyance is set aside or rectified; until that event the declaration contained in the document speaks for itself.'

In the majority of cases it is unlikely that there will be any express agreements as to beneficial interests in the property. Evidence that some informal agreement was made may be adduced but this is unlikely to be treated as having been intended to create enforceable legal relations. In this respect Lord Pearson said in *Gissing* v *Gissing*:

'I think it must often be artificial to search for an agreement made between husband and wife as to their respective ownership rights in property used by both of them while they are living together. In most cases they are unlikely to enter into negotiations or conclude contracts or even make agreements. The arrangements which they make are likely to be lacking in precision and finality which an agreement would be expected to have ...'

In cases where there is neither an express nor an acceptable informal agreement the court will look for evidence of a common intention that both parties were to have an interest in the property. This evidence will be based on the conduct of the parties, according to Lord Diplock in *Gissing* v *Gissing*, and will include evidence of contributions, direct and indirect, to the deposit, the mortgage instalments and the housekeeping expenses.

In the absence of agreements of significance the doctrine of resulting trusts will be applied to ascertain the interests of a couple in jointly owned property, subject of course to the presumption of advancement and resulting trust referred to above. The principles to be applied will vary according to whether the case is one where the house is taken in joint names or the name of one party alone. In *Burns* v *Burns* [1984] Ch 317 May LJ summarised the position in each situation as follows:

Where the house is taken in joint names:

'... both the man and the woman are entitled to a share in the beneficial interest. Where the house is bought outright and not on mortgage, then the extent of their respective shares will depend on a more or less arithmetical calculation of the extent of their contributions to the purchase price. Where, on the other hand, as is more usual nowadays, the house is bought with the aid of a mortgage, then the court has to assess each party's respective contributions in a broad sense; nevertheless, the court is only entitled to look at the financial contributions, or their real or substantial equivalent, to the acquisition of the house; that the husband may spend his weekends redecorating or laying a patio is neither here nor there, nor is the fact that the woman has spent so much of her time looking after the house, doing the cooking and bringing up the family.'

Where the house is taken in only one of two names, usually, but not always, the man's name:

'Where a matrimonial or family home is bought in the man's name alone on mortgage by the mechanism of deposit and instalments, then if the woman pays or contributes to the initial deposit this points to a common intention that she should have some beneficial interest in the house. If thereafter she makes direct contributions to the instalments, then the case is a fortiori and her rightful share is likely to be greater. If the woman, having contributed to the deposit, but although not making direct contributions to the instalments, nevertheless uses her own money for other joint household expenses so as to enable the man the more easily to pay the mortgage instalments out of his money, then her position is the same. Where a woman has made no contribution to the initial deposit, but makes regular and substantial contributions to the mortgage instalments, it may still be reasonable to infer a common intention that she should share the beneficial interest from the outset, or infer a fresh agreement after the original conveyance that she should acquire such a share. It is only when there is no evidence on which a court can reasonably draw an inference about the extent of the share of the contributing woman that it should fall back on the maxim 'equity is equality'. Finally, when the house is taken in the man's name alone, if the woman makes no 'real' or 'substantial' financial contribution towards either the purchase price, deposit or mortgage instalments by means of which the family home was acquired, then she is not entitled to any share in the beneficial interest in that home even though over a very substantial number of years she may have worked just as hard as the man in maintaining the family, in the sense of keeping house, giving birth to and looking after and helping to bring up the children of the union.'

The dictum in *Burns* v *Burns* indicates that the contributions to the acquisition of the house may be either direct or indirect. Direct contributions include payments towards the deposit on purchase and payment of mortgage instalments. Indirect contributions include payments towards household expenses, which otherwise might be borne by the party paying mortgage instalments, and which enable that party to meet these instalments or pay off the mortgage sooner. In *Gissing* v *Gissing* the House of Lords considered that the indirect contribution must be referable to the acquisition of an interest in the house, in that the other party could not have done without that assistance. But, there are a number of Court of Appeal decisions which seem to depart from this dictum and to allow indirect contributions to be taken into account even if not referable to the acquisition of an interest in the house: see *Hazell* v *Hazell* [1972] 1 WLR 301. But also see *Lloyds Bank plc* v *Rosset* [1990] 2 WLR 867; *Hammond* v *Mitchell* [1991] 1 WLR 1127 (Chapter 7, section 7.9), and cases referred to in Chapter 7, section 7.10.

Improvements made to the house which enhance its value may give an interest or greater interest in the house to the party making them. In *Pettitt* v *Pettitt* the House of Lords could not agree on whether such improvements would give an interest or greater interest. The position is now dealt with by s37 Matrimonial Proceedings and Property Act 1970 which states:

'Where a husband or wife contributes in money or money's worth to the improvement of real or personal property in which or in the proceeds of sale of which either or both of them has or have a beneficial interest, the husband or wife so contributing shall, if the contribution is of a substantial nature and subject to any agreement to the contrary express or implied, be treated as having then acquired by virtue of his or her contribution a share or an enlarged share, as the case may be, in that beneficial interest.'

Note that s37 only applies to married couples, not unmarried couples, and that the contribution must be 'of a substantial nature' and referable to the acquisition of an interest in the property. Thus, do-it-yourself work of a substantial nature could be taken into account, such as the erection of a glasshouse or installing a central heating system. But matters such as repainting and keeping the house will not: see *Gissing* v *Gissing*.

If one party has not made any contributions towards the acquisition of the property or an interest in it, or his or her contributions are not referable to the acquisition of an interest in the property, then subject to section 6.5, there is no question of that party obtaining an interest in the property. In *Burns* v *Burns* the plaintiff and defendant lived together for almost 20 years as if married and had two children of their relationship. The house they lived in was paid for by the defendant with part cash and part mortgage. The mortgage was paid off by the defendant while the plaintiff was not earning. When the plaintiff returned to work she used her earnings to purchase furniture, fixtures and fittings for the house and did some painting and redecoration. The relationship broke up and the plaintiff sought a declaration as to whether she had a beneficial interest in the house. The Court of Appeal held that she had no interest in the house, she had made no contributions referable to the acquisition of an interest in the property and a common intention that she should have an interest in the property could not be inferred from the fact that the relationship had lasted 19 years. She was not entitled to bring proceedings under matrimonial legislation because of the nature of the relationship.

This decision, and indeed this area of law, has now been thrown into considerable doubt by the decision of the Court of Appeal in *Midland Bank plc* v *Cooke* [1995] 4 All ER 562. The resulting trust which arose in the case was based on initial contribution to the acquisition of the property. A house was purchased in 1971 for £8,500 in the husband's sole name. The purchase was financed by a mortgage of £6,450 with the balance provided from the husband's savings and a wedding gift from his parents. The wife's half share of the wedding gift gave rise to a presumption of a 6.74 per cent share in the property by way of resulting trust, and her share was quantified on this basis at first instance. She appealed against this quantification and the Court of Appeal awarded her a beneficial half interest in the matrimonial home. Waite LJ delivered the judgment, with which Stuart-Smith LJ and Schiemann LJ agreed. It was held that the court was not bound to deal with the matter on the strict basis of the trust resulting from the cash contribution to the purchase price. In the absence of any express agreement between the husband and wife, the court would assess the proportion of beneficial shares by undertaking a survey of the whole course of dealing between the parties and would take into consideration all conduct. Although distinguishable from *Burns* v *Burns* on the basis that at least some interest did arise by way of conventional purchase money resulting trust, the overall effect of the decision is to cast considerable doubt on the earlier authority and to demolish the rationale behind the House of Lords' authority of *Lloyd's Bank* v *Rosset* (see Chapter 7, section 7.9). In particular, Waite LJ clearly envisaged that relief will be available in equity even if no agreement has been made between the parties:

> 'If the parties themselves testify on oath that they have made no agreement, there is no scope for equity to make one for them. That is a submission which ... I would reject instinctively on the ground that it runs counter to the very system of law – equity – on which it seeks to rely. Equity has traditionally been a system which matches established principle to the demands of social change ... There will inevitably be numerous couples,

married or unmarried, who have no discussion about ownership ... It would be anomalous, against that background, to create a range of home-buyers who were beyond the pale of equity's assistance in formulating a fair presumed basis for the sharing of beneficial title, simply because they had been honest enought to admit that they never gave ownership a thought or reached any agreement about it.'

Although the principles referred to apply to both married and unmarried couples, it is not necessarily the case that the court will apply them to all unmarried couples. The nature of the relationship must be considered and it must have the same degree of commitment as marriage, as Griffiths LJ pointed out in *Bernard* v *Josephs* [1982] Ch 391.

'... but the nature of the relationship between the parties is a very important factor when considering what inferences should be drawn from the way they have conducted their affairs. There are many reasons why a man and a woman may decide to live together without marrying, and one of them is that each values his independence and does not wish to make the commitment of marriage; in such a case it will be misleading to make the same assumptions and to draw the same inferences from their behaviour as in the case of a married couple. The judge must look most carefully at the nature of the relationship, and only if satisfied that it was intended to involve the same degree of commitment as marriage will it be legitimate to regard them as no different from a married couple.'

7

Constructive Trusts

7.1 Introduction

7.2 Unauthorised profits by fiduciaries

7.3 'Strangers'

7.4 Using a statute as an instrument of fraud

7.5 Property obtained through unlawful conduct

7.6 Mutual wills

7.7 Proprietary estoppel

7.8 Vendor of land

7.9 The 'fair and reasonable' cases

7.1 Introduction

There is no satisfactory definition of what a constructive trust is and it is doubtful whether one could be formulated. All that can be said is that a constructive trust arises by operation of law; it does not depend upon the intentions, either express or implied, of those who are affected by it. The constructive trust has been imposed in a number of broad categories but the boundaries of these categories are vague. This is probably deliberate as the constructive trust is really a residual category of trust, to enable the imposition of a fiduciary relationship, with its consequent proprietary rights and duties to account.

The aim of constructive trusts appears to be to preserve property rights affected by unconscionable conduct on the part of those considered as constructive trustees in the eyes of equity. The property may have been taken by the constructive trustee from the beneficiary under the constructive trust, or it may be property that the beneficiary did not possess but which he should possess in the eyes of equity. For example, if X, a trustee, wrongly took 1,000 shares in A Co from the trust, for himself, and bought 1,000 shares in B Co for himself, when they were offered to him for the benefit of the trust, he would be a constructive trustee of all these shares for the beneficiaries under the trust: see *Boardman* v *Phipps* [1967] 2 AC 46.

It is easy to see why he should be treated as a constructive trustee of the shares while he actually possesses them, plus any profits. However, once X sells or otherwise disposes of the shares he is no longer a constructive trustee of them. But the fact that he was once a constructive trustee of them gives rights and remedies to the beneficiaries. Assuming that the shares were sold to a bona fide purchaser for value without notice, the beneficiaries could not recover the shares themselves: see *Bassett* v *Nosworthy* (1673) Rep t Finch 102. There would still be rights of action against X personally and against the proceeds of sale of the shares. If X still had the proceeds of sale, or used them in the purchase of something identifiable, for example, a motor car, then the beneficiaries could seek to exercise the proprietary remedy of 'tracing' so as to recover the proceeds: see *Re Hallett's Estate* (1880) 13 Ch D 696 and Chapter 21. But, if X had dissipated the proceeds of sale so that he had nothing to show for them, for example, by applying it in living expenses, then the beneficiaries would have a personal remedy against X for the amount that represented the value of the shares and profits on them, which they should otherwise have had. Whether the beneficiaries sue X personally or seek to 'trace' is a matter for them but 'tracing' will be important where X is insolvent. This is considered in Chapter 21.

The main aim in imposing a constructive trust will be either:

1. Recovery of the constructive trust property if the constructive trustee still possesses it.
2. To trace its proceeds if the constructive trustee has disposed of it and there is something to show for it.
3. To enable a personal action to be brought against the constructive trustee: see *Re Montagu* [1987] 2 WLR 1192.

The categories considered below are concerned with whether or not the court will impose a constructive trust and not with the consequences of such a trust. It will be seen that in many of the cases considered in each category the aims of those claiming that a constructive trust arises are essentially different; compare *Keech* v *Sandford* (1726) Sel Cas t King 61 and *Boardman* v *Phipps* [1967] 2 AC 46.

Constructive trustees are not subject to the same duties as express trustees nor do they possess any of the powers of express trustees. This arises from the nature of the trust itself – as a means of protecting property rights – the duties of constructive trustees probably vary from case to case. At a minimum it might be said that they have a duty to hand over the trust property or its proceeds or an equivalent in money.

In English law the constructive trust is a substantive institution imposed within the boundaries of defined categories and leading to certain consequences. In other jurisdictions, particularly America, it is looked upon as a remedial institution. In *Beatty* v *Guggenheim Exploration Co* (1919) 225 NY 380 Cardozo J explained the American approach:

'A constructive trust is the formula through which the conscience of equity finds expression. When property has been acquired in such circumstances that the holder of the legal title may not in good conscience retain the beneficial interest, equity converts him into a trustee.'

The English approach differs from the American approach in that it distinguishes between the circumstances in which a constructive trust will be imposed and the remedies that are available. For example, if X claimed that his agent, Y, held monies on a constructive trust he would have to satisfy the court that the circumstances of the case were such that they fell into one of the broad categories where English law imposes constructive trusts. If he could do this, then the remedies referred to earlier would be available. The execution of these remedies would be independent of the constructive trust. But, in American law it seems that it is not necessary to satisfy the first stage; the constructive trust may be imposed in any circumstances which in the opinion of the court justify its imposition. There are dangers in this approach, which probably lie behind the reluctance of English courts to adopt it:

1. The uncertainty as to the circumstances in which a constructive trust might arise would only serve to increase the volume of litigation.
2. The proprietary nature of the constructive trust could have far reaching consequences for third parties, in particular ordinary creditors who might find the beneficiaries under the constructive trust taking priority over them. For example, if X appointed Y as his agent and Y had acted corruptly as agent, obtaining profits for himself, and then became insolvent, then X could, by obtaining a constructive trust, take priority over Y's other creditors. The arbitrary imposition of such a remedy would make nonsense of the order of payment on insolvency and leave ordinary creditors in considerable uncertainty.
3. The imposition of a constructive trust will often affect the property rights of the constructive trustee. He may be divested either partially or totally of such property. If the courts were to impose such trusts arbitarily it would leave considerable uncertainty as to ownership. This is particularly so in the context of matrimonial property; some attempts have been made in England to impose constructive trusts in this area.

The imposition of constructive trusts in defined categories in English law does not mean that the courts are inflexible in their approach. The boundaries of these categories are vague and as Slade J said in *English* v *Dedham Vale Properties* [1978] 1 WLR 93:

'I do not think that the categories of fiduciary relationships which give rise to constructive trusteeship should be regarded as falling into a limited number of strait-jackets or as being necessarily closed. They are, after all, no more than formulae for equitable relief ...'

Moreover, Lord Browne-Wilkinson suggested recently in *Westdeutsche Landesbank Girozentrale* v *Islington London Borough Council* [1996] 2 All ER 961 that the introduction of the remedial constructive trust in English law might provide a suitable basis for developing restitutionary remedies. See Chapter 28, section 28.1, for further details.

7.2 Unauthorised profits by fiduciaries

In dealing with this category of constructive trust the first question is: Who is a fiduciary? Unfortunately, there is no clear answer to this question. The cases in which the courts have held a fiduciary relationship to exist are numerous. It is possible to find common factors binding some of these cases together, and it is also possible to treat certain specific relationships as giving rise to fiduciary duties and being therefore fiduciary relationships. Common factors which are discernible in the cases include:

1. Where one person takes property or an advantage which in equity should belong to another – a secret profit. For example, X, as trustee, takes trust property for himself, or takes for himself the benefit of an opportunity which he was supposed to use for the benefit of the trust: see *Boardman* v *Phipps* [1967] 2 AC 46 (below).
2. Where there is a conflict of interest and duty. If a relationship is such that one person is under a duty to act in the interests of another in a particular matter, and in breach of that duty he allows his own personal interests to take precedence, then there is a conflict of interest and duty. For example, if a trustee renews a lease of trust property for himself instead of for the trust, or purchases trust property for himself instead of for the trust, such a conflict would arise: see *Keech* v *Sandford* (1726) Sel Cas t King 61 and *Ex parte Lacey* (1802) 6 Ves 625, and Chapter 13.
3. Where one person reposes trust or confidence in another. For example, X enters into a contract with Y on a matter on which he is ignorant or inexperienced, and Y, knowing of X's ignorance and inexperience takes advantage of them, knowing that X is relying on him to act in his, X's, interests. If Y was a solicitor who took personal advantage of his client, the fiduciary relationship might arise: see *O'Sullivan* v *Management Agency* [1985] 3 All ER 351 and *Finers* v *Miro* [1991] 1 WLR 35.

The difficulty with trying to use common factors as a means of identifying fiduciary relationships is that they will often overlap, and they are not an exhaustive guide to the instances in which constructive trusts have been imposed for breach of fiduciary relationships. An alternative is to consider the main relationships which the courts have regarded as carrying fiduciary duties with them:

1. *Trustee and beneficiary.* This is the most obvious fiduciary relationship since the trustee is put in a position to manage and deal with the trust property for the benefit of the beneficiary. Should the trustee seek to take personal advantage, such as secret profits, from this relationship, he will be a constructive trustee of them: see *Boardman* v *Phipps* [1967] 2 AC 46 (below).
2. *Director and company.* A director is in a fiduciary relationship to his company and is expected to put the company's interests first. Should a director seek to

take for himself a lucrative contract offered to his company he will be a constructive trustee of the benefits: see *Regal (Hastings) Ltd* v *Gulliver* [1942] 1 All ER 378. This is discussed in more detail in the following pages.

3. *Principal and agent.* An agent is in a fiduciary relationship with his principal, and should he abuse his position to the detriment of his principal for his own personal gains, he will be liable to account for those gains to his principal: see *Boardman* v *Phipps* [1967] 2 AC 46.

4. *Partners.* Partners are in a fiduciary relationship with each other and any unauthorised benefits taken by one partner from the partnership assets will be held on a constructive trust: see *Clegg* v *Edmondson* (1857) 8 De GM & G 787.

The above four categories are only the main fiduciary relationships from which liability under a constructive trust might arise. Others that might be mentioned include promoters of a company who owe a fiduciary duty to the company: see *Erlanger* v *New Sombrero Phosphate Co* (1878) 3 App Cas 1218; employees who breach the trust and confidence placed in them by their employers: see *Canadian Aero Services* v *O'Malley* (1973) 40 DLR (3d) 371; and employees and others who repose trust and confidence in another: see *Tate* v *Williamson* (1866) 2 Ch App 55. These are established cases, and a fiduciary relationship could arise in almost any situation, so that it is pointless, if not impossible, to list these. This point was made by Fletcher Moulton J in *Re Coomber* [1911] 1 Ch 723:

'Fiduciary relations are of many different types; they extend from the relation of myself to an errand boy who is bound to bring me back my change up to the most intimate and confidential relations which can possibly exist between one party and another where one is wholly in the hands of another because of his infinite trust in him. All these are cases of fiduciary relation, and the Courts have again and again, in cases where there has been a fiduciary relation, interfered and set aside acts which, between persons in a wholly independent position, would have been perfectly valid. Thereupon, in some minds there arises the idea that if there is any fiduciary relation whatever any of these types of interference is warranted by it. They conclude that every kind of fiduciary relation justifies every kind of interference. There is no class of case in which one ought more carefully to bear in mind the facts of the case, when one reads the judgment of the Court on those facts, than cases which relate to fiduciary and confidential relations and the action of the Court with regard to them ...'

Note the emphasis in the latter part of this judgment on the fact that the interference in different fiduciary relationships gives rise to different consequences.

Assuming that the court finds a fiduciary relationship as established in a particular case, the next issue is in what circumstances the fiduciary will be held liable to account as a constructive trustee. It must be emphasised that the imposition of a constructive trust is not the sole course of action that might be taken against a fiduciary. The fiduciary may have a contractual relationship, enabling those whom he owes fiduciary duties to sue him for breach of contract, for example, where there is an agency agreement or a partnership agreement. The fiduciary may be sued in negligence or deceit; he might be liable to account, or an injunction might be asked for. But the constructive trust is probably the most important weapon in the hands of those to whom fiduciary duties are owed, so as to protect their proprietary rights arising out of the relationship. (For a recent example of the benefits of a constructive trust, and its 'remedies', as compared to the rights in a debtor-creditor relationship see *Attorney-General for Hong Kong* v *Reid and Others* [1993] 3 WLR 1143.)

The grounds upon which a constructive trust has been imposed on a fiduciary are numerous and varied but they include:

Unauthorised remuneration

A trustee or other fiduciary is not entitled to remuneration for the execution of his fiduciary duties. If a trustee receives remuneration he will be liable to account for it; this rule can be traced back to 1734 where it was said in *Robinson* v *Pett* (1734) 3 P Wms 132:

> 'A trustee ... shall have no allowance for his care and trouble: the reason of which seems to be, for that on these pretences, if allowed, the trust estate might be loaded, and rendered of little value.'

There are a number of exceptions under which trustees can receive remuneration but these are applied strictly by the court. The exceptions are dealt with in Chapter 13, section 13.2. The rule on unauthorised remuneration also applies to company directors, as Bowen LJ said in *Hutton* v *West Cork Railway* (1883) 23 Ch D 654: 'It is not implied from the mere fact that he is a director that he is entitled to be paid for it.' But it is usual to find that a company's articles allow for directors' fees to be paid. There are a number of statutory and other limitations, but it is not proposed to deal with these here. Unauthorised remuneration may take other forms, such as a commission received by the fiduciary for business. In *Williams* v *Barton* [1927] 2 Ch 9 a trustee was liable to account for a commission he received from a firm of valuers, of which he was a member, for introducing the trust estate to the firm for a valuation.

Unauthorised transactions

A fiduciary may not enter into transactions on his own behalf which he was under a duty to enter on behalf of those to whom he owed the fiduciary duty. A trustee may not renew a lease for himself which was formerly held by him on trust. In *Keech* v *Sandford* (1726) Sel Cas t King 61 it was held that the rule was applied to avoid the dangers of conflict of interest and duty, and in that case it was considered irrelevant that the landlord would not renew the lease to the trust. As Lord King LC said:

> 'I very well see, if a trustee, on the refusal to renew, might have a lease for himself, few trust estates would be renewed to a cestui que trust ... the trustee is the only person of all mankind who might not have the lease ...'

The implications and effects of this rule are considered further at Chapter 13, section 13.3. The rule is applied in all the main categories of fiduciary.

In *Thompson's Trustee* v *Heaton* [1974] 1 WLR 605 it was applied to partnership property and in *Cook* v *Deeks* [1916] 1 AC 554 the Privy Council held that directors could not take contracts for themselves which were negotiated for the benefit of the company. The motives of the directors seem to be irrelevant in such cases. While in *Cook* v *Deeks* their motives were plainly improper on the evidence, even directors who believed they were acting in the best interests of the company have been held liable as constructive trustees in entering unauthorised transactions. In *Regal (Hastings) Ltd* v *Gulliver* [1942] 1 All ER 378, Regal's board of directors formed a subsidiary company for the purpose of acquiring the leases of two cinemas. The subsidiary was to have a share capital of £5,000 with £2,000 paid up. The landlord would not renew the leases unless all the shares were paid up. As Regal could not find more than the £2,000 it paid up on the subsidiary's shares. Four of the directors and the company solicitor put up £500 each for shares, and the company chairman found friends to put up the remaining £500. Regal was eventually taken over by another company and as a result the shares in the subsidiary were sold at a substantial profit. The purchasers of Regal brought proceedings against the four directors, the solicitor and the chairman, to recover the profits they had made on the subsidiary's shares, on the ground they had made a secret profit. The chairman escaped as he had not made a secret profit, the solicitor escaped because those to whom he owed a fiduciary duty as agent, namely the board of directors, had approved of his purchase. But the other four directors had to account; they had acted in breach of their fiduciary duty in purchasing the shares in the subsidiary and the company had not approved of this, as it could have, by ratifying the matter in general meeting. As Lord Russell said:

> 'I am of the opinion that the directors standing in a fiduciary relationship to Regal in regard to the exercise of their powers as directors, and having obtained these shares by reason and only by reason of the fact that they were directors of Regal and in the course of the execution of that office, are accountable for the profits which they have made out of them. The equitable rules laid down in *Keech* v *Sandford* ... applies to them in full force.'

This case shows the application of a constructive trust in a rigid manner; there had been a breach of fiduciary duty and its' full consequences followed on. The breach was in many respects a technical one, since the directors could have called a shareholders' meeting at any time and had their breach of fiduciary duty ratified by the company. This had not been done before they sold the shares. Further, the purchasers of the shares were obtaining an undeserved reduction in the price they had agreed to pay. The decision may be justified in law but perhaps not in commercial reality. This conflict between the law of constructive trusts and commercial practicality is difficult to resolve. The former is designed to prevent abuse, yet often this so-called abuse arises because the initial company consciously turned down the chance to benefit.

The decision in the *Regal* case should be contrasted with the approach adopted by the Canadian court in *Peso Silver Mines* v *Cropper* (1966) 58 DLR (2d) 11 where several directors of Peso took up prospecting claims which the company had itself turned down because it considered them to be highly speculative and financially unattractive. After the company rejected the claims Cropper and some other directors, who had unsuccessfully urged the company to take up the claims, formed a company to take them. Peso's board was informed of this. The claims proved highly profitable and Peso's board demanded an account. The Canadian Supreme Court refused to apply the strict rule in *Regal* (*Hastings*) v *Gulliver*; they held that the company's deliberate act in refusing to take up the claims released the directors so that they could form a separate company to exploit the claims themselves. This seems a fairer interpretation or balancing of the effect of constructive trusts and commercial reality.

Purchase of property

Generally a fiduciary may not purchase property which he holds in a fiduciary capacity. In the case of trustees the rule is strictly applied and any such purchase can be set aside at the instance of the beneficiaries: see *Ex parte Lacey* (1802) 6 Ves 625. The reason for this is that the trustee is both vendor and purchaser at the same time and an obvious conflict arises between his duty as trustee to get the highest price and his interest as purchaser to pay the lowest price. The matter is considered in depth in Chapter 13, section 13.5. The position is similar where directors are involved, as dicta in *Boardman* v *Phipps* [1967] 2 AC 46 make clear.

Sale of property

A fiduciary who sells his own property to those to whom he stands in a fiduciary relationship may find the transaction set aside or a claim for an account of profits on the basis of constructive trusteeship. In this type of case the danger is overcharging by the fiduciary for his own benefit. The problem has not been common in the context of trustees but it has been known to arise in the context of directors, especially at the stage of promotion of a company. In *Erlanger* v *New Sombrero Phosphate Co* (1878) 3 App Cas 1218 the House of Lords held Erlanger liable to account for the secret profit he made on selling an island to a company he was forming for £110,000, but which he had purchased for £55,000 a short time previously. These facts were not revealed to those invited to subscribe for the shares: see also *Emma Silver Mining Co* v *Lewis* (1879) 4 CPD 396. In *Bentley* v *Craven* (1853) 18 Beav 75 the rule that a fiduciary may not sell his property to those to whom he owes fiduciary duties was applied in the context of a partnership. In that case the defendant was a partner in a sugar refining business and also carried on business as a sugar dealer. He purchased some sugar as part of his dealer's business which he resold to the partnership at a profit. Despite the fact that the price was fair he was nevertheless liable to account for the profit.

Competition

A fiduciary must not enter into competition with a business he holds in his fiduciary capacity. This rule applies to trustees, but in this context the courts only apply constructive trusteeship if actual competition is proved, otherwise the trustee might be deprived of earning a living: see Chapter 13, section 13.4 and *Re Thomson* [1930] 1 Ch 203. Partners are under a statutory duty not to compete with their partnership under s30 Partnership Act 1890. In the case of directors the position is less clear. Older cases such as *London and Mashonaland Exploration Co* v *New Mashonaland Exploration Co* (1891) 1 WN 165 suggest that a director may compete with his company, but dicta of Lord Denning in *Scottish Co-operative Wholesale Society* v *Meyer* [1959] AC 324 suggest that directors should refrain from such competition, and the provisions in the Companies Act 1985 tend to support this.

Confidential information

A fiduciary who misuses confidential information or knowledge he acquires in his fiduciary capacity will be liable to account as a constructive trustee for any profits made. The leading case on this is *Boardman* v *Phipps* [1967] 2 AC 46. The facts of this case were as follows:

The estate of a testator, which was held on trust for his wife for life with remainders over to his children, included a substantial minority holding of shares in a textile company, Lester & Harris Ltd. The trustees were dissatisfied with the returns on the shares in this company and considered this was due to bad management. Boardman, the trustees' solicitor, and Phipps, a beneficiary who was in textiles himself, both of whom supported the trustees' view, attended an annual general meeting of the company; they expressed their dissatisfaction with the company's affairs and tried unsuccessfully to have Phipps elected as a director. Boardman and Phipps then decided to acquire the shares in the company and on this they had the approval of two of the trustees but not the third, who was the widow of the deceased and senile at the time. An offer was made for the outstanding shares but it was only partly successful. Afterwards Boardman entered into negotiations with the directors of the company, apparently as representative of the trustees, for a division of the assets between the trust and the majority shareholders. These negotiations were not authorised by the trustees and although unsuccessful Boardman gained much information from them about the company's business and the value of its assets. On the basis of this information Boardman and Phipps made another offer for the outstanding shares in the company. This offer was preceded by a letter to all the beneficiaries informing them of the proposal and seeking their consent. The offer was successful and enabled Boardman, Phipps and the trustees to take full control of the company, which Phipps then reorganised. Substantial distribution of surplus capital was made to themselves as shareholders, so they all made handsome profits. However, a beneficiary entitled to a share in remainder brought an action claiming that Boardman and Phipps held the shares they acquired in the company as constructive trustees, and that they were liable to account for the profits they had made thereon. Wilberforce J upheld these claims against Boardman and Phipps. The Court of Appeal affirmed this decision and the House of Lords, by a majority of 3 to 2, upheld the decision of the lower courts.

The majority (Lords Cohen, Hodson and Guest) applied the principles behind constructive trusts strictly and it seems that the minority (Viscount Dilhorne and Lord Upjohn) differed in that they were prepared to take a more flexible approach towards fiduciary duties. All were agreed that Boardman stood in a fiduciary capacity to the trustees, as he was called upon from time to time to give them advice. Tom Phipps was a fiduciary because he had been a co-adventurer with Boardman. The case turned on whether, as fiduciaries, they were liable to account, because they had represented themselves as acting for the trustees in the negotiations for a division of the assets and had obtained information in so doing which had prompted them to acquire more shares in the company, ultimately for themselves. This information gave them the opportunity to make a profit but the information was not 'property' as such, as Lord Cohen said: 'Information is, of course, not property in the strict sense of the word.' Lord Upjohn went further:

> 'In general, information is not property at all. It is normally open to all who have eyes to read and ears to hear. The true test is to determine in what circumstances the information has been acquired. If it has been acquired in such circumstances that it would be a breach of confidence to disclose it to another then courts of equity will restrain the recipient from communicating it to another … I protest at the idea that information acquired by trustees in the course of their duties as such is necessarily part of the assets of the trust which cannot be used by the trustees except for the benefit of the trust … if such information is trust property, not all the trustees acting together could … give (it) away …'

There seems little between the majority and the minority on the issue of whether information can be property. The judgments differ on when a trustee or fiduciary will be accountable as a constructive trustee when he uses information acquired as such. Lord Cohen took a strict view:

> '… the mere use of any knowledge or opportunity which comes to the trustee or agent in the course of his trusteeship or agency does not necessarily make him liable to account. In the present case had the company been a public company and had the appellants bought the shares on the market, they would not, I think, have been accountable. But, the company is a private company and not only the information but the opportunity to purchase these shares came to them through the introduction which Mr Fox (the active trustee) gave them to the board of the company …'

This judgment suggests that as Boardman and Phipps got the information and could only have got it in acting in the trusts, they were liable to account in this particular case. This view may be contrasted with the approach taken by Lord Upjohn, who accepted the argument that the use of the information was outside the fiduciary roles because the trust did not want to use it and could not use it. He said:

> '… there was no question whatever of the trustees contemplating the possibilty of a

purchase of further shares in the company ... The reasons for this attitude are worth setting out in full: (a) The acquisition of further shares in the company would have been a breach of trust, for they were not authorised by the investment clause in the will; (b) ... it must have been obvious to those concerned that no court would sanction the purchase of further shares in a small company which the trustees considered to be badly managed ... (c) the trustees had no money available for the purchase of further shares ...'

Lord Upjohn then went on to outline the circumstances in which, in his view, a fiduciary would be liable to account for the use of confidential information

' ... it is ... given to him (1) in circumstances which, regardless of his position as a trustee, would make it a breach of confidence for him to communicate to anyone for it has been given to him expressly or impliedly as confidential, or (2) in a fiduciary capacity, and its use would place him in a position where his duty and his interest might possibly conflict.'

The decision is another unfortunate example of the uneasy relationship between constructive trusts and the business community. This is further complicated by the fact that despite being held to be a constructive trustee Boardman was also awarded nominal payment in lieu of services rendered. See further Chapter 13, section 13.4.

The rules as to the use of confidential information are applied strictly to directors so that a director is barred from utilising any opportunity to profit from information received which is within the scope of his company's business, whether or not the company could have utilised the opportunity. These points arose in *IDC v Cooley* (1972) 1 WLR 443. Cooley was appointed a director of IDC, which specialised in managing building projects, in order to help the company gain business in the public sector. Previously he had worked for the Midlands Gas Board. The Eastern Gas Board approached Cooley about a construction contract in a private capacity and it became clear to him that he could have the contract for himself if he could be released from his obligations with IDC. He 'retired' from IDC through supposed ill- health, formed his own business and took the contract on which he made a substantial profit. IDC sought to recover these profits. Roskill J held that he was liable to account as he had a fiduciary duty to pass on information to IDC which was of interest to them, and had allowed his interests and his duties to conflict. Argument that IDC could never have had the contract itself was rejected because as Roskill J pointed out:

'When one looks at the way the cases have gone over the centuries it is plain that the question whether or not the benefit would have been obtained but for the breach of trust has always been treated as irrelevant.'

IDC succeeded in obtaining a profit which they would not have got for themselves if Cooley had fulfilled his duty. This may appear strange but the alternative would be to permit Cooley to profit out of breach of fiduciary duty.

7.3 'Strangers'

There are a number of instances in which a constructive trust may be imposed upon a 'stranger', which must be considered. For these purposes 'stranger' includes all persons who do not have duties in respect of the property apart from the constructive trust. For example, if X was an express trustee for A and B, X would not be a 'stranger' to the trust, but if Y who had no connection with the trust took it upon himself to intermeddle with the trust property, he would be a 'stranger'. It should also be noted that the term 'trust' in this category is used in a broad sense.

Not all strangers may be held liable as constructive trustees; a constructive trust will only be imposed if the stranger has been guilty of 'knowing receipt or dealing' with trust property or 'knowing assistance' in a dishonest and fraudulent design relating to trust property. These are considered below but it is convenient to consider the various categories into which a 'stranger' might fall.

Bona fide purchaser for value of the legal estate without notice

If X, as trustee, sold trust property to Y, who was a bona fide purchaser without notice, then Y would not be a constructive trustee of the property he purchased for the beneficiaries. This is because he takes free from all their equitable rights: see *Bassett* v *Nosworthy* (1673) Rep t F 102. The remedy of the beneficiaries will be against the trustees for any losses suffered and so far as the trust is concerned it will apply to the proceeds of sale – there will, in effect, have been overreaching of the trust property: see *Re Montagu* [1987] 2 WLR 1192.

Innocent volunteers

An innocent volunteer is one who has received trust property without consideration and in good faith without notice of the trust, for example, if X, a trustee, distributed trust funds to Y who was told by X it was a gift from X himself. An innocent volunteer is not a constructive trustee. This much seems clear from *Re Diplock* [1948] Ch 465, as the following passage from the judgment in that case illustrates:

> 'Suppose that the sole trustee of (say) five separate trusts draws £100 out of each of the trust banking accounts ... and gives it to his son. A claim by the five sets of beneficiaries to follow the money of their respective trusts would be a claim against the son. He would stand in no fiduciary relationship to any of them ...'

These latter words negative the idea of a constructive trust on the innocent volunteer. Other parts of the judgment support this view, for example, the right of the innocent volunteer to rank pari passu where he has mixed his own funds with those he received in the purchase of an article. This does not mean that the innocent volunteer is allowed to keep funds he receives without notice that they have come to him wrongly. The equitable remedy of tracing is available against him: see also *Re Montagu*. This is considered further in Chapter 21.

Purchaser and volunteers taking with notice of the trust

Purchasers or volunteers taking trust property with notice of the trusts affecting it cannot take free from those trusts and, consequently, are constructive trustees. They would fall within the category of 'knowing receipt or dealing'. Notice for these purposes includes both actual and constructive notice: see *Nelson* v *Larholt* [1948] 1 KB 339 and below.

Agents

Fiduciaries, particularly trustees, frequently appoint agents to carry out certain duties for them. Under s23(1) Trustee Act 1925 and s9 Trusts of Land and Appointment of Trustees Act 1996 trustees have wide powers of delegation to agents: see Chapter 18, section 18.7. The question which arises is in what circumstances, if any, an agent may be liable as a constructive trustee. An agent is, of course, a stranger to the trust but he will frequently have to deal with the trust property; for example, an investment adviser who buys and sells stock and shares on behalf of the trust. However, the agent will not be a constructive trustee merely because he acts as such. The position was made clear by Lord Selbourne LC in *Barnes* v *Addy* (1874) 9 Ch App 244:

'... strangers are not to be made constructive trustees merely because they act as the agents of trustees in transactions within their legal powers, transactions, perhaps of which a Court of Equity may disapprove, unless those agents receive and become chargeable with some part of the trust property, or unless they assist with knowledge in a dishonest and fraudulent design on the part of the trustees ...'

Agents can only be made constructive trustees if they have knowingly received or dealt with trust property in breach of trust or knowingly assisted in a breach of trust. In *Barnes* v *Addy* funds were settled in trust to be held as to one-half for A's wife and children, and as to the other half for B's wife and children. As sole surviving trustee, A divided the trust fund so that he remained sole trustee of one half for his wife and children and he appointed B as sole trustee of the other half. The solicitors who acted in the matter had advised A against appointing B as sole trustee of half of the fund, but nevertheless drew up the necessary deeds at A's direction. B sold the trust property shortly after he became trustee, misapplied the proceeds of sale and became bankrupt. B's wife and children sued the solicitors alleging they were constructive trustees. This claim was dismissed as the solicitors had no notice or suspicion that B might behave dishonestly; they had acted within their powers throughout and had based their advice on the risks which arise generally from the appointment of a sole trustee.

The decision in *Barnes* v *Addy* shows that an honest agent acting within the scope of his powers cannot be a constructive trustee. It does not matter that he acts negligently in the exercise of those powers because the constructive trust is imposed here for dishonesty or want of probity, not negligence. However, the position is different if the so-called honest agent has deliberately or wilfully closed his eyes to the situation. In *Williams-Ashman* v *Price* [1942] Ch 219 a firm of solicitors, who at all times had a copy of the trust deed in their possession, paid out money to persons who were not beneficiaries, and also invested trust funds in unauthorised investments. The court held that they were not constructive trustees because they had not actually been aware that they were acting in breach of trust. As Bennett J said:

'... an agent in possession of money which he knows to be trust money, so long as he acts honestly, is not accountable to the beneficiaries interested in the trust money unless he intermeddles in the trust by doing acts characteristic of a trustee and outside the duties of an agent.'

The proper course of action in a case such as this would be to sue in negligence, assuming that there was no recourse against the trustees themselves for failing to delegate properly under s23(1) Trustee Act 1925 or for failing to supervise properly under s30(1) Trustee Act 1925.

Intermeddlers

An intermeddler or 'trustee de son tort' was defined by AL Smith LJ in *Mara* v *Browne* [1896] 1 Ch 199:

'... if one, not being a trustee and not having authority from a trustee, takes upon himself to intermeddle with trust matters or to do acts characteristic of the office of trustee, he may thereby make himself what is called in law a trustee of his own wrong – ie a trustee de son tort, or, as it is also termed, a constructive trustee ...'

For example, if X is trustee of £10,000 and asks Y to act as trust solicitor and Y made distributions from the fund to beneficiaries without X's consent, he would be a trustee de son tort. The cases seem to classify the trustee de son tort as either a constructive trustee, as in *Mara* v *Browne*, or as an express trustee, depending on the circumstances. In *Life Association of Scotland* v *Siddall* (1861) 3 De GF & J 60, a woman who took it upon herself to sell trust property and receive the proceeds of sale was held to be behaving as if there was a written declaration of an express trust, and the limitation periods applicable to express trusts rather than constructive trusts were applied to the case.

A constructive trust will be imposed on a stranger if he has been guilty of 'knowing receipt or dealing' or 'knowing assistance'. Knowing receipt or dealing may arise in three ways:

1. Where the stranger knowingly receives trust property in breach of trust. The degree of knowledge necessary to hold the stranger a constructive trustee is considered below, but for present purposes it includes both express and constructive notice that receipt is in breach of trust. For example, if money was given to a beneficiary under a will, who knew full well that he had been

overpaid, he would be a constructive trustee of the excess. In *Nelson* v *Larholt* [1948] 1 KB 339 an executor of a will drew eight cheques on the estate bank account in favour of the defendant, who cashed them. It was alleged that the defendant was a constructive trustee because he had received cheques which were intended to discharge the executor's personal debts but which had been drawn on the estate account. He should have been put on inquiry by the circumstances. Denning J (as he then was) held that the defendant was indeed a constructive trustee. In *International Sales & Agencies* v *Marcus* [1982] 3 All ER 551, over £30,000 belonging to the plaintiff company was applied in paying the personal debts of one of its directors, which were owed to the defendant. The defendant knew that the money was being paid from the company funds as the cheque was drawn on the company's bank account, and that it was an improper application of those funds. He was therefore a constructive trustee.

2. Where the stranger receives trust property without notice of the trust but afterwards becomes aware of the trust and deals with it in a manner inconsistent with the terms of the trust. This might arise in a number of ways, for example, if T, a trustee, gave his son £1,000 as a gift by way of a cheque drawn on T's bank account, and all the money in that account was misappropriated from the trust, a fact unknown to his son at the time, then the son would be an innocent volunteer against whom only tracing would be available. But if the son subsequently became aware that the £1,000 had been taken from the trust and immediately decided to spend it to avoid repayment, he would become a constructive trustee: see *Re Diplock* [1948] Ch 465. The same principle might apply to a stranger who received money from a company and who later became aware that it had been given to him in breach of trust but nevertheless went ahead and spent it.

3. Where the stranger receives trust property knowing it to be such but without breach of trust and subsequently deals with the property in a manner inconsistent with the trusts. This category was referred to by Peter Gibson J in *Baden Delvaux* v *Société Generale* [1993] 1 WLR 509. It seems that this was the basis of the decision of Bacon V-C in *Lee* v *Sankey* (1873) LR 15 Eq 204. In that case a firm of solicitors was employed by two trustees of a will trust to receive trust moneys. The solicitors received such moneys knowing they were trust moneys and afterwards paid them to one trustee without obtaining a receipt from both trustees. The solicitors were liable as constructive trustees.

Cases of 'knowing assistance' are concerned with situations where the stranger has knowingly assisted in a dishonest and fraudulent design on the part of trustees: see per Lord Selbourne in *Barnes* v *Addy* (1874) 9 Ch App 244, cited above. This category was considered in detail by Peter Gibson J in *Baden Delvaux* v *Société General* who said that four elements must be established before a case can be treated as being in the 'knowing assistance' category. These were:

1. The existence of a trust. On this he said the trust need not be a formal trust but

it is sufficient if there is a fiduciary relationship between the 'trustee' and the property of another person. Directors of a company are treated as trustees for these purposes because of the fiduciary nature of the duties they owe to the company: see *Selangor United Rubber Estates Ltd* v *Cradock (No 3)* [1968] 1 WLR 1555 and *Karak Rubber* v *Burden (No 2)* [1972] 1 WLR 602 (below).

2. The existence of a dishonest and fraudulent design on the part of the trustee of the trust. Peter Gibson J pointed out that no distinction should be drawn between 'dishonest' and 'fraudulent' for these purposes. He accepted the dicta of the court in *Belmont Finance Corp Ltd* v *Williams Furniture Ltd* [1979] Ch 250 where the Court of Appeal made it clear that it was insufficient that there was misfeasance or a breach of trust which fell short of dishonesty.

3. The assistance by the stranger in that design. This is a question of fact in each case.

4. The knowledge of the stranger. This encompasses the first three elements just mentioned. He should know there is a trust but this does not require him to know all the details of the trust. He should know of a dishonest and fraudulent design, but this does not mean that he should know of this in detail; it is enough that he knows that something of a dishonest and fraudulent nature is being carried out. As to assistance, he must know that his acts are assisting in the implementation of such a design.

The type of knowledge which were necessary to hold a stranger liable as a constructive trustee for either knowing receipt or dealing or knowing assistance had also been the subject of some debate. Most of the cases are concerned with the knowing assistance category where the aim has been to establish that a bank or some other agent assisted the trustee in a dishonest and fraudulent design, or to recover losses which the trustee could not meet or when the trustee had absconded. It is noteworthy that in such cases it is not necessary that the party whom it is claimed is a constructive trustee should have or have had the trust property vested in him. The constructive trust arises because of his 'knowing assistance'. The elements outlined by Peter Gibson J in the *Baden Delvaux* case show that knowledge is the most important matter to be established in the 'knowing assistance' cases, as it encompasses the first three elements. The possible types of knowledge relevant for the purposes of constructive trusteeship in accordance with the *Baden Delvaux* test were also considered by Peter Gibson J. They were:

1. Actual knowledge. This was a question of fact and needed no explanation.

2. Wilfully shutting one's eyes to the obvious. This category was referred to by Buckley LJ in *Belmont Finance* v *Williams Furniture* (before), who said: 'If he wilfully shuts his eyes to dishonesty ... he may be found to have involved himself in the fraudulent character of the design ...'

3. Wilfully and recklessly failing to make such enquiries as an honest and reasonable man would make. This category was also drawn from the judgment of Buckley LJ in *Belmont Finance* v *Williams Furniture*. It might arise, for example, where a

trust solicitor having before him some evidence tending to suggest that the trustees are misappropriating trust moneys from investments he has sold on their behalf, fails to make enquiries on the evidence he has before him.

4. Knowledge of circumstances which would indicate the facts to an honest and reasonable man. This category did not require dishonesty to be proved on the part of the stranger, unlike the three categories above. Support for this category could be found in the judgment of Ungoed-Thomas J in *Selangor United Rubber Estates* v *Cradock (No 3)* [1968] 1 WLR 1555. In *Consul Development Pty Ltd* v *DPC Estates Pty Ltd* (1975) 132 CLR 373 the Australian High Court considered this type of knowledge as relevant for a constructive trust. In his judgment Gibbs J said:

> '... it does not seem to me to be necessary to prove that the stranger who participated in a breach of trust and fiduciary duty with knowledge of all the circumstances did so actually knowing that what he was doing was improper. It would not be just that a person who had full knowledge of all the facts could escape liability because his own moral obtuseness prevented him from recognising an impropriety that would have been apparent to an ordinary man.'

5. Knowledge of circumstances which would put an honest and reasonable man on inquiry. On this Peter Gibson J said in the *Baden Delvaux* case:

> '... It is little short of common sense that a person who actually knows all the circumstances from which the honest and reasonable man would have knowledge of the relevant facts should also be treated as having knowledge of the facts ...'

The types of knowledge referred to in the first three categories above all involve dishonesty and there was no dispute in the cases that such knowledge on the part of the stranger to the trust would render him liable as a constructive trustee. However, categories 4 and 5 seem to have been disapproved as types of knowledge which would import constructive trusteeship. In *Carl Zeiss Stiftung* v *Herbert Smith & Co (No 2)* [1969] 2 Ch 276 the Court of Appeal seemed to view 'dishonesty' as the appropriate yardstick. Sachs LJ limited his discussion to categories (1)–(3) above while Edmund Davies LJ referred to 'want of probity' and nothing less as required. In *Belmont Finance* v *Williams Furniture* Goff LJ said: 'it would be dangerous and wrong to depart from the safe path of the principle as stated by Lord Selbourne LC (in *Barnes* v *Addy*) to the uncharted sea of something not innocent ... but still short of dishonesty'. Despite these dicta, all from the Court of Appeal, there are several cases, at first instance, where a constructive trust has been imposed when the stranger's conduct had fallen short of dishonesty. These include the *Selangor* case, the *Baden Delvaux* case and *Karak Rubber Co Ltd* v *Burden (No 2)* [1972] 1 WLR 602. In the *Selangor* case Ungoed-Thomas J concluded that

> '... the knowledge required to hold a stranger liable as a constructive trustee in a dishonest and fraudulent design, is knowledge of circumstances which would indicate to an honest, reasonable man that such a design was being committed or would put him on inquiry, which the stranger failed to make, whether it was being committed.'

Brightman J reached similar conclusions in the *Karak* case as did Peter Gibson J in *Baden Delvaux*. In all of these, the stranger's knowledge is viewed in an objective sense. All the cases involved commercial transactions, the first two involved circular cheque transactions. It is useful to outline the facts of the *Selangor* case, which were as follows:

Selangor's rubber plantations in Malaya were nationalised with compensation leaving Selangor with £232,000 in cash but no business. Cradock decided to take over Selangor by purchasing its shares but he had little money to do so. He devised a scheme, unlawful under the Companies Act 1985, by which he would use the company's money to purchase its shares. He made a successful offer to buy Selangor shares and used a banking company called Contanglo to buy the shares. He then arranged a loan with his bankers, the District Bank, to pay for the shares and for Selangor's account to be transferred to the District Bank. When the takeover had been completed Cradock appointed his nominees to the Selangor board and they resolved to lend all Selangor's money to a company called Woodstock, owned by Cradock. Woodstock re-lent the money to Cradock who then paid off the loan from the District Bank. Cradock disappeared and it was alleged that the District Bank was liable for Selangor's losses as constructive trustees. This claim was upheld on the ground that in the circumstances the bank should have realised Cradock was using the company's money to pay for the shares.

In contrast the more recent first instance cases showed a tendency to follow the approach of the Court of Appeal decisions referred to above, namely *Belmont Finance* and *Carl Zeiss Stiftung*. In *Re Montagu's Settlement Trusts* [1987] 2 WLR 1192 an unsuccessful claim was made to hold a beneficiary under a settlement of chattels liable as a constructive trustee of chattels he received from the trustees in breach of the trust. There was no evidence that he had knowledge that his receipt or dealing with them was in breach of trust. Megarry V-C summarised his conclusions on 'knowledge' as follows:

> '... (2) In considering whether a constructive trust has arisen in a case of knowing receipt of trust property, the basic question is whether the conscience of the recipient is sufficiently affected to justify the imposition of such a trust.
> (3) Whether a constructive trust arises in such a case primarily depends on the knowledge of the recipient, and not on notice to him; and for clarity it is desirable to use the word "knowledge" and avoid the word "notice" in such cases.
> (4) For this purpose, knowledge is not confined to actual knowledge, but includes at least knowledge of types (2) and (3) in the *Baden* case ... for in such cases there is a want of probity which justifies the imposition of a constructive trust.
> (5) Whether knowledge of the *Baden* types (4) and (5) suffices for this purpose is at best doubtful; in my view, it does not, for I cannot see that the carelessness involved will normally amount to a want of probity.
> (6) For these purposes, a person is not to be taken to have knowledge of a fact that he once knew but has genuinely forgotten: the test (or a test) is whether the knowledge continues to operate on that person's mind at the time in question ...'

The question of 'knowledge' sufficient to hold a person liable as a constructive trustee was also considered by Alliot J in *Lipkin Gorman* v *Karpnale Ltd* [1987] 1

WLR 987 (but see judgment of the Court of Appeal, [1989] 1 WLR 1340 below which represents the more relevant of the case's appeals as the House of Lords' decision, [1991] 3 WLR 10 considered the matter on different grounds) who took the view that 'want of probity is a key aspect in the approach the court should take' and followed *Re Montagu's Settlement*. He then went on to point out that there were differences in the courts' approach to the two types of constructive trusteeship:

'In *knowing receipt*, fraud is irrelevant. The recipient will be liable, if with want of probity on his part he had actual or constructive knowledge that the payor was misapplying trust money and the transfer to him was in breach of trust. In *knowing assistance*, the stranger to the trust must be proved subjectively to know of the fraudulent scheme of the trustee when rendering assistance, or to shut his eyes to the obvious, or to have wilfully and recklessly failed to make such inquiries as a reasonable and honest man would make.'

In *Lipkin Gorman* v *Karpnale Ltd*, C, a partner in a firm of solicitors misappropriated clients' money which he used in gambling. C was subsequently convicted of theft. The firm sought to recover the money from the casino where he gambled and from their bank on the basis that each was a constructive trustee. The claim against the casino on the basis of knowing receipt failed as the staff there did not have actual knowledge that C was gambling with trust funds nor did they have constructive knowledge of his misuse of trust funds. But the claim against the bank on the basis of knowing assistance succeeded at first instance as the bank manager was, on the judge's findings at first instance (but see below) aware that C's gambling was out of control, that his personal accounts were operating irregularly and that he had access to clients' accounts, but either shut his eyes to the obvious or wilfully and recklessly failed to make proper inquiries.

On appeal, however, the Court of Appeal concluded that the evidence did not justify the judge's findings concerning the bank manager, so that the bank's appeal was upheld: see [1989] 1 WLR 1340. The Court of Appeal also concluded that the relationship between a bank and its customer is contractual and, accordingly, the bank cannot be liable as a constructive trustee in respect of funds in its customer's account unless it is also in breach of its duty of care towards its customer. In this case the evidence did not disclose a breach of the bank's duty of care to its customer in contract or tort.

In this case May LJ stated, at p1355:

'In my opinion, ... there is at least strong persuasive authority for the proposition that nothing less than knowledge, as defined in one of the first three categories stated by Peter Gibson J in *Baden, Delvaux and Lecuit* v *Société Generale* ... [see above], of an underlying dishonest design is sufficient to make a stranger a constructive trustee of the consequences of that design.'

In *AGIP (Africa) Ltd* v *Jackson and Others* [1989] 3 WLR 1367 Millett J came to the conclusion that to make a stranger to a trust liable for 'knowing assistance', constructive notice is not sufficient. He stated that: 'Dishonest furtherance of the dishonest scheme of another is an understandable basis for liability; negligent but honest failure to appreciate that someone else's scheme is dishonest is not.' But, as his lordship pointed out, if such a stranger to a trust were suspicious of wrongdoing but nevertheless omitted to make enquiries because 'he did not want to know' or because he considered it to be 'none of his business', such conduct would be dishonest and such a person would, from the point of view of civil liability, be considered to have actual knowledge.

Millett J's conclusion was upheld by the Court of Appeal, see [1991] Ch 547, with Fox LJ giving the leading judgment.

In *Eagle Trust plc* v *SBC Securities Ltd* [1993] 1 WLR 489, Vinelott J pointed out that to hold a stranger liable as a constructive trustee, knowledge falling within categories (1), (2) or (3) of the classification in *Baden Delvaux* is necessary to establish liability, although, as his lordship continued:

'... in the absence of any explanation by the defendant, that kind of knowledge could be inferred and would be, if the circumstances were such that an honest and reasonable man would have inferred from them that the money was probably trust money and was being misapplied.'

In this particular case, however, the facts excluded any such inference.

See also the decision in *El Ajou* v *Dollar Land Holdings plc and Another* [1994] 2 All ER 685 in which the Court of Appeal ruled that a company could be held to have constructive knowledge by virtue of the knowledge of an employee (even if not a director) if the employee concerned was de facto a controlling mind of the company.

The recent line of case law on constructive trustees and 'knowing assistance' came to a head in the decision of the Privy Council in *Royal Brunei Airlines Sdn Bhd* v *Philip Tan Kok Ming* [1995] 3 All ER 97 (PC) The facts of the case are relatively straightforward. The defendant, Mr Tan, was the principal director of, and shareholder in, Borneo Leisure Travel ('BLT'), a Brunei incorporated travel agency. Under a standard form agreement BLT held various monies from ticket sales on trust for Royal Brunei Airlines. BLT went insolvent. However, despite the existence of the trust it was BLT's practice to use part of the ticket sales by paying these into its own bank account under a standing order, then using that money for its own business purposes. In holding Mr Tan liable as a constructive trustee on behalf of the airline for the money wrongfully paid into BLT's account the Privy Council reviewed the case law on the test to determine whether or not a stranger was to be held a constructive trustee. Marking a fundamental shift from the test laid down in the *Baden Delvaux* case the Privy Council ruled that the test should be:

1. the existence of a trust;
2. the breach of trust by the trustee. For these purposes Lord Nicholls (who delivered the Privy Council's recommendation) stated that it did not matter what was the state of mind of the trustee, a breach of trust being a breach of trust regardless of any intention or dishonesty;
3. the assistance by the stranger in the breach of trust. Again this remains a question of fact;

4. the keystone of holding the stranger as a constructive trustee is the need to establish the stranger's dishonesty in providing the assistance. Lord Nicholls considered that the five level test of knowledge in the *Baden Delvaux* case should be forgotten in this context. Rather the test which now appears to be applicable is that of an objective test with a hint of subjectivity. Per Lord Nicholls:

'Honesty has a connotation of subjectivity, as distinct from the objectivity of negligence. Honesty, indeed, does have a strong subjective element in that it is a description of a type of conduct assessed in the light of what a person actually knew at the time, as distinct from what a reasonable person would have known or appreciated. Further, honesty and its counterpart dishonesty are mostly concerned with advertent conduct, not inadvertent conduct. Carelessness is not dishonesty. Thus for the most part dishonesty is to be equated with conscious impropriety.' (p105j – p106a)

The practical effect of the new test of dishonesty will, invariably, mean a narrowing of the circumstances in which a stranger can be held to be a constructive trustee. Unfortunately, because of the large sums of money involved in these cases, the clarity of the recommendations made in the *Royal Brunei Airlines* case will not prevent counsel from continuing to pursue technical arguments. This occurred in a subsequent case, *Brinks Ltd* v *Abu-Saleh and Others (No 3)* (1995) The Times 23 October, which is discussed in Chapter 28, section 28.2. Two final points arise out of the Privy Council's decision. The first is, in accordance with Lord Nicholls' suggestion, the possibility that the new test will also apply whether the stranger has procured the breach of trust or merely assists in it. In this regard, a streamlining of the test for liabilities would be welcomed. Second, and of some note, is the Privy Council's implicit affirmation of the decision in *El Ajou* v *Dollar Land Holdings plc and Another* (above), whereby for all intents and purposes Mr Tan was held to be BLT, with his state of mind being imputed to BLT who, accordingly, were also held to have acted dishonestly.

7.4 Using a statute as an instrument of fraud

Cases where a statute is being used as an instrument of fraud are grounds for the imposition of constructive trusts. In fully-secret trusts, the trust is enforced in spite of its failure to meet the requirements of s9 Wills Act 1837 in order to prevent fraud. It will not lie in the mouth of a legatee to assert that a legacy, given to him apparently absolutely in the will, is his, because the obligations he accepted as to how it should be dealt with after the testator's death do not comply with s9: see Chapter 5 above. In *Bannister* v *Bannister* [1948] 2 All ER 133 this principle was applied to a trust of land, which was not evidenced in writing in accordance with s53(1)(b) Law of Property Act 1925. In that case the defendant sold two cottages to her brother-in-law on the basis of an oral agreement that she could live in one of them as long as she wished, free of rent. The conveyance on sale made no mention of this agreement. The brother-in-law brought an action for possession of the cottage after having given her notice to quit on the ground that she was nothing more than a mere licensee. The county court judge granted possession but the Court of Appeal imposed a constructive trust in favour of the defendant. The brother-in-law had used the absence of writing under s53(1)(b) as a means of defeating the trust which had been effectively agreed to by him prior to the sale.

7.5 Property obtained through unlawful conduct

A constructive trust will be imposed to prevent anyone guilty of murder or manslaughter or other serious crimes from benefiting from their criminal conduct. In *In the Estate of Crippen* [1911] P 108, Crippen murdered his wife, and as she had no will, he would have inherited her substantial estate under the intestacy rules. However, he was convicted and hanged and the issue arose as to whether his mistress was entitled to take the wife's estate through the terms of Crippen's will, made in favour of his mistress. The court held that the wife's estate must be distributed without reference to any rights that Crippen or those claiming through him might otherwise have had.

The doctrine also applies in Scotland where it was recently applied in the decision in *Hunter's Executors, Petitioners* (1992) The Scotsman 17 June. H, having been found guilty of murdering his wife, could not benefit under the terms of his wife's will. Similarly nor could the beneficiaries named in default benefit under the will, as this would necessitate an indirect tracing of their interest 'through' the husband. Rather the wife's estate would be distributed under the rules of intestacy, albeit with the husband being barred from gaining any interest.

The same rule applies to cases of manslaughter, so in *Re Giles* [1972] Ch 544, a woman who was convicted of the manslaughter of her husband through diminished responsibility could not benefit from his estate. Note that the Forfeiture Act 1982 may provide relief in some of these cases today. Property obtained through theft would appear to be subject to constructive trusts and in the Australian case of *Black v Freedman* (1910) 12 CLR 161 O'Connor J said:

> 'Where money has been stolen it is trust money in the hands of the thief and he cannot divest it of that character.'

The *Westdeutsche* case [1996] 2 All ER 961 now authoritavely resolves that, in English law, property obtained by theft is subject to a constructive trust. This will, of course, facilitate a tracing right in equity.

Finally, a recent decision, peculiar to its facts, is found in *Davitt v Titcumb* [1990] Ch 110. X and Y purchased a property, as equitable tenants in common, secured by a mortgage. X was subsequently convicted of murdering Y. After applying the proceeds of the endowment policy to pay off the mortgage, Scott J, held that X could not claim any interest in the property's net proceeds after sale. Rather the entire net proceeds were deemed vested in Y's personal representatives.

7.6 Mutual wills

A mutual will is created where several persons, usually a husband and wife, make wills in similar terms generally in each other's favour with a gift over to a third party. However the principle applies regardless of who the ultimate beneficiary is (see *Re Dale (deceased)*, *Proctor* v *Dale* [1993] 3 WLR 652), on the basis of an antecedent agreement which includes a term that each will not revoke without the other's consent. There is nothing to prevent either party revoking the agreement at any time before either of them dies: see *Stone* v *Hoskins* [1905] P 194. It is a recognised principle that a will is always revocable up until death. But where mutual wills are concerned, revocation may give rise to an action for breach of contract against the party who has revoked. When one party has died the situation changes completely if the surviving party revokes. This is because the party who has suffered as a result of the breach can, while alive, always alter his will after the breach, but this is, obviously, not so on death. In such circumstances a constructive trust is imposed on the survivor for the benefit of those entitled under the agreement: see *Re Hagger* [1930] 2 Ch 190 and *Re Cleaver* [1981] 1 WLR 939.

There are, however, practical, or possibly only theoretical difficulties with mutual wills. The decision in *Re Oldham* [1925] Ch 75 confirms the courts' insistence that there be mutual intention on the parties involved rather than mere coincidence. However, to what property does this mutual intention attach? Is it the property at the time of the wills being signed, or at the death of the first testator, or at the death of the second? Practically the first presents fewer difficulties but neither of them is trouble free.

7.7 Proprietary estoppel

The principles of proprietary estoppel may lead to the imposition of constructive trusts in order to protect the rights acquired thereunder. One aspect of proprietary estoppel is the rule in *Dillwyn* v *Llewellyn* (1862) 4 De GF & J 517 which is that if the legal owner of property promises to give it to another and that other expends money or otherwise acts to his detriment on the faith of the promise, the legal owner may be ordered to convey the property or to hold it subject to the rights acquired by the other. The legal owner would be a constructive trustee of the property in the circumstances: see *Re Basham* [1987] 1 All ER 405. Another aspect of proprietary estoppel is that laid down in *Ramsden* v *Dyson* (1866) LR 1 HL 129. This arises where a person expends money or acts to his detriment in relation to land in the mistaken belief that it belongs to him and the legal owner being aware of the mistake refrains from correcting it.

Both aspects of estoppel involve detriment giving rise to an equitable right in favour of the party who acted to his detriment. The reason the equitable right arises is because it would be unconscionable for the legal owner to assert his rights free from this obligation and if he sought to do so the court would impose a constructive trust upon him.

Scarman LJ in *Crabb* v *Arun District Council* [1976] Ch 179 concluded that estoppel cases involved three questions.

Is an equity established?

Oliver J in *Taylor Fashions* v *Liverpool Victoria Trustees Company* [1982] QB 133 determined that an equity will be established whenever the assertion of strict legal rights is found by the courts to be unconscionable.

What is the extent of the equity?

This is a matter to be decided on the facts of each case, by looking at the extent to which the plaintiff was encouraged to expend money or act to his detriment on the basis of the mistaken belief.

What relief should be granted?

This, again, is a matter dependent on the facts of each case. A conveyance may be ordered as in cases such as *Pascoe* v *Turner* [1979] 1 WLR 431; in other cases the plaintiff may be given a lesser interest. As each case depends on its facts it seems inappropriate to compare them. The following are worthy of consideration:

In *Inwards* v *Baker* [1965] 2 QB 29, in 1931 a father suggested to his son, who was looking for a site for a bungalow, that he should build on the father's land. The son acted on this suggestion and built the bungalow and lived in it. In 1951 the father died and in 1963 the trustees of his will, Miss Inwards (his mistress) and his children of their relationship, to whom the father left his estate on death, sought possession of the bungalow. The Court of Appeal held that the son had built the bungalow on the father's land with the father's encouragement and was entitled to remain in possession as a licensee so long as he wished to use it as his home.

In *Jones (AE)* v *Jones (FW)* [1977] 1 WLR 438 a father retired from London to Suffolk shortly after his second marriage. He asked one of his two sons to come and live near him and bought, for £4,000, a house for the son to live in when the son finally agreed to move to Suffolk. The house was put into the father's name but the son paid him £1,000 of the price and offered to pay more which the father refused saying: 'The place is yours'. The son paid no rent but he paid the rates. On the father's death, intestate, in 1972 his second wife became his administratrix and she claimed the house was hers and that the son ought to pay her rent. He refused so she sought possession against him. The Court of Appeal held that the father's conduct led the son to believe that he could regard the house as his home for the rest of his days. As the father would have been estopped from turning the son out of the house, the wife was equally estopped from doing the same. She could not obtain possession from him as he would be entitled to live there for as long as he wished.

Greasley v *Cooke* [1980] 1 WLR 1306. In 1938 D began work as a maid in a widower's house and looked after his four children. In 1946 the maid and the widower's eldest son began living together as man and wife in the house. The widower died in 1948 leaving the house to two sons equally, one being the eldest son. The maid looked after the eldest son and his mentally ill sister without receiving any payments and on the basis of assurances by the two sons who owned the house that she could remain in the house as long as she wished. On the death of the eldest son, intestate, his share in the house passed to the next-of-kin. The maid sought a declaration that she was entitled to remain in the house rent free for the rest of her life. The Court of Appeal held that the assurances to the maid by the two sons who owned the house raised an equity in her favour and it was to be presumed that she acted on those assurances. Accordingly the declaration was granted.

In *Baker* v *Baker* (1993) The Times 23 February the Court of Appeal had to consider the claim of a father who had assisted his son in purchasing a house in return for rent-free accommodation for life. The court rejected the father's claim to an interest in the property based on his contribution insofar as this had never been the underlying purpose of his assistance. Rather the father was entitled to be compensated for the loss of his rent-free accommodation for life (having left the house following a family dispute); this being in contrast to any right to recover the actual contribution made towards the property's purchase.

In *Crabb* v *Arun District Council* [1976] Ch 179, P and D were neighbouring landowners. P's property was landlocked with no right of way to the public highway. P had a plot of land, which he had sold without reserving a right of way over it to his landlocked land, after being led by D to believe that D would give him access through his land. But for this P would have reserved a right of way. D subsequently said they would only give P the right of way if he paid them £3,000. The Court of Appeal held that P was entitled to the right of way as D had, by words and conduct, led him to believe it would be granted. He did not have to pay £3,000 for it.

The principles of proprietary estoppel were considered as useful guidelines in *Grant* v *Edwards* [1986] Ch 638 in deciding whether the plaintiff in that case was entitled to a share of the proceeds of sale of the property. This decision shows that in appropriate cases the court may impose a constructive trust where a couple, A and B, set up house together in a property which is in the name of B alone, and A establishes a common intention between A and B, acted on by A to her detriment, that A should have a beneficial interest in the property. In *Re Basham* the plaintiff acted to her detriment on the faith of a belief encouraged by her step-father that she would inherit his estate by working in his businesses without payment for many years and caring for him and his home. The stepfather died intestate and the plaintiff was not entitled to anything on his intestacy. It was held that the plaintiff was entitled to the estate as she had established a case in proprietary estoppel in the circumstances. *Re Basham* was distinguished in *Windeler* v *Whitehall* (1990) 154 JP 29.

7.8 Vendor of land

This is the oldest type of constructive trust dating back to *Lady Foliamb's Case* in 1651, cited in *Daire* v *Beversham* (1661) Nels 76. When a written contract for the sale of land is capable of being specifically enforced the equitable doctrine of conversion operates and from the date of exchange to the date of completion the vendor holds the land on a constructive trust for the purchaser subject to his right to receive the purchase money. The constructive trust operates from the moment conversion takes place: see *Lysaght* v *Edwards* (1876) 2 Ch D 499.

The vendor is an unusual type of constructive trustee because he still retains an interest in the property which he is entitled to protect: see *Shaw* v *Foster* (1872) LR 5 HL 321. He can remain in the property until completion of the contract and is entitled to an equitable lien for the purchase money on the property: see *Re Birmingham* [1959] Ch 523. On the other hand, the vendor must preserve the property, so far as reasonably possible, in the state in which it existed at the date of the contract: see *Clarke* v *Ramuz* [1891] 2 QB 456. If the premises are tenanted at the date of the contract and the vendor subsequently re-lets them, he will be liable for any loss which occurs to the purchaser in consequence: see *Abdulla* v *Shah* [1959] AC 124. If the vendor wrongly resells the property to a third party before completion in circumstances where the purchaser has not registered his interest, the purchaser may claim the proceeds of sale as representing the property and on obtaining them, repay from them the contract price, so retaining any profits made on the resale by the vendor: see *Lake* v *Bayliss* [1974] 1 WLR 1073.

Arguably the effect of the Law of Property (Miscellaneous Provisions) Act 1989, dealing with contracts for the sale of land, does not have a radical effect on this type of constructive trust. In support of this one looks to s2(5) which specifically provides that s2(1) does not bite in respect of constructive, resulting or implied trusts.

7.9 The 'fair and reasonable' cases

As noted at the start of this chapter, constructive trusts in this country are founded on established principles and case law. This is as opposed to the American view of constructive trusts where they are seen as weapons to prevent injustice. This reasoning, and its undeniably attractive nature, lead at one point to the development of the now infamous 'new model constructive trust theory'. Its source was primarily that of an unremarkable decision of Lord Diplock in *Gissing* v *Gissing* [1971] AC 886. In that judgment Lord Diplock stated that a constructive trust would be imposed if:

1. there was conscionable conduct on the part of the potential constructive trustee; and
2. such conduct induced the constructive beneficiaries to act as they did on the understanding that they were thereby acquiring a beneficial interest.

The difficulty with this judgment, aside from its application, arose when Denning MR effectively hi-jacked it and moulded it in line with the American view of constructive trusts. This necessarily resulted in the second, but essential, limb of Lord Diplock's test being discarded. Its application was highlighted in the controversial decisions of *Cooke* v *Head* [1972] 1 WLR 518, and earlier in *Heseltine* v *Heseltine* [1971] 1 WLR 342. Building on these Denning MR openly stated in *Hussey* v *Palmer* [1972] 1 WLR 1286, at 1289, that in future a constructive trust could be imposed by law: 'wherever justice and good conscience required it'.

This dicta was quickly applied in three linked, but distinct, fields, namely matrimonial property rights, licensees of land and registered land: see *Eves* v *Eves* [1975] 1 WLR 1338, *Binions* v *Evans* [1972] Ch 359 and *Peffer* v *Rigg* [1977] 1 WLR 285. Each, on its peculiar facts, strove to give effect to justice and prevent injustice. This was despite the established principles normally applied. However, for that reason the new model constructive trust was, with hindsight, doomed to have a short lifespan. Without established principles and reliable case law the allure of a flexible tool for justice turns into a nightmare of inconsistency, unreliability and invariably injustice as compared to the justice it purports to uphold.

Rather than permitting such a scenario, the higher courts rapidly stepped in to protect the concept of certainty. See *Chandler* v *Kerley* [1978] 2 All ER 942, *Williams & Glyn's Bank Ltd* v *Boland* [1981] AC 487 and most importantly *Lloyds Bank plc* v *Rosset and Another* [1990] 2 WLR 867.

In this case a husband had provided (from a trust fund of which he was a beneficiary), the purchase money for the matrimonial home and had arranged overdraft facilities with his bank to cover substantial renovation work in respect of the premises. The loan was secured by a charge on the house. The wife, though not having contributed financially towards the acquisition of the house, had performed work in connection with the renovations.

In an action by the bank for possession of the house on the husband's default on his overdraft, brought against the wife – the husband had by then left and did not contest the bank's claim – she argued that she was entitled to a beneficial interest under a constructive trust arising as a consequence of the work she had done on the renovations.

The wife's claim was rejected by the House of Lords. In his speech, with which the other Law Lords sitting concurred, Lord Bridge pointed out that in a situation in which the wife had used her skills in helping to renovate premises which were to be the matrimonial home, this activity could not, in itself, give rise to the inference that there was a common intention that she should have a beneficial interest in the house. (At first instance it had been found that the parties had not decided, up to the exchange of contracts, whether the wife was to have a beneficial interest.) On the contrary, it would have been very natural for a wife, in these circumstances, to use her skills with the intention of making the property ready to be lived in as soon as possible. The value of the work she had done, pro rata to what the husband had provided, was 'trifling'.

In this case, Lord Bridge explained, and the other Law Lords present expressed their agreement, the tests to be applied in these situations. In fact, his lordship indicated that the necessary agreement or common intention can arise in either of two categories of situation. He said:

> 'The first and fundamental question which must always be resolved is whether, independently of any inference to be drawn from the conduct of the parties in the course of sharing the house as their home and managing their joint affairs, there has at any time prior to acquisition or exceptionally at some later date, been any agreement, arrangement or understanding reached between them that the property is to be shared beneficially.'

A finding to this effect can, only in Lord Bridge's view, 'be based on evidence of express discussions between the partners, however imperfectly remembered and however imprecise their terms may have been'. His lordship then pointed out that:

> 'Once a finding to this effect is made it will only be necessary for the partner asserting a claim to a beneficial interest against the partner entitled to the legal estate to show that he or she has acted to his or her detriment or significantly altered his or her position in reliance on the agreement in order to give rise to a constructive trust or a proprietary estoppel.'

As 'outstanding examples' of cases falling within this first category, his lordship cited *Eves* v *Eves* [1975] 1 WLR 1338 and *Grant* v *Edwards* [1986] Ch 638. In these cases the 'excuses' given by the male partner to the female partner for not putting the shared house into joint names at least indicated that there was an understanding between them in this regard.

As Lord Bridge pointed out:

> 'The subsequent conduct of the female partner in each of these cases, which the court rightly held sufficient to give rise to a constructive trust or proprietary estoppel supporting her claim to an interest in the property, fell far short of such conduct as would by itself have supported the claim in the absence of an express representation by the male partner that she was to have such an interest.'

The second 'very different' type of situation indicated by Lord Bridge in *Lloyds Bank plc* v *Rosset* is:

> '... where there is no evidence to support a finding of an agreement or arrangement to share, however reasonable it might have been for the parties to reach such an arrangement if they had applied their minds to the question, and where the court must rely entirely on the conduct of the parties both as the basis from which to infer a common intention to share the property beneficially and as the conduct relied on to give rise to a constructive trust. In this situation direct contributions to the purchase price by the partner who is not the legal owner, whether initially or by payment of mortgage instalments, will readily

justify the inference necessary to the creation of a constructive trust. But, as I read the authorities, it is at least extremely doubtful whether anything less will do.'

Lord Bridge cited as cases which demonstrate the second category of situation, *Pettitt* v *Pettitt* [1970] AC 777 and *Gissing* v *Gissing* [1971] AC 886.

In these two cases no agreement or understanding between the parties could be shown and the non-legal owner had made no *direct* contributions.

Recent decisions demonstrate, however, a return to the efforts to give effect to justice and prevent injustice. The decision in *Midland Bank* v *Cooke* [1995] 4 All ER 562, considered in Chapter 6, section 6.4, was clearly motivated by the desire to do justice. Waite LJ expressed satisfaction with Item 8 of the Law Commission's Sixth Programme of Law Reform (Law Com no 234, p34) which recommends an examination of the property rights of home-shares on the basis that the present legal rules are 'uncertain and difficult to apply and can lead to serious injustice.' Bearing in mind a subsequent case, *Drake* v *Whipp* [1996] 1 FLR 826, which is discussed in the final chapter, it cannot be doubted that the nightmare of inconsistency and unreliability now prevails again in English law. See Chapter 28, section 28.3, for further details.

8

Setting Trusts Aside

8.1 Introduction

8.2 Section 42 Bankruptcy Act 1914

8.3 Section 172 LPA 1925

8.4 Sections 339–342 Insolvency Act 1986

8.5 Sections 423–425 Insolvency Act 1986

8.6 Statutory provisions against discrimination

8.1 Introduction

A trust which is otherwise valid may fail because it is created for immoral purposes or is unlawful on grounds of public policy. Examples where trusts are considered as created for such purposes are:

1. Where they encourage the breakdown of marriage: see *Wren* v *Bradley* (1848) 2 De G & Sm 49 in which a condition in a gift, that a woman should live apart from her husband was struck down.
2. Where they are in restraint of marriage generally, but not if only a partial restraint, for example, against marriage with a non-Jew: see *Hodgson* v *Halford* (1879) 11 Ch D 959.
3. Trusts which tend to prevent the performance of parental duties: see *Re Sandbrook* [1912] 2 Ch 271.
4. Trusts for fraudulent or illegal purposes: see *Thrupp* v *Collett* (1858) 26 Beav 125, where a trust set up to pay the fines of convicted poachers was held void.

An important, if not the most important, area involving setting trusts aside involves claims by creditors or trustees in bankruptcy to recover property from settlements made by a bankrupt. This may arise, for example, where X has gone bankrupt and it is discovered that he made a marriage settlement for the benefit of his family, into which he has been constantly placing assets, even in time of financial difficulty, and that he made further settlements when he was worried about his financial position. If X were able to avoid his creditors by the mere device of a trust this would result in injustice to his creditors. To prevent this, statutory provisions exist to enable the creditors to have the trusts set aside in certain circumstances.

The statutory provisions dealing with setting trusts aside were changed by the Insolvency Act 1985. Prior to this Act the main provisions were s42 Bankruptcy Act 1914 and s172 Law of Property Act 1925. Both provisions were repealed by the Insolvency Act 1985, the provisions of this Act were repealed and replaced by the Insolvency Act 1986. The provisions in ss339–342 and ss423–425 of the 1986 Act are similar to those formerly contained in s174 and s212 1985 Act. In this Chapter the provisions of s42 and s172 are dealt with briefly in order to assist understanding of the provisions in the 1986 Act, as are their replacements, ss174 and 212 Insolvency Act.

8.2 Section 42 Bankruptcy Act 1914

Section 42(1)

This section provided protection for creditors and was designed to prevent trusts being abused by debtors to avoid payment of their debts. Section 42(1) is concerned with cases where settlements were made within specified time limits before bankruptcy, and under its provisions the settlement could be set aside automatically provided the appropriate conditions were fulfilled. For this reason s42(1) was usually resorted to before s172 LPA, because the latter required those seeking to set aside a trust to prove an intent to defraud creditors on the part of the settlor, which could be difficult.

Section 42, which was not dependent on proving an intention to defraud creditors, operated in the following circumstances:

1. Where the settlement was made within two years of bankruptcy, then all that need be to proved to the court was the date of the settlement and the date of bankruptcy.
2. Where the settlement was made more than two years before the date of bankruptcy but less than ten years before the date of bankruptcy, then it could be set aside unless two things were proved by those seeking to uphold the settlement: that at the date the settlor made the settlement he could pay all his debts without the aid of the settled property; and that his interest in the property passed to the trustees of the settlement at the time of execution, albeit that this second requirement is still fulfilled even if the ultimate interest in the property is still reserved to the settlor: see *Shrager* v *March* [1908] AC 402.
3. For the purposes of s42 the term settlement was widely defined by s42(4) as including 'any conveyance or transfer of property'. Generally it appears that if property was disposed of to be held and preserved for the enjoyment of some other person, there would be a settlement. In *Re Tankard* [1899] 2 QB 57 gifts by a bankrupt of personal property including furniture, pictures and jewellery to

his mistress, made within two years of his bankruptcy without imposing any restrictions on the mistress's power of alienation but with the intention that she should use or retain the property for an indeterminate time, were treated as voluntary settlements under s42.

4. There were four exceptions set out by s42(1) where it did not apply. These were settlements made before and in consideration of marriage; settlements made in favour of a purchaser or incumbrancer, in good faith and for valuable consideration; settlements made on or for the wife or children of the settlor of property which has accrued to the settlor after marriage in right of his wife; and policies of assurance effected by a man on his own life for the benefit of his wife or children.

Section 42(2)

Under s42(2) settlements before and in consideration of marriage were outside the rules permitting settlements to be set aside. However, if a marriage settlement contained a covenant or a contract:

1. for the future payments of money for the benefit of the settlors wife or husband or children; or
2. for the future settlement on or for the settlor's wife or husband or children of property, wherein the settlor had not at the date of the marriage any estate or interest whether vested or contingent, in possession or remainder and not being money or property in right of the settlor's wife or husband;

then the contract or covenant would be void against the trustee in bankruptcy if the settlor was adjudicated bankrupt and the contract of convenant had not been executed at the date of bankruptcy.

The section was designed to prevent abuse of marriage settlements by settlors covenanting to settle all their after-acquired property, and taking advantage of the covenant only when in financial difficulties so as to provide a safe haven for their assets. The beneficiaries under such covenants could also claim in bankruptcy under the covenant, but if they did so their claim was postponed to that of other creditors for valuable consideration: see *Re Cumming and West* [1929] 1 Ch 534.

Section 42(3)

Section 42(3) covered situations where money was transferred to a marriage settlement before the date of bankruptcy, in pursuance of a covenant or contract to settle property on the marriage settlement. Such transfers were void under s42(3) unless the persons to whom the payment was made proved that certain conditions laid down in the subsection applied. See 'Section 42(1)' above.

If any transfer or payment to the settlement was declared void then the beneficiaries were entitled to claim for a dividend in respect of the covenant or contract, as if it had not been executed at the commencement of the bankruptcy.

8.3 Section 172 LPA 1925

If a settlement was made outside the time limits set out in s42, or for some other reason could not be set aside under s42, the creditors or trustee in bankruptcy could resort to s172 LPA 1925 in order to have the settlement set aside. Section 172(1) stated:

> 'Save as provided in this section, every conveyance of property, made whether before or after the commencement of this Act, with intent to defraud creditors, shall be voidable, at the instance of any person thereby prejudiced.'

The section applied to all forms of property: see s205(i)(xx) LPA 1925. Although, having noted this, it was unclear if it applied to money.

Intent to defraud creditors

This was the most difficult element of the section to prove. Clear evidence of an intent to defraud would often be unavailable and the plaintiff would have to rely on inferences based on the defendant's conduct. In *Twyne's Case* (1601) 3 Co 80 six 'badges' of fraud were suggested as indicative of fraud and the more badges present in the case the greater was the likelihood of fraud. These badges were:

1. Where the conveyance comprises nearly all the settlor's property.
2. The settlor retains the property even though he has purported to convey it to others, but sometimes this may be explained as a valid and legitimate mortgage.
3. Secrecy of the conveyance.
4. Conveyance after the issue of a writ against the settlor, or threat of execution on his property, by creditors.
5. Existence of a trust for the settlor's benefit at the creditors' expense.
6. Unusual and unnecessary statements in the conveyance that it was made without fraudulent intent.

It was for the court in each case to decide on the facts whether there was an intent to defraud creditors: see *Re Wise* (1886) 17 QBD 290. In *Freeman* v *Pope* (1870) 5 Ch App 538 Lord Hatherley LC suggested that an intent to defraud creditors could be inferred where a debtor made a settlement which subtracted from the property that which was the proper fund for the payment of those debts and without which the debts could not be paid. This rather simplistic test was criticised by Lord Esher in *Re Wise* who made it clear the intent to defraud had to be proved. In *Freeman* v *Pope*, a clergyman was being pressed by his creditors and had to borrow money from his housekeeper from time to time to keep them at bay. At this time the clergyman transferred his major asset, a policy of insurance on his life worth about £1,000, to his god-daughter. It was agreed that the clergyman had no intent to defraud but the creditors nevertheless sought to have the transfer of the insurance policy set aside under s172. It was held that it was not necessary to prove that as a matter of fact the clergyman had an intent to defraud his creditors; this would be presumed where he subtracted from his property an amount without which his debts could not be paid.

In comparison in *Re Wise*, Wise, a sailor, promised to marry Miss Vyse who lived in Portsmouth. Then he went to Hong Kong and there married another lady, and so laid himself open to an action for breach of promise of marriage by Miss Vyse. The marriage in Hong Kong took place in May and the following October Wise received two letters in the same post from England. One letter stated that he had become entitled to a £500 legacy and the other that he was being sued by Miss Vyse for breach of promise of marriage. Wise immediately settled the £500 on his wife and children. Subsequently, Miss Vyse obtained judgment for £500 for breach of promise, but she failed to obtain her damages and had Wise adjudicated bankrupt. The trustee in bankruptcy sought to have the settlement set aside. Wise was able to show that at the date of the settlement he was not influenced by the possibility of an award of damages being made against him. The Court of Appeal held that as the settlement had not been made with the intention of defrauding creditors, it would not be set aside. The fact that the effect of creating the settlement was to defeat creditors was not relevant; an intention to defeat them had to be proved.

Intent to defraud was not, however, limited to cases where a debtor has put his property beyond the reach of his creditors. In *Lloyds Bank* v *Marcan* [1973] 1 WLR 1387 it was held to include cases where the creditors were deprived of timely recourse to property which would otherwise have been applicable for their benefit. It did not have to be an intent to defraud when the creditors were knocking on the debtor's door. In *Re Butterworth* (1882) 19 Ch D 588 it was held that an intent to defraud creditors could be inferred where a man settled his property on his wife and family before embarking on a hazardous business venture.

Following on from this persons who were prejudiced for the purposes of s172(1) included both existing creditors and future creditors. The former class included those who were owed money at the date the settlement was made; the latter class included those who lent money after the date of the settlement: see *Re Butterworth* (1882) 19 Ch D 588. The phrase 'any person thereby prejudiced' was not confined to creditors in the strict sense of the word, it could include a divorced spouse seeking an order for financial provision: see *Cadogan* v *Cadogan* [1977] 1 WLR 1041. In any case, only creditors whose debts subsisted at the date of the order setting aside the conveyance were protected. In *Re Butterworth* the owner of a prosperous bakery business made a voluntary settlement of £500, which comprised most of his property, upon his wife and children on the eve of taking over a grocery business. He owed £100 and without the aid of the property settled he could not pay these debts. Realising that the grocery business might be risky, he wanted to minimise his loss through the settlement. Six months later he sold the grocery business for as much as he gave for it. Three years later the bakery business became insolvent and his creditors sought to set aside the settlement. It was held that although the prime object of the settlement was to defeat the grocery business creditors, the settlement was void as against all creditors since it was made with the object of placing the property beyond the creditors' reach should a failure in business occur. An intention to defraud any creditor was sufficient to cause the settlement to be set aside.

A defence was provided by s172(3) if the plaintiff made out a case that it was probably the intention of the defendant that he intended to defraud his creditors. It stated:

> 'This section does not extend to any estate or interest in property conveyed for valuable consideration and in good faith or upon good consideration and in good faith to any person not having, at the time of the conveyance, notice of the intent to defraud creditors.'

The alternative requirements of valuable consideration and good faith, and good consideration and good faith, were narrowly interpreted to mean that only valuable consideration was sufficient. The reason for this was that otherwise a settlor could, by making the settlement in favour of his family for natural love and affection, avoid the mischief of the provision entirely: see *Re Eichholz* [1959] Ch 708.

Section 172(3) required good faith. It was not clear whether this was a reference to good faith on the part of the settlor or good faith on the part of the recipient. The problem was raised in *Lloyds Bank* v *Marcan* [1973] 1 WLR 1387 (first instance), but Pennycuick V-C found it unnecessary to decide the point. In the same case the Court of Appeal did not discuss the matter. However, it was likely that the onus lay on the transferee at the very least to show his good faith.

8.4 Sections 339–342 Insolvency Act 1986

These sections are intended in part to replace s42 Bankruptcy Act 1914, and follow, in broad terms, the recommendations of the Cork Report on Insolvency Law and Practice (1982) Cmnd 8558 which pointed to three defects in s42:

1. Out-and-out gifts of money were outside the section altogether. In order to set aside such a gift there had to be recourse to the fiction that it constituted a settlement, there being an implied intention that the subject-matter of the gift be preserved as capital: see *Re Tankard* [1899] 2 QB 57.
2. Dispositions for a merely nominal consideration were caught by the section, but otherwise all dispositions for valuable consideration were outside the section, even where the consideration represented a gross undervalue, unless they were not made in good faith.
3. No transaction could be impeached under the section where the debtor had died before a bankruptcy petition had been presented against him.

The provisions of ss339–342, so far as relevant, are as follows:

s339(1) 'Subject as follows in this section and ss341 and 342, where an individual is adjudged bankrupt and he has at a relevant time (defined in s341) entered into a transaction with any person at an undervalue, the trustee of the bankrupt's estate may apply to the court for an order under this section.'

s339(2) 'The court shall, on such application, make such order as it thinks fit for restoring the position to what it would have been if that individual had not entered into that transaction.'

s339(3) 'For the purposes of this section and ss341 and 342, an individual enters into a transaction with a person at an undervalue if –

a) he makes a gift to that person or he otherwise enters into a transaction with that person on terms that provide for him to receive no consideration,

b) he enters into a transaction with that person in consideration of marriage, or

c) he enters into a transaction with that person for a consideration the value of which, in money or money's worth, is significantly less than the value, in money or money's worth, of the consideration provided by the individual.'

s340(1) 'Subject as follows in this and the next two sections, where an individual is adjudged bankrupt and he has at a relevant time (defined in s341) given a preference to any person, the trustee of the bankrupt's estate may apply to the court for an order under this section.

s340(2) 'The court shall, on such application, make such order as it thinks fit for restoring the position to what it would have been if that individual had not given that preference.'

s340(3) 'For the purposes of this and the next two sections, an individual gives a preference to a person if –

a) that person is one of the individual's creditors or a surety or guarantor for any of his debts or other liabilities, and

b) the individual does anything or suffers anything to be done which (in either case) has the effect of putting that person into a position which, in the event of the individual's bankruptcy, will be better than the position he would have been in if that thing had not been done.'

s341(1) 'Subject as follows, the time at which an individual enters into a transaction at an undervalue or gives a preference is a relevant time if the transaction is entered into or the preference given –

a) in the case of a transaction at an undervalue, at a time in the period of 5 years ending with the day of the presentation of the bankruptcy petition on which the individual is adjudged bankrupt ...

b) in any other case of a preference which is not a transaction at an undervalue, at a time in the period of 6 months ending with that day.'

s341(2) 'Where an individual enters into a transaction at an undervalue or gives a preference at a time mentioned in paragraph (a), (b) or (c) of subsection (1) (not being, in the case of a transaction at an undervalue, a time less than 2 years before the end of the period mentioned in paragraph (a)), that time is not a relevant time for the purposes of ss339 and 340 unless the individual –

a) is insolvent at that time, or

b) becomes insolvent in consequence of the transaction or preference.

but the requirements of this subsection are presumed to be satisfied, unless the contrary is shown, in relation to any transaction at an undervalue which is entered into by an individual with a person who is an associate of his (otherwise than by reason only of being his employee).'

s341(3) 'For the purposes of subsection (2), an individual is insolvent if –

a) he is unable to pay his debts as they fall due, or
b) the value of his assets is less than the amount of his liabilities, taking into account his contingent and prospective liabilities.'

Sections 339–342 are concerned with the adjustment of prior transactions and are wide enough to apply to transactions in which a bankrupt, prior to bankruptcy, settled property upon trusts. Two types of transaction are dealt with by these provisions – those at an undervalue (defined by s339(3)) and preferences (defined by s340(3)). The provisions of s339 are likely to be of greater importance in setting aside trusts because of the definition of transaction at an undervalue in s339(3). If X voluntarily settled £100,000 on trusts at 'a relevant time' within s341 for the benefit of his spouse and children and was subsequently declared bankrupt, the trust would fall within s339(3)(a). If the settlement was made on X's marriage, as a marriage settlement, then it would fall within s339(3)(b). Even if X made the settlement for valuable consideration, it would be caught by s339(3)(c) if that consideration was significantly less than the value of the property settled. For example, if X settled a Van Gogh painting he had purchased for £12 million on a trust in consideration of a conveyance of land valued at £4 million, it is likely that the settlement would fall within s339(3)(c). There may be difficulty in some cases under s339(3)(c) in determining whether the consideration is 'significantly less' than the value of the property settled. If, in the example given, the painting had never been on the market or was by an artist whose works fluctuated in value according to tastes, it might be difficult to assess its true worth. Section 340 is unlikely to be of great significance in the context of trusts. One possible application here is in the case of covenants to settle. A settlor who, say, covenanted to settle £100,000 on trusts and whose covenant was executory at 'a relevant time' might pay the money to the trustees in order to ensure that the settlement was completely constituted in the event of his possible bankruptcy. In such circumstances his conduct would appear to amount to a preference within s340(3)(b).

It is clear from the provisions of s339(1) and s340(1) that only 'the trustee of the bankrupt's estate' may apply for relief under ss339–342. The trustee in bankruptcy is not entitled to have any prior transactions entered into by the bankrupt adjusted but only those which were entered into by him at 'a relevant time'. This is defined by s341. In the case of a transaction at an undervalue, a settlement of property made by the bankrupt at any time within the five years prior to the date of the presentation of the bankruptcy petition is within the 'relevant time'. See s341(1)(a). If the transaction was entered into not less than two years before the date of the presentation of the bankruptcy petition then, under s341(2), it will not be within the 'relevant time' unless the bankrupt was insolvent at that time, or became insolvent in consequence of the transaction. 'Insolvent' is defined by s341(3). For example, if a bankruptcy petition was presented against X on 1 July 1988 and X had made three voluntary settlements, A on 1 January 1982, B on 1 June 1984 and C on 1 January 1987, only settlements B and C might be set aside under s339. Settlement A could not be set aside under s339 as it was not made at a relevant time under s341((1)(a), but some six and a half years prior to the presentation of the bankruptcy petition. Settlement B having been made some four years before the presentation of the bankruptcy petition could only be set aside if the provisions in s341(2)(a) or (b) could be satisfied, and settlement C could clearly be set aside under s341(1), being made only one year before presentation of the bankruptcy petition. If the transaction involves a preference, then the relevant time will, in general, be six months ending with the day of the presentation of the bankruptcy petition and will only be the relevant time if the requirements in s341(2)(a) or (b) are satisfied.

The court has wide powers in making orders to deal with transactions at an undervalue or preferences. Sections 339(2) and 340(2) enable it to 'make such order as it thinks fit' and s342(1), without prejudice to the generality of these provisions, sets out orders that may be made. These include vesting the property transferred as part of the transaction or its proceeds of sale, or such other property as represents it. Given the relative 'youth' of such powers it is inevitable that their usage will vary tremendously until a firm body of case law is established.

8.5 Sections 423–425 Insolvency Act 1986

These sections replace s172 LPA 1925 referred to in section 8.3 above. The Cork Report on Insolvency Law and Practice (1982) Cmnd 8558 considered s172 had many defects including:

1. It was unclear whether it applied to mere payments of money as well as dispositions of property, whether effected by an instrument or not.
2. The meaning of 'to defraud' was unclear, in particular as to whether it actually included transactions to defeat, hinder, or delay creditors or to put assets belonging to the debtor beyond their reach.
3. The provisions of s172(3) were confusing as to the meaning of 'good' and 'valuable' consideration and good faith, and their relationship with s172(1) was obscure.
4. The section did not make it clear that dispositions in favour of a bona fide purchaser for money or money's worth without notice could not be set aside.

The provisions of ss423–425 so far as relevant are as follows:

s423(1) 'This section relates to transactions entered into at an undervalue; and a person enters into such a transaction with another person if –
1. he makes a gift to the other person or he otherwise enters into a transaction with the other on terms that provide for him to receive no consideration;
2. he enters into a transaction with the other in consideration of marriage; or
3. he enters into a transaction with the other for a consideration the value of which, in money or money's worth, is significantly less than the value, in money or money's worth, of the consideration provided by himself.'

s423(2) 'Where a person has entered into such a transaction, the court may, if satisfied under the next subsection, make such order as it thinks fit for –
1. restoring the position to what it would have been if the transaction had not been entered into, and
2. protecting the interests of persons who are victims of the transaction.'
s423(3) 'In the case of a person entering into such a transaction, an order shall only be made if the court is satisfied that it was entered into by him for the purpose –
1. of putting assets beyond the reach of a person who is making, or may at some time make, a claim against him, or
2. of otherwise prejudicing the interests of such a person in relation to the claim which he is making or may make.'
s424(1) 'An application for an order under this section shall not be made in relation to a transaction except –
1. in a case where the debtor has been adjudged bankrupt ... by the trustee of the bankrupt's estate ... or (with the leave of the court) by a victim of the transaction;
2. in any other case, by a victim of the transaction.'
s424(2) 'An application made under any of the paragraphs of subsection (1) is to be treated as made on behalf of every victim of the transaction.'

Sections 423–425 are designed to enable transactions at an undervalue intended to defraud creditors to be avoided. If X created a settlement with the purpose of placing his property in it to avoid his creditors in the event of bankruptcy, it would be possible to set it aside under s423. 'Transaction at an undervalue' is defined by s423(1) and is similar in its terms to s339(3), referred to above. If a settlement falls within this definition it may only be the subject of an order under s423(2) if the conditions in s423(3) are satisfied, that is, if it was entered into by the settlor to put assets beyond the reach of present or future creditors, or to prejudice the interests of present or future creditors. Unlike the provisions of s339–342, there are no time limits placed on transactions which may be set aside by s423. In the example in section 8.4, although settlement A could not be set aside under s339, it might be set aside under s423, provided s423(3) was satisfied. The provisions of s423–425 do not depend on 'fraud' being established and should be easier to invoke successfully than s172 LPA 1925. Those who may apply for an order under s423 are defined by s424 and a victim of the transaction may apply provided that a trustee in bankruptcy has not been appointed. The court may make such order as it thinks fit under s423(2) but s425 provides that the order may include the return of property or its proceeds or property representing these. Section 425 is similar in its terms to s342 referred to in section 8.4.

8.6 Statutory provisions against discrimination

Race Relations Act 1976

This only really affects charitable trusts. See s34 particularly. That section provides for the curious situation that it is permissible to discriminate in favour of a particular race, nationality or ethnic group but not against them. Any provision contrary to the Act is disregarded with the illegal discrimination aspect removed. Aside from this statutory provision the Act does not prevent otherwise discriminatory gifts or private trusts.

Sex Discrimination Act 1975

As per the Race Relations Act this Act does not apply so as to invalidate a private trust. Further s43 specifically provides that the Act does not apply to charitable trusts which confer benefits on a single sex.

9

Trusts of Imperfect Obligation

9.1 Introduction

9.2 The 'monument' cases

9.3 The 'animal' cases

9.4 Trusts for saying masses

9.5 The perpetuity rule

9.6 Someone to execute the trust

9.7 Gifts to unincorporated associations

9.1 Introduction

A trust must generally be made for the benefit of human objects. As seen in Chapter 2, if these objects cannot be ascertained the trust is void. Where a trust does not have any human objects at all but is merely for a particular purpose, then as a general rule it is void also. This is illustrated by *Re Astor's Settlement Trust* [1952] Ch 534 where an inter vivos settlement was created by Lord Astor in 1945 which had among its objects the following:

1. The maintenance of good understanding, sympathy and co-operation between nations.
2. The preservation of the independence and integrity of newspapers.
3. The protection of newspapers from being absorbed by combines.

Roxburgh J held that the trusts failed; there were no human objects, and the trusts were for purposes and not for individuals. That is, they are trusts for imperfect obligations and void for policy reasons. This chapter addresses such trusts, the underlying policy that governs them and the exceptions to that policy. However, it must be stressed that a major exception to the policy to be discussed following is the field of charitable trusts. These are expanded upon in Chapter 10 but it is useful here to note the fine distinction between trusts for imperfect obligations and charitable trusts.

In *Re Shaw* [1957] 1 WLR 729 the playwright George Bernard Shaw left funds on trust, the income to be applied for 21 years after his death in the research of a 40 letter alphabet. This research was to include its dissemination, via one of his 'translated' plays, and promotion as a replacement for the existing 26 letter alphabet. Harmon J held this to be void as a trust for imperfect obligations. Further it was held not to be charitable being neither educational or for the benefit of the community. See Chapter 10 for the relevance of these two features in a charitable trust.

Returning specifically to trusts for imperfect obligations the reasons why the court will not uphold purpose trusts were explained by Sir William Grant MR in *Morice* v *Bishop of Durham* (1805) 10 Ves 522. In this case the testatrix bequeathed all her personalty to the Bishop of Durham upon trust for 'such objects of benevolence and liberality as the Bishop of Durham in his own discretion shall most approve of'. It was held that the gift was not charitable and it could not stand as a private trust either, because it did not have any beneficiaries, and was made purely for a purpose. Sir William Grant MR said:

'There can be no trust, over the exercise of which this Court will not assume a control; for an uncontrollable power of disposition would be ownership, and not trust. If there be a clear trust, but for uncertain objects, the property that is the subject of the trust is undisposed of ... But this doctrine does not hold good with regard to trusts for charity. Every other trust must have a definite object. There must be somebody in whose favour the Court can decree performance.'

In the same case Lord Eldon LC said:

'As it is a maxim, that the execution of a trust shall be under the control of the court, it must be of such a nature, that it can be under that control; so that the administration of it can be reviewed by the court; or, if the trustee dies, the court itself can execute the trust; a trust therefore, which in the case of maladministration could be reformed; and a due administration directed; and then unless the subject and the objects can be ascertained, upon principles familiar in other cases, it must be decided, that the court can neither reform maladministration, nor direct due administration.'

In short, the reasons which this dictum puts forward are:

1. that the purpose may not be clearly stated and therefore the trustees would be given what would be tantamount to ownership;
2. as there are no beneficiaries there is no one who can demand performance in their favour.

Thus, if the trustees were abusing their position nobody would be able to demand proper application, although those entitled in remainder or under a resulting trust if the purpose were to fail, can restrain a misapplication of funds, but without being able to enforce a proper one: see *Re Thompson* [1934] Ch 342. These problems do not arise where the trust is charitable, as the Charity Commissioners will have a supervisory role and the Attorney-General will have locus standi to enforce and control it: see Chapter 10, section 10.1.

Having stated the general attitude of the courts, the exceptions must be noted. But given the general dislike of these types of trusts the tendency appears to be to limit these exceptions on the ground that they are anomalies. In *Re Endacott* [1960] Ch 232 a testator bequeathed money to erect 'some useful memorial to myself'. In refusing to uphold this as a purpose trust Harman LJ said:

> '... there have been decisions at times which are not really to be satisfactorily classified, but are perhaps merely occasions when Homer has nodded, at any rate, these cases stand by themselves and ought not to be increased in number, nor indeed followed, except where one is exactly like another. Whether it would be better that some authority should now say those cases were wrong, this is perhaps not the moment to consider. At any rate I cannot think of this kind, the case of providing outside a church an unspecified and unidentified memorial, is the kind of instance which should be allowed to add to those troublesome anomalous and abberrant cases.'

The reasons for the court's refusal to extend these exceptions are largely those reasons referred to above for not recognising purpose trusts. As Lord Evershed MR pointed out in *Re Endacott*, to extend the exceptions would be to validate almost limitless heads of non-charitable trusts. To permit further exceptions would erode the strict rule that a non-charitable trust must have ascertained or ascertainable beneficiaries. In *Re Denley*, Goff J's distinction between 'abstract' purpose trusts and trusts which are indirectly for the benefit of ascertainable individuals even when they appear to be purpose trusts of the old fashioned, unpopular type, has opened up a new line of case law: see section 9.7.

Three conditions would appear to be necessary before the court will uphold a purpose trust contrary to the general rule that it is void:

1. The trust must be for a purpose which has been previously upheld by the court.
2. The trust must be limited in perpetuity.
3. There must be someone who will execute the purpose trust. (Note the difference with express trusts where the courts will not permit the absence of a trustee to thwart a trust.)

Each of the above conditions will be dealt with in detail below.

As Harman LJ said in *Re Endacott*, there are cases where the court has in the past upheld purpose trusts, mainly what are described as the 'monument' and 'animal' cases. Purpose trusts have also been upheld for the saying of masses in jurisdictions where such trusts are regarded as non-charitable, and in one case for the furtherance and promotion of fox hunting: see *Re Thompson* [1934] Ch 342. There are also some occasions when gifts to unincorporated associations may be regarded as purpose trusts. Unincorporated associations are dealt with below.

It is vital that purpose trusts sought to be upheld should fall within one of the recognised categories. In *Re Shaw* (above) a gift for a 40 letter alphabet did not. Some gifts can also be rather deceptive. The monuments cases all appear to have been for the erection of tombs and memorials for human beings, and therefore a monument erected to the memory of an animal would not be upheld on the principles in *Re Endacott*.

9.2 The 'monument' cases

Purpose trusts have been upheld where they have been for the erection or maintenance of monuments, tombs or graves. In *Re Hooper* [1932] 1 Ch 38 a testator left trustees £1,000 to provide 'so far as they can legally do so and ... for as long as may be practicable' for the care of:

1. A grave and monument in Torquay cemetery.
2. The care and upkeep of a vault containing the remains of the testator's wife and daughter.
3. The care and upkeep of a grave and monument in Ipswich.
4. The care and upkeep of a tablet and window in a church, to the memory of various members of the testator's family.

Maugham J held that the first three gifts for the care and upkeep of the graves were non-charitable. They were valid purpose trusts and had been limited in perpetuity, and as the trustees were willing to carry them out they should be permitted to do so. The fourth gift was charitable.

The erection of tombs and monuments will normally take place in a church or in the churchyard. Sometimes the gift can be upheld on the basis of being charitable, if it adds to or improves the fabric of the church. In *Re Hooper* the fourth gift had such an effect, namely, the erection of a tablet on the church wall and a stained-glass window. In *Trimmer v Danby* (1856) 25 LJ Ch 424 a gift of £1,000 to erect a monument to the testator's memory in St Paul's Cathedral 'among those of my brothers in art' was held only to be a purpose trust; it was not for the fabric of the church.

There are very few reported cases which deal with the point whether monuments which are not erected on church ground can be upheld as purpose trusts. In *Re Dean* (1889) North J appears to have accepted that this could be done when he said:

'... a man may if he pleases, give a legacy to trustees, upon trust to apply it in erecting a monument to himself, either in a church or in a churchyard, or even in unconsecrated ground ...'

The rule against purpose trusts is directed mainly against bequests and gifts which involve the element of maintenance of a monument, tomb or grave, as this could go on indefinitely, thereby falling foul of the concept of perpetuity, that is the tying up of, 'alienation of', property for excessive periods of time. This appears from the judgment of Hall V-C in *Mussett v Bingle* (1876) WN 170 where a testator left £300 for the erection of a monument and £200 for its maintenance. The former was upheld, the latter held void for perpetuity.

A bequest of gift for the erection or maintenance of a monument, tomb or grave or any other form of memorial may be struck down if it is considered as excessive and of benefit to nobody. The Scottish cases of *McCaig v University of Glasgow* (1907) SC 231 and *McCaig's Trustees v Kirk-Session etc* (1915) SC 426 are interesting examples. In the former the testator left all of his substantial estate to be used to build statues of himself, and towers in prominent places on his estates, while in the latter the testatrix directed that 11 bronze statues costing not less than £1,000 each should be erected in Scotland to the memory of various members of her family. In the first case Lord Kyllachy said:

> 'I suppose it would be hardly contended … if the purposes … were to be slightly varied, and the trustees were, for instance directed to lay the truster's estate waste, and keep it so; or to turn the income of the estate into money, and throw the money yearly into the sea; or to expend income in annual or monthly funeral services in the testator's memory … Such purposes I think would hardly be consistent with public policy …'

To a great degree the controversy surrounding this area has been deflected by the effect of s1 The Parish Councils and Burial Authorities (Miscellaneous Provisions) Act 1970. This permits the settlor to contract with the relevant local authority to maintain a grave, memorial or monument for a period not greater than 99 years.

9.3 The 'animal' cases

Where a gift is made for the benefit of animals generally then it will be upheld as charitable and the issue of purpose trusts will not arise. In *Re Douglas* (1887) 35 Ch D 472 a home for lost dogs was held charitable. The only test applied to permit charitable status for animals generally is that there must be some benefit to humanity. In *Re Wedgwood* [1915] 1 Ch 113 it was said this was satisfied if it checked man's tendency to cruelty or developed the better side of human nature towards animals.

A gift for a specific animal or group of animals is not charitable but it can stand as a valid purpose trust. Gifts for the benefit of a testator's dog or cat or horses and hounds are good purpose trusts. Such gifts must have as their object the care of the animals concerned, it seems. In *Re Dean* (1889) 41 Ch D 552 a testator left funds to trustees for a period of 50 years, if any of his horses and hounds should live that long, to be used for their maintenance. North J held the gift was a valid purpose trust because:

> 'Is there then anything illegal or obnoxious to the law in the nature of the provision, that is, in the fact that it is not for human beings, but for horses and dogs? It is clearly settled by authority that a charity may be established for the benefit of horses and dogs, and therefore, the making of a provision for horses and dogs, which is not a charity cannot of itself be obnoxious to the law, provided, of course, that it is not to last for too long a period …'

This dictum seems to be based on very wide grounds which might be questioned especially in the light of the dictum in *Re Endacott*. However, there is established authority apart from *Re Dean* that gifts for animals which are not charitable may be good purpose trusts. In *Pettingall* v *Pettingall* (1842) 11 LJ Ch 176 a testator left

£50 to be used to maintain his favourite black mare after his death. Knight-Bruce V-C held the gift was valid.

9.4 Trusts for saying masses

It seems that trusts for the saying of masses strictly in private and in respect of which no public benefit can be shown, may be regarded as trusts of imperfect obligation: see *Bourne* v *Keane* [1919] AC 815. For what will be regarded by the courts as public benefit in the context of trusts for the saying of masses or other religious services see, in particular, *Re Hetherington Dec'd* [1989] 2 WLR 1094 and the discussion contained in Chapter 10, section 10.11.

9.5 The perpetuity rule

A non-charitable purpose trust cannot exist for an indefinite period; to permit it to do so would offend against the rule against perpetual duration. This rule does not apply to charitable trusts which can, once the gift has vested in them, technically go on for ever because it is in the public interest that they should do so.

The rule against perpetual duration is a further reason for striking down purpose trusts. In the case of those that are upheld it is strictly applied and under it the trust must not run for longer than a period of lives in being and 21 years: see *Re Astor's Settlement* (above). The lives in being, if used, must be human lives. In an Irish decision, *Re Kelly* [1932] IR 255, an attempt was made to use a greyhound as a life in being; this was rejected. Meredith J said:

'There can be no doubt that "lives" means lives of human beings, not animals or trees in California. Lives in being are rarely used in purpose trusts.'

The perpetuity period of lives plus 21 years as applied to purpose trusts has not been affected by the Perpetuities and Accumulations Act 1964. Section 15(4) states:

'Nothing in this Act shall affect the operation of the rule of law rendering void for remoteness certain dispositions under which property is limited to be applied for purposes other than the benefit of any person or class of persons in cases where the property may be so applied after the end of the perpetuity period.'

This appears to mean that even the 80 year perpetuity period laid down in s1(1) of the Act cannot be used in purpose trusts. Similarly the 'wait and see' provisions of the Act (s3) do not apply to purpose trusts.

The perpetuity period must be set out expressly in the purpose trust, confining its duration, or there must be something which necessarily dictates that the trust will not run for longer than the perpetuity period. Where a purpose trust was for 'the lives of Her Majesty Queen Victoria and her descendants now living and during the lives and life of the survivors and survivor of them and during the period of twenty-one years after the death of such survivor', it was held good: see *Re Khoo Cheng Teow* (1932) Straits Settlements Reports 226.

The rule that the perpetuity period must be stated has been held to have been satisfied where the following phrases have been used:

1. Money for the care and upkeep of family graves 'so far as (the trustees) can legally do so': see *Re Hooper* [1932] 1 Ch 38.
2. Money bequeathed to maintain a grave 'so long as the law for the time being permitted': see *Pirbright* v *Sawley* [1896] WN 86.

In other cases, the court has been prepared to take judicial notice of the fact that the trust could not last beyond the end of the perpetuity period. This is particularly relevant in the 'animal' cases. In *Re Haines* (1952) The Times 7 November, a gift for the testatrix's cats was upheld on judicial notice being taken of the fact that cats do not live longer than 21 years. The same approach appears to have been taken in *Re Dean* (1889) (above) where, despite a 50-year period being expressly set out, the gift was upheld. The latter case is open to serious doubt because the court will not cut down any period stated in a gift to 21 years: see *Re Compton* [1946] 1 All ER 117.

Various attempts have been made to set a perpetuity period which would ensure that the purpose trust continued for a long time. One favourite was the 'royal lives' clauses, an example of which is cited above in *Re Khoo Cheng Teow*. In cases concerning the erection and maintenance of tombs, monuments and graves, testators have sought to ensure that their last resting place would be cared for as long as possible. One method of doing this is to leave funds to maintain all tombs and graves in the churchyard in which the testator hopes to be buried. This would be a charitable trust, as it is for the maintenance of the whole churchyard: see *Re Vaughan* (1886) 33 Ch D 187. Two other methods of extending the period for maintaining the grave or tombs are:

1. Making a gift on trust to one charity, with a gift over to another charity should the first charity fail to keep the tomb or grave in repair. In *Re Tyler* [1891] 3 Ch 252 a testator left £42,000 to the London Missionary Society (a charity) and left the family vault at Highgate Cemetery in their charge to maintain it and keep it in good repair but failing to do so, the money was to go to Christ's Hospital (a charity). Questions were raised as to the validity of the gift. The Court of Appeal held that that part of the gift to repair the vault was valid; it did not impose an obligation on the first charity to maintain the tomb. Such an obligation would have amounted to a trust and would have been void, but the will merely stated that the first charity would lose the gift if it failed to maintain the tomb. This direction did not affect property; instead it affected the rights of the first charity, and also took advantage of the rule that a gift to one charity followed by a gift over to another charity is completely exempt from the perpetuity rule: see Chapter 10, section 10.2. As Fry LJ said:

'If the testator had required the first donee, the London Missionary Society, to apply any portions of the fund, towards the repair of the family tomb, that would in all probability, at any rate, to the extent of the sum required, have been void as a perpetuity which was not a charity. But he had done nothing of the sort. He has given the first donee no power to apply any part of the money. He has only created a condition that the sum shall go over to Christ's Hospital if the London Missionary Society do not keep the tomb in repair ...'

The decision in *Re Tyler* should be contrasted with *Re Dalziel* [1943] Ch 277 where a testatrix gave £20,000 to St Bartholomew's Hospital 'subject to the condition that they shall use the income' for the upkeep and repair of the mausoleum and surrounding garden in Highgate Cemetery with a gift over to another charity if they failed to do so. The gift and gift over were held to be void because the testatrix had required the income to be used to maintain the mausoleum. This requirement amounted to a trust obligation.

2. Under s1 Parish Councils and Burial Authorities (Miscellaneous Provisions) Act 1970, as previously noted.

Other suggested methods for avoiding the perpertuity rule are:

1. To set up a trust in which a mere power is given to the trustees to carry out a non-charitable purpose. By this method the trustees could maintain a tomb or monument for so long as the trust existed.
2. To create a company for the execution of the purpose.
3. By the use of unincorporated associations.

These methods of 'avoidance' aside it is strongly argued that the harshness of the rules governing this field should be mitigated by further statutory exceptions. After all it should be remembered that the effect of these rules is to deprive the settlor from doing what he likes with his own property. Perhaps an amicable compromise would be the extension of ss1 and 3, Perpetuities and Accumulations Act 1964 (the 80-year perpetuity period and 'wait and see' provisions) to apply to purpose trusts.

9.6 Someone to execute the trust

As seen earlier in *Morice* v *Bishop of Durham*, Sir William Grant MR said 'there must be somebody in whose favour the court will decree performance'. There must, in other words, be someone who will execute the trust. In *Re Dean* (above) North J appears to have regarded this point as being of no importance. He could see no one who could ask the court to enforce the trust in that case, but added, 'still it cannot be said that the trust must fail because there is no one who can actively enforce it'. In more recent decisions the dicta of North J have been ignored. In *Re Astor* Roxburgh J gave as one of the reasons for his decision the fact that there was nobody who could enforce the purpose against the trustee. He found it hard to accept that the trustees would enforce the purpose against themselves. In *Re*

Endacott (above) Lord Evershed MR also assumed that this was a necessary condition.

It is necessary that somebody should give the court an undertaking to see that the purposes are carried out, as they cannot carry themselves out and the court will not do it. Normally, the trustees who are appointed to the purpose trust may be prepared to carry it out, but should they refuse to do so, and those who are interested in the property subject to the trust are unwilling to do so, it would seem that the purpose trust would fail.

9.7 Gifts to unincorporated associations

Gifts to unincorporated associations, although dealt with in this chapter on purpose trusts, are not usually purpose trusts. Indeed, it is often through poor drafting of their rule book and of gifts to them that they turn out as such. The whole position of unincorporated associations and gifts to them will be considered here.

An unincorporated association is not a distinctive legal entity in itself. It does not have the same attributes as, for example, a company which is recognised as a separate legal entity with rights and duties which are separate from those of its shareholders. In *Conservative Central Office* v *Burrell* [1982] 2 All ER 1 Lawton LJ described the concept in more detail as:

> '... two or more persons bound together for one or more common purposes, not being business purposes, by mutual undertakings, each having mutual duties and obligations, in an organisation which has rules which identify in whom control of it and its funds rest and on what terms and which can be joined or left at will.'

For example, if a number of people got together to form a golf club and drew up rules and regulations for the club, purchased a golf course and clubhouse and agreed to admit new members on payment of an annual fee of £200, there would be an unincorporated association. This association may be given a name but the name is nothing more than a convenient label to describe those who form the membership of the association in carrying out their activities as members.

Most unincorporated associations will have a rule book which sets out the rights and duties of members. The rules will, in particular, deal with the ownership of the association's assets and how these are held, usually by trustees on behalf of all the members. The rules will also give indications as to the right of a departing member vis-à-vis the association's property and the rights of the members to the association's property on dissolution. In most cases a member will not be permitted to claim that any particular share of the association's assets belongs to him, so as to enable him to sever that share when he leaves. The assets will be held for the benefit of present and future members. In most cases the assets of the association will, on dissolution, be divided between the members or, perhaps, go to a named charity. See also Chapter 6 on this point.

The manner in which the rules of an unincorporated association define the rights of the members in relation to its property is of considerable importance when considering the validity of a gift to such an association. The gift may be construed in two main ways – as a gift to the members beneficially, or as a gift only to further the purposes for which the association was formed. If the gift is construed as the second, then it may well be void as a non-charitable purpose trust. In deciding into which of these categories the gift falls, the court will have regard to the words of the gift and the rules of the association.

There are four possible ways in which a gift to an unincorporated association might take effect, assuming for present purposes that the gift cannot take effect as a charitable trust.

1. *As an absolute gift to existing members as joint tenants so that any member can sever his share and claim it whether or not he continues to be a member of the association.* A gift which takes effect in this way would enable each member of the association, if he chose, to demand his share of the gift and put it in his pocket to spend as he pleased. Whether the gift can be construed as of this type depends on showing that 'neither the circumstances of the gift nor the directions given nor the objects expressed impose on the donee the character of a trustee' per Lord Parker in *Bowman* v *Secular Society* [1917] AC 406. It is, perhaps, easier to explain this category by looking at what would not come within it. If the gift was to an association set up for purposes which did not benefit the members individually, it is unlikely it could be treated as a gift to the members as joint tenants. A gift to the members of a constituency Labour party could not be construed in this way, or a gift to 'the Communist Party': see *Re Grant's Will Trusts* [1980] 1 WLR 360; *Bacon* v *Pianta* (1966) 114 CLR 634. The wording of the gift may negative any intention to give to the members beneficially, for example, '£10,000 to X cricket club to refurbish the club house'. The nature of the association's rules may prevent the gift taking effect in this way, where they set out detailed provisions as to the members' rights in such gifts. It is, therefore, rare to find gifts of this type. An example, which might come under the first category, given by Vinelott J in *Re Grant's Will Trusts*, was the case of a testator who left a legacy to a small dining club of which he had been a member. If the gift was to the club simpliciter, and it had no rules and conferred benefits on the members alone, it could only be treated as to them as joint tenants.

2. *As an absolute gift to existing members beneficially as an accretion to the funds of the association which are subject to a contract inter se between the members.* A gift taking effect in this way goes to the members of the association beneficially but subject to the rules of the association which bind the members inter se in contract. Gifts in this category are relatively common since the majority of unincorporated associations will have rules or a rule book which members will agree to observe on joining, and in any case the court may find a contract implicit in the mutual rights and duties arising from the membership of an association, as in *Re Recher*,

below. The effect of such a gift was stated by Cross J in *Neville Estates* v *Madden* [1962] Ch 832:

'In such a case a member cannot sever his share. It will accrue to the other members on his death or resignation, even though such members include persons who became members after gift took effect. If this is the effect of the gift, it will not be open to objection on the score of perpetuity or uncertainty unless there is something in its terms or circumstances or in the rules of the association which precludes the members at any given time from dividing the subject of the gift between them on the footing that they are solely entitled to it in equity.'

There must be nothing in the rules to stop the members dividing the gift between themselves at any given time if they so choose. This is to prevent gifts which are for purposes coming within this category. What prevents the individual member severing his share in cases such as this is the contract he has made. He is bound by that contract to permit the responsible officers of the association to apply the gift in accordance with the rules and he may also ensure that they observe them in this respect. An example is *Re Recher's Will Trusts* [1972] Ch 526, where a testatrix made a bequest to the London and Provincial Anti Vivisection Society. This society was unincorporated and its object was to secure the abolition of vivisection, a non-charitable object. The members of the society were required to pay an annual subscription and abide by its constitution. Brightman J found the members of the society bound together by contract inter se and the gift was an accretion to the funds bound together by that contract. If the members want to put the subject-matter of the gift into their pockets in cases such as these, then they may do so provided they follow the rules which may enable them to do this, either by unanimous agreement or majority vote. Should the rules prohibit them doing this it is likely that the trust will be treated as a purpose trust and void, though of course it may be open to members to change their rules: see *Re Grant's Will Trusts*.

In some cases a gift in this category may specify a purpose within the powers of the association for which it is to be applied, for example, '£10,000 to the X Cricket Club to purchase a new cricket ground'. In *Re Lipinski's Will Trusts* [1976] Ch 235 Oliver J saw no reason why specifying purposes within the powers of the association should cause the gift to fail as a purpose trust. He said:

'I do not really see why such a gift, which specifies a purpose which is within the powers of the association and of which the members of the association are the beneficiaries, should fail. Why are not the beneficiaries able to enforce the trust, or indeed, in the exercise of their contractual rights, to terminate the trust for their own benefit? Where the donee association is itself the beneficiary of the prescribed purpose, there seems to me to be the strongest argument in common sense for saying that the gift should be construed as an absolute one within the second category. The more so where, if the purpose is carried out, the members can by appropriate action vest the resulting property in themselves, for here the trustees and the beneficiaries are the same persons.'

In *Re Lipinski* a gift to 'the Hull Judeans (Maccabi) Association in memory of my late wife to be used solely in the work of constructing new buildings for the association and/or improvements in the said buildings' was upheld as valid. Gifts such as this depend on a distinction drawn by Goff J in *Re Denley's Trust Deed* [1969] 1 Ch 373 between purpose trusts of an abstract or impersonal nature where there was no beneficiary, for example, a trust for abolishing vivisection, and a trust, although expressed as a purpose, which was directly or indirectly for the benefit of individuals who were ascertainable. Another example is *Re Turkington* [1937] 4 All ER 501 where a gift was made to a masonic lodge 'as a fund to build a suitable temple in Stafford'. The gift was an absolute one to the members for the time being of the lodge who were both the trustees and the members. Gifts of this nature may be defeated if the members are prohibited from dividing the assets among themselves. This would negative any inference that they were beneficiaries, as would anything which prevented them from altering the purpose. The purpose would then dominate the beneficial nature of the gift: see *Re Grant's Will Trusts*.

3. *As a gift on trust for present and future members beneficially.* If on true construction a gift is for both the present and future members of an unincorporated association without limitation as to time, this would leave the gift as void for perpetuity. This arose in *Leahy* v *Attorney-General for New South Wales* [1959] AC 457 where a testator left a 730 acre farm upon trust for 'such Order of nuns of the Catholic Church or the Christian Brothers as my executors and trustees shall select'. The orders among whom selection could be made were not all charitable, so the question arose whether the gift could take effect as a good private trust. The Privy Council held that the gift was in fact a purpose trust and void. This conclusion was based on:

a) The fact that the gift was for a selected Order which suggested it was not to the existing members of such Order only.

b) The Order selected was likely to have members all over the world and it was difficult to conclude that the testator intended to benefit these people individually.

c) It was difficult to accept that the testator intended all the individual members to become beneficial owners of a 730 acre farm.

The testator's intention was 'to create a trust, not merely for the benefit of the existing members of the selected Order, but for its benefit as a continuing society and for the furtherance of its work'. In his speech Viscount Simonds said:

'If the gift is intended for the good not only of present but future members so that the present members are in the position of trustees and have no right to appropriate the property or its proceeds for their personal benefit then the gift is invalid. It may be invalid by reason of there being a trust created, or it may be by reason of the terms that the period allowed by the rule against perpetuities would be exceeded ...'

4. *As a gift for the purposes of the association only.* A gift which can only take effect as one for the purposes of the association is clearly a purpose trust and, as such, is liable to be held void under the general rule against purpose trusts. The only

way it might avoid defeat is if it were for a purpose which is within the exceptional cases referred to in sections 9.2–9.4. However, there are no authorities on this and considering the dictum in *Re Endacott* (above) this must be doubtful. Gifts fall within this category mainly because they cannot in the circumstances be treated as gifts to the members of the association. An example is *Re Grant's Will Trusts* [1980] 1 WLR 360 in which a testator devised all his estate to 'the Labour Party Property Committee for the benefit of the Chertsey Headquarters of (the new Chertsey Constituency Labour Party)' Vinelott J held the gift was void because on the evidence before him the Chertsey CLP did not control the property given to it by subscription or otherwise. They could not alter the rules of association so as to change the purposes for which the money might be applied or to divide it among themselves. All the requirements for a gift to the members of the association were absent and it could only be treated as a gift for a purpose.

10

Charitable Trusts

10.1 Introduction

In medieval times the ecclesiastical courts had a policy of upholding gifts for pious or charitable intentions, wherever possible. Most of these gifts went to religious houses which administered them for the purposes laid down by law. The legislature, however, had a policy to restrict such gifts, motivated by the fact that they placed land in mortmain – making it inalienable and subject to a 'dead hand' – and thus disinherited heirs, lost the incidents of tenure to the Lords in the case of land and, above all, increased the power of the religious houses.

After the Reformation, when the monastic houses had been suppressed, fear of their power gave place to concern for the loss of their charitable and educational activities, and accordingly the legislature changed its policy towards charitable gifts. In 1601 the Statute of Charitable Uses was passed and by it commissioners were

147

appointed to supervise the enforcement of charitable gifts and to check the abuse of them which had arisen after the Reformation. The preamble to the 1601 Statute, often referred to as the Statute of Elizabeth, set out a list of the most common and important charitable purposes. The court has always construed these liberally and originally charitable status was established if the purpose was within the preamble.

The legislature has had to intervene on several occasions to limit the ways in which charitable status might be obtained and the courts have also limited charitable status. In the 19th century a requirement was introduced that the gift should be for the public good as well as being within the preamble. This requirement of public benefit is necessary in all purposes stated in the preamble with the exception of charitable trusts for the relief of poverty.

The Statute of Elizabeth was repealed by the Mortmain and Charitable Uses Act 1888, but this Act expressly preserved the preamble. The preamble itself was repealed by s38(4) Charities Act 1960 (whilst the 1960 Act has been, in the main, repealed by the Charities Act 1993, s38(4) has been expressly preserved). However, the effect of the preamble has been preserved in case law and the purposes in it are still treated as charitable: see *McGovern* v *Attorney-General* [1982] Ch 321. In effect it represents an index of charitable purposes which will be extended by analogy, if possible. As Lord Reid said in *Scottish Burial Reform and Cremation Society* v *Glasgow Corporation* [1968] AC 138:

'The courts appear to have proceeded first by seeking some analogy between the object mentioned in the preamble and the object with regard to which they had to reach a decision. Then they appear to have gone further and to have been satisfied if they could find an analogy between an object already held to be charitable and the new object claimed to be charitable.'

10.2 Difference between charitable and non-charitable trusts

A private trust is designed to benefit one person or a number of ascertained or ascertainable persons, while a charitable trust is designed to benefit society or a part of it.

A gift to charity is never void for uncertainty of objects. In the words of Lord Eldon in *Mills* v *Farmer* (1815) 1 Mer 55, 'uncertainty of the mode (as where no directions are given, no executor appointed, etc) cannot defeat the intention'. Therefore, gifts to 'the poor' or to trustees in trust for such charitable objects as someone other than the donor shall select are valid.

The perpetuity rules are applied to charitable trusts but subject to a number of modifications:

1. The rule against perpetual trusts does not apply to charities. A private trust is void if it will continue beyond the perpetuity period and it must be limited so as not to offend the perpetuity rule. But a charitable trust may continue for ever, so

that the capital of the trust is effectively inalienable: see *Chamberlayne* v *Brockett* (1872) 8 Ch App 206. The public interest in maintaining alienability of property is outweighed in this case by the public interest in supporting charitable objects. For a recent example of this see *Peggs and Others* v *Lamb and Others* [1994] 2 WLR 1.

2. The rule against remoteness of vesting is only modified in its application to charities. A gift to a charity must vest in it within the perpetuity period if it is to be effective. In *Re Lord Stratheden and Campbell* [1894] 3 Ch 265 an annuity to a military regiment on the appointment of the next lieutenant-colonel was void since the next holder of that office might be appointed more than 21 years after the gift took effect. This decision is now subject to the Perpetuities and Accumulations Act 1964 and its 'wait and see' provisions. The rule as to remoteness of vesting does not apply to cases where a gift is made to one charity with a gift over to another in the occurrence of certain events. This is because the gift is devoted to charity throughout and there is only a change of charitable objects. In *Re Tyler* [1891] 3 Ch 252 a gift to charity A, subject to that charity maintaining the testator's tomb and, if it failed to do so, a gift over to charity B, was valid. But, if A had been a non-charity in this case the gift would have been void.

A gift with a general intention of charity does not fail because the directions of the donor as to the mode cannot be carried out. In such circumstances other objects as like as possible to those that have failed will be chosen, and the court will sanction a scheme for carrying out the trusts in favour of the new objects. This is known as the cy-près doctrine and it has no equivalent in the realm of private trusts. The cy-près doctrine is explained in Chapter 11.

In private trusts the trustees must act unanimously, unless the trust instrument states otherwise, while in administering a charitable trust a majority of the trustees binds the minority: see *Re Whiteley* [1910] 1 Ch 600. Similarly charities are not caught by the operation of s34(2) Trustee Act 1925 which restricts the number of trustees for a private trust of land. Indeed, it is not uncommon for charities, which often have land as part of their property, to have ten or more trustees.

Charitable trusts are given certain tax advantages which are not available to private trusts. Charitable status is often sought for this reason alone and the court is therefore cautious in granting such status. The following are the main tax advantages given:

1. The income of a charity, in so far as it is applied for the charitable objects of the charity concerned, is exempt from income tax (s505 ICTA 1988) and corporation tax (s9(4) ICTA 1988).
2. A 50 per cent remission of rates on hereditaments occupied by the charity wholly or mainly for its charitable purposes, the previous preferential treatment in respect of local rates, changed to the community charge and now the council tax,

has however declined over recent years. The previous remission for this tax has been steadily been eroded, resting now (albeit this is by no means clear) on the local authority having a discretion to waive liability.

3. Remission from VAT in certain cases.
4. No charge is made to inheritance tax for transfers (whether on death or inter vivos) to any charity.
5. As a rule of trusts charities are also exempt from capital gains tax (CGT) subject to the gain realised on disposal of any asset being applied to the charitable purpose (Taxation of Charitable Gains Act 1992, s256).

10.3 Definition of charity

Because of their origins charities are difficult to define exhaustively by statute as this could prove to be unduly restrictive. As Viscount Simonds said in *IRC* v *Baddeley* [1955] AC 572: 'There is no limit to the number and diversity of ways in which a man will seek to benefit his fellow men.' Further, 'any statutory definition might well produce a fresh spate of litigation and provide a set of undesirable artifical distinctions' per Sachs LJ in *Incorporated Council of Law Reporting* v *Attorney-General* [1972] Ch 73.

Charity is a matter of law; the donor's own opinion as to what is or is not a charitable trust is irrelevant. The court decides whether a particular object is or is not charitable. In *Re Hummeltenberg* [1923] 1 Ch 237 a testator bequeathed a legacy to set up a college to train persons as spiritualist mediums, which he stated to be charitable. On this Russell LJ said:

'In my opinion the question whether a gift is or may be operative for the public benefit is a question to be answered by the court by forming an opinion on the evidence before it.'

The donor's motive for making a gift will not prevent it from being charitable if the object is charitable in law. In *Re King* [1923] 1 Ch 243 a bequest for the erection of a stained glass window in a church was primarily intended by the testator as a memorial to himself but this did not prevent the gift being considered as charitable for the advancement of religion. See also *Re Hooper* [1932] 1 Ch 38.

The meaning of 'charity' or 'charitable' in the legal sense is quite different from the popular sense in which these words are used. This was considered by Lord MacNaghten in *Commissioners of Income Tax* v *Pemsel* [1891] AC 531:

'No doubt, the popular meaning of the words "charity" and "charitable" does not coincide with their legal meaning; and no doubt it is easy enough to collect from the books a few decisions which seem to push the doctrine of the court to the extreme, and to present a contrast between the two meanings in an aspect almost ludicrous. But, still, it is difficult to fix the point of divergence, and no one has yet succeeded in defining the popular meaning of the word "charity" ... How far then, it may be asked, does the popular meaning of the word "charity" correspond with its legal meaning? "Charity" in its legal sense comprises four principal divisions: trusts for the relief of poverty; trusts for the advancement of education; trusts for the advancement of religion; and trusts for other purposes beneficial to the community, not falling under any of the preceding heads ...'

Many things which are charitable in the legal sense would hardly be treated as charitable in the popular sense, for example, the printing and publishing of law reports: see *Incorporated Council of Law Reporting* v *Attorney-General* (below); or a trust to encourage football amongst students: see *IRC* v *McMullen* [1981] AC 1. The popular meaning seems to be closely tied with the relief of need. The purpose of the law of charity is to provide a framework within which objects may be treated as charitable if they fulfil a number of conditions.

10.4 Requirements of a charitable trust

Because of the privileges accorded to charities by law it is not surprising that certain conditions must be satisfied before a trust can achieve charitable status. There appear to be three main requirements:

1. The trust must be of a charitable nature within the spirit and intendment of the preamble to the Statute of Elizabeth as interpreted by the courts and extended by statute.
2. It must promote a public benefit of a nature recognised by the courts as a public benefit.
3. The purposes of the trust must be wholly and exclusively charitable.

As will be seen the actual requirements of each of the three varies according to the particular type of charity in question.

If a trust satisfies its' three conditions it will normally be entitled to charitable status. Once this is granted the trust will be registered as a charity by the Charity Commissioners and will be subject to their powers and duties as laid down in legislation such as the Charities Act 1960. The interests of charities are protected by the Attorney-General as was explained by Lord Eldon LC in *Attorney-General* v *Brown* (1818) 1 Swans 261:

> 'It is the duty of the King as parens patriae, to protect property devoted to charitable uses, and that duty is executed by the officer who represents the Crown for all forensic purposes. On this foundation rests the right of the Attorney-General in such cases to obtain by information the interposition of a Court of Equity.'

The duty of the Attorney-General is to protect the interests of the public in the proper administration of charities.

10.5 Charitable objects

The preamble to the Statute of Elizabeth contained the following list of charitable objects:

'The relief of aged, impotent, and poor people, the maintenance of sick and maimed soldiers and mariners, schools of learning, free schools, and scholars in universities; the repair of bridges, ports, havens, causeways, churches, seabanks and highways, the education and preferment of orphans; the relief, stock, or maintenance of houses of correction; marriage of poor maids; supportation, aid, and help of young tradesmen, handicraftsmen, and persons decayed; the relief or redemption of prisoners or captives; and the aid or ease of any poor inhabitants concerning the payment of fifteens, setting out of soldiers and other taxes.'

The preamble was, as previously noted, repealed by the Charities Act 1960, however, s38(4) of this Act provided that:

'... any reference in any enactment or document to a charity within the meaning, purview and interpretation of the Charitable Uses Act 1601, or of the preamble to it, shall be construed as a reference to a charity within the meaning which the word bears as a legal term according to the law of England and Wales.'

The preamble is sometimes used by the courts as a starting point for determining whether an object is charitable, if this is in issue. But the following points should be noted on the preamble:

1. The courts do not give it a literal construction so that if an object for which charitable status is claimed is not within it, this does not mean it will be refused charitable status. The court, it would appear, considers two things – first, the 'spirit and intendment' of the preamble and second, the effect of the cases on the preamble. This is because charity is an evolving subject and must keep pace with changing social needs and attitudes so that the court is frequently asked to consider whether objects are charitable which may not have been dealt with by the preamble or the cases. As Lord Wilberforce said in *Scottish Burial Reform and Cremation Society* v *Glasgow Corporation* [1968] AC 138:

   'It is now accepted that what must be regarded is not the wording of the preamble itself, but the effect of the decisions given by the court as to its scope, decisions which have endeavoured to keep the law as to charities moving according as new social needs arise or old ones become obsolete and satisfied.'

2. That being noted it should be borne in mind that in the 19th and early 20th century the courts took a liberal attitude as to what was within the 'spirit and intendment' of the preamble. A case decided then, upholding an object as charitable, does not necessarily mean that such an object would be treated as charitable today because the public benefit requirement (see section 10.11) was not as strictly applied then. As Lord Upjohn said in the *Scottish Burial Reform* case:

   'I conclude by saying that the authorities show that the "spirit and intendment" of the preamble to the Statute of Elizabeth has been stretched almost to breaking point. In the nineteenth and early twentieth centuries this was often due to a desire on the part of the courts to save the intentions of the settlor or testator from failure from some technical rules of law. Now that it is used so frequently to avoid the common man's liability to rates or taxes, this generous trend of the law may one day require consideration.'

The problem of charitable status being abused in order to reap tax advantages is considered at section 10.11.

3. The facts of the *Scottish Burial Reform* case illustrate how the court will determine how an object which has not been considered for charitable status before will be dealt with. In that case the issue was whether a society which was devoted to the promotion of cremation as a means of disposing of human corpses was charitable. The House of Lords held that it was, even though no case had previously held cremation or its promotion as charitable. As Lord Reid said:

'The preamble specifies a number of objects which were then recognised as charitable. But in more recent times a wide variety of other objects have come to be recognised as also being charitable. The courts appear to have proceeded first by seeking some analogy between an object mentioned in the preamble and the object with regard to which they had to reach a decision. Then they appear to have gone farther, and to have been satisfied if they could find an analogy between an object already held to be charitable and the new object claimed to be charitable.'

The use of the preamble as a means of determining charitable status was considered by the Goodman Committee on Charity Law and Voluntary Organisation in 1976 which recommended its replacement by an updated version, their report said at para 32:

'The preamble to the Act of 1601 is written in language inappropriate to contemporary concepts and it has led, and will lead, to mental gymnastics if it is to encompass within its terms the many forms of human endeavour now or hereafter deserving to fall within the scope of charity, while excluding those which lie outside. What we suggest ... would be beneficial to produce an updated version of the preamble to the Act of 1601 ...'

The committee included a very long list of objects which were deemed to be charitable. The purpose of the list is, like the preamble, to provide a starting point for determining charitable status since the idea of a definition of charity seems to be impossible in that, unlike a list, it would not allow for flexibility in extending charitable status to deserving objects.

In *Commissioners of Income Tax* v *Pemsel* [1891] AC 531 Lord MacNaghten categorised charity in its legal sense as comprising four principal divisions, namely:

1. Trusts for the relief of poverty.
2. Trusts for the advancement of education.
3. Trusts for the advancement of religion.
4. Trusts for other purposes beneficial to the community, not falling under any of the preceding heads.

This classification is frequently cited in the textbooks and used as a basis for explaining charity. However, Lord Wilberforce gave three warnings as to its use in the *Scottish Burial Reform* case:

'... first that, since it is a classification of convenience, there may well be purposes which do not fit neatly into one or other of the headings, secondly, that the words used must not be given the force of a statute to be construed, and thirdly, that the law of charity is a moving subject which may well have evolved since 1891.'

There are a number of objects which do not fall neatly within the first three of the categories mentioned by Lord MacNaghten. Examples are the relief of aged and impotent people, 'the education and preferment of orphans', 'the supportation, aid and help of young tradesmen'. All of these qualify as objects of charity without necessarily being poor or being within the other categories set out by Lord MacNaghten.

The main objects of charity are, however, contained in Lord MacNaghten's classification and for this reason it will be used here to explain the main charitable purposes.

10.6 Trusts for the relief of poverty

'Poverty' is a vague term and it can mean different things at different times and in different places. Some attempts have been made to define the term but they are by no means conclusive. In *Re Coulthurst* [1951] Ch 661, Evershed MR said:

'It is quite clearly established that poverty does not mean destitution; it is a word of wide and somewhat indefinite import; it may not unfairly be paraphrased for present purposes as meaning persons who have to "go short" in the ordinary acceptation of that term, due regard being had to their status in life, and so forth. Poverty is a relative term and it may cover "ladies of limited means" as in *Re Gardom* [1914] 1 Ch 662, even though in absolute terms they are financially better off than members of "the working classes" which are not considered as poor persons: *Re Drummond* [1914] 2 Ch 90.'

A charitable gift for the relief of poverty need not be expressly stated as being such. The court is prepared to uphold gifts for the poor which are expressed in general or indefinite language. In *Re Dudgeon* (1896) 74 LT 613 Stirling J said:

'It appears to me that the cases cited on behalf of the charity do show this, that it is not necessary to find poverty expressed in so many words but that the Court will look at the whole gift, and if it comes to the conclusion that the relief of poverty was meant, will give effect to it, though the word "poverty" is not to be found in it. Gifts where the court has read in an intention to relieve distress include the following: widows and orphans in a particular place; *Attorney-General* v *Power* (1809) 1 Ball & B 145; distressed gentlefolk: *Re Young* [1951] Ch 344; unsuccessful literary men: *Thompson* v *Thompson* (1844) 1 Coll 381, etc.'

A gift can only be charitable under this head if it is intended for persons who are actually poor. In *Re Sanders' Will Trusts* (1954) a gift was made 'to provide or assist in providing dwellings for the working classes and their families resident in the area of Pembroke Dock'. Harman J held that the gift was not charitable as the expression 'working classes' did not indicate poor persons. This does not mean, however, that poverty cannot be implied into a gift for the working classes in certain cases. In *Re Niyazi's Will Trusts* [1978] 1 WLR 910 a testator left the residue of his estate, worth about £15,000, to be used for 'the construction of or as a contribution towards the construction of a working men's hostel' in Famagusta, Cyprus. It was held that the gift was charitable and the term working men's hostel connoted poverty, as the building would not be grandiose considering the amount available to build it, its facilities would only give basic requirements, so only the relatively poor would be its occupants. It was also possible to infer the relief of poverty as the object of the gift in *Re Niyazi*, from the size of the sum of money given. This has been frequently used in the past and in *Re Lucas* [1922] 2 Ch 52 a gift to 'the oldest respectable inhabitants in Gunville to the amount of 5/- per week each' was held charitable on this basis. Another decision which illustrates that a gift under this head must only be for the poor is *Re Gwyon* [1930] 1 Ch 255 where a testator left a fund to be applied in providing knickers for boys of Farnham and district subject to a number of qualifications. Eve J refused to to give charitable status saying, 'it does not follow that a gift to all and sundry in a particular locality and not expressed to be for the poor ought to be construed as evidencing an intention to relieve poverty'.

The preamble to the Statute of Elizabeth refers to the relief of the aged, impotent and poor. These words fall to be read disjunctively: see *Re Robinson* [1951] Ch 198 and *Re Lewis* [1955] Ch 104. Aged and impotent persons may qualify as objects of charity without necessarily being poor. This does not mean that 'impotent millionaires' are a charitable object. There has to be 'relief' of impotence so that only those who can benefit in a practical way are eligible: see *IRC v Baddeley* [1955] AC 572 which equated relief with need. In turn such need cannot be purely for amusement purposes: see *Rowntree Housing Association v Attorney-General* (below). A further reason why a trust for 'impotent millionaires' is not charitable is that put forward by Lindley LJ in *Re Macduff* [1896] 2 Ch 451, that no trust is charitable if it excludes the poor.

These matters were considered in *Rowntree Housing Association v Attorney-General* [1983] 1 All ER 288 which concerned a number of schemes put forward by the Rowntree Housing Association, an incorporated charity, for the provision of housing for the elderly. On the terms 'aged impotent and poor' Peter Gibson J said:

> 'Looking at those words without going to authority and attempting to give them their natural meaning, I would have thought that two inferences therefrom were tolerably clear. First, the words "aged, impotent and poor" must be read disjunctively. It would be as absurd to require that the aged must be impotent or poor as it would be to require the impotent to be aged or poor, or the poor to be aged or impotent. There will no doubt be many cases where the objects of charity prove to have two or more of the three qualities at the same time. Second, essential to the charitable purpose is that it should relieve aged, impotent and poor people. The word "relief" implies that the persons in question have a need attributable to their condition as aged, impotent or poor persons which requires alleviating, and which those persons could not alleviate, or would find difficulty in alleviating themselves from their own resources. The word "relief" is synonymous with "benefit".'

So far as gifts for the 'aged' are concerned, it appears that the sixties age group is the minimum although no precise age limit has been set. In *Re Cottam* [1955] 1

WLR 1299 a trust to build flats for persons over 65 fell within this head of charity. In *Re Robinson* [1951] Ch 198 a gift for old people over 65 of Hazel Slade, near Hednesford, was also considered to fall under this head. See also *Re Wall* (1889) 42 Ch D 510. Perhaps the easiest solution is to look to the current retirement ages?

'Impotent' means some infirmity or failing such as blindness or paralysis, or addiction to drink or drugs. Gifts for the benefit of such persons or institutions which cater for these problems are charitable. In *Re Lewis* [1955] Ch 104 bequests of £100 each to 10 blind girls and 10 blind boys in Tottenham was held to be for the impotent while in *Re Vagliano* [1905] WN 179 a gift to an asylum was considered to fall under this head also. It also appears that these trusts can be extended slightly to associated ancillary purposes. See for example *Re Dean's Will Trusts* [1950] 1 All ER 882 which dealt with the provision of accommodation for relatives of the critically ill. However, the limit of this particular limb is best shown by the decision in *Re Coxen* [1948] Ch 747.

Trusts for the relief of poverty need not satisfy the requirement of public benefit and therefore they stand in a special category so far as charitable status is concerned. It appears, however, that it is only trusts for the relief of poverty which are exempted from this requirement; trusts for the aged and the impotent must still satisfy this test. This point is dealt with below in section 10.11. For the possibility of amending the objects of certain local charities for the relief of poverty in prescribed circumstances, see s2 Charities Act 1985.

10.7 Trusts for the advancement of education

The preamble refers to 'the maintenance of schools of learning, free schools and scholars in universities' and 'the education and perferment of orphans'. The meaning of 'education' has expanded since then and in *Incorporated Council of Law Reporting for England and Wales* v *Attorney-General* [1972] Ch 73 Buckley LJ said the term now applied 'to the improvement of a useful branch of human knowledge and its public dissemination'. However, there has been some difficulty in defining what 'education' does or does not include. It seems well established that the mere increase of knowledge will not do. There must be teaching or instruction bringing about improvement in an area of useful knowledge. In *Re Shaw* [1957] 1 WLR 729 a trust to inquire into a new alphabet and disseminate the results of such research failed because this involved nothing educational; it merely tended to increase knowledge. As to what is 'educational' or amounts to 'useful knowledge' in the charitable sense, this is considered below.

There is little doubt that the founding, maintenance and support of educational establishments is charitable and the cases go back a long way on this. The same is also true of gifts to establish professorships, scholarships and other academic awards. All of these are aimed at 'teaching' or 'instruction' either directly or indirectly. Difficulties have arisen where gifts have been made which do not have 'teaching' as such as their main object. In such cases it seems that the gift will qualify if it can be shown to have some element of instruction.

It is now well established that the word 'education' is not limited to mere teaching for the purposes of the law of charity. The encouragement of activities which improve artistic taste or which have aesthetic merit is charitable. Thus in *Royal Choral Society* v *IRC* [1943] 2 All ER 101, the Royal Choral Society had as its object 'to form and maintain a choir in order to promote the practice and performance of choral works, whether by way of concerts or choral pageants in the Royal Albert Hall or as otherwise decided from time to time'. The question arose whether it was charitable and therefore exempt from income tax. The Court of Appeal held that it was. In giving judgment Lord Greene MR said:

> '... the Solicitor General argued that nothing could be educational which did not involve teaching ... I protest against that narrow conception of education ... a body of persons established for the purpose of raising the artistic taste of the country and established by an appropriate document which confines them to that purpose, is established for educational purposes, because the education of artistic taste is one of the most important things in the development of a civilised human being.'

This, and the subject nature of such 'artistic taste' is the cause of much discussion and controversy, dealt with subsequently in this section.

In *Re Shaw* [1952] Ch 163 a trust for encouraging good manners and etiquette was upheld as charitable. The widow of George Bernard Shaw left the residue of her estate for 'the making of grants, contributions and payments to any foundation ... having for its objects the bringing of the masterpieces of fine art within the reach of the people of Ireland of all classes in their own country ... The teaching promotion and encouragement in Ireland of self control, elocution, oratory, deportment, the arts of personal contact, of social intercourse and the other arts of public, private, professional and business life'.

As to this Vaisey J said:

> '... education includes ... not only teaching, but the promotion or encouragement of these arts and graces of life which are, after all, perhaps the finest and best part of the human character.'

'Education' also includes the search for or research of original manuscripts and other items of scientific or historical interest. See *Re Hopkins' Will Trusts* [1965] Ch 669. The objects of the donee, the Francis Bacon Society, were to encourage the study of the works of Bacon, a philosopher, lawyer, statesman and poet, and to encourage the study of evidence that Bacon was the author of the plays commonly attributed to Shakespeare. Wilberforce J held that the trust was charitable, after referring to the cases on the meaning of 'education' he said:

> 'I think the word "education" as used by Harman J in *Re Shaw* [1957] 1 WLR 729 must be used in a wide sense, certainly extending beyond teaching, and that the requirement is that, in order to be charitable, research must be either of educational value to the researcher or must be so directed as to lead to something which will pass into the store of

educational material, or so as to improve the sum of communicable knowledge in an area which education may cover – education in this last context covering literary taste and appreciation.'

See also *Re British School of Egyptian Archaeology* [1954] 1 WLR 546.

One problem area is that of sports and other associated authorities, without formal instruction and encouraged by schools, universities and the like. There is now no doubt that such activities are charitable as for the advancement of education if carried out as part of the activities of the school or university. In *IRC* v *McMullen* [1981] AC 1 the Football Association set up a trust known as the Football Association Youth Trust, the main objects of which were 'the furtherance of education of Schools and Universities in any part of the United Kingdom encouraging and facilitating the playing of Association Football or other games and sports at such Schools and Universities and thus assisting to ensure that due attention is given to the physical education and character development of pupils at such Schools and Universities'. It was held that this was a charitable trust because the aim of the settlor was to promote the physical education and development of pupils at schools as an addition to such part of their education as related to their mental education. Education could not be restricted to mean formal instruction in the classrooms or the playground because the idea of education as set out by the Education Act 1944 expressly recognised the contribution that extra-curricular activities and voluntary societies or bodies could make to the statutory system of education. As Lord Hailsham LC said:

'I reject any idea which would cramp the education of the young within the school or university syllabus, confine it within the school or university campus, limit to the formal instruction, or render it devoid of pleasure in the exercise of skill.'

In *Re Mariette* [1915] 2 Ch 284 a not dissimilar problem arose. In this case a testator bequeathed:

1. £1,000 to the Governors of Aldenham School for the purpose of building squash courts or for some similar purpose to be determined by the housemasters;
2. £100 to the headmaster for the time being upon trust to use the interest to provide some prize for some event in the school athletic sports.

Eve J held the gift was for the advancement of education, and charitable because:

'It is necessary ... in any satisfactory system of education to provide for both mental and bodily occupation, mental occupation by means of the classics and those other less inviting studies to which a portion of the day is devoted, and by bodily occupation by means of regular organised games. To leave 200 boys at large and to their own devices during their leisure hours would be to court catastrophe; it would not be educating them, but would probably result in their quickly relapsing into something approaching barbarism. For these reasons I think it is essential that in a school of learning ... there should be organised games as part of the daily routine, and I do not see how the other part of the education can be successfully carried on without them.'

The promotion of sport purely for sport's sake in general is not charitable and these cases should be carefully distinguished from *IRC* v *McMullen* and *Re Mariette*. In *Re Nottage* [1895] 2 Ch 649 a bequest to purchase a perpetual trophy for yacht racing was held not to be charitable, while in *Re Clifford* [1912] 1 Ch 29 a gift to aid angling was also refused charitable status. The current limit appears to have been established in *Re Dupree's WT* [1945] Ch 16 where £5,000 was left to establish an annual chess tournament for boys and young men under 21 resident in the city of Portsmouth. Vaisey J upheld the gift as charitable but warned against the 'slippery slope' – if chess, why not draughts? if draughts, why not bezique? and so on, stating these would have to be dealt with when they came up for consideration. Although on this point see the effect of the Recreational Charities Act 1958, discussed at section 10.9.

In deciding whether a trust is for the advancement of education the court has to determine whether the object of the trust is in fact 'educational'. This can lead to many difficulties. In *Re Delius* [1957] Ch 299 Roxburgh J held that a trust to promote the musical works of the composer Frederick Delius was charitable. If the judge could arrive at this conclusion in respect of Delius's work then it might be asked if the same conclusion would be arrived at in respect of the works of, say, Elvis Presley or The Beatles and, if so, how. This point came to the fore in *Re Pinion* [1965] Ch 85 in which the Court of Appeal had to consider a bequest by a testator of his studio and contents, including pictures, furniture, china, glass, and objets d'art, to be kept intact and displayed to the public. The court refused charitable status. In giving judgment Harman LJ held there was neither public utility nor educational merit in the collection being kept together as a museum. He said:

> 'Here it is suggested that education in the fine arts is the object ... there is a strong body of evidence here that as a means of education this collection is worthless. The testator's own paintings ... are said by competent persons ... to be "atrociously bad" ... Apart from pictures there is a haphazard assembly ... of furniture and objects of so-called "art" about which expert opinion is unanimous that nothing beyond the third rate is to be found ... It was said that this is a matter of taste ... but here I agree with the judge that there is an accepted canon of taste on which the court must rely, for it has itself no judicial knowledge of such matters, and the unanimous verdict of the experts is as I have stated ... I can conceive of no useful object to be served in foisting upon the public this mass of junk. It has neither public utility or educative value ...'

It appears that if public utility or educational value are called into question the court will ask for expert opinion on the matter and rely on this evidence in reaching a decision as to charitable status.

A further common complication in respect of educational charities concerns that of politics masquerading as education. In so far as the main, or principle, purpose of the cahrity is educational and its political element is purely ancillary then the trust will succeed. See *Re Scowcroft* [1898] 2 Ch 638. However, the position is different when the political nature of the trust is more than ancilllary. See section 10.10.

The requirement of public benefit is a necessary element in all trusts for the advancement of education for which charitable status is sought. It is in this field that most of the major issues on the public benefit requirement have arisen, as settlors have sought means to obtain income-tax free funds to educate their children or their employees' children. This requirement is considered in section 10.11.

10.8 Trusts for the advancement of religion

There is no comprehensive definition of religion for the purposes of charity law. Gifts to any organisation or body of persons believing in a god will be upheld provided they are not subversive of all religion and morality, for then they would not satisfy the public benefit requirement. Gifts to sects such as Roman Catholics: see *Dunne* v *Byrne* [1912] AC 407; Quakers: *Re Manser* [1905] 1 Ch 68; Baptists: *Re Stickland* [1936] 3 All ER 769; the Salvation Army: *Re Fowler* (1914) 31 TLR 102; and Jewry: *Neville Estates* v *Madden* [1962] Ch 832, are all valid objects in this respect. There appears no reason why other religions, such as Buddhism and Islam, should not be entitled to charitable status also. There are many dicta supporting the definition of such religions as charitable, and local authorities give them rate relief. Regulations under the Charities Act 1960 assume their charitable status, and the Charity Commissioners register their organisations as charitable. The problem of what religion means for charitable purposes was considered in *Re South Place Ethical Society* [1980] 1 WLR 1565. In this case an ethical society sought charitable status for itself and its reading rooms. One issue was whether ethics was a religion. On this Dillon J held it was not because ethics, being concerned with belief in the excellence of truth, love, and beauty but not belief in anything supernatural, did not in his view meet the two essential attributes of religion, namely, faith and worship; faith in a god and worship in that god. He said:

> 'Religion, as I see it is concerned with a man's relations with god, and ethics are concerned with a man's relations with man. The two are not the same ...'

It is essential that a trust be for the 'advancement' of religion in order to qualify for charitable status. This means that it must advance some religious doctrine either directly or indirectly. In *United Grand Lodge of Ancient Free and Accepted Masons* v *Holborn Borough Council* [1957] 1 WLR 1080, Freemasonry was held non-charitable for this reason, as it did not advance religion but instead required its members to believe in a Supreme Creator and live a good moral life. Donovan J added:

> 'To advance religion means to promote it, to spread its message even wider among mankind; to take some positive steps to sustain and increase religious belief; and these things are done in a variety of ways which are described as pastoral and missionary.'

Religion can be advanced in a variety of ways. It may be done by the spread of the religion itself. However, the actual spreading of dissemination cannot be passive; rather there must be some form of contact with the outside world. Therefore the trust in *Holmes* v *Attorney-General* (1981) The Times 12 February, was upheld due to their occasional public sermons. In contrast see *Gilmour* v *Coates* [1949] AC 426.

The maintenance of missionary establishments: *Commissioners of Income Tax* v *Pemsel* (1891); the distribution of Bibles and other religious books: *Attorney-General* v *Stepney* (1804); and gifts to missionary societies such as the Church Missionary Society: *Re Clergy Society* (1856), are all charitable. Gifts to provide aid and support for the clergy are also charitable, the only requirement here being that the gift be related to religion in some way. Gifts to establish a bishopric: *Attorney-General* v *Bishop of Chester* (1785); to provide for a clergyman's stipend: *Attorney-General* v *Sparks* (1753), or to provide a pension for a clergyman: *Attorney-General* v *Parker* (1747), are all charitable. Gifts for providing and maintaining places of worship: *Re Parker* (1859); for the provision of furniture and ornaments in such places: *Re Manser* (1905); to maintain any part of the fabric of the church such as the chancel: *Hoare* v *Osborne* (1866); the bells: *Turner* v *Ogden* (1787); the organ: *Attorney-General* v *Oakover* (1736), or the churchyard or burial ground: *Re Vaughan* (1886), are all charitable. Gifts to provide stipends for church officials such as the organist or sexton are also charitable: *Attorney-General* v *Oakover* (1736), and gifts to maintain and repair a parsonage or vicarage are also charitable: *Attorney-General* v *Bishop of Chester* (1785).

Frequently gifts are made to clergymen, not beneficially but as the holder of their office. Such gifts are considered to be charitable, if made to the clergyman by virtue of his office, and he is expected to apply the money for the advancement of religion. A legacy of £10,000 to 'Rev Jones' would prima facie be considered as a gift to him for the religious aspects of his office. Sometimes a settlor sets out particular purposes which he desires the money to be put to and it is then necessary to ensure that the purposes specified are for the advancement of religion, otherwise charitable status cannot be given to the gift. The cases on this area are far from clear and, in some, unnecessary distinctions have been drawn. In *Re Simson* [1946] Ch 299 a gift 'to the Vicar of St Luke's Church, Ramsgate for his work in the parish' was held to be charitable because, as Romer J said:

'A gift to a Vicar for his work in the parish merely means that it is to be used for the purposes of such part of his work (that is to say, his functions connected with the cure of souls in the particular district) as lies within the particular parish.'

This decision should be contrasted with *Farley* v *Westminster Bank* [1939] AC 430 in which the testatrix bequeathed the residue of her estate in equal shares to the vicars and churchwardens of two named parishes 'for parish work'. This was held by the House of Lords to be non-charitable because, as Lord Russell said:

'The words in brackets (for parish work) mean that the gift is not a gift for ecclesiastical or religious purposes in the strict sense, but it is a gift for the assistance and furtherance of those various activities connected with the parish church which are found, I believe, in every parish, but which, unfortunately for the donees here, include many objects which are not in any way charitable in the legal sense of that word.'

It would seem that the gift in *Farley's* case could have been applied in giving the children of the parish an outing to the seaside or providing a dinner for elderly parishioners. These would have nothing to do with religion. But the decision seems very strict and when compared with the liberal attitude taken by the courts in respect of students' unions, it might be asked if the same result would be reached today: see *London Hospital Medical College* v *IRC* [1976] 1 WLR 613; and also *Attorney-General* v *Ross and Others* [1985] 3 All ER 334. Other cases in which gifts were made to clergymen by virtue of their office include *Re Eastes* [1948] Ch 257, in which a gift of residue, made to the vicar and churchwardens of St George's Church 'for any purposes in connection with the said church which they may select', was held charitable. The fact that the gift gave a discretion as to its application did not allow the vicar and churchwardens to use the gift for non-charitable purposes. In *Re Stratton* [1931] 1 Ch 197 a bequest was made to the Vicar of Mortlake on trust 'to be by him distributed at his discretion among such parochial institutions or purposes as he shall select'. Charitable status was refused because the gift could be used for non-charitable purposes, as 'parochial institutions' were not necessarily religious institutions. This reasoning had been adopted in the earlier decision of *Dunne* v *Byrne* [1912] AC 407 the Privy Council refused charitable status to a gift of residue left 'to the Roman Catholic Archbishop of Brisbane and his successors to be used and expended wholly or in part as such Archbishop may judge most conducive to the good of religion'. Because, according to Lord MacNaghten:

'... a thing may be "conducive" and in particular circumstances "most conducive", to the good of religion in a particular diocese or in a particular district without being charitable in the sense which the Court attached to the word, and indeed without being in itself in any sense religious.'

It seems that all things conducive to the good of religion are not necessarily religious themselves. For example, purchasing a new motor car for a bishop might be conducive to the good of religion if it replaced an unreliable vehicle so that he got to church punctually. It seems that *Dunne* v *Byrne* is a rather strict application of rules of construction. The solution seems to be for the donor to either make no specifications for the intended use or specify wholly charitable ones; or alternatively for the intended use to be expressed purely as a desire and not a firm intention: see Chapter 2.

10.9 Trusts for other purposes beneficial to the community

Under this category are grouped a great variety of general purposes more or less conducive to the public good, within the 'spirit and intendment' of the preamble, taking into account changed social conditions. Not all trusts that benefit the community are automatically charitable and the court has found it difficult to determine precisely what the term includes and excludes. In *Attorney-General* v *National Provincial Bank* [1924] AC 262 Viscount Cave said:

'Lord MacNaghten did not mean that all trusts for purposes beneficial to the community are charitable, but that there were certain charitable trusts which fell within that category.'

The modern approach of the court in deciding whether a trust falls within this category was explained by Russell LJ in *Incorporated Council of Law Reporting* v *Attorney-General* [1972] Ch 73, where the issue was whether the object of preparing and publishing law reports was a charitable object for a purpose beneficial to the community. He said:

'In a case such as the present, in which in my view the object cannot be thought otherwise than beneficial to the community and of general public utility I believe the proper question to ask is whether there are any grounds for holding it to be outside the equity of the Statute: and I think the answer to that is here in the negative. I have already touched upon its essential importance to our rule of law ... It cannot I think be doubted that if there were not a competent and reliable set of reports of judicial decisions, it would be a proper function and responsibility of government to secure their provision for the due administration of the law.'

This approach appears to be that a matter which is beneficial to the community will be treated as entitled to charitable status unless there are reasons for excluding it. Russell LJ also rejected a case by case approach to the fourth head, as it was suggested that the provision of a court house had already been held charitable within the fourth head. Of this approach he said 'this seems to me to be too narrow or refined an approach'. The need for analogy seems of little help in dealing with the fourth head. Another approach which has been suggested to determining whether an object is beneficial to the community is by asking if it provides for some of the 'indispensibles of a settled community': see *Incorporated Council of Law Reporting (Queensland)* v *Commissioner of Taxation* [1971] AL JR 552.

The authorities in this category do not admit of orderly classification mainly because of the vague nature of the test of whether a gift is charitable or not. In *Re Foveaux* [1895] 2 Ch 501 Chitty J said of this class:

'Cases arise such as the present, in which it is not easy to ascertain whether a particular institution is or is not a charity. Charity in law is a highly technical term. The method employed by the Court is to consider the enumeration of charities in the Statute of Elizabeth bearing in mind that the enumeration is not exhaustive. Institutions whose objects are analogous to those mentioned in the statute are admitted to be charities; and again institutions which are analogous to those already admitted by reported decisions are held to be charities. The pursuit of these analogies obviously requires caution and circumspection. After all, the best that can be done is to consider each case as it arises upon its own special circumstances.'

There is little point in setting down a list of all the objects which might be regarded as charitable, being beneficial to the community; some of the more important objects only are considered here.

Trusts for animals

These trusts arose to prevent cruelty to animals and they were based on their tendency to improve the morality of the human race, as cruelty to animals was degrading to man: see *Re Foveaux* [1895] 2 Ch 501. However, they have now been extended to include, in the ambit of charity, gifts in favour of animals generally or a class of animals. In *Re Wedgwood* [1915] 1 Ch 113 a testatrix left her residuary estate to her brother upon secret trusts to apply it for the protection and benefit of animals. The testatrix had been interested in seeking more humane ways of slaughter. The Court of Appeal held that the gift was charitable as tending to promote public morality by checking the innate tendency to cruelty, ameliorating the condition of the brute creation and stimulating humane sentiments in men towards the lower animals, thereby elevating the human race.

It appears that a gift for animals must have some benefit to mankind in order to be charitable. Accordingly a dogs' home: *Re Douglas* (1887) 35 Ch D 472; a hospital for sick animals: *University of London* v *Yarrow* (1857) 1 De G & J 72; and even a trust for feeding the birds: *Swifte* v *Attorney-General* [1912] 1 IR 133, have been held to be charitable, as they all benefited mankind in some way. But this was not so in *Re Grove-Grady* [1929] 1 Ch 557 where the testatrix left her residuary estate upon trust to found an animals' society whose objects included the acquisition of land 'for the purpose of providing a refuge or refuges for the preservation of all animals, birds or other creatures not human ... and so that all such animals, birds and other creatures not human shall there be safe from molestation or destruction by man'. In rejecting a claim for charitable status Russell LJ said:

> 'If this trust is carried out according to its tenor, no animal within the area may be destroyed by man no matter how necessary that destruction may be in the interests of mankind or in the interests of the other denizens of the area or in the interests of the animal itself, and no matter how painlessly such destruction may be brought about. It seems to me impossible to say that the carrying out of such a trust necessarily involves benefit to the public.'

Trusts aimed at the abolition of vivisection are not charitable: see *National Anti-Vivisection Society* v *IRC* [1948] AC 31. This decision of the House of Lords reversed earlier authorities, notably *Re Foveaux* (above) which had stated the contrary. One ground for this appears to be that such trusts lack public benefit, while another expressed in the speeches was that the object was political (see section 10.10). The second ground appears to be somewhat narrow, but on the first the decision may be supported in that the material benefits gained by vivisection outweigh moral considerations. As Lord Simonds said:

> 'The ... point is fundamental ... It is whether the court, for the purpose of determining whether the object of the society is charitable may disregard the finding of fact that any assumed public benefit in the direction of the advancement of morals and education was far outweighed by the detriment to medical science and research and consequently to the public health. which would result if the society succeeded in achieving its object, and that on balance, the object of the society, so far from being for the public benefit, was gravely injurious thereto.'

Recreational charities

This category is concerned with the provision of sporting and recreational facilities and whether they are charitable. Sport in itself is not charitable: see *Re Nottage* (1895) and *Liverpool City Council* v *Attorney-General* (1992) The Times 1 May, but if it is an incident of a general education it may be: see *McMullen* v *IRC* (1981). In some cases sport has been held charitable where it has tended to promote the efficiency of the public services. In *Re Gray* [1925] Ch 362 a trust for the promotion of sport in the Army was held charitable because it promoted the physical efficiency of the soldiers. Contrast this with *IRC* v *City of Glasgow Police Athletic Association* [1953] AC 380 where the promotion of sport and athletics among policemen was held not charitable. The rationale behind the latter decision was that the association's objects were too wide and therefore could not be described as wholly and exclusively charitable. Lord Normand said in considering *Re Gray* (1925) and similar cases:

> 'As I shall not have occasion to refer to these cases again I will say now that so far as they are founded on the principle that gifts exclusively for the purpose of promoting the efficiency of the armed forces are good charitable gifts, they are in my opinion, unassailable, but that the decision that the actual gifts were of that nature is more doubtful. I would hold further that gifts or contributions exclusively for the purpose of promoting the efficiency of the police forces and the preservation of public order are by analogy charitable gifts.'

This strongly suggests that *Re Gray* may, on its facts, not have been wholly and exclusively charitable, and this is best explained with reference to the case's links to the army.

It appears that if the social or recreational aspect of a gift is too great it will not be admitted as charitable: see *Williams' Trustees* v *IRC* [1947] AC 447; *IRC* v *Baddeley* [1955] AC 572. The introduction of words such as 'social' and/or 'recreational' in a gift appear to render the ambit of a gift too wide and possibly embracing non-charitable objects. In this respect the decisions in *Williams' Trustees* v *IRC* and *IRC* v *Baddeley* put in doubt the charitable status enjoyed by many institutions, especially village halls and recreation grounds. To clarify the position the Recreational Charities Act 1958 was passed. In *IRC* v *Baddeley* [1955] AC 572 land was conveyed to trustees upon trust to permit the property to be:

> '... used by the leaders for the time being of the Stratford Newtown Methodist Mission for the promotion of the religious social and physical well-being of persons resident in the County Boroughs of West Ham and Leyton ... by the provision of facilities for religious services and instruction and for the social and physical training and recreation of such aforementioned persons who for the time being are in the opinion of such leaders likely to become members of the Methodist Church and of insufficient means to otherwise enjoy the advantages provided ... and by promoting and encouraging all forms of such activities as are calculated to contribute to the health and well-being of such persons.'

The question arose whether the conveyances of the land could be stamped at a reduced rate on the grounds that the purposes were charitable. It was held by the

House of Lords that the purposes set out were not charitable as they were wide enough to include non-charitable objects. In addition, the requirement of public benefit was not satisfied.

The Recreational Charities Act 1958 was passed as a result of observations made by the House of Lords in respect of recreational charities in *IRC* v *Baddeley*. The Act extended the definition of recreational charities and clarified the law. Section 1 of the Act provides:

'1) Subject to the provisions of this Act it shall be deemed always to have been charitable to provide or assist in the provision of facilities for recreation or other leisure time occupation, if the facilities are provided in the interests of social welfare. Provided that nothing in this section shall be taken to derogate from the principle that a trust or institution to be charitable must be for the public benefit.'
2) The requirement of the foregoing subsection that the facilities are provided in the interests of social welfare shall not be treated as satisfied unless –
a) the facilities are provided with the object of improving the conditions of life for the persons for whom the facilities are primarily intended, and
b) either –
i) those persons have need of such facilities as aforesaid by reason of their youth, age, infirmity or disablement, poverty or social and economic circumstances; or
ii) the facilities are to be available to the members or female members of the public at large.'
3) Subject to the said requirement, subsection (1) of this section applies in particular to the provision of facilities at village halls, community centres and women's institutes, and to the provision and maintenance of grounds and buildings to be used for the purposes of recreation or leisure-time occupation, and extends to the provisions of facilities for those purposes by the organising of any activity.'

For a recent application of this Act see *Guild (Executor Nominate of the late James Young Russell* v *IRC* [1992] 2 WLR 397

Miscellaneous

The following list of objects have also been held as charitable under this head:

1. Gifts for saving life, for example, to the Royal National Lifeboat Association: *Thomas* v *Howell* (1874) LR 18 Eq 198; and the Royal Humane Society: *Beaumont* v *Oliveira* (1869) 4 Ch 309.
2. Preservation of places of historic interest or natural beauty: *Re Verrall* [1916] 1 Ch 100; *Re Cranstoun's WT* [1949] 1 Ch 523.
3. Museums: *British Museum* v *White* (1826) 2 S & S 594; public libraries: *Abbott* v *Fraser* (1874) 6 PC 96; botanical gardens: *Harrison* v *Southampton Corp* (1854) 2 Sm & G 387.
4. Encouragement of useful arts such as horticulture and good housewifery: *Re Pleasants* (1923) 39 TLR 675; and agriculture by means of a show: *IRC* v *Yorkshire Agricultural Society* [1928] 1 KB 611.
5. Relief of the national debt: *Newland* v *Attorney-General* (1809) 3 Mer 684.

6. Maintenance of efficiency among soldiers by a bequest to a regiment or a volunteer corps for their general purposes: *Re Lord Stratheden and Campbell* [1894] 3 Ch 265; a prize for a competition among cadets: *Re Barker* (1909) 25 TLR 753; a gift to provide books for an officers' mess: *Re Good* [1905] 2 Ch 60; and a gift to promote sport in the army: *Re Barker* (above).

7. A trust for the benefit of the inhabitants of a particular place: *Goodman* v *Saltash Corporation* (1882) 7 AC 633; in *Attorney-General* v *Mayor of Dartmouth* (1883) 48 LT 933 a gift to the uses of the town of Dartmouth was held charitable.

8. A trust for the benefit of a particular class of inhabitants of a place: *Re Christchurch Enclosure Act* (1888) 36 Ch D 520; for example, for the residents of a certain village to cut turf or firewood or graze cows on certain land. This particular category is anomalous and cannot be related to the Statute of Elizabeth. It logically involves the proposition that purposes which are not charitable in the world at large are charitable if their operation is confined to a specified locality. Some limitations have been put on this category by the House of Lords in *Houston* v *Burns* [1918] AC 337 where a gift 'for such public benevolent or charitable purposes in connection with the parish of Lesmahagow or the neighbourhood as the trustees might select' was held non-charitable. How far this limitation goes is unclear.

9. Trusts for municipal purposes. Some of these purposes have been set out in the Statute of Elizabeth, eg the repair of bridges and highways. Other purposes include the prevention of encroachment by the sea: *Attorney-General* v *Brown* (1818) 1 Swans 265; supplying a town with water: *Jones* v *Williams* (1767) Amb 651; providing a court house or a house of correction: *Attorney-General* v *Heelis* (1824) 2 S & S 77; endowment of a village club: *Re Mann* [1903] 1 Ch 232.

10. Relief of the sick. The provision of hospitals and medical facilities: *Re Resch's WT* [1969] 1 AC 514; except where these are being provided on a commercial basis: *Re Smith* [1962] 1 WLR 763; or are not for the public, or a sufficiently large part of the public.

11. Maintenance of the police force: *IRC* v *City of Glasgow Police Athletic Association* [1953] AC 380; and the provision and maintenance of a fire brigade: *Re Wokingham Fire Brigade Trusts* [1951] Ch 373.

10.10 Political objects and charity

The court will not permit a trust, which has among its objects matters which are essentially political, to attain charitable status. In *McGovern* v *Attorney-General* [1982] Ch 321 Slade J gave several reasons for this, namely:

1. The court will have no adequate means of judging whether a proposed change in the law is for the benefit of the public.

2. Even if the evidence enabled the court to form an opinion that a change in the law was desirable, it must still decide a case on the principle that the law is right

as it stands, since to do otherwise would be to usurp the functions of the legislature.
3. The court would risk prejudicing its reputation for political impartiality, if it promoted political objects.
4. Where the trust was to secure a change in foreign law the court was bound to consider, as a matter of public policy, the risk of prejudicing the relations of this country with the foreign country.

In summarising the reasons for his decision in *McGovern* v *Attorney-General* to refuse charitable status to a trust set up by Amnesty International, which had among its objects the relief of prisoners of conscience and the release of prisoners of conscience in foreign countries, Slade J set out the following conclusions on trusts for political purposes:

1. Even if it otherwise appears to fall within the spirit and intendment of the preamble to the Statute of Elizabeth, a trust for political purposes falling within the spirit of Lord Parker's pronouncement in *Bowman's* case can never be regarded as being for the public benefit in the manner which the law regards as charitable. Note also *Webb* v *O'Doherty and Others* (1991) The Times 11 February, where Hoffmann J held that political campaigning, 'in the sense of seeking to influence public opinion on political matters', is not a charitable activity, so that funds of a students' union (an educational charity) could not be used in connection with a 'stop the Gulf War' campaign: see also in this context *Baldry* v *Feintuck* [1972] 1 WLR 552. But where the political purposes are only ancillary to some charitable purpose – for example, education, as in *Attorney-General* v *Ross* [1985] 3 All ER 334 – the trust will not be thereby disqualified from being of charitable status.
2. Trusts for political purposes falling within the spirit of this pronouncement include, inter alia, trusts of which a direct and principal purpose is either:
   a) to further the interests of a political party, or
   b) to procure changes in the law of this country, or
   c) to procure changes in the law of a foreign country, or
   d) to procure a reversal of government policy or of particular decisions of governmental authorities in this country, or
   e) to procure a reversal of government policy or of particular decisions of governmental authorities in a foreign country.

Gifts to the political parties have always been refused charitable status. In *Bonar Law Memorial Trust* v *IRC* (1933) 49 TLR 220 and in *Re Hopkinson* [1949] 1 All ER 346, gifts to the Conservative and Labour parties respectively, were refused charitable status. One case which appears to stand on its own in this area is *Re Scowcroft* (1898) (above) where a gift was made for the maintenance of a club and reading room to be used 'for the furtherance of Conservative principles and religious and mental improvement and to be kept free from intoxicants and dancing'. It was held that the gift was charitable as it could be carried out without the political object being predominant. It is submitted that the case would be decided otherwise today, as it is one which on its facts is not wholly and exclusively charitable.

Organisations are frequently set up to procure changes in the law or have as one of their objects a change in the law. If the organisation's sole aim is changes in the law, then it will be refused charitable status: see *National Anti-Vivisection Society* v *IRC* [1948] AC 31 (above). If, however, the organisation only presses for change in the law as a matter incidental to its main purposes, then it appears that this will not remove charitable status. Each case is a question of fact, but it is submitted that the court would be unlikely to strip an organisation such as the National Society for the Prevention of Cruelty to Children of charitable status, merely because it pressed for changes in the law on child care at an appropriate time.

It is not possible to avoid the ban on charitable status for political trusts by wrapping them up with the advancement of education or religion. In *Bowman* v *Secular Society* [1917] AC 406 the society sought charitable status. It had among its objects the abolition of religious tests, the disestablishment of the Church, the secularisation of education and the alteration of the law touching religion or marriage, or the observance of the Sabbath. It was held that these objects were political, as they were aimed at changing the law, and the court had no means of judging if they were for the public benefit. In *Re Bushnell* [1975] 1 WLR 1596 a testator directed that his residue be held on trust for 'the advancement and propagation of the teaching of Socialised Medicine' and 11 managers were to be appointed to apply the income 'towards furthering the knowledge of the Socialist application of medicine to public and personal health and well-being and to demonstrating that the full advantage of Socialised Medicine can only be enjoyed in a Socialist State'. This was to be done by public lectures and the distribution of leaflets and pamphlets on the subject. The question arose whether this was a charitable trust for the advancement of education. Goulding J held that the main object of the trust was political, as the testator was trying to promote his own theory of socialised medicine by propaganda, and there was no attempt to educate the public as such.

In some cases the court appears to have adopted what might be regarded as an over-sensitive approach to trusts which have a 'political' element and refused charitable status. In *Re Koeppler* [1985] 2 All ER 869 the Court of Appeal pointed out that a trust would not be refused charitable status merely because it touched upon political matters. An endowment for a chair in politics at a university would not be refused charitable status. The principles in cases such as *McGovern* v *Attorney-General* are designed to prevent charitable status being given to trusts of a party political nature and to trusts designed to change the law or governmental policy. In *Re Koeppler* the testator had organised a series of conferences under the name Wilton Park for over 33 years with the object of bringing together politicians, academics, civil servants, industrialists and journalists so that they could exchange views on political, economic and social issues of common interest. The conferences were unofficial and did not follow any party political line. By his will the testator left a large bequest to 'the institution known as Wilton Park ... for the benefit ... of the said institution as long as Wilton Park remains a British contribution to the formation of informed international public opinion and to the promotion of greater co-operation in Europe and the West in general'. This gift was held charitable because the main object of Wilton Park was the advancement of education. As Slade LJ said, 'the activities of Wilton Park ... constitute, so far as I can see, no more than genuine attempts in an objective manner to ascertain and disseminate the truth'. The last words of the gift 'so long as' etc were construed as mere conditions precedent which had to be satisfied at the testator's death if the gift was to be effective at all.

10.11 The requirement of public benefit

Introduction

A valid charitable trust must promote some public benefit as well as being within the definition of the Statute of Elizabeth. Therefore, a trust which lacks the quality of public benefit is a private trust and it will be void if it fails to satisfy the test of certainty of objects required for private trusts. There are two legs to the test: whether a trust is for the public and not too narrow a group of people; and whether it is beneficial in an objective, and not just the donor's subjective, view. The requirement's content varies from head to head of the classes of the statute, from poverty, to which it does not apply at all, to education, where the 'public' nature of gifts seems particularly difficult to establish.

The question whether a purpose will or may operate for the public benefit is to be answered by the court forming an opinion on the evidence before it. As pointed out by Browne-Wilkinson V-C in *Re Hetherington Dec'd* [1989] 2 WLR 1094, following dicta in *National Antivivisection Society* v *IRC* [1948] AC 31, 42, 65, a trust for the advancement of education, the relief of poverty or the advancement of religion, will prima facie be regarded as charitable and assumed to be for public benefit unless the assumption is rebutted in any given case: see *Gilmour* v *Coats* [1949] AC 426, below. In some cases the purpose may be so beneficial as to make it absurd to call such evidence, but in other cases the element of public benefit may be more debatable. If the court regards the matter as incapable of proof then it will decline to recognise the trust as being charitable: see *McGovern* v *Attorney-General* [1982] Ch 321.

The requirement of public benefit does not apply to charitable trusts for the relief of poverty; note the presumption which the court is prepared to make: see above. In many ways the relief of poverty is in itself regarded as for the public benefit. However, there is a limit to how narrow a class can be in such a trust. If it is to relieve poverty among named individuals it is not charitable, and would be essentially a private trust in character. In *Re Scarisbrick's Will Trusts* [1951] Ch 622 a testator left property on trust 'for such relations of my said son and daughters as in the opinion of the survivor of my said son and daughters shall be in needy circumstances ...' It was held that the gift was a good charitable trust for the relief of poverty even though it was confined to relations of the donor, as it was excepted from the public benefit requirement. This exception was not limited to perpetual or continuing trusts but covered a trust for immediate distribution because, according to Jenkins LJ:

> 'I see no sufficient ground in the authorities for holding that a gift for the benefit of poor relations qualifies as charitable only if it is perpetual in character ... If a gift or trust on its true construction does extend to those in need amongst relations in every degree even though it provides for immediate distribution, then, inasmuch as the class of potential beneficiaries becomes so wide as to be incapable of exhaustive ascertainment, the impersonal quality, if I may so describe it, supplied in continuing gifts by the element of perpetuity, is equally present ...'

The decision in *Re Scarisbrick's WT* followed a line of cases going back over 200 years in which the courts have upheld gifts for 'poor relations' as charitable provided the trust did not have personal qualities associated with a private trust. These decisions are recognised as being anomalous but because of their antiquity the court will not overrule them: see, for example, Lord Green MR in *Re Compton* [1945] Ch 123, who regarded overruling them as 'quite impossible'. The 'poor relations' cases were extended to 'poor employees' by *Re Gosling* [1900] WR 300 and to the 'poor members of a club' in *Re Young* [1955] 1 WLR 1269. These extensions of the 'poor relations' cases were considered doubtful and in *Dingle* v *Turner* [1972] AC 601 the House of Lords were asked to review them. In that case the testator left his residuary estate so that on the death of his wife £10,000 should be set aside on trusts 'to apply the income thereof in paying pensions to poor employees of E Dingle & Co Ltd'. When the testator died in 1950 there were over 600 employees of the company and as many former employees. The House held that the trust was charitable and refused to overrule the extension of the poor relations cases. On this Lord Cross said:

> '... the "poor members" and "poor employees" decisions were a natural development of the "poor relations" decisions and to draw a distinction between different sorts of "poverty" trusts would be quite illogical and could certainly not be said to be introducing "greater harmony" into the law of charity. Moreover, though not as old as the "poor relations" trusts "poor employees" trusts have been recognised as charities for many years; there are now a large number of such trusts in existence; and assuming, as one must, that they are properly administered in the sense that the benefits under them are only given to people who can fairly be said to be, according to current standard, "poor relations" to treat such trusts as charities is not open to any practical objection.'

Lord Cross then went on to discuss how far this anomaly might be extended. It appears that it will not be extended by analogy, so that a trust for the education of relations would not be upheld. To do so would cut at the root of the objective of the public benefit test. This is considered below. Note that poverty is only excepted from public benefit on narrow grounds. There is only one other exception to the public benefit requirement, namely the 'founder's kin' cases under which scholarships at schools or colleges give preference to the donor's descendants: see *Caffoor Trustees* v *Commissioners of Income Tax, Colombo* [1961] AC 584.

The test – educational trusts

As noted the public benefit test applies in some degree to all charitable trusts other than those for the relief of poverty. The test can be traced to the Court of Appeal decision in *Re Compton* [1945] Ch 123 which held that a trust for the education of the lawful descendants of three named persons was not charitable. The reasoning of Lord Greene MR proceeded on the basis of a distinction between personal and impersonal relationships. If the trust was based on the former it was a private trust, and if it was based on the latter it was a public trust, satisfying the public benefit element necessary in all charities. This reasoning was approved in the House of Lords decision in *Oppenheim* v *Tobacco Securities Trust Co* [1951] AC 297. In this case a trust was set up by the British-American Tobacco Co to be applied 'in providing for the education of children of employees or former employees of the British-American Tobacco Co Ltd' and its subsidiaries. The total number of eligible employees at the time was about 110,000. The House of Lords held that the trust was not charitable (Lord MacDermott dissenting). The public benefit test laid down by Lord Simonds was as follows:

> 'The question is whether that class of persons can be regarded as a "section of the community" as to satisfy the test of public benefit. These words "section of the community" have no special sanctity, but they conveniently indicate (1) that the possible beneficiaries must not be numerically negligible, and (2) that the quality which distinguishes them from other members of the community, so that they form by themselves a section of it, must be a quality which does not depend on their relationship to a particular individual. It is for this reason that a trust for the education of members of a family or, as in *Re Compton*, of a number of families cannot be regarded as charitable. A group of persons may be numerous, but if the nexus between them is their personal relationship to a single propositus or to several propositii they are neither the community nor a section of it for charitable purposes.'

The personal/impersonal relationship distinction upon which the public benefit test rests is difficult to apply in practice and seems to produce a number of anomalies. One anomaly which was raised in argument and referred to by Lord Simonds was:

> '... the appellant sought to fortify his case by pointing to the anomalies that would ensue from the rejection of his argument. For, he said, admittedly, those who follow a profession or calling, clergymen, lawyers, colliers, tobacco-workers and so on, are a section of the public; how strange then it would be if, as in the case of railwaymen, those who follow a particular calling are all employed by one employer. Would a trust for the education of railwaymen be charitable, but a trust for the education of men employed on the railways by the Transport Board not be charitable? ... My Lords, I am not impressed by this sort of argument and will consider it on its merits, if the occasion should arise, the case where the description of the occupation and the employment is in effect the same, where in a word, if you know what a man does, you know who employs him to do it.'

It would appear that the only solution to this problem, applying the *Oppenheim* test, is to treat the relationship as impersonal, but this leads to another exception. Another anomaly referred to by Lord MacDermott in his dissenting speech is that the manner in which the trust is framed may make a difference. He said:

> 'It was conceded in the course of the argument that, had the present trust been framed so as to provide for the education of the children of those engaged in the tobacco industry in a named country or town, it would have been a good charitable disposition, and that even though the class to be benefited would have been appreciably smaller and no more important then the class here.'

For example, if the trust was for tobacco workers in a particular area where a tobacco company was the main or sole employer, it would be valid if framed as such.

A continual headache since *Oppenheim*'s case has been what is or is not a personal relationship and what is or is not a public relationship. In *Re Mead's WT* [1961] 1 WLR 1244 Cross J, as he then was, said 'there appears to be no principle by reference to which it can be answered'. Lord MacDermott took up this point in *Oppenheim*'s case:

> ' ... the *Compton* test may often prove of value and lead to a correct determination. But, ... I find myself unable to regard it as a criterion of general applicability and conclusiveness. In the first place I see much difficulty in dividing the qualities or attributes, which may serve to bind human beings, into classes, into two mutually exclusive groups, the one involving individual status and purely personal, the other disregarding such status and quite impersonal. ... After all, what is more personal then poverty, blindness or ignorance? Yet more would deny that a gift for the education of the children of the poor or blind was charitable ...'

Lord Cross considered this problem in *Dingle* v *Turner* and said:

> '... at the end of the day one is left where one started with the bare contrast between "public" and "private". No doubt some classes are more naturally describable as sections of the public than as private classes while other classes are more naturally describable as private classes than as sections of the public. The blind, for example, can naturally be described as a section of the public; but what they have in common – their blindness – does not join them together in such a way that they could be called a private class. On the other hand, the descendants of Mr Gladstone might more reasonably be described as a "private" class than as a section of the public, and in the field of common employment the same might well be said of the employees in some fairly small firm. But if one turns to large companies employing many thousands of men and women most of whom are quite unknown to one another and to the directors the answer is by no means so clear. One might say that in such a case the distinction between a section of the public and a private class is not applicable at all. ... In truth the question whether or not the potential beneficiaries of a trust can fairly be said to constitute a section of the public is a question of degree ... Much must depend on the purpose of the trust ...'

This judgment seems to support the approach to public benefit which Lord MacDermott put forward in *Oppenheim*'s case, namely, to look at the facts of each case and in the light of all relevant circumstances and considerations to ask if the trust was of a public nature.

There are a number of judgments which suggest that an important factor in deciding public benefit and, hence, whether charitable status should be given, is the tax advantages that would accrue to the beneficiaries. As noted earlier in section 10.2, charities enjoy exemption from many taxes. If a company can get charitable status for an educational trust for children of its employees, this amounts to a valuable 'fringe benefit' which is being effectively subsidised by the taxpayer. This point was made by Lord Cross in *Dingle* v *Turner*:

> 'Charities automatically enjoy fiscal privileges which with the increased burden of taxation have become more and more important and in deciding that such and such a trust is a charitable trust the court is endowing it with a substantial annual subsidy at the expense of the taxpayer ... To establish a trust for the education of the children of employees in a company in which you are interested is no doubt a meritorious act: but, however numerous the employees may be, the purpose which you are seeking to achieve is not a public purpose. It is a company purpose and there is no reason why your fellow taxpayers should contribute to a scheme which by providing "fringe benefits" for your employees will benefit the company by making their conditions of employment more attractive ... For the same sort of reason a trust to promote some religion among the employees of a company might perhaps safely be held to be charitable provided that it was clear that the benefits were purely spiritual ...'

It is arguable that the *Oppenheim* decision was influenced by fiscal considerations and it is clear that decisions such as *IRC* v *Educational Grants Association* [1967] Ch 123 were influenced by such considerations.

In a number of cases the issue of public benefit will not be concerned with the personal/impersonal relationships distinction because the trust is to obtain a charitable object without reference to persons. For example, if the trust was for 'the advancement of learning the English language' the *Oppenheim* test is not relevant. In this type of case 'public benefit' will be concerned with matters as to whether the gift in itself is for a beneficial purpose. In many cases this will be assumed: see *Re Pinion* in section 10.7 but, if it is in question, the court will call for evidence from experts on this matter. In *National Anti-Vivisection Society* v *IRC* [1948] AC 31 the House of Lords accepted overwhelming evidence that the objects of the National Anti-Vivisection Society were not for a beneficial purpose and removed its charitable status: see section 10.9. Lord Simonds went on to add that the notion of what was for the public benefit could change from time to time:

> 'A purpose regarded in one age as charitable may in another be regarded differently ... A bequest in a will of a testator dying in 1700 might be held valid on the evidence before the court but on different evidence held invalid if he died in 1900. So too, I conceive that an anti-vivisection society might at different times be differently regarded.'

Just because old decisions suggest that an object was for the public benefit, this does not mean that it will be so regarded for all time. In the case of trusts once established as charitable but possibly no longer capable of being so regarded, the position, it seems, is that the trustees should apply to the Charity Commissioners or the court for a cy-près scheme.

Attempts have been made to evade the difficulties the public benefit test throws in the way of certain trusts for limited classes attaining charitable status. In

Oppenheim's case Lord MacDermott, dissenting, suggested that if the trust there had been framed to benefit the inhabitants of a particular town or village in which, by coincidence, all the employees or ex-employees lived, then a good charitable trust would have existed. This suggestion has the diffculty that complete strangers may benefit from the trust. In *Re Koettgen's WT* [1954] Ch 252 the public benefit test was sidestepped by including in the trust a stated preference for a defined class of individuals. In deciding that case, Upjohn J held that as the public nature of the trust is decided at the time the primary class of beneficiaries is ascertained, a stated preference is irrelevant. This decision is open to doubt and was disapproved by Lord Radcliffe in *Caffoor Trustees* v *Commissioner of Income Tax, Colombo* [1961] AC 584 and by Pennycuick J in *IRC* v *Educational Grants Association* [1967] Ch 123, where it was said that such a trust was not wholly and exclusively charitable. In *Re Koettgen's* a testatrix bequeathed her residuary estate upon trust 'for the promotion and furtherance of commercial education'. She then outlined in wide terms the eligible beneficiaries and added 'it is my wish that the trustees shall give preference to any employees of John Batt & Co or any members of the families of such employees'. She then added that not more than 75 per cent of the total income for any year was to be devoted to the preferred class. The question arose whether the trust was charitable. Upjohn J stated that it was, for the reasons given above. The decision should be contrasted with *IRC* v *Educational Grants Association* in which an association was established for the advancement of education and had a close relationship with Metal Box Ltd from which it received most of its income. On average 76–85 per cent of the association's income was applied for the education of children of persons having some tie with Metal Box Ltd. Relief from income tax was claimed on the ground that the trust was charitable. Pennycuick J refused charitable status on the grounds that it was neither for the public benefit nor wholly and exclusively charitable instead. It was a trust for the public with preference for a private class. In giving his reasons he said:

> 'I find considerable difficulty in the *Koettgen's* decision. I should have thought that a trust for the public with a preference for a private class comprised in the public might be regarded as a trust for the application of income at the discretion of the trustees between charitable and non-charitable objects ...'

The test – religious trusts

The public benefit test applies to trusts for the advancement of education, as the *Oppenheim* case indicates, and also trusts for the advancement of religion.

Gilmour v *Coates* [1949] AC 426 deals with a trap in the public benefit test into which religious trusts may fall. In this case the income of a trust was to be applied for the purposes of a Carmelite convent, if it was charitable. The convent housed a community of cloistered nuns who devoted themselves to prayer and meditation and did not engage in any activities outside their community. They believed their prayers and meditation benefited the public by causing the intervention of God. The question arose whether the convent was a charitable body. The House of Lords held that it was not; it did not satisfy the public benefit requirement. This was because the fact that prayer benefited the public was a matter which was not susceptible of proof in a court of law, and the court could act only on proof not faith or belief. Note that the case was concerned with whether the work itself of the cloistered nuns was charitable, in particular whether there was public benefit in their intercessory prayers. The case was not concerned with whether there is public benefit in having orders of nuns or in religion generally. This is accepted. On the issue of public benefit and intercessory prayer, Lord Simonds said:

> 'I would speak with all respect and reverence of those who spend their lives in cloistered piety ... But, my Lords, whether I affirm or deny, whether I believe or disbelieve, what has that to do with the proof which the court demands that a particular purpose satisfies the tests of benefit to the community? Here is something which is manifestly not susceptible of proof. But, then it is said, this is a matter not of proof, but of belief: for the value of intercessory prayer is a tenet of the Catholic faith, therefore in such prayer there is benefit to the community. But it is just at this "therefore" that I must pause. It is, no doubt, true that the advancement of religion is, generally speaking, one of the heads of charity. But, it does not follow from this that the court must accept as proved whatever a particular church believes. The faithful must embrace their faith believing where they cannot prove: the court can only act on proof.'

The position in this regard has been clarified in the recent judgment of Browne-Wilkinson V-C in *Re Hetherington Dec'd* [1989] 2 WLR 1094 where it was held that two gifts for the saying of masses were valid charitable trusts.

On the vital issue of 'public benefit' in this regard it was held that the celebration of a religious service in public – and the public nature of such service will be assumed unless the public are expressly excluded – is, in view of its 'edifying and improving effect', a sufficient public benefit in itself. A further public benefit will arise, where, as in *Re Hetherington Dec'd*, a payment is made to the officiating priest which reduces pro tanto the amount by way of stipend to which he would otherwise be entitled from diocesan funds.

In an earlier case concerning trusts for the saying of masses, *Re Caus* [1934] Ch 162, Luxmoore J had also accepted such trusts as having charitable status. Some doubt had, however, arisen as to the validity of this conclusion in view of the House of Lords' subsequent ruling in *Gilmour* v *Coates*, above. That *Re Caus* can however be reconciled with *Gilmour* v *Coates* was clearly demonstrated in the judgment in *Re Hetherington Dec'd*. Browne-Wilkinson V-C indicated in *Re Hetherington Dec'd*, that Luxmoore J's views in *Re Caus* could not be supported insofar as he suggested that religious services per se, even of a purely private nature, are charitable. However, Luxmoore J's second ground for upholding the charitable nature of the trust – the payments to the priest for celebrating the services – could be regarded as being of benefit to the public. Accordingly the trusts for saying masses in *Re Caus* were correctly designated as charitable in view of this second finding of public benefit, and nothing in *Gilmour* v *Coates* contradicted this conclusion.

The decision of the House of Lords in *Bourne* v *Keane* [1919] AC 815, also considered in *Re Hetherington Dec'd*, overruled certain earlier decisions and held that trusts to say masses for the dead were lawful and not for superstitious uses. But it appears the House had not specifically considered whether they were charitable.

Trusts for other purposes beneficial to the community

In the case of charitable objects falling within Lord Macnaghten's fourth category of purposes beneficial to the community, the public benefit is especially important. Such objects must be of general public utility, but this does not mean that all objects of general public utility are charitable; some may be and some may not: see Lord Cave LC in *Attorney-General* v *National Provincial and Union Bank of England* [1924] AC 262. If the object is of general public utility it may well satisfy the public benefit test automatically, but this is not always so. In some cases falling under the fourth category, a distinction has been drawn between a gift for 'a section of the public' and a gift for 'a fluctuating body of private individuals'. The latter phrase seems to have been first used in *Verge* v *Somerville* [1924] AC 496 in which a testator bequeathed his residuary estate to a repatriation fund 'for the benefit of New South Wales returned soldiers'. The Privy Council held the object was charitable under the fourth category and, on whether the trust was of a sufficiently public character, Lord Wrenbury said:

> 'To ascertain whether a gift constitutes a valid charitable trust so as to escape being void on the ground of perpetuity, a first inquiry must be whether it is public – whether it is for the benefit of the community or of an appreciably important class of the community. The inhabitants of a parish or town, or any particular class of inhabitants, may for instance, be the objects of such a gift, but private individuals, or a fluctuating body of private individuals cannot.'

It is not entirely clear what a fluctuating body of private individuals is. In *Williams's Trustees* v *IRC* [1947] AC 447 the House of Lords refused to hold a gift to provide cultural facilities for 'the Welsh people in London' as charitable. This decision seems to have treated the class as a fluctuating body of private individuals. However, Lord Cross criticised this term in *Dingle* v *Turner*:

> 'I get little help from the supposed contrast for as I see it one and the same aggregate of persons may well be describable both as a section of the public and as a fluctuating body of private individuals. The ratepayers of the Royal Borough of Kensington and Chelsea, for example, certainly constitute a section of the public; but would it be a misuse of language to describe them as a "fluctuating body of private individuals"? After all, every part of the public is composed of individuals and being susceptible of increase or decrease is fluctuating. So at the end of the day one is left where one started, with the contrast between "public" and "private".'

This would suggest that the term 'fluctuating body of private individuals' is of little help in ascertaining if a trust is for the public benefit. The issue should be looked at along the lines laid down in *Oppenheim*'s case.

The leading case in applying the public benefit test to the fourth category is *IRC* v *Baddeley* [1955] AC 572, the facts of which are set out in section 10.9. One of the grounds for refusing charitable status was that the gift did not satisfy the public benefit requirement. On this point Viscount Simonds drew a distinction:

> '... between a form of relief extended to the whole community yet by its very nature advantageous only to the few and a form of relief accorded to a selected few out of a larger number equally willing and able to take advantage of it'.

The *Verge* v *Somerville* case was within the former category, as it was generally available to anyone who fell within the object for which the trust was intended to provide relief. The *Baddeley* case was within the latter category, as it provided a form of relief to a limited class only, namely Methodists; this relief was not extended to the whole community. As Viscount Simonds said: 'they are a class within a class'. This decision does not mean that in general Methodists are not treated as a section of the community; it means that in the context of this particular gift they were not a section of the community.

Many charitable trusts aim at carrying out their objects overseas rather than in the United Kingdom. For example, a missionary society may be set up to carry out its work in Latin America, or a fund set up to relieve poverty amongst poor refugees or victims of natural disaster, or to advance education abroad. In the Report of the Charity Commissioners for 1963, it was expressly stated that the Commissioners entertained no doubt that the relief of poverty, the advancement of education and the advancement of religion were charitable even if done abroad. One limitation was imposed on trusts for the relief of poverty executed abroad, namely, that the poverty had to be inferred from observable cases and not merely inferred from statistics.

Charitable trusts for other purposes beneficial to the community must, if executed abroad, be of benefit to the community of the United Kingdom: see per Evershed MR in *Dreyfus (Camille and Henry) Foundation Inc* v *IRC* [1954] AC 39. Benefit to the United Kingdom need not be material or direct, but it must not be too remote. Thus, charities with general humanitarian objects, for example, cancer research, can benefit the United Kingdom community if carried out abroad. If the purposes are the provisions of local public works such as roads or irrigation, they will be charitable only if they are a reasonable direct means to ending poverty in observable cases. They would not be charitable if their purpose was the general economic improvement of another country.

In the case of Commonwealth countries it appears that anything which could be considered as a valid charitable trust under the fourth head – for the benefit of the community, in the United Kingdom – will also be charitable if done there: see Charity Commissioners Report for 1963. One wonders whether EEC countries might also qualify since 1972.

Section 1(2) Recreational Charities Act 1958

It should be remembered that charities relying on this Act must still have a public benefit element. This is found in s1(2) which requires the charitable facilities in question to be provided 'in the interests of social welfare' as defined by subss (a) and (b). The former subsection requires the benefit to be by way of 'improving the conditions of life' for those persons in need due to their 'youth, age, infirmity, disablement, poverty or social and economic circumstances'. These appear to almost wholly replicate the existing heads of charity. The latter, subs (b), is more specific and concerns provision of facililities for women at large.

10.12 Requirement that a trust be wholly and exclusively charitable

The third requirement for a valid charitable trust is that each and every object or purpose designed must be of a charitable nature. Failing this, there is no way of discriminating what part of the trust property is intended for charitable purposes and what part for non-charitable purposes, and the uncertainty in this respect invalidates the whole trust.

Where it is asserted that a trust is non-charitable on the grounds that it introduces non-charitable as well as charitable purposes, a distinction has to be drawn between those non-charitable activities authorised by the trust instrument which are merely subsidiary or incidental to a charitable purpose, and those non-charitable activities so authorised, which in themselves form part of the trust purpose. In the latter case, but not the former, the reference to non-charitable activities will deprive the trust of its charitable status. In *Incorporated Council of Law Reporting* v *Attorney-General* [1972] Ch 73 it was argued that the fact that law reports were used by lawyers in order to earn their professional fees was not a reason for refusing charitable status. This was an inevitable consequence of publishing law reports, and such consequences were not to be considered as defeating the main purpose of the trust. In *Re Coxen* (above) a trust for hospitals was not defeated as a charitable trust merely because it directed that up to £100 should be set aside annually to provide a dinner for the trustees. This was merely ancillary and treated as encouraging the better administration of the trust rather than intending personal benefit for the trustees. But in *McGovern* v *Attorney-General* [1982] Ch 321 Slade J found some of the objects of the trust to be charitable and some not to be, and the trust was refused charitable status: see section 10.10.

Where the word 'or' is used in outlining purposes to which a gift is to be put, then generally it is considered as giving alternatives for the use of the property. If one of the alternative purposes is not a charity, then the gift will not be considered to be charitable; it is not wholly and exclusively charitable.

Where the words used were 'charitable or benevolent': *Chichester Diocesan Fund and Board of Finance* v *Simpson* [1944] AC 341; 'such charitable or public purposes as my trustees think proper': *Blair* v *Duncan* [1902] AC 37; and 'public, benevolent or charitable purposes': *Houston* v *Burns* [1918] AC 337, the gifts were held to be non-charitable. The trustees could have properly applied the funds to both charitable and non-charitable purposes.

If the word 'or' is used between two purposes both of which are charitable in themselves, then the gift is charitable. In *Re Bennett* [1920] 1 Ch 305 a gift for 'charity or other public objects in the parish of Faringdon' was held charitable. The word 'other' was held to be vital in this case, and Eve J considered that it allowed him to read public objects ejusdem generis with charity.

Where the word 'and' is used between two purposes and the first is charitable, then generally the second is read in conjunction with the first. Where a gift is made for 'charitable and public purposes' as suggested by Lord Davey in *Blair* v *Duncan* (1902), or 'charitable and benevolent' purposes as in *Re Best* [1904] 2 Ch 354, or 'charitable and deserving objects' as in *Re Sutton* (1885) 28 Ch D 464, the gift is wholly and exclusively charitable. The word 'and' does not always permit the second purpose to be read in conjunction with the first, as was pointed out in the Privy Council case of *Attorney-General of The Bahamas* v *Royal Trust Co* [1986] 1 WLR 1001, where a testator left a bequest 'for any purposes for and/or connected with the education and welfare of Bahamian children and young people'. The authorities clearly indicate that a gift for 'welfare' is not charitable, and so the issue was whether this word could be read conjunctively with 'education'. The Privy Council held that it could not, because it was difficult to see how a purpose connected with a child's education could be treated as anything but for its welfare. Welfare had to be given some separate meaning, otherwise it became otiose and therefore it had to be construed disjunctively.

Where a third word is introduced, the use of the word 'and' between two only of the three words, usually the last two, will not necessarily make a gift charitable if each of the words is not for an exclusively charitable object. In *Williams* v *Kershaw* (1835) 5 Cl & F 111n a gift for 'benevolent, charitable and religious purposes' was held bad even though the only non-charitable aspect of the gift was 'benevolent' and in *Re Eades* [1920] 2 Ch 353 a gift for 'religious, charitable and philanthropic purposes' was held bad. The judgment of Sargant J in *Re Eades* indicates that the matter is one of construction on the facts of each case. It tends to suggest that where three words are used the use of 'and' between the last two is nothing more than a grammatical connection to end a sentence. The decision in *Re Ward* [1941] Ch 308 should be contrasted with the cases already cited. The gift was for 'educational or charitable or religious purposes' and was held charitable as each of the words used involved an exclusively charitable object.

A settlor may direct that a fund is to be apportioned between charitable and non-charitable purposes. Such a gift is charitable only to the extent of the fund directed to the charitable purpose.

If the executor or trustee defaults in making an apportionment between a non-charitable purpose and a charitable purpose, then the court will apportion the property equally between the two classes of objects. The same rule will apply if there is a discretion to apportion in whatever shares the executor or trustees think fit. In *Salusbury* v *Denton* (1857) 3 K & J 529 a testator bequeathed a fund to his widow and directed that in her will she should leave it 'part to the foundation of a charity school ... for the benefit of the poor at Offley as she may prefer, and the remainder to be at her disposal among my relations in such proportions as she may direct'. No will or apportionment was made by the widow. It was held that the fund should be divided into two equal parts, one for the charitable purposes and one for the non-charitable purposes on the principle that 'equity is equality'.

If the non-charitable purpose is void in a case of apportionment then only that part of the funds devoted to them will fail: see *Re Clarke* (1923) 2 Ch 407. But, if it is impossible to quantify the funds applicable to either the charitable purpose or the non-charitable purpose then the whole gift will fail for uncertainty: see *Re Coxen* [1948] Ch 747.

10.13 Administration of charities

Whilst not essential to the study of charities on an academic level it is noteworthy that recent years have seen a spate of legislation on the area aimed, primarily, at the proper running and administration of charities. In particular the 1993 Charities Act effectively repeals all of the 1960 Act, and whilst the key provisions (for example ss13 and 14, 'Cy-près') remain unchanged, it is useful to note the general headings of the Act's provisions as follows:

Part I – Charities Commissioners and the Official Custodian of Charities

Part II – Registration and names of charities

This includes, as introduced by the now mostly repealed Part I Charities Act 1992, tougher provisions on how charities are to be registered and the ability of the Charity Commissioners to scrutinise new applications and existing charities much more closely.

Part III – Commissioners' information powers

Again, as introduced by the Charities Act 1992, the Charity Commissioners' powers are expanded. Included in this is s11 which makes it an offence to 'knowingly' or 'recklessly' supply false or misleading information to the Commissioners; the maximum penalty is the current maximum (if summary proceedings are brought) or two years imprisonment and a fine (if proceedings are by way of indictment).

Part IV – Application of property cy-près and assistance and supervision of charities by Court and commissioners

The former s13 Charities Act 1960 is re-stated in an unamended form as this Act's s13 (therefore practically there is no change for cy-près purposes).

However, the Act retains the newly introduced provisions, formerly in the 1992 Act, regarding Charity Trustees' rights to apply gifts of unknown donors cy-près with full protection from any claims by 'late' applicants demanding the return of their donation *after* proper public notices have been given and have expired.

Section 32 confirms the increased role of the Charity Commissioners who are now empowered to take legal action on behalf of the Attorney-General (ex officio) in respect of all matters (except the winding up of charitable companies pursuant to s63(1)). This avoids the need for the Commissioners to have to refer most applications to the Attorney-General, thereby potentially saving on time and costs.

Part V – Charity land

These provisions, ss36–40, confirm the liberalisation of the investment of charitable property and the way in which charities can deal in land. Of particular note is s38 which permits trustees to take out a mortgage on 'charitable' land to fund an existing loan without the need for a Court order so long as:

1. the loan is necessary for the particular purposes of the charity;
2. the terms of the proposed loan are reasonable, with the charity being viewed as a prospective borrower; and
3. due regard has been given to the ability of the charity to repay the proposed sum (after taking into account the terms of the loan).

For the purposes of the above (s38(2)) it is sufficient for the trustees to have sought advice from an independent party (ie not linked to the transaction) who is reasonably believed to be qualified to give such financial advice.

Part VI – Charity accounts, reports and returns

Part VII – Incorporation of charity trustees

Part VIII – Charitable companies

Part IX – Miscellaneous

Sections 70 and 71 empower the 'Secretary of State' (ie any of Her Majesty's Principal Secretaries of State) to enact provisions freeing charities from the provisions of the Trustee Investment Acts 1961. Specifically these sections envisage a relaxing of the requirement for an equal split of trust property between 'narrower' and 'wider' forms of investment.

Sections 72 and 73 reinforce the tougher line being taken on charities and potential trustees by excluding individuals from eligibility as a trustee if they have convictions for any 'fraudulent' or 'dishonest' offence.

Sections 74 and 75 deal with small charities.

Part X – Supplementary

Schedules

The main schedules are:

1. Schedule 1 – Constitution of the Charity Commissioners.
2. Schedule 2 – Exempt charities.
3. Schedule 7 – Repeals.

Of note is the fact that s38(4), which repealed the Preamble to the Statute of Elizabeth (the basis of the definitions of charitable purposes), has not been repealed. Therefore, whilst the Preamble remains repealed it is still necessary to look to case law to determine if a potential charity has an accepted charitable purpose: *McGovern* v *Attorney-General* [1982] Ch 321.

Commencement

The main provisions of the 1993 Act came into force on 1 August 1993.

11

The Cy-près Doctrine

11.1 Introduction: flow chart

11.2 Charitable purpose still exists

11.3 Amalgamations, gifts for purposes or institutions

11.4 Cases of initial failure

11.5 Cases of subsequent failure

11.6 Statutory provisions and cy-près

11.1 Introduction: flow chart

As discussed in Chapter 6 the usual presumption when a gift fails, and there is no provision in default, is that of a resulting trust in favour of the donor. However, in cases where the gift is for charitable purposes the doctrine of cy-près, or its alternatives, might be applied. In essence this ensures that in appropriate cases the gift is still applied for charitable purposes akin to the original objects for which it was given.

Prior to the Charities Act 1960 the cy-près doctrine was restricted by case law which dictated that it could only be applied if the original purposes were 'impossible or impracticable': see *Re Dominion Students' Hall Trust* [1947] Ch 183. The Act, by operation of ss13 and 14, reformed this.

However, before discussing the application of the cy-près doctrine it is useful to consider the circumstances in which a gift to charity can fail. These are detailed in the following flow chart.

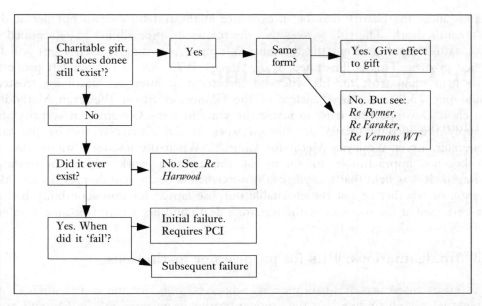

Following each of the above situations in turn:

11.2 Charitable purpose still exists

Obviously if the charitable purpose for the gift still exists then it is simply a matter of vesting the property in the appropriate parties. For these purposes the date for deciding when the charitable purpose still exists is the date at which it is effectively dedicated to charity. This is important because if a gift has been given to charity it will forever, subject only to any express provisions of the donor, be used for charitable purposes. Hence if the original charitable purpose no longer exists, being impossible or impracticable, then cy-près will automatically be invoked. Two cases that highlight the importance of this and the date at which a gift to charity is deemed to be effected are *Re Slevin* [1891] 2 Ch 236 and *Re Moon's WT* [1948] 1 All ER 300. Thus in *Re Slevin* a testator left a legacy to an orphanage. The orphanage was in existence at the testator's death but was closed down shortly afterwards, and before the assets of the estate were administered. The question arose whether the bequest could be applied cy-près. It was held that the gift could be applied cy-près; lapse of a gift can only occur during a testator's lifetime except where the testator provided for a resulting trust on failure of the charity or on its ceasing to exist. The legacy became the property of the charity at the testator's death even though it might not obtain the receipt of it until some later date.

Sometimes a gift may be made to charity as a remainder after a life interest has fallen, for example, '£10,000 to my wife for life, remainder to charity X'. In these circumstances the charity may be in existence at the testator's death but not at the life-tenant's death. The rule here is that the matter of impossibility is determined at the testator's death and not the life-tenant's death. Accordingly, such a gift will be applied cy-près. This is illustrated by *Re Moon's WT* where a testator left property to be held upon trust for his wife and directed that after her death his trustees should pay £3,000 'to the Trustees of the Gloucester Street Wesleyan Methodist Church at Devonport on trust to invest the same in some Government security and to apply the income thereof to mission work in the district served by the said Gloucester Street Wesleyan Methodist Church'. When the testator's widow died it had become impracticable to carry out the mission work which the testator envisaged. It was held that the gift could nevertheless be applied cy-près because the question of whether or not the charitable purpose lapsed for impracticability had to be ascertained at the moment of the testator's death and not when it became payable.

11.3 Amalgamations, gifts for purposes or institutions

In an effort to ensure the dedication of property to charity the courts often go to extreme lengths in finding that the original charitable purpose does in fact still exist and is capable of fulfilment.

Therefore they have held that there is no lapse if a gift is made to a named charity which has ceased to exist before the date the gift took effect but where its charitable work is nevertheless being carried on. In such cases it is really unnecessary to apply the cy-près doctrine because the charity is still in existence, albeit functioning under a different name. This is illustrated by *Re Faraker* [1912] 2 Ch 488 where the testatrix died in 1911 leaving a legacy of £200 'to Mrs Bailey's Charity Rotherhithe'. There had been a charity of this name founded in 1756 to benefit poor widows but in 1905 the Charity Commissioners had, by a scheme, consolidated this charity with several other similar charities for the benefit of the poor. The question arose whether the gift had lapsed. It was held that the gift had not lapsed as the charity was still in existence subject to the consolidation made by the Charity Commissioners. The charity had not changed, only the machinery of it had changed. In reaching this conclusion Farwell LJ pointed out that:

> '... one has to consider not so much the means to the end as the charitable end which is in view, and so long as that charitable end is well established the means are only machinery, and no alteration of the machinery can destroy the charitable trust for the benefit of which the machinery is provided.'

The construction applied in *Re Faraker* is perfectly acceptable where the charity concerned is one which no one has power to terminate. However, if it is one which can be terminated and its funds disposed of elsewhere, then there is nothing to prevent the doctrine of lapse operating. In *Re Stemson's WT* [1970] Ch 16 a testator left the residue of his estate to an incorporated charity which was dissolved shortly before his death and all its funds passed to another charity which did not have similar charitable objectives. Plowman J held that as the gift was to a charity liable to termination under its constitution it had lapsed; *Re Faraker* did not apply. In *Re Lucas* [1948] Ch 424 Lord Greene MR also pointed out that the principle in *Re Faraker* would not apply to cases where a gift was made for a particular aspect of the charity's work which was impossible to carry on after a scheme of amalgamation with other charities. Thus, for example, if £10,000 was bequeathed to 'X Charity for the aged for the upkeep of their premises at Blackacre' and no other purpose, cyprès would be impossible if the charity closed that home or the lease of it expired and was not renewed.

There is no lapse if the gift is construed as a gift for the purposes of a named institution rather than the institution itself.

This category differs from the principle in *Re Faraker* in that here the charity has ceased to exist but its work is nevertheless continuing and the gift is for the work of the charity rather than the charity itself. *Re Faraker* was concerned with the effect of administrative schemes on charities.

This principle was applied in several cases concerning hospitals after they were taken over by the Minister of Health under the National Health Service Act 1946. In many cases testators had bequeathed property to hospitals which were taken over and their wills came into effect, without alteration, after 1946: see *Re Meyer's WT* [1951] Ch 534. The leading case is *Re Vernon's WT* [1972] Ch 300n where a testatrix, who made her will in 1937, directed that her residuary estate be divided in equal shares among several named charities including 'Coventry Crippled Children's Guild'. At the date of the will there was an organisation called the 'Coventry and District Crippled Children's Guild' which ran homes and orthopaedic clinics. This organisation was incorporated under the Companies Act 1919 and eventually its work was taken over by the National Health Service in 1946. The organisation was dissolved and struck off the register of companies but its work was still being carried on in the homes and clinics at the testatrix's death in 1960. In 1949 an unincorporated body called 'the Coventry and District Cripples' Guild' was founded, its main object being the support of cripples; it had no clinics. The question arose as to how the bequest to the Coventry Crippled Children's Guild should be applied. Buckley J held the gift was meant for the organisation in existence at the date the testatrix made her will in 1937, viz the Coventry and District Crippled Children's Guild, even though it had been misdescribed. There was nothing in the gift to indicate that the gift was to be construed as one on trust for the purpose of the Guild. Therefore, although the institution had ceased to exist, its charitable purpose had not, as its work was being carried out at a hospital and a clinic by the Minister of Health.

In *Re Vernon's WT* Buckley J, in the course of his judgment, drew a distinction between gifts made to charitable institutions which are incorporated and charitable institutions which are unincorporated:

'Every bequest to an unincorporated charity by name without more must take effect as a gift for a charitable purpose. No individual or aggregate of individuals could claim to take such a bequest beneficially ... A bequest to a corporate body, on the other hand, takes effect simply as a gift to that body beneficially, unless there are circumstances which show that the recipient is to take the gift as trustee.'

This principle was not applied directly in *Re Vernon's WT* itself but in *Re Finger's WT* [1972] Ch 286 Goff J applied it to the facts before him. In this case a testatrix, who made her will in 1930, directed that her residue be divided equally among several named charities including the National Radium Commission (an unincorporated charity) and the National Council for Maternity and Child Welfare (an incorporated charity). Both charities ceased to exist between the date of the will and the date of the testatrix's death in 1965 but their work was taken over and still being carried on by other organisations. The question arose whether either or both of these gifts had lapsed. It was held that, first, the gift to the National Radium Commission did not lapse and could be applied cy-près. It was a gift to an unincorporated organisation and, therefore, it took effect as a gift for its charitable purposes and there was nothing in the words of the gift to the contrary; and, secondly, the gift to the National Council for Maternity and Child Welfare was a gift to a corporate body and, prima facie, it took effect as a gift to that body beneficially unless circumstances showed it was to take as trustee. There were no such circumstances and on the principle in *Re Vernon's WT* the gift failed. However, on the facts, it was possible to find a general charitable intention behind the gift because the testatrix regarded herself as having no relatives and her will showed an intention to benefit charity generally. On this basis cy-près was available.

Some difficulties arise out of the principles set out by Buckley J in *Re Vernon's WT*. A distinction is drawn between incorporated and unincorporated charities, which leads to possible failure of gifts because the charity to which they are given happens to be incorporated whereas the same gift might be upheld if given to an unincorporated charity. Thus, for example if a testator, in his will made in 1944 left £10,000 to Hospital A and £10,000 to Hospital B, and the former was incorporated but the latter unincorporated, then, on the formation of the National Health Service and takeover of these hospitals, the gift to A would fail but the gift to B might not, if it came into effect at a later date: see *Re Meyer's WT* [1951] Ch 534.

The principle in *Re Vernon's WT* only applies if the gift is one to an unincorporated charity by name *without more*. Thus, if a gift in terms similar to those used in *Re Rymer* (below) were to come before the court today, it would still be decided in the same way because it is not a gift to an unincorporated charity *without more*. The detailed directions in that gift would prevent the principle in *Re Vernon's WT* being applied: see *Re Finger's WT*.

11.4 Cases of initial failure

As stated, this arises where property is donated to a particular charity which has ceased to exist at the date the gift has taken effect. Thus, if a testatrix made a will in 1960 leaving £10,000 to 'X Charity' which ceased to exist in 1970 and the testatrix died in 1980 leaving her will unchanged, it would be necessary to decide if the cy-près doctrine applied. The gift to X Charity clearly cannot take effect and cy-près is concerned to see if the money can be applied to another charity with similar or nearly similar objects.

Before cy-près can be applied in cases of initial impossibility it is vital that there be a general charitable intention behind the gift. This means that it must be shown that the donor wished to benefit charity or a particular kind of charitable object in general, as opposed to one particular or named charitable organisation. Thus, if a testator left £10,000 to X Charity in his will and directed that if the charity should cease to exist before his death the money should fall into residue, then cy-près would not be available; there is no general charitable intention. In these circumstances the gift to the charity is deemed to have lapsed. In *Biscoe* v *Jackson* (1887) 35 Ch D 460 a testator directed in his will that his trustees set aside £10,000 from his personal estate for charitable purposes and out of the £10,000 apply £4,000 'in the establishment of a soup kitchen in the parish of Shoreditch and of a cottage hospital adjoining thereto'. It was impossible to obtain land to carry out the provisions of the will and the next-of-kin claimed the fund. But, it was held that the gift showed a general charitable intention to benefit the poor of Shoreditch and the stated objectives were only two out of several possible methods of achieving the testator's stated objective. As Cotton LJ said:

> '... looking at this whole clause, we see an intention on the part of the testator to give £10,000 to the sick and the poor in the parish of Shoreditch, pointing out how he desires it to be applied; and that particular mode having failed, as we must for the purposes of this appeal assume to be the case, then the intention to benefit the poor of Shoreditch, being a good charitable object, will have effect given to it according to the general principle laid down long ago by this court, by applying it cy-près'.

This decision should be contrasted with *Re Rymer* [1895] 1 Ch 19 where a testator bequeathed £5,000 'to the rector for the time being of St Thomas' Seminary for the education of priests in the diocese of Westminster'. The testator died in 1893. At the time the will was made St Thomas' Seminary was in existence and providing for the education of priests in the Westminster diocese. However, at the date of the testator's death it had ceased to exist and all its students had been transferred to a seminary in Birmingham. The question arose whether the legacy had lapsed or whether it should be applied cy-près.

It was held as there was no general charitable intention behind the legacy; cy-près could not be applied; the legacy lapsed. As Lindley LJ said:

'It is a gift of £5,000 to a particular seminary for the purposes thereof, and I do not think it is possible to get out of that. I think the context shows it. I refer to the masses, the choice of candidates and so on'.

The court leans against the lapse of charitable bequests and attempts to apply the cy-près doctrine wherever possible. In *Re Roberts* [1963] 1 WLR 406 Wilberforce J said: 'The courts have gone very far in the decided cases to resist the conclusion that a legacy to a charitable institution lapses, and a number of very refined arguments have been found acceptable with a view to avoiding that conclusion.'

Sometimes it is possible to infer from the manner in which a testator has set out gifts to various charities a general charitable intention, so as to apply the cy-près principle to any doubtful gift contained in the will. This is illustrated by *Re Satterthwaite's Will Trusts* [1966] 1 WLR 277 in which a testatrix left her whole estate in equal shares to nine named animal societies which had apparently been selected at random from a London telephone directory. Six of the societies named were well known charities; one was non-charitable being the National Anti-Vivisection Society; one completely unidentifiable; and one referred to as the 'London Animal Hospital'. A veterinary surgeon who once practised under this trade name the 'London Animal Hospital' claimed the bequest despite the fact that he had ceased to so practise long before the testatrix made her will. The Court of Appeal held that the bequest to the 'London Animal Hospital' was a gift by descriptive title which indicated an intention to benefit a charity and not the proprietor of a business especially as there was no evidence that the testatrix had ever known of this business. The bequests, by reason of the description of the beneficiaries, showed a general charitable intention, namely, animal kindness. The gift was applicable cy-près.

There are limits to the application of this principle. It cannot be used to infer that a gift to a well known and clearly named non-charitable organisation should take effect in some way which is charitable. This was pointed out in *Re Jenkins' WT* [1966] Ch 249 where a testatrix directed that the residue of her estate be divided into seven equal shares; six were given to known charitable organisations and the seventh to the British Union for the Abolition of Vivisection, a non-charitable body. The question arose whether the share given to the British Union should be held on charitable trust on the ground that the will disclosed a general charitable intention. It was held that the fact that one non-charitable gift was found among a number of charitable gifts did not permit the court to infer that the testatrix meant the non-charitable gift to take effect as a charitable gift. Buckley J observed:

'If you meet seven men with black hair and one with red hair you are not entitled to say that here are eight men with black hair. Finding one gift for a non-charitable purpose among a number of gifts for charitable purposes the court cannot infer that the testator or testatrix meant the non-charitable gift to take effect as a charitable gift when in terms it is not charitable, even though the non-charitable gift may have a close relation to the purposes for which the charitable gifts are made.'

When a gift is made to a named charitable organisation, and there is no evidence that it ever existed, then the court may infer a general charitable intention on the basis that the testator used a specific name with a particular charitable aim in mind, even if he did not care enough for the particular organisation to check its correct name. When this rule can be applied will depend on the facts of each case. In *Re Harwood* [1936] Ch 285 a testatrix made a will in 1925 leaving £200 to the Wisbech Peace Society and £300 to the Peace Society of Belfast. At the testatrix's death in 1934 the Wisbech Peace Society had ceased to exist. There was, however, no evidence that the Belfast Peace Society had ever existed. It was held that the bequest to the Wisbech Peace Society had lapsed and could not be applied cy-près. The bequest to the Peace Society of Belfast could be applied cy-près as it indicated a means of benefiting charity and had a general charitable intention. Quaere: whether a gift to promote peace is a good charitable object.

11.5 Cases of subsequent failure

Supervening impossibility arises where a gift is made to a charity which has ceased to exist after the gift has taken effect. In such circumstances there is no need to show a general charitable intention in order to apply the gift cy-près. Once property has been effectively dedicated to a charity it is always held for charitable purposes: see *Re Slevin* and *Re Moon's WT* (above).

11.6 Statutory provisions and cy-près

Before the Charities Act 1960 came into force it was only possible to apply the cy-près principle where the object of a trust had become impossible or impracticable. It was not permissible to use the cy-près doctrine in a case where the trust was considered an uneconomic way of effecting the charitable object or where it was considered that the charitable object was no longer appropriate or suitable in the light of the changing needs of society.

In order to avoid absurd results the courts did, in the years preceding the Charities Act 1960, give the test of impossibility or unpracticability an increasingly wide construction. This still had its limitations and not every sensible alteration needed in a charitable trust could be effected. As a result s13 Charities Act 1960 was enacted to solve the problem. It provided for various circumstances in which the original purposes of a charitable gift can be altered in order to allow property to be applied cy-près. While the 1960 Act has been repealed, and replaced by the Charities Act 1993, ss13 and 14 are re-enacted unamended and provide as follows; s13(1):

'a) where the original purposes, in whole or in part:
i) have been as far as may be fulfilled; or
ii) cannot be carried out, or not according to the directions or spirit of the gift; or

b) where the original purposes provide a use for part only of the property available by virtue of the gift; or

c) where the property available by virtue of the gift and other property applicable for similar purposes can be more effectively used in conjunction, and to that end suitably, regard being had to the spirit of the gift, be made applicable to common purposes; or

d) where the original purposes were laid down by reference to an area which was then but which has ceased to be a unit for some other purpose, or by reference to a class of persons or to an area which has for any reason since ceased to be suitable, regard being had to the spirit of the gift, or to be practical in administering the gift; or

e) where the original purposes, in whole or in part, have, since they were laid down:

i) been adequately provided for by other means; or

ii) ceased, as being useless or harmful to the community or for other reasons, to be in law charitable; or

iii) ceased in any other way to provide a suitable and effective method of using the property available by virtue of the gift, regard being had to the spirit of the gift.'

The provisions of s13 were applied in *Re Lepton's Charity* [1972] 1 Ch 276. In 1716 a testator devised certain lands upon trust to pay the rents and profits up to a sum of £3 per annum to the Protestant dissenting minister at Pudsey, and the residue of the income to go to the poor and aged at Pudsey. In 1716 the annual income was £5. In 1967 it was £792 and the minister was still receiving only £3. The question arose whether the court had power under s13 to raise the annual payment to the minister to £100. The court held that under paras a) (ii) and e) (iii) it was clear that the intention underlying the gift was plainly defeated when in modern conditions a derisory £3 was being paid to the minister out of £791 and when, in 1715, he took three-fifths of the annual income. The scheme to pay him £100 would be sanctioned.

The provisions of s13(2) still make it clear that the conditions other than impossibility required for a cy-près application have not been affected by the section. However, students should not confuse the doctrine of cy-près with the inherent right of charities, subject to any extraneous terms imposed on their property, to convert or sell their property so long as the proceeds are still applied to the original charitable purposes. This was confirmed in the decision in *Oldham Borough Council v Attorney-General* [1993] Ch 210 which affirmed the concept that property is not per se charitable, unless for example it is an historic site, or there was an express provision in the original gift linking the property to the charity's original charitable purpose, and can therefore be disposed of with the proceeds then being subject to the original charitable purposes.

Section 14 Charities Act 1960 (now s14 of the 1993 Act, unamended) was enacted in order to overcome the difficulties which previously arose when money was collected for a particular charitable purpose and then that purpose turned out to be unattainable. Thus, if, as in *Re Ulverston and District New Hospital Building Trusts* [1956] Ch 622 money is collected from various sources to build a hospital and it subsequently becomes clear that the object is unattainable, there is no general charitable intention behind the gift enabling a cy-près application. The money must be returned to the donors. Prior to the passing of s14 trying to trace the donors of such funds was a considerable problem. The provisions of s14 overcome such difficulties. Section 14 provides:

'(1) Property given for a specific charitable purpose shall be applicable cy-près as if given for charity generally where it belongs:
a) to a donor who cannot be identified or found after reasonable advertisements or inquiries,
b) to a donor who has executed a written disclaimer.
(2) Property is conclusively presumed to belong to unidentifiable donors without the need for advertisements or inquiries if it is:
a) the proceeds of cash collections or collecting boxes in which donations are indistinguishable from one another,
b) the proceeds of any lottery, competition, entertainment, sale or similar money raising activity after allowing for expenses.
(3) The Court may order that money or property belongs to donors who cannot be identified where:
a) it would be unreasonable to return the money to the donors, bearing in mind the amounts to be returned and the expenses involved in doing so,
b) it would be unreasonable, regard being had to the nature, circumstances and amount of the gifts and the lapse of time for the donors to expect it to be returned.'

The recent growth in small charities (currently defined as those with annual incomes of less than £5,000) has resulted in a new cy-près scheme being enacted in ss74 and 75 of the Charities Act 1993. Essentially, subject to procedural formalities and limitations, where there are express provisions (ie attached to the charitable property) to the contrary, the charity's trustees can, broadly, transfer, share or divide its assets in favour of other charities. The governing proviso, much like s13, is that the trustees must be satisfied:

'(a) that the existing purposes of the charity (or, as the case may be, such of them as it is proposed to replace) have ceased to be conducive to a suitable and effective application of the charity's resources; and
(b) that the purposes [of the charity or charities] specified in the resolution are as similar in character to those existing purposes as is practical in the circumstances.'

12

Appointment, Retirement and Removal of Trustees

12.1 Appointment

12.2 Who may be a trustee?

12.3 Number of trustees

12.4 Vesting of trust property

12.5 Termination of trusteeship

12.6 Trusts of Land and Appointment of Trustees Act 1996

12.1 Appointment

Introduction

The first trustees of a trust are usually appointed by the settlor or the testator in the trust instrument or the will creating the trust. If no trustees are appointed in the trust instrument or the will this will not cause the trust to fail. The court will appoint trustees to carry out the trust under the provisions discussed below, 'equity will not want for a trustee'.

Sometimes a trust may contain detailed provisions as to the appointment of trustees. It may be that a power to appoint trustees is given to a particular person and frequently in an inter vivos settlement the settlor may reserve this power to himself. The extent and effect of such a power is very much a matter of construction of the trust instrument.

Where there are first trustees appointed by the trust instrument or will, the trust property will vest in them (on vesting, see section 12.4) and they will hold it jointly until such time as they die, retire or are removed and the trust property will always vest in the survivors or survivor of them: see ss1 and 3 Administration of Estates Act 1925.

EXAMPLE:
S appoints T1, T2, T3 and T4 to hold Blackacre on trust for X and Y, his infant sons. The trust was created in 1970.

T1 died in 1971. The property then vested in T2, T3 and T4.

T2 retired in 1973. The property vested in T3 and T4.

T3 was removed in 1975. The property then vested in T4 as sole trustee.

T4 died in 1976. The property then vested in the personal representative of T4 subject to the trusts. Under s18(2) Trustee Act 1925 the personal representative of T4 can take up the trusteeship if he chooses. If he does not, then the provisions of s36 Trustee Act 1925 will come into operation.

Section 36 Trustee Act 1925

This statutory provision confers wide powers to appoint new trustees. It applies to all trusts, including Settled Land Act trusts unless the contrary appears in the trust instrument and, under it, a new trustee may be appointed in place of a trustee who:

1. is dead – this includes a trustee nominated in the trust instrument who dies before the testator: see s36(8); or
2. remains out of the United Kingdom for more than 12 months – this means an uninterrupted period of 12 months. In *Re Walker* [1901] 1 Ch 601 the power was held not to apply where the trustee had visited London for one week in the 12 months; or
3. desires to be discharged from all or any of his trusts or powers; or
4. refuses to act in the trusts – this includes disclaimer; or
5. is unfit to act in the trusts – is bankrupt or the likes as in *Re Roche* (1842) 2 Dr & War 287: or
6. is incapable of acting in the trusts – this means some personal incapacity such as old age and infirmity: *Re Lemann's Trusts* (1883) 22 Ch D 633; mental disorder: *Re East* (1873) 8 Ch App 735; but not bankruptcy or absence in an enemy country: *Re May's WT* [1941] Ch 109; or
7. is an infant; or
8. has been removed under a power contained in the instrument creating the trust: s36(2).

The persons who may appoint a new trustee or trustees under s36 are also set out in s36(1). They are:

1. the person or persons nominated for the purpose of appointing new trustees by the instrument, if any, creating the trust, or, if no such person or persons exist,
2. the surviving or continuing trustees or trustee for the time being, or the personal representatives of the last surviving or continuing trustee

If no person in these categories is available to make the appointment, the court would appear to have the power to appoint in the last resort under s41 TA 1925.

Mode of appointment

Section 36(1) requires an appointment of a new trustee to be in writing. In many cases a deed of appointment will be executed for reasons which will be apparent on reading section 12.4. But no particular form is necessary except that a deed will be required if there is not to be a separate instrument vesting property in the trustee: s40(1) LPA 1925.

Appointment of additional trustees

Section 36(1) allows the appointment of additional trustees when a vacancy has arisen. If X, one of two trustees, retires from his trusteeship, it is possible to appoint Y and Z to act in the trusts. This is because the section permits the appointment of 'one or more persons ... to be trustee or trustees in the place of the trustee'. Section 36(6) permits the appointment of additional trustees where there is no vacancy in the trust. This power can only be exercised where there are not more than three trustees of the trusts at the time of appointment. As with s36(1), the appointment must be in writing, and the persons who make the appointment will be either the person or persons nominated to do so, or the trustee or trustees for the time being.

The effect of an appointment under s36 is dealt with by s36(7) which provides:

'Every new trustee appointed under this section as well before as after all the trust property becomes by law, or by assurance, or otherwise vested in him, shall have the same powers, authorities and discretions, and may in all respects act as if he had been originally appointed a trustee by the instrument, if any creating the trust.'

Appointment by the court

Section 41(1) TA 1925 provides:

'The court may whenever it is expedient to appoint a new trustee or new trustees, and it is found inexpedient, difficult or impracticable so to do without the assistance of the court, make an order appointing a new trustee or new trustees either in substitution for or in addition to any existing trustee or trustees, or although there is no existing trustee.'

This power rests on it being 'inexpedient, difficult or impracticable' to make an appointment out of court. It has been used in the following instances:

1. Where all the trustees named predeceased the testator: see *Re Smirthwaite* (1871) LR 11 Eq 251.
2. Where the trustee was incapable of acting because of old age or some other infirmity such as mental illness: see *Re Lemann's Trusts* (1883) 22 Ch D 633.
3. Where there was doubt as to whether the statutory or an express power of appointment was exercisable: see *Re Woodgate* (1857) 5 WR 448.
4. Where the trustee was in enemy occupied territory: see *Re May's WT* [1941] Ch 109.

In exercising the power under s41 the court can remove a trustee against his will, and replace him. However, it appears as a matter of construction that s41 does not empower the court to simply remove a trustee without replacing him. The section can also be used to appoint additional trustees in difficult cases. Where a person has a statutory or express power to nominate trustees of a trust, the court will not exercise its powers under s41 so as to interfere with this: see *Re Hodson's Settlement*

(1851) 9 Hare 118. Even if trustees are nominated whom the court believes could have been bettered, it will not interfere. If it concludes that the trustees nominated are unsuitable it can call for a fresh nomination. Several unsuitable nominations may be regarded as a refusal to nominate and the court would make its own choice in such a case: see *Re Gadd* (1883) 23 Ch D 134.

The court has an inherent jurisdiction to supervise trusts and trustees. Before statutory powers were given this could be used to appoint trustees in difficult circumstances. This power is rarely used today as the statutory power is so wide.

The Judicial Trustee Act 1896 also gives the court power to appoint a trustee. This power is used in appointing a trustee to administer settled land, or a deceased's estate where the administration by the ordinary trustees has broken down, and it is not desired to put the estate to the full expense of administration by the court. The Act offers a means of continuing the administration where, for example, the original trustees cannot carry this on because they are ill. The appointment of a judicial trustee is purely at the court's discretion and an application for such an appointment should be by way of originating summons nominating a suitable person. The trustee appointed is an officer of the court, subject to its control and supervision.

The court may also appoint a trustee under the provisions of the Public Trustee Act 1906. This power is rarely exercised because of the expense involved and the fact that the powers of the public trustee to act in a trust are severely limited by the statute. Appointment of the public trustee is made where it is difficult or impossible to find someone who will act as trustee.

Where the court is asked to appoint trustees it will follow the principles laid down in *Re Tempest* (1866) LR 1 Ch App 485, where under a settlement created by will two trustees were appointed, one of whom predeceased the testator. The persons to whom the power of appointing new trustees was given were unable to agree on a selection. A petition was presented asking the court to appoint X as trustee. One beneficiary opposed this petition on the ground that X was connected to a branch of the family with which the testator had not been on friendly terms and had excluded from the management of his property. It was held that X should not be appointed a trustee by the court, and in making an appointment the following principles would be applied:

1. The court will have regard to the wishes of the persons by whom the trust has been created, if expressed in the instrument creating the trust, or clearly to be collected from it. If the author of the trust has in terms declared that a particular person, or a person filling a particular character, should not be a trustee of the instrument, there cannot be the least doubt that the court would not appoint a person whose appointment was so prohibited.
2. The court will not appoint a person to be trustee with a view to the interest of some persons interested under the trust, in opposition either to the wishes of the testator or to the interest of other beneficiaries. It is of the essence of the duty of every trustee to hold an even hand between the parties interested under the trust.

3. The court will have regard to whether an appointment will promote or impede the execution of the trust, for the very purpose of the appointment is that the trust may be better carried into execution. Thus the appointment of a person under a disability, for example a minor, or a person living abroad, will not be contemplated.

12.2 Who may be a trustee?

As a general rule the right to be a trustee is similar to the right to hold property. An appointment of a minor as a trustee of land is void under s20 LPA 1925 and an alien may hold any property on trust with the exception of a British ship: see s17 Status of Aliens Act 1914.

It is increasingly common for trust property to be vested in a sole custodian trustee (whose powers and duties are defined by s4(2) of the Public Trustee Act 1906). The remaining trustees then become managing trustees who exercise the powers and discretion conferred on the trustees generally and, whilst they have access to the trust property, this is vested solely in the custodian trustee. The benefit of such an arrangement is that the day-to-day administration can be dealt with by the managing trustees, who can then be easily replaced without the need to transfer the trust property.

A corporation may act as a trustee or co-trustee with another individual or corporation, in respect of either realty or personalty. The appointment of certain corporations which specialise in trust work is encouraged by the 1925 legislation. These are known as 'trust corporations' and they will normally take on trusteeship for profit only. The term 'trust corporation' includes the Public Trustee, the Treasury Solicitor and the Official Solicitor or corporations entitled to act as custodian trustee by the rules made under the Public Trustee Act 1906. At present, to be a corporate custodian trustee three conditions must be fulfilled:

1. The corporation must be constituted under the law of the United Kingdom or any other member state of the EU.
2. The corporation must be empowered by its constitution to undertake trust business in England and Wales.
3. The corporation must be incorporated by special Act or Royal Charter, or else be a registered company with an issued capital (stocks and shares) of at least £250,000 of which at least £100,000 has been paid up in cash.

12.3 Number of trustees

As a general rule there is no minimum number of trustees required by law and a sole trustee can act in the trusts whether this has been the design of the settlor or caused by death and retirement of trustees. Two matters should be noted on the position of a sole trustee:

1. A sole trustee, other than a trust corporation, cannot act effectively in some cases. Under s27(2) LPA 1925 and s18(1) SLA 1925 a sole trustee of land cannot give a valid receipt for the proceeds of sale or the capital money, notwithstanding anything to the contrary in the instrument. Accordingly an application under s41(1) TA 1925 might be appropriate.
2. There is no obligation to keep up the original number of trustees. This is now provided for by s37 TA 1925 which states that it shall not be obligatory to appoint more than one trustee where only one was originally appointed, or to fill up the original number of trustees where more than two trustees were originally appointed.

Statutory provisions impose a limitation on the maximum number of trustees where there is a settlement of land or a trust for sale of land. Section 34 TA 1925 provides that in the case of pre-1926 settlements with more than four trustees, no new trustees could be appointed until the number was reduced to below four. As regards post 1925 settlements, s34(2) provides:

1. The number of trustees shall not in any case exceed four, and where more than four persons are named as such trustees, the four first named, who are able and willing to act, shall alone be the trustees, and the other persons named shall not be trustees unless appointed on the occurrence of a vacancy.
2. The number of the trustees shall not be increased beyond four.

The provisions of s34 do not apply to pure personalty, nor according to s34(3) do they apply to:

1. Land vested in trustees for charitable, ecclesiastical, or public purposes.
2. Where the net proceeds of sale of the land are held for like purposes.
3. The trustees of a term of years absolute limited by a settlement on trusts for raising money, or of a like term created under the statutory provisions relating to annual sums charged on land.

12.4 Vesting of trust property

This is dealt with by s40 TA 1925 which dispenses with the need for conveyances of the trust property into the name of a new trustee jointly with the continuing trustees. Under s40 automatic vesting of the trust property will occur. Section 40(1) deals with deeds which appoint a new trustee and it states:

'i) If the deed contains a declaration by the appointer to the effect that any estate or interest in any land subject to the trust or in any chattel so subject, or the right to recover or receive any debt or other thing in action so subject, shall vest in the persons who by

virtue of the deed become or are the trustees for performing the trust, the deed shall operate, without any conveyance or assignment, to vest in those persons as joint tenants and for the purposes of the trust estate interest or right to which the declaration relates ...
ii) If the deed is made after the commencement of this Act and does not contain such a declaration, the deed shall, subject to any express provision to the contrary therein contained, operate as if it had contained such a declaration by the appointer extending to all the estates interests and rights with respect to which a declaration could have been made.'

The object of the section is to satisfy s40 LPA: see now s2 Law of Property (Miscellaneous Provisions) Act 1989.

Section 40(2) deals with cases where a trustee retires from the trust. It states:

'a) If the deed contains such a declaration as aforesaid by the retiring and continuing trustees, and by the other person, if any, empowered to appoint trustees, the deed shall, without any conveyance or assignment, operate to vest in the continuing trustees alone, as joint tenants, and for the purposes of the trust, the estate, interest, or right to which the declaration relates.
b) If the deed is made after the commencement of this Act and does not contain such a declaration, the deed shall, subject to any express provision to the contrary therein contained, operate as if it had contained such a declaration by such persons as aforesaid extending to all the estates, interests and rights with respect to which a declaration could have been made.'

Certain property is expressly excluded from the operation of s40 by s40(4) and must be expressly conveyed into the names of the trustees. This includes:

1. Land conveyed by way of mortgage for securing money subject to the trust, except land conveyed on trust for securing debts or debenture stock.
2. Land held under a lease which contains a covenant not to assign or dispose of the land without licence or consent, unless before the execution of the deed such licence or consent has been obtained.
3. Any share stock, annuity or property which is only transferable in books kept by a company or other body, or in a manner directed by or under an Act of Parliament.

The reason behind the first provision is to avoid bringing the trusts on to the title and avoid the mortgagor having to investigate the appointment of the trustees so as to ensure that he is paying the money to the right persons. The second is designed to avoid technical breaches of covenants against assignment in the lease, and the third is necessary because of the normal method by which company shares are transferred, by registration in the books of the company.

In any cases where it is difficult or impossible to vest property in trustees the court can make a vesting order under ss44–56 TA 1925.

The provisions of s40 only apply where the appointment of the new trustee is made by deed. If the appointment is made by writing only under s36, this would not in itself be sufficient to bring about automatic vesting and appropriate instruments of transfer would have to be executed. It would appear advisable to make appointments of trustees by deed wherever possible.

12.5 Termination of trusteeship

This can be done in four ways: disclaimer, death, retirement, and removal. Each will be considered separately.

Disclaimer

A person appointed as a trustee is not obliged to take up the office and may disclaim it at any time before acceptance, the cost of disclaimer being borne by the trust: see *Re Tryon* (1844) 7 Beav 496. However, there can be no disclaimer after acceptance: see *Re Lister* [1926] Ch 149. In strict terms a person who has disclaimed has never been a trustee, as the disclaimer operates by way of avoidance. Also, once disclaimed the disclaiming trustee cannot, of his own volition, re-activate his appointment.

A disclaimer is usually effected by deed but this is not essential, it can be oral or inferred from conduct, or even from the fact that a long time has elapsed since the appointment of the trustee and he has done nothing: see *Re Clout and Frewere's Contract* [1924] 2 Ch 230.

Death

On the death of a trustee his trusteeship automatically terminates. If there are surviving trustees then the trust estate will vest in them automatically. Trustees will invariably hold the trust estate as joint tenants and the principle of jus accrescendi will operate. The powers of the deceased trustee also accrue to the survivor or survivors according to s18(1) TA 1925 which provides:

> 'Where a power or trust is given or imposed on two or more trustees jointly, the same may be exercised or performed by the survivors or survivor of them for the time being, except (3) … Subject to the restrictions in … receipts by a sole trustee.'

On the death of a sole or last surviving trustee the trust estate devolves on his personal representatives who according to s18(2) shall be capable of exercising any power or trust available to the sole or last surviving trustee. The personal representatives are not obliged to accept the trust and they may appoint new trustees under the provisions of s36(1) TA 1925.

Retirement

A trust may contain an express power permitting a trustee to retire. Apart from this, a trustee can retire when a new trustee is appointed in his place under s36(1). If no new trustee is to be appointed then he may retire under the provisions of s39(1) TA 1925 which state:

> 'Where a trustee is desirous of being discharged from the trust, and after his discharge there will either be a corporation or at least two individuals to act as trustees to perform

the trust, then if such trustee as aforesaid by deed declares that he is desirous of being discharged from the trust, and if his co-trustees and such other person, if any, as is empowered to appoint trustees, by deed consent to the discharge of the trustee, and to the vesting in the co-trustees alone of the trust property, the trustee desirous of being discharged shall be deemed to have retired from the trust, and shall, by the deed, be discharged therefrom under this Act, without any new trustee being appointed in his place.'

Removal

There appears to be room in the provisions of ss36 and 41 TA 1925 for the removal of trustees but these provisions can only be used where the trustee being removed is being replaced at the same time. The grounds for removal under s36(1), set out above, include where the trustee has been outside the United Kingdom for 12 months, refuses or is unfit to act in the trusts, or is incapable of acting in the trusts. The jurisdiction under s41 is not based on any specific grounds.

The court has an inherent jurisdiction to remove a trustee and appoint a new one in his place or even to remove him without appointing a replacement. There is little authority on this area and the principles for the exercise of this jurisdiction were discussed in *Letterstedt* v *Broers* (1884) 9 App Cas 371. In this case the Board of Executors of Cape Town were the sole surviving executors and trustees of the will of Jacob Letterstedt. A beneficiary alleged misconduct on their part in the administration of the trust, and claimed that the board were unfit to act in the trusts and should be removed. The allegations were not substantiated by the beneficiary but all trust and respect between the trustees and beneficiaries had broken down. The Privy Council considered that in deciding whether to remove the trustees under the court's inherent jurisdiction, the main guide should be the welfare of the beneficiaries. On the facts it was decided to remove the trustees, for as Lord Blackburn said:

'It is quite true that friction or hostility between trustees and the immediate possessor of the trust estate is not itself a reason for the removal of trustees. But where the hostility is grounded on the mode in which the trust has been administered, where it has been caused wholly or partially by substantial overcharges against the trust estate, it is certainly not to be disregarded. Looking therefore at the whole circumstances of this very peculiar case, the complete change of position, the unfortunate hostility that has arisen and the difficult and delicate duties that may yet have to be performed, their Lordships can come to no other conclusion than that it is necessary, for the welfare of the beneficiaries, that the Board should no longer be trustees.'

12.6 Trusts of Land and Appointment of Trustees Act 1996

The Trusts of Land and Appointment of Trustees Act 1996, which came into force on 1 January 1997, contains provisions in Part II which create general powers for beneficiaries to direct trustees to retire and to direct the appointment of new trustees. The trust beneficiaries must be of full age and capacity and, together, must be absolutely entitled to the trust property. The beneficiaries' powers are subject to the restriction, discussed earlier, on the number of trustees which is imposed by the Trustee Act 1925. Section 21(5) Trusts of Land and Appointment of Trustees Act 1996 provides for the exclusion of the beneficiaries' powers in express trusts. The powers will, also, not apply where a person is nominated for the purposes of appointing trustees by the instrument creating the trust. Finally, in respect of express trusts created pre-commencement, provision is made in s21(4) for surviving settlors to exclude the powers.

13

Trustee Fiduciary Duties

13.1 Introduction

13.2 Remuneration of trustees

13.3 The rule in *Keech* v *Sandford*

13.4 Secret profits

13.5 Purchase of trust property

13.6 Purchase of beneficial interests

13.7 Indemnity

13.1 Introduction

Much of what was said in Chapter 7 on constructive trusts, especially on breach of fiduciary duty is applicable to trustees. It is necessary to look at the fiduciary position of a trustee in some detail.

As a general rule a trustee is not permitted to receive any benefit from his position qua trustee. That position is of personal confidence towards the beneficiaries. The duties he owes the beneficiaries must not in any circumstances be permitted to come into conflict with his personal interests. Should they do so, he will be liable to account to the beneficiaries for any profits made by him as a result. In *Bray* v *Ford* [1896] AC 44 Lord Herschell said:

'It is an inflexible rule of a Court of Equity that a person in a fiduciary position ... is not, unless otherwise expressly provided, entitled to make a profit; he is not allowed to put himself in a position where his interest and his duty conflict. It does not appear to me that this rule is, as has been said, founded upon principles of morality. I regard it rather as based on the consideration that human nature being what it is, there is danger, in such circumstances, of the person holding a fiduciary position being swayed by interest rather than duty, and thus prejudicing those whom he was bound to protect. It has, therefore, been deemed expedient to lay down this positive rule. But, I am satisfied that this might be departed from in many cases, without any breach of morality, without any wrong being inflicted, and without any consciousness of wrong-doing.'

The fiduciary duty is strictly applied to trustees and it is not in general relevant that the trustee acted honestly or has put in considerable time and effort executing the trusts. But, as Lord Herschell indicated in *Bray* v *Ford* (above) there are instances when the duty may not apply because the trust instrument expressly provides that the fiduciary duty shall not apply in a particular situation. Even where it is improperly departed from, the trustee may not be aware of wrong-doing, though the consequences still follow.

Where the trustees are put by the settlor or testator in a position where their own interests and duties conflict, and have not put themselves in that position, different considerations apply. In *Sargeant and Another* v *National Westminster Bank plc and Another* (1990) The Times 10 May, the Court of Appeal ruled that trustees for sale of land which was already subject to agricultural tenancies in their favour, were not obliged to relinquish these tenancies before selling the land concerned. This was despite the fact that if the land were sold free from the tenancies it would bring a considerably higher price than if sold subject to them.

13.2 Remuneration of trustees

Remuneration authorised by trust instrument

If a trust instrument expressly permits, a trustee may charge for his services to the trust without being in breach of his fiduciary duty. Express charging clauses are strictly construed by the court, as is illustrated by *Re Chapple* (1884) 27 Ch D 584, where a testatrix appointed her solicitor as trustee of her estate and provided that he should continue to act as solicitor in relation to her property and affairs and should 'make the usual professional charges'. The taxing master disallowed all items which were not of a strictly professional character. The solicitor appealed. It was held that the clause had to be construed restrictively; it only permitted the solicitor to charge for professional services in respect of which he could be properly employed. This did not include any of the things which a trustee could do himself without the services of a solicitor. See also *Re White* [1898] 2 Ch 217 which links the express charging clause to the amount of money in the trust fund.

A charging clause in favour of a trustee in a will is regarded as a legacy to the trustee equivalent to the profit he will make under it, and no claim is maintainable if the trustee attests the will: see s15 Wills Act 1837 and *Re Trotter* [1899] 1 Ch 764; *Re Pooley* (1888) 40 Ch D 1.

Remuneration authorised by the court

The court has an inherent jurisdiction to authorise the payment of remuneration to trustees for both past and future services nothwithstanding prior acceptance of the unpaid office: see *Bainbridge* v *Blair* (1845) 8 Beav 588.

In exercising its inherent jurisdiction the court has to balance two conflicting influences. First, that the office of trustee is gratuitous and the interests of the beneficiaries must be protected against the claims of the trustees, especially unjustified claims. Second, that the trust should be well administered and regard paid to the nature of the trust, the experience and skill of a particular trustee, the amounts which he seeks to charge compared with what other trustees might require to be paid for their services, and any other circumstances which may be relevant, per Fox LJ in *Re Duke of Norfolk's Settlement Trusts* [1981] 3 All ER 220.

The inherent jurisdiction can be exercised to give a trustee remuneration either for past or future services or to increase the remuneration of a trustee where the level is unacceptably low. In *Re Duke of Norfolk's Settlement Trusts* [1981] 3 WLR 455 the court exercised its inherent jurisdiction to award remuneration for past services rendered by the trustees which were beyond the scope of their duties and, on appeal, increased the general level of remuneration they were entitled to in future under the charging clauses in the trust instrument. The need for the exercise of the inherent jurisdiction arose because the trustees had, in that case, carried out redevelopment work on real estate owned by the trust in London and it was held the work involved in this was mainly beyond trusteeship. In the same case a claim was made for £50,000 as remuneration for services rendered in rearranging the trust affairs so as to minimise liability to capital transfer tax. This was not allowed, since it is an inherent duty of trustees to review the trust investments with regard to tax liability. In *Re Keeler's Settlement Trusts* [1981] 1 All ER 888 the court exercised its inherent jurisdiction to permit trustees to keep remuneration they had taken in breach of their fiduciary duty and ordered an inquiry as to future remuneration for some of the trustees. In that case the trustees had paid themselves directors' fees in companies the shares in which belonged to the trust. Three of the trustees were working full time for the companies while one was not. All were permitted to keep past remuneration but only those three working for the companies were authorised to receive future remuneration. An influential factor in this case was the fact that the trustees had been mistaken as to their right to remuneration and had acted in good faith.

Remuneration authorised by statute

Various statutory provisions enable trustees to charge remuneration in certain circumstances. Three provisions to be noted are:

1. Section 42 TA 1925, which permits a trust corporation appointed by the court to charge such remuneration for its services as trustees as the court may think fit.
2. Section 9 Public Trustee Act 1906, which authorises the Public Trustee to charge such fees as are fixed by the Treasury and authorised by the Lord Chancellor regardless of any provision in the trust instrument.
3. Section 1 Judicial Trustee Act 1896, which enables a person appointed as a judicial trustee to receive remuneration.

The rule in Cradock v Piper

This is an anomalous rule which has been disapproved of from time to time and is not to be extended, per Cotton LJ in *Re Corsellis* (1887) 34 Ch D 675. Under the rule a solicitor-trustee is entitled to charge his usual professional costs for work done for both himself and his co-trustees in an action or matter in court, provided his activities have not increased the expenses.

The action or matter in court need not be of a hostile nature; friendly actions in chambers fall within the rule, and in *Re Corsellis* a solicitor was allowed his profit costs on an application for an order to allow maintenance in favour of an infant beneficiary. This was held to fall within the rule.

The rule in *Cradock v Piper* is restricted to allowing the solicitor his professional costs in the action. Solicitors do not have any special position before the law in respect of trusts they administer. They will often include an express charging clause in the trust instrument, but where no such clause exists, a solicitor trustee can permit any of his partners to do non-court work for the trust provided it would be proper to employ an outside solicitor in the case. In such cases the solicitor trustee must not receive any benefit, either direct or indirect, from the work done by his firm: *Clack v Carlon* (1861) 30 LJ Ch 639.

Agreement with beneficiaries

A trustee may contract with the beneficiaries for remuneration. Beneficiaries who are sui juris and absolutely entitled will be bound by such agreements. Such agreements are rare because of the danger that undue influence may be alleged against the trustees: see *Ayliffe v Murray* (1740) 2 Atk 58.

Trust assets abroad

If property belonging to the trust is situated abroad and the law of the country where it is situated allows trustees to receive remuneration and English trustees receive such remuneration, they will not be bound to account for it unless they went out of their way to obtain it. In *Re Northcote's WT* [1949] 1 All ER 442 the trustees held assets in England and in New York for the purpose of administering an estate under a will. They were automatically entitled to remuneration under New York law for their work in administering the assets in New York. A claim was made by the beneficiaries in England that remuneration received by the trustees in New York was held on constructive trusts. This claim was rejected as the remuneration had come to the trustees without their volition and by reason of their obligation to deal with the assets in New York.

13.3 The rule in *Keech* v *Sandford*

This is a particular application of the rule that a trustee must not allow his interests and duties to conflict, which is concerned with the renewal of leases. In *Keech* v *Sandford* (1726) Sel Cas t King 61 a market lease was bequeathed by a testator to a trustee to hold for an infant. Before the expiration of the lease the trustee applied for a renewal on behalf of the trust and was refused. The lessor said it would only be granted if the trustee held the lease beneficially. The trustee applied for and received a renewal for his own benefit but it was held that he was a trustee of this for the infant and liable to account for all the profits. As Lord King LC said:

> 'I must consider this as a trust for the infant, for I very well see, if a trustee, on the refusal to renew, might have a lease for himself, few trust estates would be renewed to a cestui que trust. Though I do not say there is a fraud in this case, yet he (the trustee) should rather have let it run out than to have had the lease to himself. This may seem hard that the trustee is the only person of all mankind who might not have the lease, but it is very proper that the rule should be strictly pursued, and not in the least relaxed; for it is very obvious what would be the consequences of letting trustees have the lease on refusal to renew to the cestui que trust.'

The rule in *Keech* v *Sandford* may, at first sight, appear harsh, but it is intended to prevent a possible conflict between interest and duty on the part of the trustee. It is probably applied strictly as a matter of policy, since the main danger is that if a trustee felt he might be able to renew a lease for himself he might not do his best for the trust. The rule raises a presumption at law against a trustee of personal incapacity to retain the benefit of the renewed lease which cannot be rebutted. In *Protheroe* v *Protheroe* [1968] 1 WLR 519 the Court of Appeal applied the rule to a case where a husband held a lease for himself and his wife as beneficial joint tenants. The lease was of the matrimonial home and after the couple separated the husband was offered the opportunity to purchase the freehold reversion. The wife claimed that the freehold was held upon the same trusts as the lease, while the husband claimed that the wife's interest was confined to the lease. The wife's contention was accepted, because as Lord Denning MR said:

> '... although the house was in the husband's name, he was a trustee of it for both. It was a family asset which the husband and wife owned in equal shares. Being a trustee, he had an especial advantage in getting the freehold. There is a long established rule of equity from *Keech* v *Sandford* downwards that if a trustee, who owns the leasehold, gets in the freehold, that freehold belongs to the trust and he cannot take the property for himself.'

The rule in *Keech* v *Sandford* is also applied to other categories of fiduciaries but with less stringency, so that it throws the onus on them to show they have not abused their position. It has been applied to personal representatives, agents, partners and mortgagees. The special situation of a tenant for life since 1925 should be noted carefully, because the case below, *Re Biss*, partly concerns a pre-1925 tenant for life. The general rule in *Re Biss* still applies, but under s107 SLA 1925 a tenant becomes a trustee and thus is in a fiduciary position anyway. This problem was considered in *Re Biss* [1903] 2 Ch 40, where Romer LJ held that the rule applied to those who occupied a 'special' relationship, while Collins MR said the rule applied to those occupying a fiduciary or quasi-fiduciary position. A tenant for life of a lease may not renew it for himself but only for those entitled under the terms of the trust, including himself. This is because of the need to ensure that he does not use his power of sale for his own personal advantage and to the detriment of the remaindermen. It is unclear what amounts to a 'special' relationship or a quasi-fiduciary relationship. In *Re Biss* it appears that a mere beneficiary might well be in such a relationship and bound by the rule if he abused his position. In that case a lessee died intestate and his widow took out letters of administration to his estate. She sought to renew the lease but the lessor refused renewal to her. Her son, who was a beneficiary of the estate, sought a renewal for himself and this was granted. The widow's claim that he held the lease for the benefit of the estate was rejected because, as Collins MR said:

> '... is he [the son] entitled to go into the facts to shew that he had not, in point of fact, abused his position, or in any sense intercepted an advantage coming by way of accretion to the estate? He did not take under the will or a settlement with interests coming after his own, but simply got a possible share upon an intestacy in case there was a surplus of assets over debts. It seems to me that this obligation cannot be put higher than that of any other tenant in common against whom it would have to be established, not as a presumption of law, but as an inference of fact, that he had abused his position.'

This dictum suggests that if anyone in a 'special relationship or quasi-fiduciary relationship', whatever these may be, has abused his position, the rule may apply, whereas it always applies as a matter of law to a fiduciary such as a trustee.

13.4 Secret profits

A trustee must not take any profits from his position as trustee unless these have been authorised by the trust instrument, the beneficiaries, if sui juris, or the court. The position on profits was summarised by Lord Hodson in *Boardman* v *Phipps* [1967] 2 AC 46:

> '... no person standing in a fiduciary position, when a demand is made upon him by the person to whom he stands in the fiduciary relationship to account for profits acquired by him by reason of the opportunity and the knowledge, or either, resulting from it, is entitled to defeat the claim upon any ground save that he made profits with the knowledge and assent of the other person.'

Profits may arise in several ways, and only the more important ones are considered here.

Director's fees

Trustees may well find that the trust estate comprised substantial shareholdings in family or public companies. In such circumstances it may be necessary for the trustees to appoint one of their number as a director of the companies concerned to ensure that the interests of the trust are protected. Any director's fees received by a director-trustee are subject to the general rule that the trustee must not profit from his trust. In *Re Macadam* [1946] Ch 73 trustees had a power to appoint two directors to a company in which the trust had a substantial shareholding. The trustees appointed two of their number as directors and the issue arose whether they could retain directors' fees received by them. Cohen J held they were liable to account. He said:

> '... although the remuneration was remuneration for services as director of the company, the opportunity to receive that remuneration was gained as a result of the exercise of a discretion vested in the trustees, and they had put themselves in a position where their interest and duty conflicted. In those circumstances, I do not think this court can allow them to make a profit out of doing so ...'

It is well recognised that a trustee director may be vital to the interests of the trust and in certain instances he will be allowed to retain the director's fees. These are:

1. Where the trust instrument, either expressly or impliedly, authorises the trustee to retain them: see *Re Llewellin's Will Trusts* [1949] Ch 225.
2. Where the trustee became a director before becoming a trustee as happened in *Re Dover Coalfield Extension* [1908] 1 Ch 65, where company A purchased shares in company B and appointed X, a director of A, to be a director of B to look after A's interest in that company; later it was discovered that X needed a share qualification in B to continue as one of its directors. Consequently, A transferred some of its shares to X to meet the requirement. When A was wound up its liquidator claimed the director's fees received by X on the basis that he was a trustee for A by reason of his shareholding. This was rejected, as X had become a director before he became a trustee and the director's fees were not procured by reason of his position as a trustee.
3. Where the trustee secures the directorship by use of his own personal shareholding in the company. For this exception to apply it is necessary to show that he would have been appointed a director even if he had used the trust shareholding to vote against himself: see *Re Gee* [1948] Ch 284.
4. Where the court exercises its inherent jurisdiction to permit retention of directors' fees in whole or in part: see *Re Keeler's Settlement Trusts* [1981] 1 All ER 888 (above).

Competition

A trustee may be liable to account for profits made by him where he enters into competition with a business belonging to his trust: see *IDC* v *Cooley* [1972] 1 WLR 443. In this case the defendant was a distinguished architect working within the gas industry for some years. Whilst employed by the plaintiffs as a director the defendant attempted to convince them to use a local Gas Board in a project. His employers flatly rejected this, and subsequently the Gas Board contracted with him personally after he had left the plaintiffs, feigning illness. The court held him liable to account to the plaintiffs for the profits.

They rejected his arguments that the contract had come to him in his personal capacity, not as an employee of the plaintiffs. They also said that it was irrelevant that the Gas Board had come to him after refusal by the plaintiffs. In his capacity of director, and with his peculiar specialism, he had a duty to obtain such contracts solely for his company.

This rather harsh and possibly impractical attitude seems to have been mitigated in part in various Commonwealth decisions. See especially *Queensland Mines Ltd* v *Hudson* (1978) 18 ALR 1.

The decisions in this area do not give any clear guidance as to the position. In *Re Thomson* [1930] 1 Ch 203 it was held that an executor could not go into a business which directly competed with the trust business. This decision would seem to apply to trustees but it contains many special features; first, the business was of a specialised nature, yacht broking; second, it was in a small town where there was no other such business; third, the executor had gained his knowledge of yacht broking through dealing with the estate; fourth, he set up in competition in the same premises where the trust had carried on its business and, fifth, he threw the trust business out of those premises. This decision may be contrasted with *Moore* v *McGlynn* [1894] 1 IR 74, an Irish decision, in which Chatterton V-C refused to grant an injunction to prevent an executor competing with a business in his testator's estate but was prepared to remove him as executor. The business was a general grocery and hardware shop with a sub-post office. The judgment here suggests that there was no evidence produced by the plaintiffs of the executor abusing his position.

Misuse of opportunities and information

A trustee may be offered the opportunity to acquire property for the benefit of the trust, for example, shares or land at less than market value. If the trustee takes these benefits for himself then the decision in *Boardman* v *Phipps* (see Chapter 7) suggests that he will be liable to account for the property so acquired, plus any profits. The position is similar where he misuses information. Not all opportunities and information which a trustee learns of in the course of his trust are subject to his fiduciary obligations. The position was explored hypothetically by Lord Upjohn in his dissenting judgment in that case, though of course it should be remembered that as a dissent it is not binding.

> 'There is, in my view, and I know of no authority to the contrary, no general rule that information learnt by a trustee during the course of his duties is property of the trust and cannot be used by him ... The real rule is, in my view, that knowledge learnt by a trustee in the course of his duties as such is not in the least property of the trust and in general

may be used by him for his own benefit or for the benefit of other trusts unless it is confidential information which is given to him (1) in circumstances which, regardless of his position as a trustee, would make it a breach of confidence for him to communicate to anyone for it has been given to him expressly or impliedly as confidential, or (2) in a fiduciary capacity, and its use would place him in a position where his duty and his interest might possibly conflict. Let me give one or two simple examples. A, as trustee of two settlements X and Y holding shares in the same small company learns facts as trustee of X about the company which are encouraging. In the absence of special circumstances (such as, for example, that X wants to buy more shares) I can see nothing whatever which would make it improper for him to tell his co-trustees of Y who feel inclined to sell that he has information that this would be a bad thing to do. Another example: A as trustee of X learns facts that make him and his co-trustees want to sell. Clearly he could not communicate this knowledge to his co-trustees of Y until at all events the holdings of X have been sold for there would be a plain conflict, reflected in the prices that might or might possibly be obtained ...'

Later he gave another example:

'Blackacre is trust property and next to it is Whiteacre; but there is no question of the trustees being interested in a possible purchase of Whiteacre as being convenient to be held with Blackacre. Is a trustee to be precluded from purchasing Whiteacre for himself because he may have learnt something about Whiteacre while acting as trustee of Blackacre? I can understand the owner of Whiteacre being annoyed but surely not the owners of Blackacre, they have no interest in Whiteacre and their trustees no duty to perform in respect thereof ...'

Other cases

If a trustee receives any profits from his trust he must account for them. The variety of ways in which the profits might come to him are almost without limit. In *Barrett* v *Hartley* (1866) LR 2 Eq 789 a trustee was held liable to account for profits made in selling wines and spirits to a public house belonging to the trust, even though these were supplied from his own wine merchant's business at normal rates. In *Williams* v *Barton* [1927] 2 Ch 9 a trustee was held liable to account for a commission he received as employee of a firm of stockbrokers through introducing the trust to the firm for the purpose of valuing its securities. In *Sugden* v *Crossland* (1856) 3 Sm & G 192 a payment of £75 to a trustee on his retirement had to be accounted for. In all of these cases there was a conflict or possible conflict of interest and duty.

13.5 Purchase of trust property

A trustee cannot as a general rule purchase trust property for himself. This is sometimes called 'the self-dealing rule' and according to Megarry V-C in *Tito* v *Waddell (No 2)* [1977] Ch 106 the rule is a disability on a trustee rather than a duty. The effect of a purchase of trust property by a trustee is that the transaction is voidable at the instance of any interested beneficiary no matter how fair, open and honest it may have been. As Lord Eldon LC said in *Ex parte James* (1803) 8 Ves 337:

> 'This doctrine as to purchases by trustees, assignees, and persons having a confidential character, stands much more upon general principle than upon the circumstances of any individual case. It rests upon this; that the purchase is not permitted in any case, however honest the circumstances; the general interests of justice requiring it to be destroyed in every instance.'

The rationale behind 'the self-dealing rule' is that if the trustee were permitted to purchase trust property he would be both vendor and purchaser. As vendor he should obtain the highest price for his beneficiaries; as purchaser he would naturally want to give the lowest price. Apart from this the trustee would be in a position to fix the terms of sale, the time of sale, reserve prices and appoint agents to sell; in all of these there is a danger that he might let his interests and duties conflict. The rule is absolute. It covers both cases where the trustee has taken advantage and where he has not, because as Lord Eldon LC said in *Ex parte Lacey* (1802) 6 Ves 625:

> 'It is founded upon this; though you may see in a particular case, that he has not made advantage, it is utterly impossible to examine upon satisfactory evidence in the power of the Court, by which I mean the power of the parties, in ninety-nine cases out of a hundred, whether he has made advantage, or not. Suppose a trustee buys an estate; and by the knowledge acquired in that character discovers a valuable coal-mine under it; and locking that up in his own breast enters into a contract with the cestui que trust: if he chooses to deny it how can the Court try that against that denial ...'

The rule is based on the difficulty in most cases of proving that the trustee had taken advantage of his position in purchasing trust property.

The rule extends beyond mere purchases of trust property by the trustee himself, and any transaction which has as its object evasion of the letter of the rule but not its spirit will be set aside. Purchase by the trustee in the name of a nominee or spouse or children will be set aside: see *Re Sherman* [1954] Ch 653. Purchase by a company in which the trustee has a substantial shareholding will be set aside: see *Re Thompson* [1985] 2 All ER 720. But, if the trustee has a small shareholding in the purchasing company the court will only set the transaction aside if the trustee fails to show it was fair and honest: see *Farrar* v *Farrars Ltd* (1888) 40 Ch D 395.

There are a number of instances in which the self-dealing rules will not apply. The most obvious is when the trust instrument permits the trustee to purchase (see later). Further, if the trustee contracts to purchase trust property before becoming a trustee but only completes the transaction afterwards, it is inapplicable because there was no conflict of interest and duty at the moment the contract was formed: see *Re Mulholland's WT* [1949] 1 All ER 460. If the trustee had retired from the trust a long time before the purchase it will not normally be set aside but this does not apply to recently retired trustees: see *Wright* v *Morgan* [1926] AC 788. It seems the rule will not apply to a trustee who has disclaimed his trust or has no active duties to perform: see *Clark* v *Clark* (1884) 9 App Cas 733. See also Settled Land Act 1925, s68 which enables a tenant for life of settled land to purchase the property.

It appears from the Court of Appeal decision in *Holder* v *Holder* [1968] Ch 353 that the self-dealing rule will not be applied if the alleged trustee can satisfy the court that it is not applicable on the facts. In *Holder* v *Holder* a testator left his residuary estate to be divided between his wife and children and appointed one of his sons as an executor. The residuary estate comprised two farms of which the executor son was tenant and these were to be sold in the course of administration of the estate. The executor son ineffectively renounced his executorship and afterwards purchased the farms for himself. Seven years later another beneficiary sought to have the purchase set aside. On the facts the court refused to set aside the purchase for the following reasons:

1. The son never really assumed the duties of executor; he signed a few cheques for trivial sums and endorsed insurance policies but he never interfered in the administration of the estate before he renounced.
2. He took no part in instructing the valuer who fixed the reserves or in the preparations for the auction.
3. Everybody in the family knew of the renunciation and the reason for it, namely, that he wished to be a purchaser.
4. He made no secret of the fact that he intended to buy the farms.
5. He acquired no special knowledge of the farms as executor; he had managed them as tenant and what he knew of them he knew as tenant.
6. In any event, the beneficiary claiming to set aside the transaction had acquiesced in the purchase by the son.

The special circumstances of this case illustrate the discretionary nature of equitable rules and disabilities. In giving judgment Danckwerts LJ pointed out that the court could sanction a purchase of trust property by a trustee and that the matter must be viewed as involving a rule of practice. Harman LJ also pointed out that even if they were wrong on the self-dealing issue, the beneficiary who was seeking to set aside the transaction was barred by acquiescence.

The effect of the self-dealing rule is that the beneficiaries are entitled to have the property purchased returned to the trust. If the trustee has transferred it on to a third party they can recover it from him unless he is a bona fide purchaser for value without notice: see *Cookson* v *Lee* (1853) LJ Ch 473. The price paid will have to be returned to the trustee or third party. In some cases the trustee may have resold at a considerable profit and the beneficiaries may opt to adopt this sale and get the trustee to account for the profit: see *Barker* v *Carter* (1835) 1 Y & Coll Ex 250.

As noted, trusts often expressly give the trustees the right to purchase. This is commonly linked to the consent or conditions of a third party. In addition the court may give a trustee permission to purchase trust property on certain terms but this will normally be given only if there are no objections by beneficiaries. In most cases permission may be given to the trustee to bid at auction for the trust property upon terms and conditions laid down by the court as to reserve price or time of sale: see *Farmer* v *Dean* (1863) 32 Beav 327.

13.6 Purchase of beneficial interests

In *Tito* v *Waddell (No 2)* [1977] Ch 106 Megarry V-C stated this 'the fair-dealing rule' in the following terms:

'The fair-dealing rule is that if a trustee purchases the beneficial interest of any of his beneficiaries, the transaction is not voidable ex debito justitiae, but can be set aside by the beneficiary unless the trustee can show that he has taken no advantage of his position and has made full disclosure to the beneficiary, and that the transaction is fair and honest.'

As this statement indicates, the trustee may purchase beneficial interests under his trust but runs the risk that a beneficiary may challenge the purchase afterwards in which case the trustee bears the onus of showing he took no advantage of his position, disclosed all relevant information to the beneficiary and that the transaction was fair and honest. The danger here is that the trustee may be guilty of undue influence.

The majority of cases in this area are concerned with examining facts to see if the trustee has abused his position. In *Dougan* v *MacPherson* [1902] AC 197 the House of Lords set aside the purchase of a beneficial interest by a trustee-beneficiary from his brother, another beneficiary. The evidence showed that the trustee had concealed information as to the value of the trust property and had a valuation at the time of purchase showing the beneficial interest to be worth much more than he paid: see also *Coles* v *Trecothick* (1804) 9 Ves 234.

In *Re Thompson's Settlement* [1988] Ch 99, Vinelott J considered the situation where trustees were granting leases of trust property to companies and partnerships in which they were directors and beneficiaries. On its facts he held that the leases were granted in breach of the fair dealing rule, although they had been at a commercial rent. Accordingly the leases were voidable.

13.7 Indemnity

Section 30(2) TA 1925 provides:

'A trustee may reimburse himself or pay or discharge out of the trust premises all expenses incurred in or about the execution of the trusts or powers.'

This provision gives a trustee the right to be indemnified in respect of such out of pocket expenses as are properly incurred by him in the administration of the trust. If a trustee paid the costs of renewing a lease for the benefit of the trust out of his own pocket because of cash flow difficulties with the trust fund, he will be entitled to recover these expenses from the trust: see *Dowse* v *Gorton* [1891] AC 190. A trustee's right to be indemnified under s30(2) is not in breach of his fiduciary duties unless the right is abused.

Where a trustee is entitled to an indemnity, reimbursement will normally come out of the capital of the trust, so far as the beneficiaries are concerned. The trustee has a right to a first charge on all the trust property, both capital and income, for his expenses. These points were considered in *Stott* v *Milne* (1884) 25 Ch D 710 where the trustees of a freehold estate of which the plaintiff was the tenant for life brought an action on counsel's advice, to restrain two persons from interfering with the trust property. The trustees were out of pocket as a result of the action and sought to recover their costs from the annual rents of the property. The plaintiff insisted on receiving the full rents without any deductions. It was held that the trustees had a first charge on all the trust property, both capital and income, for their expenses and could therefore retain them out of the income until provision could be made for raising them out of capital. As between the beneficiaries themselves, however, the costs should be borne out of the capital so that the plaintiff had a claim on the capital to the extent that his income had been reduced.

The trustee's first charge or lien is in priority to the claims of both the beneficiaries and third parties and it is not affected by the assignment of beneficial interests: see *Re Knapman* (1881) 18 Ch D 300. The trustees can apply to the court at any time to enforce the charge; they are not bound to delay this until the trust property is sold off. If the court considers that early enforcement of the charge would destroy the trusts it can delay this and in such circumstances the trustees are entitled to the title deeds of the property: see *Darke* v *Williamson* (1858) 25 Beav 662. A trustee who has committed a breach of trust is only entitled to enforce his right to an indemnity after he has made good the breach of trust: see *Re Knott* (1887) 56 LJ Ch 318.

Any expense properly incurred by the trustee is one in respect of which he is entitled to be indemnified. Some of the more important examples are as follows:

1. Cost of renewing leases: see *Ex parte Grace* (1799) 1 Bos & P 376.
2. Calls paid on trust shares: see *Hardoon* v *Belilos* [1901] AC 118.
3. Liabilities incurred in continuing a trust business where authorised to do so: see *Re Evans* (1887) 34 Ch D 579.
4. Damages and costs awarded against the trustees to a third party who brought an action against the trustees as owners of the trust property. For example, in *Re Raybould* [1900] 1 Ch 199 an executor had authority to continue operating a colliery which belonged to the estate of the testator. As a result of mining operations the surface of the land subsided, thereby damaging the property of adjoining landowners who sued in tort for damages and succeeded. The executor sought and obtained an indemnity for the damages and costs awarded against him, as they had arisen from the reasonable management of the colliery.
5. Payment of statute-barred debts: see *Budgett* v *Budgett* [1895] 1 Ch 202.

A trustee can claim an indemnity under s30(2) for the costs of litigation where the court has given permission to sue or to defend, or where the action was in any case properly brought or defended: see *Walters* v *Woodbridge* (1878) 7 Ch D 504. Normally, a trustee should seek directions from the court before he brings the action and will be entitled to receive his costs whether he wins or loses: see *Re Beddoe*

[1893] 1 Ch 547. If directions are not sought from the court he may not receive his costs if he loses, especially if the court considers that the litigation was speculative or that settlement out of court should have been made by the trustees. In *Re England's ST* [1918] 1 Ch 24 an indemnity for costs was refused to trustees who sued tenants of trust property for £193 based on a report including items for which the tenants were not liable. The tenants paid £110 into court. This the trustees refused to accept and obtained only £90 on judgment, with costs of £600 against them. The fact that the trustee is defending charges made against him personally will not deprive him of his right to an indemnity for legal costs. In *Re Spurling's Will Trusts* [1966] 1 All ER 745 a trustee received an indemnity where he successfully defended claims that he had acted in breach of trust. Of course, if allegations of misconduct made against the trustee were well founded he would not be entitled to an indemnity: see *Walters* v *Woodbridge*. Note *Holdings and Management Ltd* v *Property Holdings and Investment Trust plc* [1989] 1 WLR 1313 where the plaintiff company, as maintenance trustee in respect of a block of flats, was held not to be entitled under s30(2) to reimbursement of legal costs, when it had put forward a scheme for improvement which was opposed by the tenants and when it had applied to the court for directions as to whether the scheme was within its powers. In the course of the hearing a compromise was reached favourable to the tenants. This was not in substance 'a conventional application by a trustee for directions'.

There are two cases where a beneficiary will be personally liable to indemnify trustees for costs they have incurred, and they are a departure from the general rule that the trustee is only entitled to an indemnity from the trust property:

1. Where trust is for a single beneficiary who is of full age and absolutely entitled: see *Hardoon* v *Belilos* [1901] AC 118. Some authorities also believe the principle may apply where there is more than one beneficiary, following *Matthews* v *Ruggles-Brise* [1911] 1 Ch 194.
2. Where the settlor is the beneficiary under the trust so that the trusteeship is nominal: see *Hardoon* v *Belilos* [1901] AC 118.

In *Hardoon* v *Belilos* a stockbroker bought shares in a bank and registered them in the name of Hardoon thus making him a trustee of them. The shares were resold to Belilos who left them in Hardoon's name. The bank went into liquidation and a claim of £402 was made on Hardoon for calls on the shares, who sought and obtained an indemnity from Belilos. In giving judgment Lord Lindley said:

'... where the only cestui que trust is a person sui juris, the right of the trustee to indemnity by him against liabilities incurred by the trustee by his retention of the trust property has never been limited to the trust property; it extends further, and imposes upon the cestui que trust a personal obligation enforceable in equity to indemnify his trustee. This is no new principle but as old as trusts themselves.'

14

Investment of Trust Funds

14.1 Introduction

14.2 Express powers of investment

14.3 The Trustee Investments Act 1961

14.4 Investment advice

14.5 Investment in mortgages

14.6 Reform of the investment powers of trustees

14.7 Investment under express powers

14.8 Land

14.9 Retaining investments which cease to be authorised

14.10 Altering the power of investment

14.1 Introduction

The main purpose of creating trusts is that assets can be held by the trustees to provide an income for the beneficiaries and, in certain circumstances, a capital sum. It is essential that the trust funds should be properly invested so as to achieve these aims.

The trustees will, in the case of any well-drawn trust instrument, have express wide powers of investment. Insofar as these powers do not cover all possibilities relating to investment or do not exist at all, then the statutory provisions of the Trustee Investments Act 1961 will apply. (Note: when considering their powers of investment trustees have as their primary duty, subject to any express provisions in the trust to the contrary, to preserve the trust fund rather than overtly seek its advancement. If the trustees are unsure of the scope of their duty and/or powers they should seek legal advice: see *Nestlé* v *National Westminster Bank* [1993] 1 WLR 1260.) Indeed the overriding duty of the trustees in determining how to invest the trust fund pursuant to their statutory powers, but subject to any express provisions to the contrary (both of which are dealt with subsequently in this chapter) is that of acting for the overall benefit for the beneficiaries regardless of their personal social or

218

political views. This was confirmed by Megarry V-C, in *Cowan* v *Scargill* [1984] 2 All ER 750, in which the judge ruled that the coal miners' union policy of investing in areas with the primary purpose of advancing the coal mining industry was contrary to the trustees' duty to the beneficiaries insofar as those investments were made regardless of any benefit to the beneficiaries.

The provisions of the Trustee Investments Act 1961 are rather narrow in the types of investment permitted, and frequently, in order to extend or supersede its provisions, trustees are given wide powers to invest the trust funds as if they were the absolute owners. The 1961 Act is now regarded as out of date and proposals have been made for reform. These are considered in section 14.10.

14.2 Express powers of investment

Where there is an express power of investment contained in the trust instrument it is normally construed according to the ordinary and natural meaning of the words used; the court will not impose a restrictive interpretation. It is the duty of trustees seeking to argue that a particular investment falls within the clause to prove that it actually does so. In *Re Harari's Settlement Trusts* [1949] 1 All ER 430 a settlement gave the trustees power to invest 'in or upon such investments as to them may seem fit'. The question arose whether this power gave them the right to invest outside the usual range of trustee investments. It was held that it did. Jenkins J said:

> 'It seems to me that I am left free of construe this settlement according to what I consider to be the natural and proper meaning of the words used in their context, and so construing the words ... I see no justification for implying any restriction. I think the trustees have power ... to invest in any investments which, ... they "honestly think are desirable investments".'

The word 'invest' is frequently used in trust instruments and in several cases the question has arisen of whether an investment clause so worded permits the purchase of assets which yield capital gains rather than income. In *Re Wragg* [1919] 2 Ch 58 a testator left his estate on trust for his children in equal shares. The trustees were given power to 'invest' in any stocks, funds, shares and securities or other investments as they in their absolute discretion thought fit. They were to have the same power of investing as if they were absolutely and beneficially entitled to the property. The trustees asked the court if they had the power to 'invest' in real property. According to P O Lawrence J the word 'invest' had as one of its meanings 'to apply money in the purchase of some property from which interest or profit is expected'. The power given to the trustees permitted them to purchase real estate if it was bought as an investment. This case should be contrasted with *Re Power's Will Trusts* [1947] Ch 572 where the trust instrument contained an investment clause which required 'all money to be invested by the trustee in any manner which he may in his absolute discretion think fit in all respects as if he were the sole beneficial owner of such monies including the purchase of freehold properties in

England and Wales'. The trustee asked the court if this permitted him to purchase a house with vacant possession for the rent free occupation of the beneficiaries. Jenkins J held that the clause did not permit this because the use of the word 'investment' connoted a yield of income. It did not authorise the purchase of a house for rent free occupation as that would not produce income.

It would appear that if the trustees are to have power to allow a beneficiary to occupy a property rent-free, then such a power must be expressly included in the trust instrument, otherwise the power of investment will have to be altered (see Chapter 10, section 10.9). Powers to invest in land would appear to be limited to buying property for purposes such as renting it or working it to produce income, as with agricultural land. Question: would it have been in order if the trustees in *Re Power* had proposed to buy the property for the beneficiary to occupy and operate as a hotel?

Sometimes a trust instrument will give the trustees power to lend money. Where this power exists, it will only be considered as authorising an investment on personal security – there is no security beyond the obligation of the borrower to repay – if clear provisions exist: see *Khoo Tek Keong* v *Ching Joo Tuan Neoh* [1934] AC 529 PC.

Some investment clauses may give the trustees power to vary investments. It has been held that such a power is implied in any event: see *Re Pratt's Will Trusts* [1943] Ch 326. In any case the Trustee Investment Act includes such a power.

A power of investment 'with the consent of' some third party is valid: see *Re Wise* (1954) LT News 116. Normally such a power is considered as not having fiduciary obligations attached to it unless the context dictates otherwise.

14.3 The Trustee Investments Act 1961

Introduction

This Act applies to all trusts and wills which before and after the passing of the Act granted investment powers less than those conferred by the Act.

The Act confers powers of investment in cases where no such powers are contained in the trust instrument and it supplements investment powers where these are limited. For example, if the trust simply gave a power to invest in land, then the TIA 1961 would apply to the extent that it was desired that the trust funds should be otherwise invested.

It is possible to exclude the powers of the TIA 1961 completely from a trust by an express provision to that end: see s1(3) TIA 1961.

Division of the trust fund

The first schedule to the TIA 1961 sets out a list of investments which are authorised investments under it. Schedule 1 Part I contains a list of the safest investments of all and the trustees do not require advice in making these investments as there are unlikely to be fluctuations in capital value. Schedule 1 Part II contains a list of investments upon which the trustees must obtain advice. Both Part I and Part II investments are referred to as 'narrower range investments'. Schedule 1 Part III contains 'wider range investments' and on these the trustees must obtain advice: see s1(4) TIA 1961. As to what investments fall within each of the three parts, it is simply a matter of looking at the definition in force at the time of the investment.

The trustees have power to put any amount of the trust funds in narrower-range investments regardless of whether they fall within Schedule 1 Part I or Part II. However, if they wish to invest in wider range investments or to retain such investments they must divide the trust fund into two parts equal at the time of division and not in any other proportions: s2(1) TIA 1961. The fund's valuation is determined at the time of division by a qualified third party, for example an accountant. Once such a division has been made no property can be transferred from one part of the fund to another unless there is a compensating transfer in the other direction: see s2(1)(b) TIA 1961.

Property belonging to the narrower range must be invested in narrower range investments only. Any property within the narrower range part which is not so invested must be transferred either to the wider range, with a compensating transfer in the other direction, sold off or reinvested in narrower range investments: see s2(2) TIA 1961.

In contrast property belonging to the wider range can be invested in either wider range investments or any combination of wider range and narrower range investments.

EXAMPLE:

X sets up a trust for his children, without any powers of investment. The total value is £200,000 and includes:

1. £20,000 National Savings Certificates (narrower range, Part I).
2. £50,000 British Government Stock (narrower range, Part II).
3. £50,000 shares in ICI (wider range, Part III).
4. Various holdings in private companies worth £80,000 (unauthorised).

If the trustees wish to invest all in the narrower range then they must sell off the two latter assets and reinvest them in narrower range investments.

If the trustees wish to invest in wider range investments they must divide the fund into two equal parts of £100,000.

1. The Saving Certificates (£20,000) and Government Stock (£50,000) will fall within the narrower range.
2. The ICI shares (£50,000) will fall within the wider range.
3. The £80,000 proceeds of sale of shares in private companies will fall within both parts of the trust fund. The £30,000 worth of shares falling within the narrower

range must be sold off as soon as possible and invested in narrower range investments. The £50,000 worth of shares falling within the wider range must be sold also but these can be reinvested in either narrower range or wider range investments. There is no duty to invest all of the funds in the wider range in wider range investments; it may be in any combination of narrower and wider range investments or in wider range investments only.

Accruals of property to the trust fund after the division of the fund has taken place are to be apportioned between each part of the trust fund so that each part increases in value by the same amount: see s2(3)(b) TIA 1961. This does not apply to accruals to the trustee as owner or former owner of property comprised in either part of the fund, for example, a bonus issue of shares arising by virtue of shares held in the wider range: see 2(3)(a) TIA 1961.

Under s2(4) TIA 1961 where the trustee has to withdraw funds from the trust in the exercise of any power or duty, for example, under the power of advancement under s32 Trustee Act 1925, then he has a choice as to whether such a withdrawal should come from the narrower or the wider range. No compensating transfers are necessary in such a case but they may be advisable if the trustee is to comply with his duties of diversification under s6 TIA 1961.

The investments permitted by TIA 1961

These are set out in the first schedule to the Act, and the reader is referred to that schedule. The following matters should however be noted:

Narrower range Part I

This contains a limited range of investments and includes: Defence Bonds, National Savings Certificates, National Savings Income Bonds, National Savings Deposit Bonds and deposits in the National Savings Bank and National Savings Capital Bonds, added by the Trustee Investments (Additional Powers) Order 1988, SI 1988/No 2254.

There is no provision in this range or elsewhere in Schedule 1 for permitting investment in deposit accounts in ordinary high street banks such as Lloyd's Bank or the Midland Bank. Money can only be put in a deposit account in such banks under the provisions of s11 Trustee Act 1925 which states:

'Trustees may, pending the negotiation and preparation of any mortgage or charge, or during any other time while an investment is being sought for pay any trust money into a bank to a deposit or other account, and all interest, if any, payable in respect thereof shall be applied as income.'

Narrower range Part II

This is mainly a list of various types of securities in government, local authority and nationalised industries.

Two investments set out here of particular importance are those mentioned in Part II, paras 12 and 13. They are deposits in a building society (para 12), and mortgages of freehold property in England and Wales or Northern Ireland and of leasehold property in those countries of which the unexpired terms at the time of investment is not less than 60 years, and in loans on heritable security in Scotland (para 13). The former should be contrasted with Part III para 2 which makes shares in a building society a wider range investment. Mortgages are dealt with in detail below. Recently the Trustee Investments (Additional Powers) Order 1991 s1(1991) No 999 included fixed and variable interest securities issued in the UK in the EBRD (European Bank for Reconstruction and Development).

Wider range investments

The most important of these is 'any securities issued in the United Kingdom by a company incorporated in the United Kingdom, being securities registered in the United Kingdom and not being securities mentioned in Part II of this Schedule.'

The reference to Part II of the schedule refers to Part II para 6, which provides that debentures in a United Kingdom company are an authorised investment.

For debentures or shares to be authorised investments under Part II and Part III respectively they must satisfy five conditions:

1. They must be shares or debentures in a company incorporated in the United Kingdom.
2. The companies concerned must be quoted on the Stock Exchange (Part IV para 2(a)).
3. The shares or debentures must be fully paid up or be issued on terms that they are to be fully paid up within nine months from the date of issue (Part IV para 2(b)).
4. The company must have an issued and paid up capital of at least £1 million pounds (Part IV para 3(a)).
5. The company must have, in each of the preceding five years, paid a dividend on all its shares. (Part IV para 3(b)).

Special range investments

A trustee may be given express power by the trust instrument to retain or invest in certain securities which fall outside the scope of the TIA 1961, or to invest in certain shares falling within the wider range. Such securities are known as 'special range' investments: see Schedule 2 para 1. For example, a settlor may direct that the trustees may retain shares in his family company.

Where the trust fund includes special range property this must be carried to a separate part of the fund and dealt with outside the TIA 1961 provisions. The provisions of s2(1) apply in the normal way to property which is not included in the special range: Schedule 2 para 2.

If special range property is converted into other forms of property, then it must be transferred to the narrower or wider range part or apportioned between them, and compensating transfers made to ensure that the funds benefit equally. In short, the property becomes subject to TIA 1961 provisions if it does not remain in its special range form: see Schedule 2 para 3.

There are no provisions requiring the trustees to withdraw money from the narrower range and the wider range equally. They can withdraw funds from one or other of these exclusively to purchase special range investments if the trust gives such powers of purchase, for example where the settlor authorises the trustees to purchase and retain shares in a private company.

14.4 Investment advice

No investments can be made under TIA, other than under Schedule 1 Part I, without advice. Under s6(2) the trustee is required when making Schedule 1 Parts II and III and special range investments to 'obtain and consider proper advice on the question of whether the investment is satisfactory' having regard to:

1. The need for diversification of investments of the trust fund, in so far as is appropriate to the circumstances of the trust: see s6(1)(a).
2. The suitability to the trust of investments of the description proposed: see s6(1)(b).

Under s6(4) 'proper advice' for the purposes of s6(2) means 'the advice of a person who is reasonably believed by the trustee to be qualified by his ability in and practical experience of financial matters', such as a stockbroker or accountant.

The trustees are required to obtain advice not only when they are initially making investments for the trust but also from time to time as is appropriate under s6(3). If one of the trust investments was doing badly or had reached the height of its value the trustees ought to seek and consider advice as to whether it is appropriate to sell it off.

If one of the trustees is in a position to give investment advice to his fellow trustees then he can do this under s6(4), and the provisions of s6(2) and (3) are then irrelevant. These provisions also apply to an officer or servant of a trust corporation giving advice where the trust corporation is a trustee of the trust.

In all cases the advice given to trustees must either be in writing or subsequently confirmed in writing if given orally: see s6(5). Failure to do this means that the trustee shall not be treated as having obtained advice. Such failure, or a failure to get advice at all, leaves the trustees open to a personal action against them by the beneficiaries if things go wrong. See Chapter 20 in particular.

14.5 Investment in mortgages

Introduction

Under Schedule 1 para 13 trustees are empowered to invest in mortgages of freehold land or leasehold property of at least 60 years unexpired term at the time of investment.

One problem which appears without an answer in this area is whether mortgages must be legal first mortgages or whether second or equitable mortgages would be satisfactory. There is no guidance in the TIA 1961 on this matter. The pre-1926 law on this area was clear. In *Chapman* v *Browne* [1902] 1 Ch 785 the Court of Appeal held that a second mortgage was an improper investment for trustees as they would not get the protection of the legal estate. In *Swaffield* v *Nelson* (1876) WN 255 the Court of Appeal also stated that equitable mortgages were unauthorised and that this had always been assumed to be the case. It would therefore appear that the safest course for trustees is to invest in only legal first mortgages. The reasons behind the decision in *Chapman* v *Browne* on second mortgages may now be regarded as no longer relevant since a trustee can protect the priority of a second mortgage by registration under the Land Charges Act 1972.

Advice on mortgage investments

Under s8(1) Trustee Act 1925 three matters are laid down, which, if followed by a trustee in investing in mortgages, will protect him from breach of trust:

'a) that in making the loan the trustee was acting on a report as to the value of the property made by an able practical surveyor or valuer instructed and employed independently of any owner of the property AND
the amount of the loan does not exceed two-thirds of the value of the property as stated in the report AND
the loan was made under the advice of the surveyor or valuer expressed in the report.'

It is up to the trustee to choose a competent surveyor or valuer to give him the advice. He must ensure that the surveyor or valuer is employed independently of the owner of the property, and this includes the mortgagor: see *Shaw* v *Cates* [1909] 1 Ch 389. The loan must not exceed two-thirds of the value of the property as stated in the report. This does not mean that a trustee is always safe in investing two-thirds based on the surveyor's valuation; two-thirds is regarded as the maximum safe limit and in particular cases a lower limit may be appropriate. Regard must be had to what the surveyor has recommended as a suitable investment. This may well be less than two-thirds. In *Shaw* v *Cates* trustees lent £4,400 on the security of two partially built houses, this being two-thirds of their value as contained in the schedule to a surveyor's report. The report was one which valued these two houses and two others already built at £9,180 and recommended all four as suitable investments for a mortgage of two-thirds of £9,180. The trustees did not consult the valuer further on their investment. It transpired that the valuer was the rent-collector for the mortgagor. The houses proved to be inadequate securities and the beneficiaries sued the trustees for the losses suffered by the trust. Parker J held the trustees liable because the surveyor was not an independent surveyor as required by the Act, and the advance made was not in any event the advance advised by the surveyor because he was dealing with the mortgage of all four properties, not just two. In considering the case Parker J made the following remarks on s8(1)(b) and (c):

'I dissent entirely from the position ... that once they have ascertained the value of the property they are, whatever its nature and whatever method of valuation they have adopted, at least prima facie justified in advising an advance of two-thirds of its value. Such a position in my opinion defeats the object of the section in making what the legislature has recognised as the standard minimum of protection which a prudent man will require, into a standard of the normal risk which, whatever the nature of the property, a prudent man will be prepared to run ... It is as true now as it was before the Act that the maximum sum which a prudent man can be advised to lend upon a mortgage depends on the nature of the property and all the circumstances of the case. If the property is liable to deteriorate or is specially subject to fluctuations in value, or depends for its value on circumstances, the continual existence of which is precarious, a prudent man will ... require a larger margin for his protection ...

To advise an advance of two thirds of the value of four properties is not the same thing as advising an advance of two thirds of the value of any one or more of the properties apart from the others or other. This is more especially the case where one of the properties is not at the date of the report an income bearing property. ... In the present case the income of three of the four properties originally proposed to be mortgaged was sufficient to provide, with a considerable margin, for the payment of interest on the amount proposed to be advanced, although the other property was unlet.'

There is no duty imposed upon the trustee to obtain a surveyor's valuation which satisfies s8. However, if he fails to do so he is unlikely to obtain any relief under s61 TA 1925 which protects a trustee from the consequences of a breach of trust if he acted honestly and reasonably and ought fairly to be excused. In *Re Stuart* [1897] 2 Ch 583 a valuation requested by a trustee stated the amount for which the property was a good security, but did not state the value of the property or its suitability as an investment. The trustee advanced more than two-thirds of the stated valuation and the valuer was instructed by the solicitor acting for the mortgagor. The trustee admitted liability for the loss but argued that he should be relieved under what is now s61 TA 1925. Stirling J refused this because the valuations did not satisfy (what is now s8 TA 1925). He said:

'It was ... rightly contended that this was not necessarily a fatal obstacle to the application of the section. Still, I think those requirements cannot be left out of consideration. The legislature ... dealt with the duties of trustees in regard to investments and laid down certain rules for their guidance which in some respects relaxed those previously existing and are in themselves reasonable, and they appear to me to constitute a standard by which reasonable conduct is to be judged.'

There is also some limited relief for trustees who fail to satisfy s8 in the provisions of s9 TA 1925. These provisions only apply 'when a trustee shall have improperly advanced trust money on a mortgage security which would at the time of the investment, have been a proper investment in all respects for a less sum than was actually advanced thereon'. This provision was considered by Kekewich J in *Re Walker* (1890), who said of it:

> 'That I understood to mean that the impropriety consists in the amount invested. If the investment is otherwise improper – as, for instance, if a man invests in a mortgage of trade buildings when he is only entitled to invest in mortgage of agricultural land – he cannot claim the benefit of the section, and say "I might take the value of two-thirds of the advance, although not the whole." He must establish the propriety of the investment independently of the value, and then he has the benefit of the section to save him from any loss greater than that which would have been incurred by advancing too large a sum on what otherwise would be a proper security.'

For example, the trustees were able to claim the benefit of s9 in *Shaw* v *Cates* because the investment in itself was a proper or authorised investment leaving aside any matters of valuation. In such cases the trustee is only liable for the excess over what would otherwise have been a proper advance, with the security being regarded as an authorised investment for the smaller sum.

However, the above aside, it is invariably best for the trustees to comply fully with the provisions of s8. By so acting they generally provide themselves with a full defence against any future actions for breach by improper investments. See in particular *Re Chapman* [1896] 2 Ch 763 which involved a property which decreased in value through no fault of the trustees.

EXAMPLE:
X, a trustee, advances £10,000 by mortgage on a property, which is otherwise an authorised security under the trust, and valued at £12,000. The property falls in value by £6,000 and a proper advance on it at the time of investment would have been £8,000 under s8(1)(b). X is only liable for £2,000, the difference between £8,000 and £10,000, under s9, and not the difference between its present value of £6,000 and the sum of £10,000 advanced.

A mortgage can be made without advice or without any report as to the value of the land under s10(2) TA 1925. This provides that trustees, a tenant for life, or a statutory owner when selling freehold land or leasehold property with at least a 500 year term to run, can, where the proceeds are liable to be invested, contract that the payment of any part, not exceeding two-thirds of the purchase money, shall be secured by a legal mortgage, or a mortgage by demise, or a mortgage by sub-demise for a term of at least 500 years.

14.6 Reform of the investment powers of trustees

The Trustee Investments Act has, for a substantial period, been viewed as inappropriate to modern economic and financial conditions. As early as 1982, the

Law Reform Committee recommended extensive changes in trustee powers of investment in its report *The Powers and Duties of Trustees* (1982) Cmnd 8733. Such reform commenced in 1996 and further reform is imminent. The Charity Trustee Investments Act 1961 Order 1995 (SI 1995/1092) relaxed the requirements of the Trustee Investments Act 1961 by enabling charitable trustees to invest up to 75 per cent of their funds in wider-range investments as defined in the Act. The Trustee Investments (Division of Trust Fund) Order 1996, which came into force on 11 May 1996, extended this relaxation to all trusts. On 7 April 1997 ss33–36 Pensions Act 1995 came into force. These sections extend the investment powers of trustees of pension funds which are trust schemes. Trustees of such trusts are thereby given the same power to make investments, subject to the need for diversification and obtaining and considering proper advice, as if they were absolutely entitled to the assets of the fund.

In May 1996 the Treasury issued a Consultation Document, *Investment Powers of Trustees*, which proposes repeal of the Trustee Investment Act by means of an order under the Deregulation and Contracting Out Act 1994. The consultation process terminated on 31 August 1996 and repeal of the Act is likely to occur in the near future. General limitations on investment powers, discussed in section 14.7, will continue to provide protection for beneficiaries.

14.7 Investment under express powers

General principles

Generally, trustees when investing trust moneys must avoid investments which are of a speculative or hazardous character. The mere fact that they have wide powers of investment, for example an absolute discretion as if they were absolute and beneficial owners, does not mean they can make any investment they like. They must always consider whether the proposed investment is one which is prudent and correct for them as trustees to make. As Lord Watson said in *Learoyd* v *Whiteley* (1887) 12 App Cas 727:

> 'As a general rule the law requires of a trustee no higher degree of diligence in the execution of his office than a man of ordinary prudence would exercise in the management of his own private affairs. Yet he is not allowed the same discretion in investing the moneys of the trust as if he were a person sui juris dealing with his own estate. Businessmen of ordinary prudence may, and frequently do, select investments which are more or less of a speculative character; but it is the duty of a trustee to confine himself to the class of investments which are permitted by the trust, and likewise to avoid all investments of that class which are attended with hazard. So, so long as he acts with honest observance of these limitations, the general rule already stated will apply.'

In *Learoyd* v *Whiteley* trustees invested £3,000, on the security of a mortgage, in a brickfield, following competent advice given by a firm of valuers. The valuer's report was based on the assumption that the brickfield remained a going concern but went on to emphasise that it was nearly worked out. The trustees acted on the report, ignoring this caveat; the brickfield eventually failed and the proceeds of sale did not cover the mortgage debt. The trustees were sued for the loss and held liable as they had not acted with ordinary prudence but had made a hazardous investment.

This does not mean that the trustee is expected to act as an insurer of the trust fund. In *Re Godfrey* (1883) 22 Ch D 727 Bacon V-C said:

'No doubt it is the duty of a trustee, in administering the trusts of a will, to deal with property entrusted into his care exactly as any prudent man would deal with his own property. But the words in which the rule is expressed must not be strained beyond their meaning. Prudent businessmen in their dealings incur risk. That may and must happen in almost all human affairs.'

The distinction is between a prudent degree of risk on the one hand, and hazard on the other.

Trustees will not be held liable for mere errors of judgment either in making investments or retaining them. It is recognised, with the benefit of hindsight, that a trustee may have made the wrong decision, but this is not in itself a breach of trust; it has to be shown that he acted imprudently or in wilful default. In *Re Chapman* (1896) (above) trustees held several mortgages of agricultural land and, because of an agricultural depression which caused the value of the properties to decline, they decided to hold their mortgages and wait for a more favourable time for realisation. The beneficiaries sued for breach of trust but this was rejected. As Lindley LJ said:

'There is no rule of law which compels the Court to hold that an honest trustee is liable to make good loss sustained by retaining an authorised security in a falling market, if he did so honestly and prudently in the belief that it was the best course to take in the interest of all parties. Trustees acting honestly, with ordinary prudence and within the limits of their trust, are not liable for mere errors of judgment. Any loss sustained by the trust estate under such circumstances falls upon and must be borne by the owners of the property – ie the cestuis que trust – and cannot be thrown by them on their trustees, who have done no wrong, though the result may prove that they possibly might have done better.'

A higher duty of care is expected from professional trustees such as trust corporations which specialise in the business of trust management. In *Bartlett* v *Barclays Bank Trust Co* [1980] Ch 515 Brightman J considered that because they hold themselves out as having expertise which it would be unrealistic to expect the ordinary prudent man to have, they must be judged by the standard of skill and expertise they profess to have.

Controlling interests in a company

Where trustees have a controlling interest in a company they are expected to act in relation to it in the same manner as an ordinary prudent man of business, and the ordinary prudent man of business will act in such a manner as is necessary to safeguard his investment by:

1. Taking appropriate action by making enquiries of, or consulting the directors, or in the last resort, convening a general meeting to replace one or more of the directors, when facts come to his knowledge that the company's affairs are not being conducted as they should be.
2. Ensuring that he has sufficient information to enable him to make a responsible decision from time to time, either to let matters proceed as they are proceeding, or to intervene if he is dissatisfied.

In *Bartlett* v *Barclays Bank Trust Co* [1980] Ch 515 the bank held 99.8 per cent of the shares in a private company, as trustee under the terms of a family trust. The board of directors of the company did not, for various reasons, include a representative or nominee of the bank. The bank contented itself with information on the company's affairs received by its representative at annual general meetings. The board made hazardous investments in the form of property speculation and it was held that the bank was liable for the losses caused to the trust, as it had failed to take adequate steps to protect the interests of the trust.

In *Re Lucking's Will Trusts* (1968) Cross J considered various methods by which a trustee who has a controlling interest could place himself in a position in which to make informed decisions as to how to protect his asset. These were all based on the ultimate right of the trustee to act by virtue of his majority.

1. By running the business himself as managing director.
2. By becoming a non-executive director and having the business managed by someone else.
3. By appointing a nominee to the board to report to him from time to time on the company's affairs.
4. By the receipt of copies of the agenda and minutes of board meetings, the receipt of monthly management accounts in the case of a trading concern, or quarterly reports.

14.8 Land

The Trusts of Land and Appointment of Trustees Act 1996 prevents, subject to two exceptions, the creation of further settlements under the Settled Land Act 1925 as from 1 January 1997. Pre-existing settlements continue to be governed by the Settled Land Act 1925 and references to this Act herein will now only be relevant to such settlements. Under s73 Settled Land Act extensive powers of investment are set out which apply to settled land settlements.

Under s73(1)(xi) SLA 1925, it is provided that the purchase of freehold land or leasehold property of 60 years unexpired term at the time of purchase is an authorised investment for the purposes of the SLA.

From 1 January 1997 any trust of property which consists of or includes land now becomes a trust of land. The Trusts of Land and Appointment of Trustees Act

1996 specifically provides in s6(3) for trustees of land to purchase land by way of investment, for occupation by any beneficiary, or for any other reason, provided that they pay due regard to the rights of the beneficiaries.

14.9 Retaining investments which cease to be authorised

Under s4 TA 1925 it is provided that:

> 'A trustee shall not be liable for breach of trust by reason only of his continuing to hold an investment which has ceased to be an investment authorised by the trust or by the general law.'

This provision must now be read in the light of the TIA provisions, particularly s6(3), which requires a trustee to determine at what intervals he should take advice on the question of retaining investments. It would appear that a trustee must be considered liable, if he retains an unauthorised investment without observing the requirements of s6(3). The provisions of s4 would only appear to be appropriate where the sole reason for the breach is the fact that the investment became unauthorised: see *Re Chapman*.

14.10 Altering the power of investment

The court has no inherent jurisdiction to alter or enlarge express powers of investment contained in a trust instrument except in cases of emergency. In *Re Tollemache* [1903] 1 Ch 955 the court refused to alter investment powers under its inherent jurisdiction merely because this would be in the interests of the beneficiaries; there was no emergency. Emergencies for these purposes might only include cases where the trustees needed to sell investments urgently, for example to carry out urgent repairs to trust buildings, despite a direction to retain them.

Alteration of the powers of investment can only be made under s57 Trustee Act 1925 or the Variation of Trusts Act 1958. The distinction between these provisions is that s57 only permits the court to make the alteration if it is 'expedient' while the Variation of Trusts Act 1958 only gives the court power to approve a variation on behalf of those who are unable to do so themselves. The consent of all other beneficiaries must be obtained to the variation. It would seem that the choice between these provisions in making an application for variation of investment powers will depend on the circumstances of each case. See in this context *Anker-Petersen* v *Anker-Petersen and Others* [1991] LSG 1 May at p32, and see Chapter 19, section 19.3.

In *Anker-Petersen* v *Anker-Petersen and Others*, on an application for an extension of trustees' investment powers, to invest in any kind of assets as if they were beneficial owners and to delegate to investment managers, Judge Paul Baker QC, in allowing the application, pointed out that in a case like this, where beneficial interests were unaffected, an application under s57 Trustee Act 1925 was to be preferred to an application under s1 of the Variation of Trusts Act 1958. In this case, there was no opposition to the proposed changes. The application had been made under s57 Trustee Act 1925 and, alternatively, under s1 of the Variation of Trusts Act 1958.

After the passing of the Trustee Investments Act 1961 a series of decisions headed by *Re Kolb's Will Trusts* [1962] 3 All ER 811 held that the new powers of investment in the 1961 Act should be taken as sufficient for trustees and that an application for widening investment powers would only be entertained by the court if there were special circumstances. The effect of these decisions was to discourage such applications. It is now recognised that the provisions of the 1961 Act are out-of-date and the courts are prepared to grant investment powers wider than those in the 1961 Act. In *Mason* v *Fairbrother* [1983] 2 All ER 1078 inflation was considered to be 'special circumstances' enabling the grant of wider powers of investment. In that case the Co-operative Society pension fund was granted wider powers; it had previously been confined to investing in the Co-operative Society and under the 1961 Act. Then, in *Trustees of the British Museum* v *Attorney-General* [1984] 1 WLR 418 Megarry V-C held that the line of decisions headed by *Re Kolb* should no longer be followed. Instead, the court should be ready to grant an extension of investment powers in suitable cases, judging each case on its merits and without being constrained by the 1961 Act. Note was taken of the recommendations of the Law Reform Committee (see Chapter 17, section 17.10) for the replacement of the 1961 Act. Megarry V-C suggested five guidelines to be considered in deciding what extended investment powers should be conferred:

1. The extent of provision for advice and control, because the wider the investment powers the more important these would become.
2. Where very wide investment powers are being considered it would be appropriate to divide the trust fund so that a fraction of it is in safe or relatively safe investments.
3. The combined effect of width, division, advice and control should be considered as they interact.
4. The size of the fund should be considered as greater risks may be justified with a larger fund.
5. The object of the trust should be considered so that if it requires greater capital resources greater risks may be justified.

In the *British Museum* case Megarry V-C sanctioned extended investment powers to the trustees of the British Museum so as to enable them to make higher risk investments with part of the trust fund in order to have sufficient capital resources to keep pace with the inflation of prices in museum pieces generally.

This decision was followed by Hoffmann J in *Steel* v *Wellcome Trustees Ltd* [1988] 1 WLR 167 in which paid trustees sought the court's approval for a draft scheme, already negotiated with the Attorney-General, who had no objections to it, to extend their powers of investment to acquisition of any property as if they were beneficial owners of the investment fund, except that they had, by the scheme, to observe certain guidelines and either to obtain advice from qualified external advisers or delegate investment powers to such advisers. In following the principle established in *Trustees of the British Museum* v *Attorney-General* that every application should be judged on its own merits, Hoffmann J found in the *Wellcome Trustees* case that, 'having regard ... to the size of [the] fund [involved], the eminence of the trustees, the provisions of the scheme for obtaining and acting on advice and the quality of advice available, as well as the special circumstances pertaining', it was not necessary to require that part of the fund should be invested in narrower range investments. Contrast the position in the *Trustees of the British Museum* case.

15

Conversion and Apportionment

15.1 Introduction

15.2 The duty to convert

15.3 The duty to apportion

15.4 The windfall principle

15.5 The rule in *Allhusen* v *Whittall*

15.6 Apportionment Act 1870

15.7 Proposals for reform

15.1 Introduction

As a preliminary to making authorised investments it is often necessary for the trustees to sell certain assets belonging to the trust which are in the form of unauthorised investments.

The questions which arise here are which assets are they bound to sell and when? – this is the duty to convert; and how should the income from unauthorised assets be dealt with pending sale? – this is the duty to apportion.

15.2 The duty to convert

Conflicting claims

Where property is left to persons in succession, for example to A for life, remainder to B, the life tenant (A) will be entitled to all the income as it arises, or the use of the trust property, and the remainderman (B) will take the capital on A's death. If the trust fund is not properly invested unfairness could result to either the life tenant or remainderman. If the fund were invested in high income investments this might well be at the expense of preserving the trust capital. On the other hand, if investments were low yielding they might benefit the remainderman by capital appreciation at the life tenant's expense. In such cases it is the duty of the trustee to

234

keep an even hand between these conflicting claims, not favouring the life tenant at the remainderman's expense and vice versa.

Where the trust property consists of authorised investments, then normally this problem will not arise if the trustees fulfil their duty to diversify the trust funds under s6(1)(a) TIA 1961.

The rule in Howe v Dartmouth

Under *Howe* v *Dartmouth* (1802) 7 Ves 137 there is a duty to convert:

Where by will, a bequest of residual personality is left to persons in succession, for example 'to A for life remainder to B absolutely' and there is no intention on the part of the testator that the property be enjoyed in specie, then the trustees must realise such parts of the trust estate as are:

1. Of a wasting or hazardous nature.
2. Of a reversionary nature.
3. Unauthorised investments under the law or the will.

The rule was summarised in *Hinves* v *Hinves* (1844) 3 Hare 609 where Wigram V-C said:

'... where personal estate is given in terms amounting to a general residuary bequest to be enjoyed by persons in succession, the interpretation the Court puts upon the bequest is that the persons indicated are to enjoy the same thing in succession; and in order to effectuate that intention, the Court as a general rule converts into permanent investments so much of the personalty as is of a wasting or perishable nature at the death of the testator and also reversionary interests. The rule did not originally ascribe to testators the intention to effect such conversions, except in so far as a testator may be supposed to intend that which the law will do, but the Court, finding the intention of the testator to be that the objects of his bounty shall take successive interests in one and the same thing, converts the property, as the only means of giving effect to that intention. But, if the will expresses an intention that the property as it existed at the death of the testator shall be enjoyed in specie, although the property be not in the technical sense specifically bequeathed, to such a case the rule does not apply.'

Howe v *Dartmouth* operates on the presumption that the testator intended a fair benefit to be received by both life tenant and remainderman, but he is not in a position to know what his assets will be at the moment of his death. If some assets are hazardous and retained in their present form then it would be impossible to keep the balance between them. For example, if the residue comprises the copyright of a book, this may now produce very high income but in, say, 10 years' time, when the life tenant dies, be virtually worthless.

Cases where the rule is inapplicable

The duty to convert does not arise under *Howe* v *Dartmouth* in the following cases:

1. Where the bequest in the will is not a residuary one but specific or general, for

example '£20,000 worth of my shares in X Co Ltd to my son for life remainder to his children'. If X Co Ltd shares are unauthorised, no duty to convert will arise under *Howe* v *Dartmouth*. In fact, according to *Re Van Straubenzee* [1901] 2 Ch 779 there is no duty to convert here at all. However, the trustees may fall foul of investment provisions in the will or under TIA 1961 should they retain the investment.

2. Property passing under the intestacy rules.

3. Where the gift is one of residuary realty. In such cases if the land is freehold or leasehold of at least 60 years unexpired term then it will be an authorised investment under s73(1)(xi) SLA 1925.

4. Where the property is settled by deed inter vivos. Such instruments must be observed strictly in accordance with their terms, for the settlor's intention is that the specific property be enjoyed successively: see *Re Van Straubenzee*.

5. Where there is express or implied exclusion of the rule such as:
   a) An express clause that the rule in *Howe* v *Dartmouth* shall not apply. This is nearly always the case with modern trusts.
   b) Where there is an intention that the life tenant enjoy the property in specie: see *Marshall* v *Bremner* (1854) 2 Sm & G 237.
   c) Where the will states that all beneficiaries shall enjoy the property in the form it exists at the testator's death: see *Re Gough* [1957] Ch 323.
   d) An express provision that no item in the estate be sold.
   e) A provision in the will conferring a discretion to sell assets if and when expedient, for example, a power to retain or sell or convert: see *Re Bates* [1907] 1 Ch 22.
   f) Where the trustee or some other person has a discretion as to what part of the estate should be converted: see *Re Bates* [1907] 1 Ch 22.
   g) Where the will directs that the property is only to be converted on the death of the life tenant: see *Alcock* v *Sloper* (1833) 2 My & K 699.

15.3 The duty to apportion

Introduction

Where there is a duty to convert the trustees must execute it as soon as possible. It will be most unlikely that they could do this immediately because the administration of the testator's estate will have to be carried out first.

The duty to apportion will arise where there is a duty to convert. This duty applies to ensure that the income from unauthorised investments is distributed fairly between capital and income – at least this was the aim of the rule, but it is very doubtful if it happens at present as the life tenant is only entitled to receive income at the rate of 4 per cent of the capital value of unauthorised investment. It is possible that a higher rate might now be applied in the light of the decision in

Bartlett v *Barclays Bank* [1980] Ch 515 on the matter of low interest rates formerly awarded in breach of trust cases.

Valuations for apportionment

Pending conversion there will be an equitable apportionment between the life tenant and the remaindermen of all the income actually received in respect of unauthorised property: see *Gibson* v *Bott* (1802) 7 Ves 89.

The life tenant will receive an income which represents the current yield on authorised investments and this was fixed at 4 per cent in *Re Baker* [1924] 2 Ch 271. In *Re Berry* [1962] Ch 97 the 4 per cent figure was applied but at present it must be regarded as wholly out of line with the current yield on authorised investments which is about 10 per cent. It may be advisable for trustees to ask the court for guidance on this matter as the decision in *Bartlett* v *Barclays Bank* [1980] Ch 515 suggests that the court is prepared to recognise that this rate is unrealistic in the present climate of interest rates.

The income received by the life tenant is based on the capital value of the unauthorised investments and a distinction must be made between cases where the trustees have a power to postpone conversion and those where they do not:

1. If the trustees have a power to postpone conversion then the unauthorised property will be valued at the date of death. In *Re Parry* [1947] Ch 23 a testator left his residuary personalty on trust for sale and conversion, with a power to postpone sale. The property was left to named persons in succession. Romer J held that as there was a power to postpone conversion it was difficult to think of a better date for valuing the property for the purposes of apportionment than the date of death. He said:

   '... if there is no duty on the executor to sell at once, or within a year, or at any other time I can see no reason for assuming a notional conversion at once, or within a year, or at any other time. The essential equity, however – the balance between the successive interests – remains equally compelling even where there is no immediate obligation to convert and property is retained for the benefit of the estate as a whole. It is accordingly rational, and indeed obvious, to substitute a valuation of the testator's assets in the place of a hypothetical sale; and, if so, it is difficult to think of a better date for the valuation than the day the testator died and the assets passed to his executors.'

2. If there is no power to postpone conversion the date for valuing the property for the purposes of apportionment will be one year from the testator's death. This is based on the common law presumption that an estate will be administered within one year of the testator's death. In *Re Fawcett* [1940] Ch 402 the testatrix bequeathed her residuary estate, which included a number of unauthorised investments, to trustees on trust for her nephews and nieces for life with remainder to their children. There was no power to postpone conversion. Farwell J held that the life tenant was entitled to receive 4 per cent interest per annum

based on the value of those investments at the first anniversary of the testatrix's death.

The income which the life tenant receives is taken out of the actual income arising from the unauthorised asset in so far as it can meet this. If it cannot, the balance is met out of the capital when it is sold. Any excess is added to the capital of the trust fund. In *Re Fawcett* (above) Farwell J said:

> 'In order to give effect to the rule it appears to me that in a case of this kind it is the duty of the trustees to have the unauthorised investments valued as at the end of the first year after the testatrix's death. During that year the executors are given time to deal with the estate as a whole. At the end of it comes the time when, in my judgment, any unauthorised investments which they still retain should be valued and the tenant for life becomes entitled to be paid 4 per cent on the valuation of the whole of the unauthorised investments. To that extent these tenants for life are entitled to receive income in each year and that income, 4 per cent on the capital value of the unauthorised investments, must be paid out of the actual income received from the unauthorised investments; that is to say, the trustees will receive the whole of the dividends which the unauthorised investments pay and there will be no apportionment. Those dividends will be applied in the first instance in paying, so far as they go, 4 per cent on the capital value of the unauthorised investments. If the income received on the unauthorised investments is more than sufficient to pay the 4 per cent, then the balance will be added to the capital and it will form part of the whole fund in the hands of the trustees. If, on the other hand, the income actually received from the unauthorised investments is not sufficient to pay 4 per cent in each year to the tenants for life, they will not be entitled to immediate recoupment out of the capital, but when the unauthorised investments are sold the trustees will then have in their hands a fund representing the proceeds of sale of the unauthorised investments ... out of those proceeds the tenants for life will be entitled to be recouped so as to provide them with the full 4 per cent during the whole period and they will be entitled to be refunded the deficit ...'

If the trustees postpone conversion improperly then the court will order an apportionment. In *Wentworth* v *Wentworth* [1900] AC 163 the trustees improperly postponed conversion beyond a date laid down by the testator, and apportionment was ordered from that date.

Calculation of apportionment

The following example illustrates the operation of apportionment.

T leaves copyrights (unauthorised investments) to A for life with remainder to B absolutely by a residuary bequest in his will. The copyrights are worth £1,200 on his death and only £1,000 one year from his death.

Royalties received:

Year	
1	£70
2	£32
3	£48

Where there is a power to postpone conversion, valuation is at the date of death. The tenant for life will receive 4% of £1,200 per year until conversion.

The income of the life tenant (A) will be 4% of £1,200 = £48

Year	Actual income	To life tenant
1	£70	£48 – surplus of £22 added to capital
2	£32	He receives all income, a £16 deficit
3	£48	£48 – no surplus

On the sale of the copyright the tenant for life will receive £16 from the capital to make up for the deficiency in Year 2.

Where there is no power to postpone conversion, valuation is one year from the date of death and so the life tenant will receive 4% of £1,000 = £40.

Year	Actual income	To life tenant
1	£70	£40 – surplus of £30 added to capital
2	£32	£32 – he receives all income, an £8 deficit
3	£48	£40 – £8 surplus added to capital

Again, on conversion, the life tenant will receive £8 from the proceeds of sale.

Reversionary interest

The essence of an interest in expectancy, for example an interest in reversion, is that it is non-income producing until the property falls into possession. As the life tenant gets older, the value of the reversionary interest increases until it finally falls into possession.

While the reversioner is alive he can console himself for the absence of income by the steady increase in the capital value of his interest in expectancy. But if the reversioner dies leaving his reversionary interest as part of his residuary estate on trust for persons in succession, then the reversionary interest would fall under the rule in *Howe* v *Dartmouth* and would have to be sold. It is recognised that early sale of a reversionary interest might often be unwise, especially if the life tenant is advanced in years. Accordingly, special provisions have been made to deal with such cases by the rule in *Re Earl of Chesterfield's Trusts* (1883) 24 Ch D 643.

Under *Re Earl of Chesterfield's Trusts* a reversionary interest which ought to be converted can be retained until it falls into possession and then it must be sold and part of the proceeds of sale paid to the life tenant as arrears of income. Only the balance is to be regarded as capital.

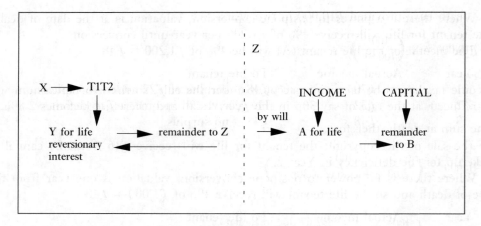

Assume Z dies on 1 January 1980 and that Y dies on 1 January 1982.

Explanation:

1. Z predeceases Y so he obtains no benefit from the reversionary interest conferred upon him by X when the trust was set up. Like any other remainderman he must wait until the life interest drops before he gets his interest.
2. Z's reversionary interest is a valuable item which will pass as part of his estate on his death. If it is left as part of his residuary estate to persons in succession then it will be subject to the rule in *Howe* v *Dartmouth* and must be sold and converted into authorised investments unless Z has excluded *Howe* v *Dartmouth*.
3. If the reversionary interest is not sold and converted then the person with a life interest in Z's residuary estate, A, would be deprived of income from an asset to which he is entitled.
4. As it may be inexpedient to sell the reversionary interest as soon as possible after Z's death, under *Re Earl of Chesterfield's Trusts* it may be retained until it falls into possession on Y's death.
5. The income which A has not received in the years between Z's death and Y's death will be calculated according to the following formula: what sum, if invested and interest paid at 4 per cent per annum compound interest, after deducting income tax at the basic rate, would have produced the sum actually received?

If the reversionary interest in this example was valued at £7,000 on X's death, but two years later, when it fell in, it was valued at £10,000 the apportionment of capital and income would be as follows:

To find the sum which must be invested at compound interest to provide a given amount in a given number of years the following formula is used:

$$\text{Sum} = \text{Amount} \; X \left(\frac{100}{100+R} \right)^{n} \quad \begin{array}{l} \text{[R is the rate of interest and} \\ \text{n is the number of years]} \end{array}$$

Applying the formula, the sum which at 4% per annum compound interest would at

X's death have provided £10,000 in two years:

$$= £10,000 = X \left(\frac{100}{100+4}\right)^2$$

Income tax has to be taken into account under the rule, so the 4% per annum will be reduced, at the rate of say 30p in the £, by 1.2% and, therefore becomes 2.8%.

The sum at death, therefore:

$$= 10,000 \text{ X } \left(\frac{100}{100 + 4 \text{ less tax at 30p}}\right)^2$$

$$= 10,000 \text{ X } \left(\frac{100}{102.8}\right) = \begin{array}{l} £9462.67 \text{ due to capital} \\ £537.33 \text{ due to income} \\ \hline £10,000.00 \end{array}$$

The rule in *Re Earl of Chesterfield's Trusts* also applies to other property not producing income. In *Re Duke of Cleveland's Estate* [1895] 2 Ch 542, it was applied to a debt which bore no interest and was not receivable immediately. In *Re Chance* [1961] Ch 593 compensation for a refusal to grant planning permission was also held to be apportionable under this rule.

Where a reversionary interest is sold before it falls into possession, then the trustee will have to invest the proceeds in the normal way. Any delay in doing so will bring into operation apportionment between the tenant for life and the remainderman.

The rule in *Re Earl of Chesterfield's Trusts* can be excluded by a contrary intention being shown in the will. A clause excluding the rule in *Howe* v *Dartmouth* will generally exclude this rule: see *Rowlls* v *Bebb* [1900] 2 Ch 107. But it is often better to add a special clause to exclude the rule.

Re Earl of Chesterfield's Trusts does not apply to realty. In such cases the life tenant keeps the actual rents and profits: see *Re Searle* [1900] 2 Ch 829.

15.4 The windfall principle

Sometimes extraordinary payments may be made to the trust which cannot be satisfactorily classified either as income or capital. This is so when payments are made by a company to the trust under such names as 'cash bonus' or 'capital profits dividend'.

If payments are made to trustee shareholders they should normally enquire into the distribution and treat it as income or capital as is appropriate. However, prima facie, whatever the payment is called it belongs to the life tenant. In *Re Bates* [1928]

Ch 682 a company sold some of its assets and distributed the profits of the sale as a cash bonus. It was held that the life tenant was entitled to the whole payment.

Where a company is being wound up or making an authorised reduction in capital then money returned is regarded as the money paid for shares and accordingly treated as capital: see *Re Armitage* [1893] 3 Ch 337. Similarly, dividends paid as part of a company's restructuring arrangements are, prima facie, deemed to form part of the trust capital: see *Sinclair* v *Lee* (1993) The Times 6 May.

Where a company takes steps to capitalise profits by using them to make a bonus issue of shares which are issued to the trustee-shareholder, they become part of the trust capital. In *Bouch* v *Sproule* (1887) 12 App Cas 385 the company directors distributed accumulated profits as a bonus dividend by alloting new shares to each shareholder, and applied the bonus dividend in payment. This was held to be a distribution of capital, as it was the company's decision to decide to capitalise profits and, provided such a decision was properly made, it bound beneficiaries claiming as shareholders.

15.5 The rule in *Allhusen* v *Whittall*

This particular aspect of the conversion and apportionment rules is concerned with the effect of the payment of debts by personal representatives out of a residuary estate left to A for life, remainder to B absolutely. If, for example, the residuary estate was worth £100,000 and producing income of £12,000 per annum, but there were debts of £25,000, it would be unjust to the life tenant if the income alone was utilised to meet these debts and if capital alone were used to meet the debts, the life tenant would obtain an advantage.

The rule in *Allhusen* v *Whittall* (1867) LR 4 Eq 295 is designed to ensure that whatever funds are used from the residue to pay debts, an adjustment should be made so that the debts are borne proportionately by the capital and income on an equitable basis. As Page-Wood V-C said in that case:

'... supposing a testator has a large sum – say £50,000 or £60,000 – in the funds, and has only £10,000 worth of debts, the executors will be justified, as between themselves and the whole body of persons interested in the estate, in dealing with it as they think best in the administration. But, the executors, when they have dealt with the estate, will be taken by the Court as having applied in payment of debts such a portion of the fund as, together with income of that portion for one year, was necessary for payment of debts.'

15.6 Apportionment Act 1870

Section 2 addresses specific questions that arise on the death of the testator or life tenant. Namely, what is to be done with the incoming periodical income, such as rents, dividends, etc, as a result? In essence that which accrues, ie is paid or is payable before death, is added to the testator's estate or paid to the life tenant. That income accruing after death goes either to the testator's beneficiary, or to the life tenant's successor life tenant, or in default of there being a successor to the fund's capital. The actual apportionment of income is a simple calculation based primarily on determining the respective days before and after death and dividing the income into the appropriate periods.

15.7 Proposals for reform

The Law Reform Committee in its 23rd report on *The Powers and Duties of Trustees* (1982) Cmnd 8733 considered the future of the rules of conversion and apportionment. It was recognised that they are generally excluded in a well-drawn will and were more honoured in breach than observance. It was considered inappropriate to abolish them altogether and put nothing in their place since they are part of the trustees' wider duty to hold an even hand between those entitled to the fund. It was recommended that *Howe* v *Dartmouth*, *Re Earl of Chesterfield* and *Allhusen* v *Whittall* be subsumed in a new statutory duty to hold a fair balance between the beneficiaries, in particular those entitled to capital and those entitled to income. It was considered that this would give the trustees the necessary degree of flexibility to enable them to have regard to the investment policy of the trust. Further, the Commission noted the artificial nature of the Apportionment Act and its inherent unfairness.

16

Duty to Distribute

16.1 Introduction

16.2 Enquiries

16.3 Section 27 Trustee Act 1925

16.4 Benjamin order

16.1 Introduction

The distribution of trust property may occur during the course of the trust, for example, the payment of income to beneficiaries or the capital share of one of several beneficiaries who has fulfilled the contingencies under the trust. Alternatively, the distribution may be of the whole trust fund. This may arise when all of the beneficiaries have reached full age and are absolutely entitled to the trust property between themselves: see *Saunders* v *Vautier* (1841) 4 Beav 115; or where the trust is one for immediate distribution as in the case of gifts under a will or on intestacy. The rule in *Saunders* v *Vautier* is probably one of the most common reasons for a distribution. It only applies if the beneficiaries are of full age, that is, have reached majority, and are absolutely entitled, having fulfilled all contingencies and conditions required of them by the trust. The rule applies to individual beneficiaries who have fulfilled these conditions concerning their share, and severing it from the remainder of the trust estate would not affect the value of the remaining property: see *Re Marshall* [1914] 1 Ch 192.

A trustee is under a duty to distribute the trust property to the persons who are rightfully entitled to it. A failure to do so is a breach of trust. Where payment was made to the wrong person on the faith of a marriage certificate which was forged the trustees were liable: see *Eaves* v *Hickson* (1861) 30 Beav 136. However, relief may now be given in such cases under s61 TA 1925 (see Chapter 20, section 20.5). Where there is doubt about the claims of beneficiaries to the trust property the safest course for the trustee is to make an application to the court for directions. This can be done by way of an originating summons which puts the particular difficulties before the court: see RSC O.85 r2.

In cases of doubt over to whom the trust property should be distributed, or if and how it should be distributed, it is inappropriate to go to court in the first instance to seek directions. An application to the court on these matters will involve expense to the trust estate and should only be used in cases of necessity. Trustees who apply to the court for their own convenience may be ordered to pay the costs of the applications themselves: see *Re Allen-Meyrick's WT* [1966] 1 WLR 499. The trustees may be able to deal with the matter out of court by obtaining proper legal advice or in cases where there are problems in finding the beneficiaries, by appropriate enquiries or by advertisements in accordance with s27 TA 1925.

16.2 Enquiries

A trustee or personal representative may, as a preliminary step to distribution, make enquiries to discover who he has to give the property to. This may arise where a gift is made to a class of beneficiaries, for example, '£10,000 to be divided equally between my nephews and nieces'. It may be difficult to ascertain who all the nephews and nieces are if the family concerned was not very close and have become scattered throughout the world. In such cases the trustees or personal representatives should enquire among the relatives to find all the beneficiaries. A family tree should be drawn up if necessary.

In cases where gifts have been made to a particular beneficiary, or a particular description of beneficiary, different considerations will apply. If a gift is made to 'my nephew John Smith' it may well be that there are three nephews of that name. In such circumstances the issue is a matter of construction. However, a gift may have been made to a named beneficiary who cannot be found. In such cases the presumption of death may apply if the beneficiary has not been heard of for seven years or more. The trustees or personal representatives should seek a declaration to this end. Otherwise they should pay the money into court after all other courses, such as advertisements under s27 TA 1925, have been adopted. However, this course of action is very much a last resort and if a more appropriate alternative exists the courts will often penalise the trustees by way of an unfavourable costs order: see *Re Cull's Trusts* (1875) LR 20 Eq 561.

16.3 Section 27 Trustee Act 1925

This section is designed to protect trustees in making distributions of trust property, or personal representatives distributing a deceased's estate, if they make the appropriate advertisements and follow the instructions laid down:

1. To advertise in the London Gazette.
2. Where land is comprised in the estate, to advertise in a newspaper circulating in the district where the land is situated.
3. To place such other advertisements or notices as a court would direct in an action for administration.

All such advertisements should give notice of the trustees' intention to distribute, and require any person interested to send in particulars of his claim, allowing not less than two months for such claims to be made. The court's directions should always be sought on the advertisements made.

If the requirements of s27(1) are satisfied then the trustees or personal representatives may distribute to the persons entitled having regard only to the claims of which they then have notice. Under s27(2) it is provided that in such circumstances they are not, in respect of the distributed assets, liable to any person of whose claim they did not have notice at the time of distribution. In *Re Aldhous* [1955] 1 WLR 459 a testator died partially intestate and his executor gave a notice to distribute in accordance with s27; the executor received no claims from persons claiming to be the testator's next-of-kin and accordingly paid the money to the Crown as bona vacantia. Subsequently, next-of-kin came forward. Danckwerts J held that the executor was protected from any claims by them through the s27 advertisements.

Where a beneficiary has failed to respond to an advertisement under s27(1) he is not deprived of his interest because s27(2) provides that nothing in the section 'prejudices the right of any person to follow the property or any property representing the same, into the hands of any person, other than a purchaser, who may have received it'. He might trace for his share or claim a refund from the recipient personally. See Chapter 21.

16.4 Benjamin order

Sometimes trustees may be faced with the problem of having a duty to distribute to a particular beneficiary who cannot be found, for example, where a settlor created a trust in his will for the benefit of his son, X. If X has disappeared in circumstances which make it unclear whether he is alive or dead, an advertisement under s27 is likely to be of little value. This is because it seems to be directed to finding unascertained rather than ascertained beneficiaries. The problem of finding a known beneficiary who may or may not be dead can be overcome by a Benjamin order. Such an order will give the trustees leave to distribute the trust property on the footing set out in the order, for example, that the particular beneficiary died before the settlor or testator, unmarried and without issue. In this form the beneficiary and his descendants could be ignored on distribution, and the trustees would be protected by the court order if he or his descendants ever appeared to claim.

The Benjamin order is not a positive declaration of rights, and the beneficiary affected by the order is not declared dead nor is his entitlement destroyed. The order is based on the probability, on the evidence before the court, that the beneficiary is dead. A result of the order is that it avoids undue delay in the administration of the estate and other administrative inconvenience but this, it seems, is not the object in making the order. In *Re Benjamin* [1902] 1 Ch 723 a testator left his estate to be divided between such of his children living at his death in equal shares. One of the testator's sons disappeared ten months before his death and on the evidence before him Joyce J granted an order permitting distribution of the estate on the footing that the son was dead. A striking example of the application of a Benjamin order is *Re Green's Will Trusts* [1985] 3 All ER 455. In this case the testatrix died in 1976 leaving a will under which she directed her trustees to hold her estate, worth over £700,000, for her son, whom she had not seen for over 30 years but still believed to be alive. She directed that if her son did not claim the estate by the year 2020, it should be applied for charitable purposes. The trustees sought a Benjamin order because the testatrix's son was last seen and heard of in January 1943 when he took off on a bombing mission to Berlin as a Royal Air Force tail gunner. The indications were that he was killed in action as neither the aeroplane nor any of its occupants were ever found. The testatrix always believed her son was alive. Nourse J granted the Benjamin order as the evidence suggested that the son was probably dead. It was pointed out that merely the fact that the testatrix believed her son to be alive was no bar to granting the order. The court was entitled to take a view as to the probabilities of his being alive entirely different from the testatrix.

17

Miscellaneous Duties of Trustees

17.1 Introduction

17.2 Best interests of beneficiaries

17.3 Accounts

17.4 Information

17.1 Introduction

The more important duties of trustees have been considered in separate chapters above. These include trustees' fiduciary duties, the duty to invest the trust funds and the duty to distribute the trust funds to those properly entitled to them. Other duties of trustees, some of which are incidentally referred to elsewhere in this textbook, are:

1. To get the trust property into the trust.
2. To familiarise themselves with the trust on appointment.
3. To adhere to the terms of the trust.
4. To exercise reasonable care in the management of the trust.
5. To act impartially between the beneficiaries.

The classic example of such impartiality is the trustees' duty to weigh up the competing interests of, say, a life tenant and a beneficiary with a remainder interest in respect of their duties to distribute or accumulate trust funds. This impartiality also extends to cover situations where there are a number of tenants with interests in possession. See *Duker* v *Lloyds Bank* [1987] 1 WLR 1324 (Deputy Judge Mowbray QC). In this instance two beneficiaries were entitled to varying shares of a testator's estate part of which comprised of shares in a private company. Beneficiary A was entitled to a majority share of the testator's estate and therefore, a majority share in the private company. Beneficiary A demanded that the executor vest the majority shareholding of the private company in A. This would have left the second Beneficiary, B, with a minority shareholding which, insofar as it was a private company, was practically worthless. The executor sought the Court's assistance and, by way of enforcing the Executor's duty of impartiality, was ordered to sell the private company's shares on the open market and then divide the proceeds between

A and B in accordance with their shares in the testator's estate.

Three further duties of some importance are considered here.

1. To act impartially between the beneficiaries.
2. To keep accounts.
3. To provide information on the trust to the beneficiaries.

17.2 Best interests of beneficiaries

A trustee has a duty to act in the best interests of his beneficiaries in all matters, whether this be in the context of investment, the sale of trust property, the conduct of litigation or the appointment of new trustees. Any failure by the trustee to do this is a breach of trust. In particular trustees must not put their own interests before those of the beneficiaries. To do so would be a breach of fiduciary duty, for example, where the trustee allows his personal political views to sway his decision as to which of two authorised investments he shall make on behalf of the trust.

The nature of this duty was considered at length by Megarry V-C in *Cowan* v *Scargill* [1985] 3 WLR 501. In this case five trustees, nominated by the National Union of Mineworkers to the mineworkers' pension trust fund refused to approve an annual investment plan for £200 million unless it were amended so that overseas investment was not increased, existing overseas investments be withdrawn when opportune, and no investments be made in energy industries competing with coal. The five trustees were seeking to further the interests of the coal mining industry by this policy but these interests were not the same as those of beneficiaries under the trust. The beneficiaries were retired miners or the wives and children of ex-miners, who had never been engaged in mining. It was held that the five trustees were in breach of their fiduciary duty as they were not putting the best interests of their beneficiaries first. In giving judgment Megarry V-C said:

> 'The duty of the trustees towards their beneficiaries is paramount. They must, of course, obey the law; but subject to that, they must put the interests of the beneficiaries first. When the purpose of the trust is to provide financial benefits for the beneficiaries, as is usually the case, the best interests of the beneficiaries are normally their best financial interests. In the case of a power of investment, as in the present case, the power must be exercised so as to yield the best return for the beneficiaries, judged in relation to the risks of the investments in question; and the prospects of the yield of income and capital appreciation both have to be considered in judging the return from the investment ...
>
> In considering what investments to make trustees must put on one side their own personal interests and views. Trustees may have strongly held social or political views. They may be firmly opposed to any investment in South Africa or other countries, or they may object to any form of investment in companies concerned with alcohol, tobacco, armaments or many other things. In the conduct of their own affairs, of course, they are free to abstain from making any such investments. Yet under a trust, if investments of this type would be more beneficial to the beneficiaries than other investments, the trustees must not refrain from making the investments by reason of the views that they hold. I

should say that I am not asserting that the benefit of the beneficiaries which a trustee must make his paramount concern inevitably and solely means their financial benefit, even if the only object of the trust is to provide financial benefits. Thus, if the only actual or potential beneficiaries of a trust are all adults with very strict views on moral and social matters, condemning all forms of alcohol, tobacco and popular entertainment, as well as armaments, I can well understand that it might not be for the 'benefit' of such beneficiaries to know that they are obtaining rather larger financial returns under the trust by reason of investments in those activities ...'

See also the decision of Sir Donald Nicholls V-C in *Harries and Others* v *Church Commissioners for England and Another* [1992] 1 WLR 1241. This considers the question as to whether or not, ethical reasons aside, the trustees of church funds could exclude certain types of investments from their portfolio.

In particular, even if the trustee has no positive duty to act, once he decides to act or use his powers the burden is on him to establish that he made proper enquiries to ensure, as far as possible, the propriety of the transaction involved: *Bishopsgate Investment Management Ltd (In Liquidation)* v *Maxwell (No 2)* [1994] 1 All ER 261.

17.3 Accounts

A trustee has a duty to keep accounts of the trust and to produce them to the beneficiaries when requested to do so: see *Pearse* v *Green* (1819) 1 Jac & W 135. The beneficiaries have a right to inspect them and demand information and explanations on them. However, the beneficiaries are not entitled to demand copies of the accounts unless they are prepared to pay for them: see *Re Watson* (1904) 49 Sol Jo 54.

Under s22(4) TA 1925 trustees are given a discretion to cause the accounts of trust property to be audited or examined by an independant accountant. Whether this discretion is exercised will depend on the nature of the trust property and the dealings in it which have taken place. However, this power should not be exercised more than once in every three years unless special circumstances require it.

17.4 Information

A trustee is under a duty to give any beneficiary information concerning the state of the trust. For this purpose the trustees should keep records of the affairs of the trust, which are available to all beneficiaries.

The beneficiary is not entitled to see all documents belonging to the trust; he cannot demand documents such as the minutes of meetings and correspondence between the trustees, which sets out reasons for the exercise or non-exercise of their discretion in a discretionary trust. To permit this might lead to the challenge of the exercise of the discretion: see *Re Londonderry's Settlement* [1965] Ch 918. The beneficiary is entitled to see title deeds and other documents relating to the trust. These points were considered in *Re Londonderry's Settlement* which concerned a family settlement created by the seventh Marquess of Londonderry. The trustees, in accordance with their powers under the trust, decided to bring it to an end and distribute the trust property among the beneficiaries according to the discretion vested in them for this purpose. The settlor's daughter was dissatisfied with the exercise of the discretion in favour of herself and her children and asked to see minutes of trustees' meetings, agendas, other documents prepared for their meetings, and correspondence between the trustees and their advisers and between the trustees themselves. The trustees supplied her with the trust accounts and copies of the appointments of capital made by them. They took the view that it would not be in the interests of the family for them to supply all the documents asked for. The Court of Appeal held that beneficiaries were prima facie entitled to the production and inspection of all trust documents in the possession of their trustees. However, to be entitled to inspect any document in the possession of the trustees the beneficiaries had to show:

1. They were documents in the possession of the trustees as trustees.
2. They contained information about the trust which the beneficiaries were entitled to know.
3. They had a proprietary interest in the documents.

Beneficiaries under a discretionary trust are not entitled to see documents containing confidential information as to the exercise of the discretion where this 'might cause infinite trouble in the family out of all proportion to the benefit which might be received from the inspection of the same'. Accordingly the settlor's daughter would not be allowed to see the documents concerned.

18

Powers of Trustees

18.1 Introduction

Where trustees are given a power to do certain things under the trust it is up to them to decide whether or not to exercise the power in appropriate circumstances. A power should be contrasted with a duty which obliges the trustee to conform with the duty imposed upon him.

The powers dealt with in this Chapter are those contained in the Trustee Act 1925. It is common to find that a trust instrument modifies these powers to suit the particular circumstances of the trust. Indeed, the settlor may even give the trustees powers not found in the Trustee Act 1925.

The main powers dealt with in this section are:

1. The regulation of the power of sale: s12 TA 1925
2. The power to give receipts: s14 TA 1925
3. The power to insure: s19 TA 1925
4. The power to compound liabilities: s15 TA 1925
5. The powers in relation to reversionary interests: s22 TA 1925
6. The power to delegate: ss23, 25 and 30 TA 1925

7. The power of maintenance: s31 TA 1925
8. The power of advancement: s32 TA 1925

18.2 Powers of sale

A power of sale may be granted either expressly or impliedly by the trust instrument, by statute or by order of the court under s57 TA 1925.

Powers of sale of land

Land can now only be held in trust under either the Settled Land Act 1925 or the Trusts of Land and Appointment of Trustees Act 1996; the former being a strict settlement, the latter being a trust for land. Under s1 SLA 1925 a power of sale is given to the tenant for life, in whom the land is vested. If any settlement purports to vest the power in the trustees of the settlement, it is exercisable by the tenant for life: ss108 and 109 SLA 1925. However, if the trustees of the settlement are the statutory owners they may have a power of sale. If the land is not subject to the SLA 1925 then there may still be an express trust for sale. According to s11(1) Trusts of Land and Appointment of Trustees Act 1996 a power to postpone sale will be implied into all such express trusts.

Powers of sale of chattels

A trust for sale may arise expressly on chattels, for example by the terms of a will, or impliedly, for example under s33 AEA 1925 on the death of a person intestate, or under the rule in *Howe* v *Earl of Dartmouth* (above). There are special provisions in the SLA 1925 dealing with the power to sell heirlooms, that is chattels which are settled so as to devolve with the settled land. Here the heirlooms can only be sold by the tenant for life with the consent of the court: s67 SLA 1925. If the chattels are settled without reference to the settled land the trustees have a power of sale under s130(1) LPA 1925, with the consent of the user for the time being of full age.

Other powers of sale

Where property is in the form of unauthorised investments for the purposes of TIA 1961 the trustees have a power to sell unauthorised investments and place the money in authorised investments. The TIA 1961 also gives the trustees a general power to change investments which are unsuitable and this carries with it a power of sale.

Under s16 TA 1925 there is a general power vested in trustees to raise money by the sale of trust property in order to pay or apply capital money for any purpose authorised by the trust instrument or by statute.

The trustees' power of sale, by operation of s12 TA 1925, is regulated insofar as trustees are entitled to:

'... sell or concur with any other person in selling all or any part of the property, either subject to prior charges or not, and either together or in lots, by public auction or by private contract, subject to any such conditions respecting title or evidence of title or other matters as the trustee thinks fit, with power to vary any contract for sale, and to buy in at any auction, or to rescind any contract for sale and to resell, without being answerable for any loss.'

18.3 Power to give receipts

Under s14(1) TA 1925 trustees are given a general power to give receipts. The section provides:

'The receipt in writing of a trustee for any money, securities, or other personal property or effects payable, transferable, or deliverable to him under any trust or power shall be a sufficient discharge to the person paying transferring or delivering the same and shall effectually exonerate him from seeing to the application or being answerable for any loss or misapplication thereof.'

Section 14(3) provides that the power to give receipts applies notwithstanding anything to the contrary contained in the trust instrument.

A sole trustee can give a valid receipt under s14(1), except in the cases set out in s14(2). These are:

1. For the proceeds of sale or other capital money arising under a trust for sale of land – s27(2) LPA requires the receipt of at least two trustees unless the trustee is a trust corporation or a sole personal representative.
2. For capital money arising under SLA 1925 – s94(1) SLA 1925 requires the receipt of at least two trustees or a trust corporation.

18.4 Power to insure

There is no duty imposed upon trustees to insure trust property by law although a settlor may include an express provision to this effect in the trust instrument. However, it may well be regarded as a failure to safeguard the trust property if they failed to insure. Under s19 TA 1925 trustees are given a power to insure, the section provides:

'A trustee may insure against loss or damage by fire, any building or other insurable property to any amount, including the amount of any insurance already on foot, not exceeding three fourth parts of the full value of the building or property, and pay the premiums for such insurance out of income thereof or out of the income of any other property subject to the same trusts without obtaining the consent of any person who may be entitled wholly or partly to such income.'

Note that s19(1) is limited to insuring against loss or damage by fire and it only allows the trustees to insure three-quarters of the value of the property. The settlor may often amend s19(1) so that other hazards such as theft and flood damage are provided for and that the full value is insured, as opposed to only three-quarters.

Section 20 TA 1925 deals with the application of insurance money. Generally, if the property destroyed or damaged by fire was subject to an SLA settlement, then the insurance money is treated as capital money: s20(1). There are detailed provisions for the application of the insurance moneys. Subsections (4) and (5) are noteworthy. The former empowers the trustees to apply the money in rebuilding, reinstating, repairing or replacing the property lost or damaged, while the latter preserves the rights of persons who could require the application of the insurance moneys in the ways stated under subs (4).

18.5 Power to compound liabilities

Trustees may well find that in the administration of the trust, difficulties which require instant decisions arise with regard to the trust property. For example, they may have to decide if it is worthwhile disputing that a debt is owed by the trust or extending the time for the payment of a debt. All these matters are dealt with by s15 TA 1925 which provides that trustees may:

'a) accept any property, real or personal, before the time at which it is made transferrable or payable; or

b) sever or apportion any blended trust funds or property; or

c) pay or allow any debt or claim on any evidence that he or they think sufficient; or

d) accept any composition or security, real or personal, for any debt or for any property, real or personal, claimed; or

e) allow any time of payment of any debt; or

f) compromise, compound, abandon, submit to arbitration, or otherwise settle any debt, account, claim, or thing whatever relating to the testator's or intestate's estate or to the trust;

... without being responsible for any loss occasioned by any act or thing so done by him or them in good faith.'

Section 15 is only concerned with external disputes, or cases in which there is some issue between the trustees on behalf of the trust as a whole and the outside world. It is not concerned with internal disputes where one beneficiary under the trusts is at issue with another. In the latter the law in *Chapman* v *Chapman* [1954] AC 429 and related cases applies.

The language of s15 is very wide so as to give trustees wide and flexible powers of compromising, and settling disputes. The power must be exercised with the interest in mind of the beneficiaries under the trust. The provision cannot be used to effect a variation of the beneficial interests under a trust, but beneficiaries surrendering their interest in certain trust property will not necessarily be a variation of the trusts. Section 15 was considered in *Re Earl of Stafford* [1980] Ch 28. In this case T died in December 1951 two months after his wife. Under his will T settled his mansion house on a strict settlement and bequeathed all his chattels to devolve with the settled land. Under the settlement the property was to be held for T's two daughters for life, then for one of T's grandsons and then to T's other grandsons. By her will T's wife left all her estate to the two daughters equally. T and his wife owned many works of art and valuable chattels and after their deaths the daughters arrived at decisions as to which belonged to the estate of their father and which belonged to the estate of their mother. The allocations they made were acted upon. Subsequently evidence showed that many chattels allocated to the wife's estate in fact belonged to T. Because of these doubts the beneficiaries under the trust in T's will, other than the two daughters, put forward a compromise regarding the disputed chattels. By the compromise the trustee would abandon a claim to half the disputed chattels and the other half would be settled on the trusts, with the daughters surrendering their interests in these. The trustees sought the decision of the court as to whether the compromise should be accepted and surrendered to the court the discretion to compromise under s15. It was held that s15 conferred wide and flexible powers of compromising and settling disputes. In exercising these powers the trustee had to take into account the interests of the beneficiaries and the value of assets recovered as against other factors which would be involved in continuing a claim for the disputed assets. In the circumstances the trustees' compromise would not be upset.

18.6 Powers relating to reversionary interests

Under s22 TA 1925 trustees are given wide powers to deal with reversionary interest or choses in action which have just fallen into possession. The powers include making arrangements for their valuation and acting upon such valuations without being responsible for any loss, and allowing any deductions for costs and expenses or executing any release so as to discharge accountable parties without being liable for the loss.

18.7 Power to delegate

Before 1925

Before 1925 the general rule was that a trustee could only delegate on the grounds of necessity: see *Ex parte Belchier* (1754) Amb 218. It was recognised that there were certain things which a man of business would never do himself but would instead delegate to a skilled agent. So, he would employ a solicitor for legal work and a stockbroker or banker for financial work. The seal of approval was put on delegation in this manner by the House of Lords in *Speight* v *Gaunt* (1883) where Gaunt, a trustee, employed Cooke, a stockbroker, to invest £15,000 of the trust funds. Cooke was a member of a reputable firm of stockbrokers and he contracted to buy shares on behalf of the trust from a jobber in the Stock Exchange. In accordance with the usual business practice Cooke brought Gaunt a bought note from the jobber and asked for the money to pay for the shares on the account day. Cooke did not complete the transaction, misapplied the money and was adjudicated bankrupt shortly afterwards with the result that the £15,000 trust money was lost. Gaunt was sued by the beneficiaries for breach of trust. He argued that he could not be held liable for the loss unless it was shown that he had failed to act as an ordinary prudent man of business would have acted on his own behalf. It was held that Gaunt was not liable, he had acted as a prudent man of business in asking Cooke to make the investments for him and nothing more could be expected of him as a trustee. If a higher standard was imposed on trustees, with regard to trust affairs than their own affairs, in respect of delegating commercial matters, then no one would become a trustee.

The trustee was, however, expected to exercise proper care in choosing his agent and to employ him in his proper line of business or proper profession. In *Fry* v *Tapson* (1884) 28 Ch D 268 a solicitor was held not to be acting in the ordinary course of his profession in introducing a surveyor to a client.

Delegation under Trustee Act 1925 s23(1)

As the case of *Speight* v *Gaunt* and the other pre-1926 cases indicated, delegation could only be made where it was necessary, particularly in the ordinary course of business. Under s23(1) Trustee Act 1925 a new principle was introduced making delegation possible by trustees whether it is necessary or not. Section 23(1) provides:

'Trustees or personal representatives may, instead of acting personally, employ and pay an agent, whether a solicitor, banker, stockbroker, or other person, to transact any business or do any act required to be transacted or done in the execution of the trust, or the administration of the testator's or intestate's estate, including the receipt and payment of money, and shall be entitled to be allowed and paid all charges and expenses so incurred, and shall not be responsible for the default of any such agent if employed in good faith.'

In *Re Vickery* [1931] 1 Ch 572 Maugham J explained the scope of s23(1):

'It is hardly too much to say that it revolutionises the position of a trustee or an executor so far as regards the employment of agents. He is no longer required to do any action work himself, but he may employ a solicitor or other agent to do it, whether there is any real necessity for the employment or not. No doubt he should use discretion in selecting an agent, and should employ him only to do acts within the scope of the usual business of the agent.'

The scope of the power of delegation under s23(1) appears clear enough. However, the scope of the responsibility of the trustee for the defaults of the agent is far from clear. The section states that the trustee shall not be responsible for the default of any agent 'if employed in good faith'. This does not mean that a trustee is protected so long as he appoints an agent in good faith and that he can leave the agent to do exactly as he pleases with the trust property and trust affairs in his hands. Section 23 does not, it is submitted, sweep away the pre-1926 law but merely adds to it. A trustee who delegates to an agent must still ensure the agent is suitable for the purpose required and supervise him properly. By so acting the trustee is more than likely to gain the protection of s61 TA 1925 in any personal action against him for breach. See Chapter20.

If it was to be concluded that s23(1) only applied to the appointment of the agent and relieved the trustee from all other responsibility with regard to the agent's position, the following results would ensue:

1. Section 23(3) would be difficult to understand, and in particular the proviso to it would be meaningless. Under s23(3) delegation is permitted in three particular cases 'without prejudice to such general power to appoint agents as aforesaid'. However, the proviso retains the trustee's previous liability. It states 'nothing in this subsection shall exempt a trustee from any liability which he would have incurred if this Act and any enactment replaced by this Act had not been passed'. If a trustee is given complete protection by s23(1) if he appoints the agent in good faith, then the words in the proviso are meaningless and the words at the beginning of s23(3) would appear to be unnecessary.

2. Section 30 TA would be quite unnecessary because a trustee need never act personally, if s23 is correctly interpreted in *Re Vickery*, and it would be little more than repetition to say that he is not liable for any loss except where the same happens through his own wilful default, as this would be caught by s23(1) in any event, with regard to his action in appointing the agent.

3. The provisions of s23(1) would be difficult to reconcile with the provision of s23(2) and s25 TA 1925, as these provide respectively for wider powers of delegation for trustees to deal with property outside the UK, and to delegate while the trustee himself is absent abroad. Under s23(2) the trustee is only given protection against losses arising 'by reason only of their having made any such appointment'. This assumes that liability under the pre-1926 law remains, and any other view would make these words meaningless. Under s25 the trustee can delegate all his powers and discretions but retains all responsibility. It is difficult to see why such a heavy burden of responsibility should be placed on a trustee who delegates under this provision as opposed to s23(1) leaving aside the fact the s25 permits delegation of discretions but s23(1) does not.

Section 9 Trusts of Land and Appointment of Trustees Act 1996 enables trustees to delegate any of their functions relating to land to any beneficiaries who are beneficially entitled to an interest in possession in the land.

Section 30 Trustee Act 1925

Section 23(1) gives the trustee some protection for the defaults of an agent 'if employed in good faith'. It is backed up by s30 TA 1925 and the general purpose of the provision appears from the dictum of Lindley LJ in *Speight* v *Gaunt* (1883) 22 Ch D 727:

'I wish most emphatically to say that if trustees are justified by the ordinary course of business in employing agents, and they do employ agents of good repute and whose fitness they have no reason to doubt, and employ those agents to do that which is in the ordinary course of their business, I protest against the notion that the trustees guarantee the solvency or honesty of the agents employed.'

The scope of s30(1) is limited as its words indicate, it states:

'A trustee shall be chargeable only for money and securities actually received by him nothwithstanding his signing any receipt for the sake of conformity, and shall be answerable and accountable only for his own acts, receipts, neglects, or defaults, and not those of any other trustee, nor for any banker, broker, or other person with whom any trust money or securities may be deposited, nor for the insufficiency or deficiency of any securities, nor for any other loss, unless the same happens through his own wilful default.'

In *Re Vickery* Maugham J pointed out that the protection given in s30(1) is limited to the situations mentioned and that the words 'for any other loss' must be construed ejusdem generis.

The key to s30(1) is the meaning of the words 'wilful default' – the trustee is not liable for losses unless they happen through his own 'wilful default'. In pre-1926 cases this phrase was construed in an objective sense and it did not relieve a trustee from acting as a prudent man of business. However, in *Re Vickery* Maugham J construed 'wilful default' in a subjective sense. He applied dicta of Romer J in *Re City Equitable Fire Insurance Co* [1925] 1 Ch 407, a case concerning the construction of the articles of association of a company and a director's liability under them. In deciding the case Romer J defined wilful default as 'either a consciousness of negligence or breach of duty, or a recklessness in the performance of a duty'. In *Bartlett* v *Barclays Bank* [1980] Ch 515 Brightman LJ defined wilful default as:

'... a passive breach of trust, an omission by a trustee to do something which, as a prudent trustee, he ought to have done ...'

However, this case was concerned with s30(1) nor was *Re Vickery* mentioned.

In *Re Vickery* (1931) itself the sole executor of a small estate appointed a solicitor called Jennens to wind up the estate and collect certain moneys totalling about £300 from Post Office savings accounts. At the time of appointment of Jennens to act as solicitor to the estate the executor had no reason to consider Jennens as unsuitable for the task. However, he was subsequently informed that Jennens had been suspended from practice twice for misconduct. The beneficiaries had objected to his appointment and to permitting moneys belonging to the estate being under his control. The executor, on learning of Jennens' past record, pressed him for payment of moneys belonging to the estate and was promised repeatedly that the money would come shortly. Eventually another solicitor was appointed to deal with the estate but by that time Jennens had absconded with the moneys from the Post Office savings accounts. The beneficiaries sued the executor for the lost money. It was held that the executor was not liable. He had only been guilty of an error of judgment which did not amount to a 'wilful default' under s30(1) TA 1925.

Delegation under ss23(2) and 23(3) Trustee Act

Section 23(2) is wider than s23(1). It permits trustees to delegate both their ministerial powers and their discretions, unlike s23(1) which only allows delegation of ministerial powers, not discretions. The purpose of s23(2) is to enable the trustees to appoint agents to deal on their behalf with trust property situated outside the UK.

Under s23(3)(a) a trustee can delegate his power to receive and give a discharge for any money or valuable consideration to a solicitor by letting him have the deeds of the property endorsed with a receipt. Under s23(3)(c) the trustee can delegate his power to receive insurance money to a banker or solicitor by giving them the insurance policy with a receipt signed by the trustee.

Delegation under s25 Trustee Act and s3(3) of the Enduring Powers of Attorney Act 1985

Section 25 Trustee Act was originally devised to enable a trustee to delegate his powers while absent abroad but, since being amended by s9 of the Powers of Attorney Act 1971, it applies even if the trustee is not abroad. Delegation can be of discretions as well as powers and under s25(1) it has to be by power of attorney attested by at least one witness: s25(3).

The basic conditions of s25 are as follows:

1. The attorney cannot be the trustee's sole co-trustee, unless a trust corporation (thereby excluding, for example, couples who purchase a house together who, prima facie, will have joint legal and beneficial interests, from appointing each other); and
2. Notice of the appointment must be given to the other trustees and any person entitled to appoint new trustees; and
3. The delegation does not last for more than 12 months; and
4. The trustee, by virtue of s25(5), remains liable for the attorney's acts and defaults. (But note *Steel* v *Wellcome Trustees Ltd* [1988] 1 WLR 167, and see Chapter 14, section 14.9, where an investment scheme was approved under which the liability of paid trustees was set at specific limits, including negligence in choosing agents or in setting and enforcing the terms of employment of such agents.)

However, an important limitation on any delegation under s25 is that it does not survive the mental incapacity of the donor: *Yonge* v *Toynbee* [1910] 1 KB 215. To rectify this, and also to highlight further limitations on trustee's power to delegate (as revealed in the decision in *Walia* v *Michael Naughton Ltd* [1985] 1 WLR 1115) Parliament enacted the Enduring Powers of Attorney Act 1985. Section 3(3) of that Act provides as follows:

'Subject to any conditions or restrictions contained in the instrument, an attorney under an enduring power, whether general or limited, may (without obtaining any consent) execute or exercise all or any of the trusts, powers or discretions vested in the donor as trustee and may (without the concurrence of any other person) to give a valid receipt for capital or other money paid.'

To grant such an enduring power the donee is required to adopt a specific form of wording. However, once this is done it is evident that, in contrast to s25, s3(3) contains few of the accepted safeguards (eg notice, 12 month's duration, continuing liability) imposed on a trustee who attempts to delegate. In response to this manifest inconsistency the Law Commission (Paper No 220, 'Delegation by Individual Trustees') has recommended that, save for the application of s3(3) in circumstances of the donor's mental incapacity, it should be repealed (along with a number of consequential, transitional amendments). It remains to be seen if this recommendation will be adopted.

18.8 Power of maintenance

Introduction

A trustee has no power to give an infant beneficiary the income from the trust as it arises, unless the trust instrument expressly authorises him to do so, even if the infant beneficiary would be entitled to receive the income if he were an adult in the same position. This is because an infant cannot give the trustees a valid receipt for the income.

Under s31(2) TA 1925 the trustees must usually accumulate the income arising on an infant's share in the trust fund and add it to capital. When the infant attains majority the accumulations are held for him absolutely and from that time onwards the trustees must pay the beneficiary all the income from the trust to which he is entitled as it arises.

It may be necessary that an infant beneficiary receive maintenance payments for his day-to-day upkeep and support, such as for school fees, clothes and food and accommodation. For this purpose s31 TA 1925 confers upon trustees a discretionary power to maintain an infant beneficiary out of his share of the income. Section 31(1) provides:

'Where any property is held by trustees in trust for any person for any interest whatsoever, whether vested or contingent then, subject to any prior interests or charges affecting that property –
i) during the infancy of any such person, if his interest so long continues the trustees may, at their sole discretion, pay to his parent or guardian, if any or otherwise apply for or towards his maintenance, education, or benefit, the whole or such part, if any, of the income of that property as may, in all the circumstances, be reasonable, whether or not there is –
a) any other fund applicable for the same purpose; or
b) any person bound by law to provide for his maintenance or education; and
ii) if such a person on attaining the age of eighteen years has not a vested interest in such income, the trustees shall henceforth pay the income of that property and of any accretion

thereto under subsection (2) of this section to him, until he either attains a vested interest therein or dies, or until failure of his interest ...'

It is clear from s31(1) that when an infant beneficiary attains 18 the trustees must pay to him the income arising from his share of the trust property if the trust cannot be brought to an end at that time. But this provision does not authorise the trustees to pay to him income accumulated on his share during infancy. This is dealt with in s31(2) which provides:

'During the infancy of any such person, if his interest so long continues, the trustees shall accumulate all the residue of that income in the way of compound interest by investing the same and the resulting income thereof from time to time in authorised investments, and shall hold those accumulations as follows:
i) If any such person –
a) attains the age of eighteen years, or marries under that age, and his interest in such income during his infancy or until marriage is a vested interest; or
b) on attaining the age of eighteen years or on marriage under that age becomes entitled to the property from which such income arose in fee simple, absolute or determinable, or absolutely, or for an entailed interest;
the trustees shall hold the accumulations in trust for such person absolutely, but without prejudice to any provision with respect thereto contained in any settlement by him made under any statutory powers during his infancy, and so that the receipt of such person after marriage, and though still an infant, shall be a good discharge; and
ii) In any other case the trustees shall, notwithstanding that such person has a vested interest in such income, hold the accumulations as an accretion to the capital of the property from which such accumulations arose, and as one fund with such capital for all purposes, and so that, if such property is settled land, such accumulations shall be held upon the same trusts as if they were capital monies arising therefrom; but the trustees may, at any time during the infancy of such person if his interest so long continues, apply those accumulations, or any part thereof, as if they were income arising during the then current year.'

The provisions in s31(2) were considered by the Court of Appeal in *Re Delamere's Settlement Trusts* [1984] 1 All ER 588. Those in para (i) are reasonably clear but the purpose of those in para (ii) is to 'defeat the interest (albeit a vested interest) of the infant in the accumulations if he dies before attaining 18 or marrying, and to cause them to rejoin the general capital of the trust property from which they arose' per Slade LJ. In *Re Delamere* s31(2) was found to be inapplicable to the settlement, but it does give a useful illustration of the problems dealt with by the provision. The trustees held £122,000 of accumulated income for the benefit of six infant beneficiaries and for tax reasons wished to know what they should do with accumulations accruing for the benefit of any infant should he die before attaining 18. If s31(2)(ii) had applied, such accumulations would have been treated as subject to the same trusts as the capital so that on the death of an infant, that infant's estate would not have received them on his death.

Nature of statutory power

The power of maintenance under s31 TA 1925 applies to all trust instruments unless the contrary is stated. It is therefore important in all cases that the trustees check to see if it has been excluded or modified for their trust. For example a common modification is the removal of an absolute discretion in respect of all of the fund by building in a limitation, for example half of the fund.

The trustees must ensure that all three conditions are satisfied for them to acquire the statutory power. These are:

1. That the beneficiary to receive maintenance is under 18 (an infant).
2. That the property or a share of it is held on trust for that infant.
3. That the income arising on the infant's share is applicable to the maintenance of the infant, and the 'intermediate income' until the infant attains his interest under the trust must be held for his benefit.

The first two conditions cause few problems and it will be clear if they are satisfied or not. The third condition, however, is more difficult. If the infant's share does not carry income there can be no maintenance. For example, '£10,000 to A when he attains 25, the income to B until then'. This gift does not carry intermediate income for A, therefore there is no power of maintenance.

There are complex rules involved in deciding who is entitled to the intermediate income under a trust. The general rule is that the income goes with the capital. This is only a very broad rule and the following is a statement of the main rules as to when a gift does or does not carry intermediate income:

Vested gifts

These gifts always carry the intermediate income unless the trust instrument provides to the contrary, for example, '£10,000 to X, the income thereof to Y for the next five years' or where the trust instrument directs that the income be accumulated and added to capital. The income is carried from the date the gift takes effect, unless it is a pecuniary legacy under a will when it is carried from the first anniversary of the testator's death.

Contingent gifts

These are gifts under which the beneficiary does not become entitled to the gift until the contingency is fulfilled, for example, '£10,000 to A if he attains 18'. The general rule is that the gift carries the income. Where the gift arises under a will the rules vary according to the nature of the gift:

1. A contingent specific bequest or devise carries the intermediate income: s175 LPA 1925; *Re McGeorge* [1963] Ch 544; for example, 'Blackacre to A when he attains 21.'
2. A contingent gift of residuary personalty carries intermediate income: *Green* v

Ekins (1742) 2 ALK 743; for example, 'All my residuary personalty to A when he attains 21.'

3. A contingent gift of residuary realty carries intermediate income: s175 LPA 1925; for example, 'All my residuary realty to A when he attains 21.'
4. A contingent general or pecuniary legacy does NOT carry intermediate income: *Re Raine* [1929] 1 Ch 716; for example, '£10,000 to A when he attains 21.' Here the income will fall into residue and go to the residuary legatee.

Three exceptional cases exist where a contingent general or pecuniary legacy will carry intermediate income.

1. Where the testator is the father of the beneficiary or in loco parentis to him and the beneficiary is an infant at the time of the gift and there is no further provision in the will. The court is prepared to infer that the gift was intended to carry intermediate income: *Harvey* v *Harvey* (1722) 2 P Wms 21. The contingency in such cases should relate to infancy, but in *Re Jones* [1932] 1 Ch 642 the court was not precluded from drawing the inference that the gift should carry intermediate income where the contingency was attaining the age of 25.
2. Where the gift is to an infant, in the will of a testator who is neither the infant's parent nor in loco parentis to him, and the will shows an intention that the gift should be used for the infant's benefit or maintenance. In *Re Churchill* [1909] 2 Ch 431 a gift for a child's maintenance was held to carry intermediate income on this rule and the same was held in *Re Selby-Walker* [1949] 2 All ER 178 where the gift was for the child's education.
3. Where the will directs that a particular legacy be set aside from the rest of the property. See *Re Medlock* (1886) 54 LT 828.

Deferred gifts
A deferred gift is one which will only take effect at some time or on the occurrence of some event in the future, for example, 'To A on the death of B.' The rules vary here according to the nature of the gift:

1. A deferred specific devise or bequest will carry intermediate income: s175 LPA 1925; for example, 'Blackacre to A after the death of my wife.'
2. A deferred gift of residuary personalty does NOT carry intermediate income; for example, 'My residuary personalty to A, two years after my death.' The income will pass to the next-of-kin under the intestacy rules.
3. A deferred gift of residuary realty will carry the intermediate income: s175 LPA 1925; *Re McGeorge* [1963] Ch 544; for example, 'All my residuary realty to my daughter after the death of my wife.'
4. A deferred general or pecuniary legacy does NOT carry intermediate income: *Rawlins* v *Rawlins* (1796) 2 Cox 425; for example, '£1,000 to A five years after my death.' The income will fall to the residuary legatee.

Exercise of the power

If the statutory power is available then the trustees must consider whether it is appropriate to use it. Section 31(1) states that the statutory power is exercisable at their sole discretion, but the trustees must use their discretion wisely, otherwise the court will order repayment of the money into the trust funds. In *Wilson* v *Turner* (1883) Ch D 521 the trustees were ordered to make refunds out of their own pockets where they had made automatic payments to the infants' father of all the income as it arose.

If the discretion is exercised in good faith the court will not interfere: *Bryant* v *Hickley* [1894] 1 Ch 324. In exercising the discretion the trustees must have regard to the matters set out in the proviso to s31(1):

1. The age of the infant.
2. His requirements.
3. The general circumstances of the case.
4. Other income, if any, available for his maintenance.

Note *Jones* v *Jones and Another* (1989) The Independent 27 January; see Chapter 2, section 2.5.

The trustees should not normally give the infant money in excess of his needs, if he has other financial resources.

Payment of the money

Under s31(1) the trustees must pay the money either to the infant's parent or guardian or apply it directly for his maintenance, education or benefit. Any surplus of income after the making of payments is accumulated and under s31(2) the trustees may use these accumulations at any time during the infancy as if they were income arising in the then current year.

A valid receipt to the trustees may be given by the parents of the infant or, in the case of a married infant, by that infant himself.

Maintenance out of capital

The court has a statutory power under s53 TA 1925 to order the disposal of a minor's beneficial interest with a view to the application of both the capital and the income for his maintenance. Powers are also given to order conveyances of property where necessary to enable maintenance.

Unlike s31, s53 permits capital to be used. This will normally be sanctioned where the minor's interest is small and produces only a small income. Court permission is nevertheless required.

Section 53 covers not only expenditure of the capital for maintenance but also capital investment for the infant, for example, the purchase of a dwelling house for the beneficiaries, or a partnership share.

Maintenance under the court's inherent jurisdiction

If a settlor has excluded the statutory power of maintenance under s31 TA 1925 then the court may exercise its inherent jurisdiction and allow maintenance out of the trust income.

The inherent jurisdiction was explained by Pearson J in *Re Collins* (1886) 32 Ch D 229:

> 'Where a testator has made provision for a family but has postponed the enjoyment, either for a particular purpose or generally for the increase of the estate it is assumed that he did not intend that these children should be left unprovided for or in a state of such moderate means that they should not be educated properly for the position and fortune which he designs them to have, and the Court has accordingly found from the earliest time that where an heir-at-law is unprovided for, maintenance ought to be provided for him.'

The inherent jurisdiction to grant maintenance is not confined to cases of emergency or necessity: see *Re Collins*. It can also be applied in cases where the beneficiary is not an infant: see *Revel* v *Watkinson* (1748).

Circumstances where the court may exercise its inherent jurisdiction include instances where the amount of capital is small, no other source of maintenance is available, and where a payment for past maintenance is required.

18.9 Power of advancement

Introduction

This power arises under s32 TA 1925 and applies to all trust instruments unless the contrary is stated, for example if there is an express trust for accumulation (see *IRC* v *Bernstein* [1961] Ch 399). Sometimes the settlor may include his own express power of advancement.

The purpose of the power is to permit trustees to advance capital to a beneficiary regardless of the type of interest which the beneficiary holds in the fund – no matter whether his interest is vested or contingent. The trustees can therefore give a beneficiary some of his entitlement before the time appointed.

EXAMPLE:

'£10,000 to A when he attains 21, in default thereof to B.'

Under this trust A cannot receive any of the capital until he attains 21. However, once he reaches 18 he is entitled to receive the income as it arises under s31 TA 1925. It may well be that A wishes to buy a house to live in or set up in business before he reaches 21. In such circumstances the trustees can exercise the power of advancement under s32 TA 1925 and give A some of the capital from the trust.

The trustees are restricted to applying or paying money 'for the advancment or benefit' of the beneficiary under the trust. These words have been construed to mean setting up the beneficiary in life as opposed to making mere casual payments to him. It covers purchasing business premises, a settlement on marriage, providing the means to enter an apprenticeship, or supplying further capital to an existing business: see per Lord Radcliffe in *Pilkington* v *IRC* [1964] AC 612.

'Advancement or benefit' also includes the discharge of a beneficiary's debts, except in very special circumstances: see *Lowther* v *Bentinck* (1874) LR 19 Eq 166; paying the debts of a beneficiary's husband: see *Re Kershaw* (1868) LR 6 Eq 322, and even an advancement to avoid tax was upheld in *Pilkington* v *IRC,* where the issue was whether money could be advanced into another trust for the beneficiary for this purpose. In *Pilkington*'s case T left a share of his residue on protective trusts for his nephew for life and then for such of his children or remoter issue as he should appoint and in default of appointment to such of the nephew's children as attained 21, in equal shares. The nephew had three children one of whom was a two year old daughter, Penelope, who was also one of the beneficiaries under a trust created in her grandfather's will, by which she received the income at 21 and the capital at 30, and if she died before then for such of her children, if any, as attained 21. The trustees of the trust under T's will proposed to advance, with the consent of the nephew, one-half of Penelope's presumptive share and pay it to the trustees of a new trust which was being set up for Penelope's benefit. The question was whether the trustees could properly so exercise the power of advancement. It was held that:

1. Section 32 did not restrict the width of the manner or purpose of the advancement. So long as an advancement was for the benefit of the person in whose favour it was made, it was no objection that other persons benefited incidentally as a result of the advancement, nor that the money advanced was settled on fresh trusts.
2. The exercise of a power of advancement which had the effect of creating a fresh settlement was analogous to the exercise of a special power of appointment and was accordingly subject to the perpetuity rule. On the facts the perpetuity rule was not satisfied and the advancement therefore failed.

It is important that the advancement is for the benefit of the beneficiary and that it is applied for the purpose specified. If the trustees make advancements without seeing that they are applied for the purposes for which they were made or know that they will not be so applied, they may be held personally liable to replace the money. An illustration of this is provided by *Re Pauling's Settlement Trusts* [1964] Ch 303. The facts were that under a marriage settlement property was directed to be held on trust for the wife for life with remainder to her children or remoter issue. The settlement contained an express power to advance to the children up to one-half of their expectant share with the written consent of the wife, their mother. The wife had four children entitled in remainder. The wife and her husband had an extravagant lifestyle and were always in need of money. In 1948 the husband sought the means to obtain a house on the Isle of Man and on legal advice the trustee advanced £8,450 for this purpose on condition that the house was settled on the wife and children. The house was to the knowledge of the trustee conveyed into the sole name of the father who subsequently mortgaged it for £5,000 and ultimately sold it, dissipating all of the money. An advance of £1,000 was also made to buy furniture for the house out of the shares of the two eldest children; this was credited to the wife's bank account and was used for her personal expenditure. A third advance was made of £2,600, out of the shares of the two eldest children, for the purpose of paying off a loan made by the trustee to the wife under another settlement. In return the children were assigned insurance policies on the wife's life. However, these were only worth £650 and the difference was lost to them. Another advance was made on the share of the third child to the extent of £3,260 to buy furniture for the family home in Chelsea. In fact the money was spent on the property in the Isle of Man and in reducing the wife's overdraft. Finally an advance of £6,500 was made out of the youngest child's share when he attained 21. This was paid into the wife's account and dissipated by her. The children brought an action against the trustee alleging the above advances were improper and each sued to recover advances purported to have been made to him or her for his or her benefit. The Court of Appeal held that:

1. An advance for a stated purpose could properly be made to a beneficiary if the trustee reasonably believed that the beneficiary could be trusted to carry out the stated purpose. However, a trustee could not advance money to a beneficiary leaving him free, legally and morally, to apply the money for the stated purpose or in any way he chose. The trustee had a responsibility to enquire if the money was applied for the stated purpose.
2. Where money was advanced for an express purpose, the beneficiary to whom it was advanced was under a duty to carry out the purpose and could not apply it for another purpose. If any misapplication came to the trustee's notice, he could not safely make further advances for a particular purpose without making sure that the money was applied for that purpose.
3. On the facts and taking into account the principles of law stated, the trustees were liable for the losses incurred by the children in respect of all of the advances above.

Restrictions on power of advancement

The proviso to s32(1) TA 1925 sets out three limitations on the power of advancement. These are:

Section 32(1)(a): money paid or applied for advancement shall not exceed altogether in amount one-half of the presumptive or vested share or interest of that person in the trust property. Again this can be, and often is, amended with the limitation of one-half being excluded.

In short, s32(1)(a) limits advancements to a maximum total of half of the beneficiary's interest.

EXAMPLE:
'£20,000 to my eldest daughter A when she marries.'

The trustees can make any number of advancements to A but these must not exceed £10,000 in total. The advancements can be made to A even if she has no intention of marrying and do not have to be returned by her.

Section 32(1)(b): if a beneficiary becomes entitled absolutely to a share in the trust fund, the money advanced shall be brought into account as part of the share.

EXAMPLE:
'£60,000 upon trust for my three children A, B and C until C attains 25.'

The presumptive share of each child is £20,000. Under s32(1)(a) the trustees can advance up to £10,000 to each of A, B and C. Should the trustees decide to make an advancement of £5,000 to A when he is 21 to set up in business, then he will only receive £15,000 when he reaches 25 for he will have received £5,000 of £20,000 presumptive share already.

Section 32(1)(c): no payment or application shall be made so as to prejudice any person entitled to prior life interest or other interest whether vested or contingent unless such person is in existence and of full age and consents in writing to the advancement. See also *Henley and Another* v *Wardell and Others* (1988) The Times 29 January, where it was held that on the true construction of the will in issue this rule applied to a power of advancement granted by the will which enlarged the statutory power.

EXAMPLE:
'To A for life, remainder to B and C in equal shares.'

As A has a life interest the capital is held on trust to produce income for his benefit, thus to make any advancements during A's lifetime would deprive him of his entitlement by reducing the income he receives. However, if A consents in writing to an advancement to either B or C then an advancement is possible, but A must be of full age. If A had an interest under a protective trust (see s33 TA 1925) then he could not safely consent to an advancement of any capital to B or C without destroying the protective trust and bringing a discretionary trust into existence. To avoid this problem s33(1)(i) TA specifically states that consent to an advancement under s32(1)(c) is not an occasion which will determine a protective trust.

Where gifts on trust are contingent upon the happening of certain events, the operation of the power of advancement may not appear elementary. The examples below illustrate some more awkward cases.

Contingent gift to a class

1. '£60,000 to the first of my sons to be called to the Bar.'
    The presumptive share of each son is prima facie £60,000 as only one son can take the gift. However, under s32(1)(a) the presumptive share of each son in such cases is the appropriate sum in relation to the number of beneficiaries. Thus, if

the settlor had three sons A, B and C the presumptive share of each would be £20,000. If no money has been advanced then the first to be called to the Bar would receive £60,000. If some money has been advanced then the first to be called to the Bar would only receive what is left. Advancements could not be recovered from those who received them.

2. '£9,000 to such of my sons A, B and C as are called to the Bar before attaining the age of 30.'

   If B received an advance of £1,000 to buy books, and was subsequently called to the Bar, he would be able to call for £2,000 under the rule in *Saunders* v *Vautier*, as being the share to which he is then absolutely entitled. At this point he also has a vested interest in the remaining £6,000, liable to be divested if A or C is called under 30. So long as that possibility exists, each of A and C has a presumptive share of £3,000, but once B has been called the trust cannot fail. If either A or C passes the age of 30 without being called, his interest ceases and that of the remaining two increases by £1,500 each and B will be entitled unconditionally if and when both pass 30 without being called.

The power of advancement under s32 does not apply to land or capital money under the Settled Land Act 1925 but only to money, or securities, or to property which is held on trust for sale: see s32(2). Under s32(3), the statutory power of advancement does not apply to pre-1926 settlements.

The power of advancement is exercisable with a power of appointment in certain instances.

EXAMPLE:

'£10,000 to such of my sons A, B and C as my widow may appoint, with remainder to my niece X absolutely.'

In this example if the power of appointment is not exercised then X will take the £10,000. The power of appointment does not exclude the power of advancement in X's favour here and the trustees can advance her up to £5,000 without needing to obtain the consent of A, B and C. However, if the widow exercises the power of appointment in favour of, for example, A, giving him £2,000, then A takes a vested interest in this, depriving X of any interest in it in the future. The settlor may well, in a settlement such as this, exclude the statutory power of advancement to prevent X gaining half the trust property.

Effect on supplementary benefits claims

For the Court of Appeal's ruling as to the extent to which, in the making of assessments to 'assessment units' of supplementary benefits and allowances by the social security authorities under the Supplementary Benefit (Resources) Regulations 1981 (SI 1981 No 1527), potential rights of dependent minors under ss31 and 32 Trustee Act 1925 should be taken into consideration: see *Peters* v *Chief Adjudication Officer* [1989] Fam Law 318.

The Court of Appeal ruled that money held on trust for such minors must be taken to be a 'capital resource', for the purpose of the regulations. The resource value for this purpose was the actual value of the minor's current interest under the trust, not the value of the interest to which he would become entitled on reaching full age. In this case it was held that 50 per cent of the value of the fund in question should be the appropriate valuation.

18.10 Control over trustees' powers

Introduction

Where a trustee is under a duty to do something, for example, to invest the trust funds in accordance with the terms of the trust instrument or the law generally, a failure on his part to comply with such a duty is a breach of trust which will be remedied by the court on the application of any interested party.

Where a trustee has a power to do something, for example, to maintain an infant beneficiary, the exercise of the power is at the discretion of the trustee and so long as it is exercised bona fide the court will not interfere.

The beneficiaries under a trust may be dissatisfied with the manner in which a trustee exercises the powers given to him and the purpose of this section is to examine the limited ways in which the exercise of such powers can be controlled.

Control by beneficiaries

The most effective method by which the beneficiaries can control the powers of the trustees is by threatening to bring the trust to an end, or actually bringing it to an end, if they are in a position to do so. Under the rule in *Saunders* v *Vautier* (1841) 4 Beav 115 where all the beneficiaries are of full age and have as between themselves an absolute, vested, and indefeasible interest in the trust property, they can call upon the trustees to hand it over to them. Subject to the following paragraphs, the rule applies to individual beneficiaries who satisfy these requirements as well as in cases where all the beneficiaries satisfy them: see *Berry* v *Green* [1938] AC 575. For example, if property was held on trust for A, B, and C contingent upon each of them attaining 25 and they were now aged 18, 16 and 14 respectively, it would be possible for A to demand that the trustees hand to him his share of the trust fund together with any accumulations of income. B and C could also demand their shares as soon as they attained full age: see *Josselyn* v *Josselyn* (1837) 9 Sim 63. The rule also applies to discretionary trusts as is indicated by *Re Smith* [1928] Ch 915 and *Re Nelson* [1928] Ch 920n. In the latter case a testator left a fund upon discretionary trusts to pay the income to his son, his son's wife and their children as they should think fit. The son, his wife and their only child joined together to demand that all the income be paid to them. The Court of Appeal held that the trustees were obliged to comply with the request because if all the members of a class joined together to demand the fund they must be treated as one person, for whose benefit the trustees were directed to apply the whole of a particular fund.

Where several beneficiaries are interested in trust funds, those who are dissatisfied with the exercise of trustees' powers may be able to call for their individual shares under the rule in *Saunders* v *Vautier*. To do this they have to show that the interests of other beneficiaries would not be harmed. In a trust for sale of land, a beneficiary could call for his share of the proceeds of sale if the land has been sold: see *Re Marshall* [1914] 1 Ch 192. However, if the land is still unsold, he could not call for a share of the land as that would affect the interests of other beneficiaries: see *Re Marshall*. The rule also applies to personalty. In *Re Weiner* [1956] 2 All ER 482 a beneficiary who was absolutely entitled to 45 per cent of a testator's estate requested the executors to transfer to him his entitlement. The other beneficiaries objected to this because the estate comprised three-quarters of the share capital in a private company and they argued that to allow this to be split to give the beneficiary his entitlement absolutely would be against their interests as it would cause them to lose control of the company. It was held that the beneficiary was entitled to a transfer of the shares in specie to his own name as the holding was easily divisible. If the position were otherwise there could never be a division of the shareholding since it must necessarily involve a loss of control.

According to the new provisions in the Trusts of Land and Appointment of Trustees Act 1996, any trustee or holder of a proprietary interest may apply for an order relating to the exercise by the trustees of any of their functions or declaring the nature or extent of any proprietary interest. Section 15 of the Act, which does not apply if the application is by a trustee in bankruptcy, outlines a number of factors to which the court must have regard.

Control by the court

The court has no power to interfere with the exercise of a trustee's discretion unless the discretion is being exercised mala fides. This is because any other rule would take the discretion away from the trustees and inevitably lead to trustees being rather reluctant to make decisions. One particular illustration of this is, however, no longer valid. In *Re Brocklebank* [1948] Ch 206 a testator directed that his small residuary estate should be held on trust for his wife for life with remainder to his children. Two trustees were appointed by the will to administer the trusts. When one of the trustees wished to retire he and the beneficiaries wished to appoint Lloyd's Bank in his place. The other trustee refused to join in this, to exercise the statutory powers under s36 TA 1925 to appoint the bank, as he considered it too expensive for such a small estate. The beneficiaries took out a summons asking the court to order the trustee to concur. The court held that the beneficiaries were not entitled to control the discretion of the trustees in this way, they could either put an end to the trust or continue to abide by the decisions of the trustees. The effect of the provisions in the Trusts of Land and Appointment of Trustees Act 1996, in giving beneficiaries powers to appoint and remove trustees, is to reverse the decision in *Re Brocklebank*.

19

Variation of Trusts

19.1 Introduction

19.2 Variation under court's inherent jurisdiction

19.3 Variation under statutory provisions

19.4 Variation of Trusts Act 1958

19.1 Introduction

As a general rule the court has no power to sanction a departure from the terms of a trust; the trustees must follow the terms laid down in the trust instrument: see *Re New* [1901] 2 Ch 534.

The general rule in this area has been much eroded in recent years by statute, especially by the Variation of Trusts Act 1958. Prior to statutory provisions the court only had a limited power to authorise trustees to depart from the terms of the trust in exceptional cases under its inherent jurisdiction. However, it was recognised that this did not permit what would be, in many cases, sensible alterations in the trust.

19.2 Variation under court's inherent jurisdiction

In *Chapman* v *Chapman* [1954] AC 429 Lord Morton classified the cases where the court could, under its inherent jurisdiction, give trustees additional powers to allow a variation in the terms of a trust. These were:

1. 'Cases in which the court has effected changes in the nature of an infant's property.'

    This is now only of historical interest. Under it, trustees were formerly permitted to convert personalty held on trust for an infant into realty on the basis that it would still be considered as personalty in the eyes of equity thereafter. The reason for this was connected with the pre-1926 law of succession, by which realty would have automatically devolved on the heir-at-law. Thus, by permitting the purchase of realty but regarding the property concerned as personalty, the rights of succession in the infant's property were not affected.

2. 'Cases in which the court has allowed the trustees of settled property to enter into some business transaction which was not authorised by the settlement.'

This exception does not extend to allowing trustees to carry out any business transaction which is outside the trust merely because it would be beneficial to the trust. It is confined to cases of emergency where circumstances have arisen which could not have been foreseen or anticipated by the author of the trust, and the consent of the beneficiaries cannot be obtained because, for example, they are infants. Thus in *Re New* (before) Romer LJ said:

'.... it not infrequently happens that some peculiar state of circumstances arises for which provision is not expressly made by the trust instrument, and which renders it most desirable, and it may be even essential, for the benefit of the estate and in the interest of all the cestuis que trust, that certain acts should be done by the trustees which in ordinary circumstances they would have no power to do. In a case of this kind, which may reasonably be supposed to be one not forseen or anticipated by the author of the trust, where the trustees are embarrassed by the emergency that has arisen and the duty cast upon them to do what is best for the estate, and the consent of all the beneficiaries cannot be obtained by reason of some of them not being sui juris or in existence, then it may be right for the court, and the court in a proper case would have jurisdiction, to sanction on behalf of all concerned such acts on behalf of the trustees ... it need scarcely be said that the court will not be justified in sanctioning every act desired by trustees and beneficiaries merely because it may appear beneficial to the estate ...'

This exception has been used to allow trustees to mortgage settled land to enable them to carry out vital repairs to the land: see *Re Jackson* (1882) 21 Ch D 786. In *Re Tollemache* [1903] 1 Ch 955 the court refused to exercise its jurisdiction under this head where it was proposed to mortgage the life tenant's interest to increase his income, even though this did not affect the remaindermen. Kekewich J held that although the proposed mortgage would have been of benefit there was no real emergency and as such the court had no inherent jurisdiction to authorise the variation.

3. 'Cases in which the court has allowed maintenance out of income which the settlor or testator directed to be accumulated.'

This has been dealt with already under the statutory power of maintenance. In *Re Collins* (1886) 32 Ch D 229 the court used its inherent jurisdiction to allow maintenance for a minor where his enjoyment of a fund was postponed on the basis that the settlor could not have intended to leave the infant unprovided for or in a state of such modest means that he could not be educated properly for the position and fortune the settlor intended him to have. It was also stated that this exception is not confined to cases of emergency or necessity.

4. 'Cases in which the court has approved a compromise on behalf of infants and possible after-born beneficiaries.'

This exception was in issue in *Chapman* v *Chapman*. In that case the court was asked to authorise the resettlement of trust funds on new trusts which avoided estate duty by the omission of a maintenance clause. The House of Lords held there was no power to do this under the inherent jurisdiction as it amounted to an alteration or re-arrangement. This exception only permitted the court to approve a compromise in cases of dispute where there were disagreements or doubts about the terms of the trust. See in particular *Allen* v *Distillers Co (Biochemicals) Ltd* [1974] QB 384, and *Mason* v *Fairbrother* [1983] 2 All ER 1078.

19.3 Variation under statutory provisions

Section 53 TA 1925

The section provides:

> 'Where an infant is beneficially entitled to any property the court may, with a view to the application of the capital or income thereof for the maintenance, education or benefit of the infant, make an order –
> a) appointing any person to convey such property; or
> b) in the case of stock or a thing in action, vesting in any person the right to transfer or call for a transfer of stock, or to receive the dividends or income thereof, or sue for or recover such thing in action upon such terms as the court may think fit.'

The effect of this provision is to empower the court to order property to be sold and conveyed so that the proceeds of sale may be used for the infant beneficiary's maintenance, education or benefit. Thus, in *Re Gower's Settlement* [1934] Ch 365 an infant remainderman's interest was mortgaged so as to provide for maintenance and education.

Section 57 TA 1925

This section provides:

> 'Where in the management, or administration of any trust property vested in trustees, any sale, lease, mortgage, surrender, release or other disposition, or any purchase, investment acquisition expenditure or other transaction is in the opinion of the court expedient but the same cannot be effected by reason of the absence of any power for that purpose vested in the trustees by the trust instrument, if any, or by law, the court may by order confer upon the trustees, either generally or in any particular instance, the necessary power for the purpose, on such terms, and subject to such provisions and conditions, if any, as the court may think fit and may direct in what manner any money authorised to be expended, and the costs of any transaction, are to be paid or borne as between capital and income.'

This section extended the powers of the court so as to allow a variation in the terms of a trust other than in cases of emergency; a variation can be made here in cases of expediency. The provisions of s57 are, however, limited in effect in the following ways:

1. The section is confined to alterations in the 'management or administration' of trust property; it does not permit a remoulding of beneficial interests. The court can only sanction arrangements which ensure that the trust property is managed as advantageously as possible in the interests of the beneficiaries. In *Re Downshire* [1953] 2 WLR 94 Evershed MR said the purpose of s57 was:

> '... to secure that trust property should be managed as advantageously as possible in the interests of the beneficiaries, and with that object in view, to authorise specific dealings with the property which the court might have felt itself unable to sanction under the inherent jurisdiction, either because no actual emergency had arisen or because of inability to show that the position which called for intervention was one which the creator of the trust could not reasonably have forseen, but it was no part of the legislative aim to disturb the rule that the court will not rewrite a trust.'

2. It does not apply to Settled Land Act settlements: see s57(4) TA 1925.

The effect of the court sanctioning an alteration in the powers of the trustees under s57 is as if the extra powers given were inserted as an overriding power in the trust instrument: see *Re Mair* [1935] Ch 562.

Most cases dealing with s57 are heard in chambers and are not reported but examples of where s57 has been used include authorising the sale of chattels in a trust preventing this: *Re Hope* [1929] 2 Ch 136; the sale of land where requisite consents have been refused: *Re Beale's ST* [1932] 2 Ch 15; and enlarging the range of permissible investments: *Re Brassey's Settlements* [1955] 1 WLR 192. See also *Anker-Petersen* v *Anker-Petersen and Others* [1991] LSG 1 May at p32; see Chapter 14, section 14.9.

Section 64 SLA 1925

The section provides:

> 'Any transaction affecting or concerning the settled land, or any part thereof, or any other land (not being a transaction otherwise authorised by this Act, or by the settlement) which in the opinion of the court would be for the benefit of the settled land, or any part thereof, or the persons interested under the settlement, may under an order of the court, be effected by a tenant for life, if it is one which could have been validly effected by an absolute owner.'

This section is wider than s57 TA 1925 according to the Court of Appeal in *Re Downshire* because, unlike s57, it is not limited to managerial or administrative acts but also allows alteration in the beneficial interests. This applies even if the beneficiaries themselves are sui juris and strongly opposed to the proposed variation: *Hambro and Others* v *Duke of Marlborough and Others* [1994] 3 All ER 332.

However, before s64 can be used, the court has to be satisfied that the proposed transaction is for the overall benefit of the settled land, or of a part of it, or of the beneficiaries.

The addition of potential new beneficiaries which gave tax advantages under

Schedule 4 of the Capital Transfer Act 1984, was permitted under s64 of the SLA in *Raikes* v *Lygon* [1988] 1 WLR 281.

Mental Health Act 1983

The Court of Protection is given wide powers, extending to that of settlement, in respect of the property of a patient who falls within its remit: see s96(1)(d) in particular.

Matrimonial Causes Act 1973

Again in the specific instance of matrimonial proceedings the court has wide-ranging powers. These extend to varying ante-nuptial or post-nuptial agreements.

19.4 Variation of Trusts Act 1958

This Act was introduced after recommendations made by the Law Reform Committee following the decision in *Chapman* v *Chapman*. The Act gives the court a discretionary power to approve arrangements or variations on behalf of four classes of persons as set out in s1(1) of the Act. The importance of the Act lies in the fact that it allows the court to remould beneficial interests. Section 1(1) provides:

'Where property, whether real or personal, is held on trusts arising, whether before or after the passing of this Act, under any will, settlement or other disposition, the court may if it thinks fit by order approve on behalf of –

a) any person having, directly or indirectly, an interest, whether vested or contingent, under the trusts who by reason of infancy or other incapacity is incapable of assenting, or

b) any person (whether ascertained or not) who may become entitled, directly or indirectly, to an interest under the trusts as being at a future date or on the happening of a future event a person of any specified description or a member of any specified class of persons, so however that this paragraph shall not include any person who would be of that description, or a member of that class, as the case may be, if the said date had failed or the said event had happened at the date of the application to the court or

c) any person unborn, or

d) any person in respect of any discretionary interest of his under protective trusts where the interest of the principal beneficiary has not failed or determined, any arrangement (by whomsoever proposed, and whether or not there is any other person beneficially interested who is capable of assenting thereto) varying or revoking all or any of the trusts, or enlarging the powers of the trusts of managing or administering any of the property subject to the trusts:

Provided that except by virtue of paragraph (d) of this subsection the court shall not approve an arrangement on behalf of any person unless the carrying out thereof would be for the benefit of that person.'

Section 1(1) is wide in its scope and includes not only variation of powers of management and administration by enlargement but also variation of beneficial interests in a trust. The term 'arrangement' referred to in the proviso to s1(1) is given a wide meaning so as to cover anything which may amount to a variation of the trust.

The scope of s1(1), although wide as to the nature of the arrangement that may be put before the court for approval, is narrow in its scope in that the court may only approve variation on behalf of the persons who fall within the provisions of s1(1)(a) to (d). The court does not have power to approve a variation on behalf of any person who is not within the categories set out in s1(1) so that the consent of all such persons to the variation must be obtained first, before the application is put before the court. The categories on whose behalf a variation may be approved are:

Persons incapable of consenting

As s1(1)(a) indicates, this permits the court to approve a variation on behalf of infant beneficiaries and also on behalf of those who are incapacitated by mental illness or senility. In *Re Whittall* [1973] 1 WLR 1027 the court approved a variation of a settlement on behalf of four infant grandchildren who would take as remaindermen, while in *Re CL* [1969] 1 All ER 1104 a variation was approved on behalf of a mental patient who had a protected life interest under a trust.

Persons entitled on a contingency

Under s1(1)(b) the court may vary a trust on behalf of persons who might become entitled at a future date or future event as members of a class which is ascertainable only at a future time. For example, variation could be approved under s1(1)(b) in a trust to 'A for life, remainder to any woman he might marry', so as to cut out the remainder if A was unmarried and had little or no prospects of marrying. But if A was married this would not be possible because s1(1)(b) specifically excludes the power to approve a variation on behalf of any person who has satisfied the contingency or who is a member of any class at the date the variation is sought. If a marriage settlement provided for ultimate remainders to the next-of-kin, a variation could not be approved on behalf of those who clearly were next-of-kin at the date the application was made to the court. In *Re Suffert's Settlement* [1961] Ch 1 the income of a trust fund was held on protective trusts for a spinster, aged 61, remainder to her issue, with ultimate remainder to her next-of-kin in default of issue. The spinster had no children and sought a variation under s1(1)(b) so as to give her the capital in the fund absolutely. At the date of the application there were three adult cousins who were interested as next-of-kin if she died at the date of the application to the court. Only one of these had consented to the variation. Buckley J held that he could approve the variation on behalf of those next-of-kin who were as yet unborn or unascertained but not on behalf of the existing next-of-kin. They fell within the exclusion to s1(1)(b) and all had to consent to the variation.

In *Re Moncrieff* [1962] 1 WLR 1344 a settlement gave S a life interest with remainder to her descendants. S had one daughter who died aged 14 and, also, an adopted son. She applied for a variation under s1(1)(b) so that £1,000 be set aside in the fund and the balance paid to her. Buckley J held that as the adopted son was within the terms of the settlement and 'ascertained' at the date of the application, approval could not be given on his behalf. In *Knocker* v *Youle* [1986] 1 WLR 934 a share of a trust fund was held for the benefit of the settlor's daughter for life, remainder to whomsoever she should appoint and in default of appointment, to the settlor's son on similar trusts. In default of appointment by him there were ultimate trusts in favour of, among others, the children of the settlor's four married sisters who at the time of the application were numerous, and it was impracticable to obtain their consent. The court refused to approve a variation on behalf of these children under s1(1)(b) because they were not persons who 'may become entitled ... to an interest' but already had an interest, albeit a contingent interest, liable to defeat by the power of appointment. They fell within the proviso to s1(1)(b) in that if the earlier trusts had failed at the date of the application to the court they would have been members of the specified class. The only way the variation could be effected was by obtaining their approval.

Persons 'unborn'

A variation can be approved on behalf of unborn persons. For example, if a trust left funds to A for life, remainder to A's children in equal shares, and A had four adult children at the date of the application, a variation could be approved on behalf of those children 'unborn' provided all the adult children consented. An application under this category should only be brought if there is a realistic possibility of further children being born. If A were a male an application would always be necessary, unless perhaps it was proved he was irreversibly infertile. But if A was female and past child-bearing age no application under s1(1)(c) would be necessary. In *Re Pettifor's WT* [1966] Ch 257 a testator set up a trust for his daughter for life, remainder to her children in equal shares. When the daughter was aged 78 it was sought to vary the trusts under s1(1)(c) so as to enable the trust fund to be distributed subject to a small sum being set aside to pay for an insurance policy to cover the possibility of further children being born. Pennycuick J dismissed the application saying:

> 'An application under the Variation of Trusts Act 1958 to cover that contingency, namely, the event of a birth of a child to a woman of seventy-eight, is misconceived and is not a proper application to make under this Act ... the court will allow funds to be distributed on the footing that at a certain age, normally in the middle or late fifties, a woman has become incapable of childbearing.'

Protective trusts

Under s1(1)(d) the court can vary the interests of persons who would become entitled to be considered as beneficiaries under a discretionary trust arising on the determination of a protective trust, so long as the protective trust has not determined. In this category, unlike s1(1)(b), it does not matter that the persons who could take under the discretionary trust, if it arose, are born or ascertained.

Benefit

Under s1(1) a variation may only be approved on behalf of any person falling with s1(1)(a) to (c) if it is for the 'benefit' of that person. 'Benefit' seems to be given a liberal interpretation, it is not confined to financial benefit but also includes moral or social benefit. In *Re CL* [1969] 1 All ER 1104 a variation was approved on behalf of an elderly mental patient whose condition was unlikely to improve; she was receiving £14,000 per annum from the settlement as life tenant and had over £7,000 from another settlement. The effect of the variation was to accelerate the remainders to her two adopted daughters; the actual loss to the life tenant was only £500 since she paid the remainder in tax and was unlikely ever to be in a position to use such income. Many variations are made to obtain fiscal advantages. The courts do not seem to object if the variation involves tax avoidance, but note the House of Lords decision in *Furniss* v *Dawson* [1984] AC 474. It seems a variation which involves tax advantages will not be approved if it is not for the moral or social benefit of the beneficiaries. In *Re Weston's Settlements* [1969] 1 Ch 223 a settlor made two settlements for the benefit of each of his two sons for life, remainder to their children. After the introduction of capital gains tax the families moved to Jersey and proposed to set up home there. An application was made to have the settlements revoked and similar trusts set up in Jersey so as to avoid capital gains tax. All the adult beneficiaries supported the application. However, the Court of Appeal refused to approve the matter on behalf of infant beneficiaries because the financial benefits were not the only benefits to consider. As Lord Denning MR said:

'But I think it necessary to add this third proposition. (iii) The court should not consider merely the financial benefit to the infants or unborn children, but also their educational and social benefit. There are many things in life more worth while than money. One of these things is to be brought up in this our England, which is still "the envy of less happier lands". I do not believe it is for the benefit of children to be uprooted from England and transported to another country simply to avoid tax. It was very different with the children of the Seale family, which Buckley J considered. That family had emigrated to Canada many years before, with no thought of tax avoidance, and had brought up the children there as Canadians. It was very proper that the trust should be transferred to Canada. But here the family had only been in Jersey three months when they presented this scheme to the court. The inference is irresistible: the underlying purpose was to go there in order to avoid tax. I do not think that this will be all to the good for the children. I should imagine that, even if they had stayed in this country, they would have had a very considerable fortune at their disposal, even after paying tax. The only thing that Jersey can do for them is to give them an even greater fortune. Many a child has been ruined by being given too much. The avoidance of tax may be lawful, but it is not yet a virtue. The Court of Chancery should not encourage or support it – it should not give its approval to it – if by so doing it would imperil the true welfare of the children, already born or yet to be born.'

The reference to the Seale family is concerned with *Re Seale's Marriage Settlement* [1961] Ch 574 in which Buckley J approved the revocation of trusts in England on behalf of infants and a resettlement on similar trusts in Canada. In this case the family were emigrating permanently to Canada, where the head of the family had obtained a new job. In *Re Weston's Settlements* the evidence before the Court of Appeal tended to suggest that the family were moving for the sole reason of avoiding tax. However it is now doubtful that such a pro-England line would still be taken by the courts today. See also *Re Remnant's ST* [1970] Ch 560 and *Re Tinker's Settlement* [1960] 1 WLR 1011 where the court considered the application of the Act in resolving 'disputes within the family'.

Exercise of jurisdiction

Before the court approves an 'arrangement' under the 1958 Act it must be satisfied that if is fair and proper in the light of the purpose of the trust as it appears from the trust instrument and any available evidence. It will not, therefore, sanction an 'arrangement which cuts at the roots of the testator's wishes and intentions.' In *Re Steed's Will Trusts* [1960] Ch 407 a testator devised property to the plaintiff on protective trusts for her life and after her death to any person she should appoint. She exercised this general power of appointment in her own favour and wanted to eliminate the protective trust to give herself an absolute interest. The only other persons potentially entitled were a possible future husband or husbands she might have – she was still unmarried – and their issue. If she committed some act, such as becoming bankrupt, this would terminate her life interest and give rise to a discretionary trust in favour of those persons. These contingencies were remote and an unlikely possibility, for even if she married she was beyond the normal age of child bearing. The Court of Appeal held that the variation would not be approved because as Evershed MR said:

> 'I propose in this judgment to forbear from entering, except where absolutely necessary, into matters of fact which might only serve to rub salt into existing wounds. Suffice it to say that the plaintiff was one who served loyally and most skilfully for a long period of time the testator and the testator's wife. In consideration for those services the testator included in his will provisions for her benefit, contained in cl 9 and cl 10. It is quite plain on the evidence that the testator, while anxious to show his gratitude to the plaintiff was no less anxious that she should be well provided for and not exposed to the temptation, which he thought was real, of being, to use a common phrase, sponged on by one of her brothers. I fully realise that the plaintiff's natural affection for that brother is not a matter which one can in any sense condemn. Blood is, after all, thicker than water, and the happiness of the plaintiff, according to her own view at any rate, is very much linked up with the assocation with that brother and the brother's daughter and wife. On the other side, however, are these trustees on whom has been placed an obligation, a duty to give effect to the intentions of the man who provided the money ...'

The court is confined to approving an arrangement on behalf of one of the four classes, set out in s1(1). It cannot approve an arrangement on behalf of other beneficiaries. If an adult beneficiary will not give his consent to the scheme, it will not bind him: see *Re Suffert's Settlement*.

Effect of order

The effect of the 1958 Act is to give the court power to approve an 'arrangement' on behalf of those who are unable to give their consent to it. The variation is not made by the court itself but the court is acting on behalf of those beneficiaries unable to give their consent. In *Re Holmden's Settlement Trusts* [1968] AC 685 Lord Reid said:

> 'Each beneficiary is bound because he has consented to the variation. If he was not of full age when the arrangement was made, he is bound because the court was authorised by the Act of 1958 to approve it on his behalf and did so by making an order. If he was of full age and did not in fact consent, he is not affected by the order of the court and he is not bound. So the arrangement must be regarded as an arrangement made by the beneficiaries themselves. The court merely acted on behalf of or as representing those beneficiaries who were not in a position to give their own consent or approval.'

The variation takes effect as soon as the order is made by the court, without the necessity for any further instrument. As equitable interests are being dealt with, one would have thought it was necessary for those adult beneficiaries giving their consent to at least sign a written document to satisfy s53(1)(c) LPA 1925 which requires the disposition of an equitable interest to be in writing and signed by the person able to dispose of it. This point was considered by Megarry J in *Re Holt's Settlement* [1969] 1 Ch 100 and he concluded it was not necessary to satisfy that provision in a variation of trusts case for two reasons:

1. By empowering the court to vary beneficial interests by an order Parliament had provided by necessary implication an exception to s53(1)(c).
2. Where the arrangement consisted of a specifically enforceable agreement for valuable consideration, the beneficial interest would have passed to the purchasers on the making of the agreement. A constructive trust existed and was outside s53(1)(c) by virtue of s53(2).

These reasons are not very convincing but it should be noted that Megarry J had in mind the fact that prior to 1969 thousands of variations of trust cases had been dealt with by the court without regard to s53(1)(c). His conclusion provides an escape for such cases but it would seem expedient that all beneficiaries whose consent is necessary to a variation should be asked to give that consent in writing signed by them.

20

Breach of Trust I: Personal Remedies

20.1 Introduction

20.2 Injunction

20.3 Personal liability

20.4 Measure of liability

20.5 Defences

20.6 Contribution and indemnity

20.1 Introduction

A trustee commits a breach of trust when he fails to carry out his duties properly or exceeds them. The various ways in which a breach of trust might occur are without limit. They include serious matters such as where the trustee absconds with the trust moneys, failing to deal with the investment of the trust funds correctly, for example, failing to follow s8 TA 1925 when investing in mortgages of land: see *Shaw* v *Cates* [1909] 1 Ch 389; or even minor matters which cause no loss, for example, failing to follow directions in the trust instrument regarding the appointment of additional trustees.

If a trustee performs his duties strictly in accordance with the law and the terms of the trust instrument he should never be in breach of trust. It is, however, very difficult for any trustee to carry through his office without at some time committing a breach. In fact in *National Trustees Co of Australasia Ltd* v *General Finance Co of Australia Ltd* [1905] AC 373 judicial approval was given to trustees committing 'judicious breaches of trust'.

It is advisable for a trustee to seek the approval of the court if he wishes to do an act which is beyond his authority. Should he neglect to do so, he may well find that he is responsible for a breach of trust and he may have to make good any loss to the trust estate.

The measure of liability for a breach of trust generally is the loss, direct or indirect, caused to the trust estate or, to put it another way, the measure of liability is compensatory and not punitive. This is dealt with in detail below.

There are several remedies available to beneficiaries for breach of trust, and each of these will be considered in turn, and then the possible defences available to trustees. The main remedies are:

1. An injunction.
2. An action against the trustee(s) in person, for loss suffered.
3. A proprietary remedy to recover the trust property.
4. An action against those who have received the trust property.

The main remedy for breach of trust is to sue the trustees personally for any loss to the trust estate. This remedy must be pursued before any proprietary remedies can be invoked: see *Re Diplock* [1948] Ch 465. But the remedy to recoup loss from the trustee personally is only worthwhile so long as the trustee is able to meet that loss. If he is insolvent or has absconded with the assets then the remedy is useless. Injunctions may be useful and are considered below. The third and fourth remedies referred to above are dealt with in Chapter 21, under the heading of tracing.

20.2 Injunction

Where a beneficiary has reason to believe that a trustee is about to commit a breach of trust he need not wait until it has happened before taking action. Instead he may obtain an injunction to restrain the threatened breach.

Examples of instances in which the court has granted injunction to prevent breaches of trust abound in the law reports. In *Fox* v *Fox* (1870) LR 11 Eq 142 an injunction was granted to prevent trustees distributing the trust property other than in accordance with the terms of the trust instrument. In *Milligan* v *Mitchell* (1833) an injunction was granted against trustees to prevent them electing ministers to the Church of Scotland who did not possess the appropriate qualifications, and in *Ludlow Corporation* v *Greenhouse* (1827) 1 Bli NS 17 an injunction was granted to prevent trustees demolishing a building.

20.3 Personal liability

A trustee's liability for breach of trust is in general limited to breaches for which he himself was responsible and generally not for those of his co-trustees, unless he himself was at fault, that is, the liability is normally personal and not vicarious. This was first recognised in *Townley* v *Sherborne* (1634) Bridg J 35 and is now statutory under s30(1) TA 1925 which provides:

> 'A trustee shall be chargeable only for money and securities actually received by him notwithstanding his signing any receipt for the sake of conformity, and shall be answerable and accountable only for his own acts, receipts, neglects or defaults, and not for those of any other trustee, not for any banker, broker, or other person with whom any trust money or securities may be deposited, nor for the insufficiency or deficiency of any securities, nor for any other loss, unless the same happens through his own wilful default.'

Section 30(1) TA 1925 does not give a trustee a blanket indemnity against breaches committed by his fellow trustees, it merely makes it clear that there is no question of one trustee being vicariously liable for the acts of a co-trustee. For example, if A and B are the trustees of a trust and A absconds with trust moneys, B will not be liable to replace them – unless B allowed the loss to occur through his own wilful default by allowing A to retain trusts funds when he should not have done so: see *Re Vickery* [1931] 1 Ch 572 and Chapter 18, section 18.7.

Where two or more trustees are liable for a breach of trust, their liability is joint and several. In such circumstances the beneficiaries are at liberty to claim the loss from any one or all of them as they choose: *Attorney-General* v *Wilson* (1840) Cr & Phil 1, 28. It is no concern of the beneficiaries to ascertain who actually committed the breach of trust because as between them and the trustees, all the trustees are equally liable for the breach of trust: *Re Harrison* [1891] 2 Ch 349. It is, however, for the beneficiaries to prove that there was a breach of trust which was due to the default of the trustees: *Re Brier* (1884) 26 Ch D 238. Should it become obvious that only one trustee was liable for a breach of trust then s30(1) will cover the other trustees against liability. See also Civil Liability (Contribution) Act 1978, following at section 20.6.

Whether a trustee is solely liable for a breach of trust or his co-trustees are also liable will depend on whether s30(1) TA 1925 applies to the particular case. Section 30(1) will not apply where a trustee knows his co-trustees are contemplating a breach of trust, or are in the act of a breach, and does nothing about it: see *Booth* v *Booth* (1838) 1 Beav 125; or tries to conceal a breach when he discovers it rather than remedying it: see *Boardman* v *Mosman* (1779) 1 Bro CC 68; or fails to supervise his co-trustees: see *Styles* v *Guy* (1849) 1 Mac & G 422. All these amount to a 'wilful default' for the purposes of s30(1). In *Re Vickery* this was defined as 'a breach of his duty, or is recklessly careless in the sense of not caring whether his act or omission is or is not a breach of his duty'.

A trustee's personal liability for any breach of trust he may have committed does not cease merely because he has retired or dies. In *Dixon* v *Dixon* (1879) 9 Ch D 587 a successful action was brought against the estate of a deceased trustee for losses caused by his breach of trust. If the trustee goes bankrupt, his personal liability does not cease either and the beneficiaries may prove in bankruptcy for the loss: see *Edwards* v *Hood-Barrs* [1905] 1 Ch 20. Whether it is worthwhile suing a bankrupt trustee is, of course, another matter. See also Limitation Act 1980, s21(3) which provides for a six-year limitation period for breach of trust actions unless procured by fraud or as against actual trust property (see section 20.5).

A newly appointed trustee will not normally be liable for a breach of trust committed before he was appointed; he is entitled to assume that the other trustees have performed their duties properly: see *Re Strahan* (1856) 8 De GM & G 291. On appointment, it is his duty to familiarise himself with the trust, and if in doing this he discovers any breaches he must take steps to remedy them, by legal action if necessary: see *Re Strahan*.

A trustee is not, prima facie, liable for the breaches committed by his successors. There are, however, some exceptions to this rule, for instance if a trustee retires in order to facilitate a breach of trust, or knowing that his co-trustees will commit a breach of trust when he retires.

In each of these cases the trustee is guilty of a breach of his duty to protect the trust property and he will be liable just as if he had committed the breach himself: see *Head* v *Gould* [1898] 2 Ch 250. The trustee will not be liable, however, if his retirement facilitated the breach unless it can be shown that he retired in contemplation of the particular breach committed: see *Head* v *Gould*. This presumably means that it is not possible to hold him liable where he knew that after his retirement some breach was likely, but not what it was in particular. In *Head* v *Gould* property was settled on Mrs Head for life with remainder to her three children. The settlement contained an express power of advancement. As Mrs Head was continually in financial difficulties her daughter asked the trustees for advances on her share to help her mother. This the trustees did and when the daughter's share was exhausted she pressed for more. The trustees refused to give her more and in the circumstances asked to be released from the trusteeship, suggesting that new trustees should be sought who were willing to make the advances. The trustees were replaced by the daughter and one Gould, a solicitor. Further advances were made to help Mrs Head, and trust property was sold off to do so. As a result the entitlement of one of the other children was lost. He sought to make both the old and the new trustees liable. Kekewich J held that as regards the old trustees they were not liable for the breaches committed by the new trustees. In order to make retiring trustees liable for a subsequent breach it had to be shown that that breach was in fact contemplated by them when the change in trustees took place and was not merely the outcome of, or rendered easy by, the change in trustees. However, the new trustees were liable. Gould as solicitor had advised on matters which were in fact a breach, and was liable, while the daughter had actively participated in the breaches. As Kekewich J said:

'In order to make a retiring trustee liable for a breach of trust committed by his successor you must show, and show clearly, that the very breach of trust which was in fact committed, was not merely the outcome of the retirement and new appointment, but was contemplated by the former trustee when such retirement and appointment took place ... It will not suffice to prove that the former trustees rendered easy or even intended, a breach of trust, if it was not in fact committed. They must be proved to have been guilty as accessories before the fact of the impropriety actually perpetrated.'

It must be noted that the previous discussion of liability addresses the trustee's civil liability. However it is also possible for a criminal liability to arise. See ss2(1)(c) and 4(2)(a) Theft Act 1968. This can result in sentences of up to a maximum, per offence, of ten years; plus a further year if the breach also involved breaching court directions, this being equated to contempt of court.

20.4 Measure of liability

The measure of liability for a breach of trust generally is the loss, direct or indirect, caused to the trust estate. Further, the onus is on the claimant to establish the causal link to the actions and loss, or possibly profit: see *Re Miller's Trust Deed* (1978) 75 LS Gaz 454. Different rules apply to the different possibilities that might arise.

1. If a trustee makes an unauthorised investment he will be liable for the loss incurred on realising it. In *Knott* v *Cottee* (1852) 16 Beav 77 a testator bequeathed his personal estate upon trust and directed the trustees to invest it in the public or government stocks or funds of Great Britain, or upon real security in England and Wales. The trustees invested in foreign stocks but in 1846 these were sold, under a court order, at a loss. In 1848 the court decreed these investments to be unauthorised and if they had been sold then they could have been sold at a profit. The question arose, what loss, if any, should the trustees be held liable for? It was held that the trustees were liable for the original sum invested less the amount received as proceeds of sale in 1846.

2. If a trustee improperly retains an unauthorised investment he will be liable for the difference between the price for which it is sold and that which would have been received if it had been sold at the proper time. In *Fry* v *Fry* (1859) 27 Beav 144 a testator, who died in 1834, directed in his will that the Langford Inn should be sold 'as soon as convenient after his decease ... for the most money that could be reasonably obtained for the same'. The trustees had difficulty in finding a buyer. In 1836 they advertised the inn for sale at £1,000, and an offer of £900 was refused. In 1843 a railway was opened depriving the inn of much of its coaching business. In 1854 the inn was again advertised for sale but no offer was received. The trustees were sued for breach of trust and found liable. It was held that the amount of damages to be awarded against the trustees should be the difference between £900 and the amount eventually received. This rule is varied slightly if the trustees were initially authorised to retain investments. Subject to any express revocation of this authority prior to 1961 any liability only arose if it resulted from the trustees' 'wilful default': see *Re Chapman* [1896] 2 Ch 763. Subsequent to this, s6(2) Trustee Investments Act 1961 requires trustees to take appropriate advice on such matters.

3. If a trustee improperly sells authorised investments he must replace them or pay the difference between the price received and the cost of replacement. In *Re Massingberd's Settlement* (1890) 63 LT 296 the trustees of a settlement had power to invest in government or real securities. In 1875 they sold off all such securities and reinvested in unauthorised mortgages. The mortgages were eventually realised and no money was lost on them. If the money had remained invested in authorised securities the yield to the trust would have been greater. The beneficiaries sued. The trustees were held liable for the difference between what

the mortgages yielded and what would have been received if the money had remained invested in the authorised securities.

4. Trustees should meet a direction to invest within a reasonable time. Failure results in them being liable for interest lost if the property is not invested: see *Attorney-General* v *Alford* (1855) 4 De GM & G 843. This is expanded if the investment relates to specific property and covers any profit lost as a result of the failure: see *Byrchall* v *Bradford* (1822) 6 Madd 235.

5. Compensation payable by trustees in respect of an action for restitution lost as a result of a continuing breach (ie the breach resulted in the trust property, a house, being sold to a bona fide purchaser for value without knowledge) was based on the highest intermediate value between the date of the breach and that of judgment. However, this requires there to have been an opportunity, even if only notional, to realise the value of the property during this period: see *Jaffray* v *Marshall* [1993] 1 WLR 1285.

6. If a solicitor, acting for both mortgagee and mortgagor, breaches his fiduciary duty by not informing the mortgagee of all relevant facts he is, prima facie, liable to remedy that breach. However, it must be shown that but for the breach of trust the 'beneficiary', ie mortgagee, would not have suffered a loss: *Target Holdings Ltd* v *Redfern (A Firm) and Another* [1995] 3 All ER 785 (HL).

The award made in cases of breach of trust is essentially one for restitution of the property lost and not for damages in the sense that these are awarded either in contract or in tort. The loss is assessed at the date of judgment and there can be no allowance for the tax the beneficiaries would have paid if they had received the full amount of capital and income: see *Re Bell's Indenture* [1980] 1 WLR 1217.

Where a profit is made as a result of a breach of trust the beneficiaries are entitled to claim it as it is subject to the trusts: see *Docker* v *Somes* (1834) 2 My & K 655. In some cases the trustees may have made unauthorised investments in different transactions, some of which produce a profit and some of which produce a loss. As a general rule they are not entitled to claim a set-off of the profits against the losses: see *Dimes* v *Scott* (1827) 4 Russ 195. However, if the profits and losses result from the same transaction or the same policy decision to adopt a particular course of action, a set-off may be permitted: see *Bartlett* v *Barclays Bank* [1980] Ch 515.

Where a loss has occurred to the trust estate as a result of a breach by the trustee, he is liable to replace the loss with interest. The rate of interest is in the discretion of the court but it is normally 4 per cent or 5 per cent if fraud related. In some cases interest has been awarded at higher rates where the trustees have profited out of the breach: see *Re Emmet's Estate* (1881) 17 Ch D 142. The 4 per cent rate is now recognised to be rather low and in *Bartlett* v *Barclays Bank* (1980) interest was awarded at the rate allowed from time to time on money in court.

20.5 Defences

Where a trustee is accused of a breach of trust he may, apart from attempting to rebut such allegations, make use of one or more of the defences which are available. These are:

Section 61 TA 1925

Under this provision the court has jurisdiction to relieve trustees from liability for certain breaches of trust. It provides:

> 'If it appears to the court that a trustee ... is or may be liable for a breach of trust ... but has acted honestly and reasonably, and ought fairly to be excused for the breach of trust and for omitting to obtain the directions of the court in the matter in which he committed such breach, then the court may relieve him either wholly or partly from personal liability for the same.'

The onus of proof is on the trustee to show that he acted 'honestly and reasonably' in order to succeed under s61: see *Re Stuart* [1897] 2 Ch 583. The section does not protect honest trustees, only honest trustees who have acted reasonably. In *Re Turner* [1897] 1 Ch 536 it was suggested that the trustee can only discharge this burden by showing that he was as prudent in his actions as he would have been in relation to his own affairs. Whether a trustee acted reasonably can only be decided by looking at the facts of each particular case. For example, if the trustee is a professional trustee such as a solicitor or a trust corporation, this will be taken into account and a heavy burden would lie on such trustees to make out a defence under s61: see *Bartlett* v *Barclay's Bank*. But, even if the trustee satisfies the conditions in the section, it is still within the court's discretion to grant him relief, wholly or partly, or at all. In exercising this discretion the court will consider the consequences of granting such relief on the beneficiaries and whether it would put them to considerable hardship: see *Re De Clifford* [1900] 2 Ch 707 and *Davis* v *Hutchings* [1907] 1 Ch 356. In *Perrins* v *Bellamy* [1899] 1 Ch 797 the trustees of a settlement mistakenly believed that they had a power of sale in the settlement and sold off some leaseholds. As a result, the income of the tenant for life was reduced and he sought to make then liable for his loss. It was held that in the circumstances the trustees had acted honestly and reasonably and ought to be excused. On s61 Kekewich J said:

> 'In the present case there is no imputation or ground for imputation of any dishonesty whatever. The legislature has made the absence of all dishonesty a condition precedent to the relief of the trustee from liability. But, that is not the grit of the section. The grit is in the words "reasonably, and ought fairly to be excused for the breach of trust" ... In the section the capulative "and" is used, it may well be argued that in order to bring a case within the section it must be shown not merely that the trustee has acted "reasonably", but also, that he ought "fairly" to be excused from the breach of trust. I venture, however, to think that, in general and in the absence of special circumstances, a trustee

who has acted "reasonably" ought to be relieved, and that it is not incumbent on the Court to consider whether he ought "fairly" to be excused ...'

Participation, consent, release or acquiescence

If a beneficiary participated in a breach of trust, affirmed it, acquiesced in it or released the trustees from the breach, then he will be unable to bring a claim against the trustees: *Fletcher* v *Collis* [1905] 2 Ch 24. Such a beneficiary cannot be heard to complain in a court of equity of a breach of trust which he himself has authorised: *Re Deane* (1888) 42 Ch D 9. To make out this defence, the trustees must show that the beneficiary actually adopted the breach of trust with full knowledge and was sui juris at that time: see *Farrant* v *Blanchford* (1863) 1 DeG J & Sm 107. See also *Overton* v *Bannister* (1884) 3 Hare 503 where a minor, who fraudulently misstated his age, was still bound.

In *Re Garnett* (1885) 31 Ch D 1 the court set aside a deed, releasing trustees from a breach of trust, which was executed by the beneficiaries at a time when they did not have suffcient knowledge of their rights and of what they were giving up by the deed. In *Fletcher* v *Collis*, under a marriage settlement property was settled on a husband for life, remainder to his wife for life, remainder to their children. At the wife's request and with the husband's consent the trustee sold off all the trust property and gave the money to the wife, who dissipated it. Afterwards the husband was adjudicated bankrupt. The children brought an action against the trustee to replace the trust property and this he did and the action was stayed. After the trustee's death in 1902 there was a surplus representing income. The trustee's executor claimed this as did the husband's trustee in bankruptcy. It was held that, as regards the husband's trustee in bankruptcy, he stood in no better position than the husband. As the husband had consented to the breach of trust he was not entitled to require the trustee to make good the loss resulting from it and he could not claim any surplus. It should be noted that knowledge of a breach is not, in itself, suffcient to establish a defence of acquiescence, even if beneficiaries knew of the breach for several years. But, if there is a long delay in pursuing a claim in such circumstances the court will presume acquiescence in the absence of an explanation for it: see *Sleemam* v *Wilson* (1871) LR 13 Eq 36.

Impounding beneficiary's interests

A trustee who has committed a breach of trust at the instigation or with the consent of a beneficiary may claim, in defence, to have that beneficiary's interest impounded to rectify the breach. The right to impound exists in equity and under s62 TA 1925. The right in equity arises in cases of concurrence or consent to breach if the beneficiary obtained a benefit from it, but is available regardless of benefit in cases of instigation of breach: see *Chillingworth* v *Chambers* [1896] 1 Ch 685. The right to impound under s62 is wider than the equitable right in that it is not dependent on showing benefit to the beneficiary. Unlike the equitable right, consent must be in writing: see *Re Somerset* [1894] 1 Ch 231. Section 62 provides:

> 'Where a trustee commits a breach of trust at the instigation or request or with the consent in writing of a beneficiary, the court may, if it thinks fit, make such order as to the court seems just, for impounding all or any part of the interest of the beneficiary in the trust estate by way of indemnity to the trustee.'

Before the court will exercise its discretion under s62 to impound a beneficial interest, it must be shown that the beneficiary knew that what he was instigating or requesting was a breach of trust; it is not sufficient that he asked the trustee to do something which he did not then know to be a breach of trust and left them to decide whether or not to do it: see *Re Pauling's ST (No 2)* [1963] Ch 576. In *Re Somerset* the husband under a marriage settlement wrote to the trustees asking them to sell certain trust property and to invest it in a mortgage of a particular estate. The trustees acted on this suggestion and lent an excessive amount on mortgage, which was not recovered, as the property proved to be an inadequate security. The husband and his children sued the trustees for the loss. The trustees admitted liability but claimed to impound the husband's interest under the trust by way of defence. The Court of Appeal held that the husband had clearly instigated, requested and consented to the investment concerned but it did not appear that he intended to be a party to the breach of trust as he had left it to the trustees to decide if the property was an adequate security. His interest would not be impounded. As Lindley LJ said:

> 'If a cestui que trust instigates, requests or consents in writing to an investment not in terms authorised by the power of investment, he clearly falls within the section: and in such a case his ignorance or forgetfulness of the terms of the power would not, I think, protect him – at all events, not unless he could give some good reason why it should, eg that it was caused by the trustee. But if all that a cestui que trust does is to instigate, request or consent in writing to an investment which is authorised by the terms of the power, the case is, I think, very different. He has a right to expect that the trustees will act with proper care in making the investment, and if they do not they cannot throw the consequences on him unless they can show that he instigated, requested or consented in writing to their non-performance of their duty in this respect. This is, in my opinion, the true construction of this section.'

Lapse of time

A trustee may be protected from a breach of trust by the Limitation Act 1980. This provides that, as a general rule, no action can be brought to recover trust property in respect of a breach of trust after six years from the date upon which the right of action accrued: see s21(3). In two cases there is no limitation period according to s21(1)(a) and (b):

> 'a) in respect of any fraud or fraudulent breach of trust to which the trustee was a party or privy; or

b) to recover from the trustee trust property or the proceeds thereof in the possession of the trustee, or previously received by the trustee and converted to his use.'

There is liability for an indefinite period in each of these cases, and it seems that the only way the claim could fail here is through the loss of evidence as a result of the passing of time. Laches cannot be raised as an alternative defence here: see *Attorney-General* v *Fishmongers' Co* (1841) 5 My & Cr 11.

A new provision was introduced by the Limitation Amendment Act 1980 which is now s21(2) Limitation Act 1980. This provision is designed to clear away a possible injustice arising under s21(1)(b) in that a trustee-beneficiary could not invoke the provisions of what is now s21(3) in his favour when the limitation period had expired. Section 21(2) reads:

'Where a trustee who is also a beneficiary under the trust receives or retains trust property or its proceeds as his share on a distribution of trust property under the trust, his liability in any action brought by virtue of subsection 1(b) above to recover that property or its proceeds after the expiration of the period of limitation prescribed by this Act for bringing an action to recover trust property shall be limited to the excess over his proper share. This subsection only applies if the trustee acted honestly and reasonably in making the distribution.'

The following illustrates the injustice s21(2) is designed to eliminate:

X is a trustee and beneficiary of a trust created by S. X distributes the trust property to himself and A, B and C in equal shares believing that this is the full class of beneficiaries. D makes a good claim to be a beneficiary also, but outside the limitation period. Prior to the enactment of s21(2) D could sue X for his full share under the old s19(1)(b) even after the limitation period had expired, so X would have lost 20 per cent of his 25 per cent share on distribution. By virtue of s21(2) X is only liable to give to D the excess over what he would have been entitled to as his (X's) proper share. X keeps 20 per cent, which would have been his proper share, and gives D the remaining 5 per cent. The defence is only available if the trustee-beneficiary acted 'honestly and reasonably' in making the distribution.

Under the Limitation Act time runs from the date of the breach of trust and not from the date on which the loss actually occurred: see *Re Somerset* [1894] 1 Ch 231. However, this can be varied if fraud is involved, with time running from when the fraud is reasonably discoverable: see s32, and also s28 which extends the time for those under a disability. Further, under the proviso to s21(3) time only begins to run against remaindermen from the date that their interest falls into possession. If the beneficiary is entitled to both an interest in possession and an interest in remainder in the same trust property, the fact that the limitation period has expired with regard to the former will not bar a claim under the latter when it eventually falls in: see *Mara* v *Browne* [1896] 1 Ch 199.

Once an action has become barred by time, then the beneficiary in respect of whom it is barred cannot benefit from proceedings brought by a beneficiary who is not barred: see s21(4). For example, if A and B had joint life interests in a trust in which the trustees committed a breach of trust in 1993 when A was 18 and B 14, A's claim would be barred in 1999 by s21(3). B's claim would not be barred since he was under a disability at the time of the breach, being a minor, and time would only run from the cessation of the disability in 1997. Should B bring an action in 2001 (before 2003 when B's claim would otherwise have time-barred), A cannot benefit from this.

It must be remembered that the Limitation Act only applies to certain stated remedies or causes of action. It does not apply to equitable remedies such as specific performance, injunctions and rescission or rectification. However, given their inherent equitable nature, lapse of time tends to act as a bar in itself. See *Weld* v *Petre* [1929] 1 Ch 33 where 20 years seems to be the maximum passage of time permitted.

Discharge in bankruptcy

Where a trustee is made bankrupt after an action for breach of trust, he will be freed from further liability when he obtains his discharge in bankruptcy, unless the breach was fraudulent: see s28 Bankruptcy Act 1914 and s128 Insolvency Act 1985.

Section 30 TA 1925

See section 20.3.

20.6 Contribution and indemnity

Where two or more trustees are jointly and severally liable for a breach of trust, any or all of them may be sued for the breach by the beneficiaries: *Attorney-General* v *Wilson* (1840) Cr & Phil 1, 28, and judgment may be executed against any of them. In order to ensure that each trustee pays his fair share of the loss, a contribution or an indemnity may be claimed in appropriate circumstances by any of the other trustees.

Contribution

The old rule of equity was that all trustees liable for a loss had to bear that loss equally and to that extent a contribution could be claimed: see *Bahin* v *Hughes* (1886) 31 Ch D 390. Since 1978 the Civil Liability (Contribution) Act has given the court power to award contributions in favour of one trustee against another on the basis of what it considers to be just and equitable having regard to the circumstances of the case. This represents a departure from the old rule that contributions had to be in equal shares if at all and allows the court to place a greater burden on the main culprit. This right, or potential right, to a contribution does not arise if the trustee can alternatively claim an indemnity.

Indemnity

A trustee may be given an indemnity for the losses against his co-trustee as opposed to a mere contribution. This may arise by the court exempting him from liability in the course of the action for breach of trust or refusing to order a contribution from a trustee. Cases where an indemnity has been awarded are:

1. Where the co-trustee was entirely to blame for the breach of trust or where the co-trustee got all the benefits of the breach. But this does not cover all cases where one trustee leaves the management of the trust to a fellow trustee who commits a breach. In *Bahin* v *Hughes* (1886) 31 Ch D 390 a testator left £2,000 to be held on trust by his daughters, Miss Hughes, Mrs Edwards and Mrs Burden, for the benefit of Mrs Bahin for life, remainder to her children. Miss Hughes managed the trust affairs alone, and invested the funds in a mortgage which was an unauthorised investment. The security proved insufficient and Mrs Bahin sued all the trustees for the loss. Mrs Edwards and Mrs Burden claimed on indemnity from Miss Hughes for the loss on the ground that they had not participated in the administration of the trust. The Court of Appeal held that no indemnity would be given. It would be wrong to allow this where one trustee acting honestly, though erroneously, commits a breach while the other trustees have done nothing at all and thereby neglected their duty more than the acting trustee.

2. If the active trustee was a solicitor whose advice or control was relied upon by the other trustees thereby causing them to participate in the breach of trust: see *Re Turner* [1897] 1 Ch 536. See also *Head* v *Gould* (above), which notes that the solicitor has to be giving advice or be in control, rather than being a merely coincidental feature.

3. If the co-trustee was a beneficiary under the trust, then the breach may be made good out of his interest as far as possible before applying the contribution rules: see *Chillingworth* v *Chambers* [1896] 1 Ch 685.

Under s10(1) LA 1980 a right of action for contribution becomes statute-barred two years after it has accrued. For these purposes the right of action accrues at the date of judgment for breach of trust (s10(3)) or if the action is compromised, at the date of the compromise (s10(4)).

21

Breach of Trust II: Tracing

21.1 Introduction

21.2 Tracing at common law

21.3 Tracing in equity: initial fiduciary relationship

21.4 Tracing in equity: property in traceable form

21.5 Tracing in equity: no inequitable results

21.6 Personal remedy against recipient

21.1 Introduction

An action against a trustee to recover losses suffered as a result of a breach of trust is a personal action and the success of such an action will depend very much upon whether or not the trustee has sufficient funds to repay the loss. If not, the beneficiaries may have to resort to tracing the trust property. Tracing or following trust property enables the beneficiaries to recover the trust property itself or that which now represents it in the hands of the person against whom the action is directed. Two main situations arise in which tracing may be necessary:

1. Where the trustee has misappropriated trust funds or otherwise dealt with them without distinguishing them from his own property. For example, if a trustee took £10,000 from the trust bank account and purchased a motor car for himself, the beneficiaries' claim would be for the motor car, as it represents the trust assets in the trustee's hands. Another example is where a careless trustee keeps trust funds in his personal bank account and on his insolvency there is money left in the account as well as assets in his estate, which were bought using the funds in the account. The beneficiaries may wish to trace any moneys left in the account which can be identified as theirs, plus assets purchased using trust money: see *Re Hallett's Estate* (1880) 13 Ch D 696 (below).
2. Where the trustee has made a distribution of trust funds in breach of trust either by overpaying some beneficiaries or paying money to persons who are not beneficiaries. Those beneficiaries who have been underpaid or unpaid may have

to trace against those wrongly paid or overpaid, if the trustee cannot repay their losses personally: see *Re Diplock* [1948] Ch 465 (below).

The main advantage in tracing trust property which has passed from the trust as a result of a breach is that the action is not defeated by the insolvency of the trustee. This is because, in equity, the action is proprietary in nature. This means that it is designed to protect the equitable interests of the beneficiaries under the trust, and to enable them to recover such property as they have an equitable interest in, against any person who has notice of it or takes subject to it. For example, if a trustee mixed trust funds with his own in his bank account and afterwards became insolvent, his trustee in bankruptcy would be in no better position than he is vis-à-vis the trust money, and the beneficiaries could, by asserting their right to trace, recover their trust funds. Their equitable proprietary interest in the funds is not defeated merely because the trustee deals with them in breach of trust.

In tracing trust property, the right to trace will nearly always be grounded in equity. However, tracing is also available at common law; it is of limited application in breach of trust but is considered in section 21.2. Tracing in equity, which is the main issue in breach of trust, is only available if three conditions are satisfied:

1. An initial fiduciary relationship.
2. Property in a traceable form.
3. No inequitable results.

These conditions are considered in sections 21.3–21.5.

21.2 Tracing at common law

Tracing at common law is quite different in its nature to tracing in equity. It is not concerned with protecting equitable proprietary interests, which were not recognised at common law in any event, but with protecting the immediate right to possession. The right to trace at common law may arise out of an immediate right to possession under a contract for bailment or hire-purchase, but cannot be classified as proprietary in the same sense as in equity. For example, if X hires a car to Y and Z steals the car from Y, Y would have an immediate right to possession under the contract of hire and could recover the car from Z by reason of this contract. Once the contract terminates the immediate right to possession reverts to X who could then sue Z for recovery of the car.

Common law tracing is of limited application in the context of breach of trust. As equitable rights or interests are not recognised at common law, a beneficiary under a trust could not trace against a trustee at law. Any tracing action against the trustee by the beneficiary must be in equity only. An action against a wrongly paid or overpaid recipient of trust funds would only be possible at law if the trustee was joined as a party to the action, for the beneficiary has no interest recognised at law.

Apart from these restrictions, tracing at law was said to be further limited because it could not be applied to recover money which had become part of a mixed fund. That is, the property being traced must be in an ascertainable form, either itself or its product. This limitation seems to have arisen from the nature of the common law right to trace, as intended to protect the right to possession. For example, if X held £10,000 in cash, not by way of trust but as, for example, Y's agent, then at law Y could trace the £10,000 so long as it remained as cash or had been applied by X in the purchase of an identifiable asset. In each case, Y could point to something to which he had a right of possession and a better title than X. In *Re Diplock* the Court of Appeal approved of dicta of Wynn-Parry J, at first instance in this case, to this effect. He said:

> '... where a person, other than the true owner thereof, pays money into an account at his bank, and does not mix that money with any other money, either his own or that of any other person, the true owner of the money can at common law follow it into that account, and further can follow it out of the account into any asset or assets which be shown to have been purchased wholly with it ...'

But if the £10,000 belonging to Y is mixed with other moneys belonging to X in X's bank account it seems that tracing at common law is no longer available because it is not possible for Y to assert an immediate right to possession against the fund as a whole, only an unidentifiable part. This point was made by the Court of Appeal in *Re Diplock*:

> 'If a volunteer pays for the property which he purchases by two separate sums of money, one being his own and the other being that given to him by the fiduciary agent, the two sums, whether in the form of two cheques or two sums of cash, become "mixed" in the very act of purchase in the only sense that matters. Their identity is lost to the eye of the common law, which is unable to detect their continued existence in the property bought as much as if both sums had been paid into the same account at a bank.'

It is far from clear why common law tracing was not available where there had been a mixture of moneys. The cases do not give any clear reasons, and decisions such as *Devaynes* v *Noble*: *Clayton's Case* (1816) 1 Mer 572 tend to suggest that moneys in a mixed fund are in fact identifiable at common law. The Court of Appeal in *Banque Belge* v *Hambrouck* [1921] 1 KB 321 seems to have suggested that there was good reason for permitting tracing at common law into mixed funds. As Atkin LJ said:

> 'The question always was, had the means of ascertainment failed? But, if in 1815 the common law halted outside the banker's door, by 1879 equity had the courage to lift the latch, walk in and examine the books: *Re Hallett's Estate*. I see no reason why the means of ascertainment should not now be available both for common law and equity proceedings.'

It is clearly established that tracing into mixed funds is available in equity, and this is the most common problem faced in breach of trust cases: see *Re Hallett's Estate*. One important development at common law has been the introduction by the

House of Lords in *Lipkin Gorman* v *Karpnale* [1991] 2 AC 548 of a change of position defence. Although such a defence is now clearly available in the common law personal action, Lord Goff expressed a desire that the defence should also be available to equitable claims. Lord Goff did not wish to define the parameters of the defence, preferring to see development on a case-by-case basis. There seem, however, to be strong suggestions in the case that the defence will only operate where a recipient of money has spent the money on extraordinary expenditure. It is conceivable that the defence may be used by volunteers when an equitable proprietary claim is established against them by tracing, and the defence may also be available to a personal claim in equity in the context of the decision in *Ministry of Health* v *Simpson*, discussed in section 21.6.

21.3 Tracing in equity: initial fiduciary relationship

Tracing in equity is not possible unless there is an initial fiduciary relationship. As Jessel MR said in *Re Hallett's Estate*, 'the moment you estabish the fiduciary relation, the modern rules of Equity, as regards following trust property, apply'. There is no problem in satisfying this requirement where X holds property on express trusts for Y, and Y wishes to trace against X, for X is in a fiduciary relationship to Y. But the requirement is that there is an initial fiduciary relationship, not merely a fiduciary relationship. If X in the example cited wrongly distributed the whole trust fund to Z rather than Y, Y could nevertheless trace against Z because at the outset the fiduciary relationship existed. By reason of this relationship Y had a beneficial interest in the trust funds, and that interest was not defeated by X's wrongful distribution to Z; Z takes subject to Y's beneficial interest. Y can trace against anyone into whose hands the trust fund passes, for they all take subject to his beneficial interest. The only exception is a bona fide purchaser for value of the legal estate without notice: see section 21.5, below.

The scope for finding an initial fiduciary relationship is almost unlimited. In every case where legal and beneficial ownership are in different persons it will exist. As Jessel MR said in *Re Hallett's Estate*:

'Has it ever been suggested, until very recently, that there is any distinction between an express trustee or an agent, or a bailee or a collector of rents, or anybody else in a fiduciary position? I have never heard, until quite recently, such a distinction suggested ... It can have no foundation in principle because the beneficial ownership is the same, wherever the legal ownership may be ... the moment you establish the fiduciary relation, the modern rules of equity, as regards following trust money, apply.'

No attempt has been made to classify all the situations in which an initial fiduciary relationship might arise. It is doubtful whether this is possible. There have, however, been two recent developments worthy of note. The Privy Council in *Re Goldcorp Exchange* [1994] 3 WLR 199 refused to classify a contractual commercial relationship as a fiduciary relationship. Such classification would have an entirely detrimental effect on general creditors in insolvency and it would appear that, in future, a fiduciary relationship will not arise in commercial relationships, entered into at arm's length and on an equal footing, unless the parties expressly intended such a relationship to arise. The House of Lords in *Westdeutsche Landesbank Girozentrale* v *Islington London Borough Council* [1996] 2 All ER 961 also rejected the contention that a fiduciary relationship arises between parties to a contract which is void for failure of consideration or mistake. According to their Lordships, money paid over under such circumstances is recoverable only by way of a personal restitution action at common law. No equitable proprietary claim exists and both *Sinclair* v *Brougham* [1914] AC 398 and *Chase Manhattan Bank* v *Israel-British Bank* [1981] Ch 105 are overruled. Lord Browne-Wilkinson explained in the *Westdeutsche* case that the *Chase Manhattan Bank* case was nonetheless correctly decided. Chase Manhatten received instructions from a client to pay over 2 million US dollars to the Israel-British bank. Because of a clerical error, the payment was made twice. Shortly afterwards the Israel-British bank became insolvent. Chase Manhattan claimed a right to trace the overpayment in equity. Goulding J held that where money was paid under a mistake, the receipt of such money, without more, constituted the recipient a trustee: the payer retains an equitable property in it and the conscience of the recipient is subjected to a fiduciary duty to respect the property right. Lord Browne-Wilkinson rejected this reasoning totally but he considered the case to have been rightly decided on the basis that the defendant knew of the mistake made by the paying bank within two days of the receipt of the money and that retention of the money with such knowledge gave rise to a constructive trust. See Chapter 28, section 28.1, for further details.

Both of the above cases are welcome developments in considering what relationships may be classified as fiduciary in the future. One further point must be made.

Tracing is available against an innocent volunteer into whose hands the trust money passes. In *Re Diplock* the executors of Caleb Diplock's estate distributed over £200,000 to a large number of charities in the belief that the direction in his will to give the residue of his estate to 'such charitable ... or benevolent ... objects' as they should select was valid. The next-of-kin successfully challenged the validity of the residuary gift on the ground that it was not exclusively charitable. The charities were innocent volunteers but, as the Court of Appeal explained, the initial fiduciary relationship was between the next-of-kin and the executors. Lord Greene MR, giving the leading judgment for the Court stated that:

> '... it appears to us to be wrong to treat the principle which underlies *Hallett's* case as coming into operation only where the person who does the mixing is not only in a fiduciary position but is also a party to the tracing action. If he is a party to the action he is, of course, precluded from setting up a case inconsistent with the obligations of his fiduciary position. But supposing that he is not a party? The result cannot surely depend on what equity would or would not have allowed him to say if he had been a party. Suppose that the sole trustee of (say) five separate trusts draws £1,000 out of each of the trust banking

accounts, pays the resulting £5,000 into an account which he opens in his own name, draws a cheque for £5,000 on that account and gives it as a present to his son. A claim by the five sets of beneficiaries to follow the money of their respective trusts would be a claim against the son. He would stand in no fiduciary relationship to any of them. We recoil from the conclusion that all five beneficiaries would be dismissed empty-handed by a court of equity, and the son left to enjoy what in equity was originally their money.'

Many tracing claims arise from wrongful distribution by the personal representatives in the course of the administration of estates. The personal representative stands in a fiduciary position to all those who are interested in the deceased's estate: see *Commissioner of Stamp Duties* v *Livingston* [1965] AC 694. In *Re Diplock* the next-of-kin were able to trace. As regards unpaid creditors of the deceased, they too can trace since on the deceased's death his personal representatives stand in a fiduciary position towards them to pay their debts: see *Salih* v *Atchi* [1961] AC 778.

For the possibility of equitable tracing of funds in the possession of persons, other than a bona fide purchaser without notice, who had been involved in a 'money laundering' scheme, and where there had been an initial fiduciary relationship, see the judgment of Millett J in *AGIP (Africa) Ltd* v *Jackson and Others* [1989] 3 WLR 1367; confirmed by the Court of Appeal: [1991] Ch 547.

21.4 Tracing in equity: property in traceable form

The common law's limitation on tracings seems to revolve around whether the property is identifiable, while in tracing in equity the limitation is whether it exists in some form. In *Re Diplock* Lord Greene MR said:

'The equitable remedies pre-suppose the continued existence of the money either as a separate fund or as part of a mixed fund or as latent in property acquired by means of such a fund. If, on the facts of any individual case, such continued existence is not established, equity is as helpless as the common law itself. If the fund, mixed or unmixed, is spent on a dinner, equity which dealt only in specific relief and not in damages, could do nothing.'

If there is no property to trace then tracing will not help. For example, if X holds property on trust for Y and wrongly distributes it to A and B, and A puts his share in a savings bank while B spends his on high living, tracing in equity will be successful against A but not B. B has neither the money he received nor anything to show for it. Those from whom he received services cannot be touched since they would, presumably, be bona fide purchasers in this context.

Tracing in equity is not defeated by mixing of funds. In breach of trust cases the mixing may occur in three main ways:

Trustee mixes trust funds with his own funds

This will normally occur when the trustee mixes the trust money with his own in an active banking account, for example, where X mixes £10,000 of trust funds with the £10,000 standing to his credit in his bank account. In such circumstances, it is for the trustee to prove what proportion of the mixed fund belongs to him otherwise the whole will be treated as trust property: see *Re Tilley's WT* [1967] Ch 1179. So far as tracing is concerned there is no difficulty here as Jessel MR explained in *Re Hallett's Estate*:

'I have only to avert to one other point ... supposing ... the moneys were simply mixed with other moneys of the trustee ... Supposing the trust money was 1,000 sovereigns, and the trustee put them into a bag, and by mistake or accident, or otherwise, dropped a sovereign of his own into the bag. Could anybody suppose that a judge in Equity would find any difficulty in saying that the cestui que trust had a right to take 1,000 sovereigns out of the bag? I do not like to call it a charge of 1,000 sovereigns on the 1,001 sovereigns, but that is the effect of it. I have no doubt of it. It would make no difference if, instead of one sovereign, it were another 1,000 sovereigns ...'

In the example given the mixture of X's £10,000 with the trust's £10,000 will cause no difficulty whatever. The trust has a charge on the account for £10,000. But, if X as trustee drew out the whole £20,000 in the account and spent it on assets, tracing in equity would still be available. In this situation Jessel MR in *Re Hallett's Estate* distinguished between the situation where only the trust money is used to buy an asset and where both the trustee's and trust money is used to buy it. He said:

'I will, first of all take his (the beneficial owner's) position when the purchase is clearly made with what I will call, for shortness, the trust money... In that case ... the beneficial owner has a right to elect either to take the property purchased, or to hold it as a security for the amount of the trust money laid out in the purchase; ... he is entitled at his election to take either the property, or to have a charge on the property for the amount of the trust money ... But ... where the trustee has mixed the money with his own ... the beneficial owner, can no longer elect to take the property, because it is no longer bought with trust money simply and purely, but with a mixed fund. He is, however, still entitled to a charge on the property purchased, for the amount of the trust-money laid out in the purchase; and that charge is quite independent of the fact of the amount laid out by the trustee ...'

If the trustee used the mixed fund to purchase assets it might so happen that the assets purchased are worthless or no longer worth what was paid for them. If X as trustee used £20,000 in his bank account, being £10,000 trust money and £10,000 of his own money, to buy shares which crash in value so as to be worthless, the issue arises as to who bears the loss. In *Re Hallett's Estate* Jessel MR pointed out that the trustee:

'... cannot be heard to say that he took away the trust money when he had a right to take away his own money ... Suppose he has a hundred sovereigns in a bag and he adds to them another hundred sovereigns of his own, so that they are commingled in such a way that they cannot be distinguished, and the next day he draws out for his own purpose

£100, is it tolerable for anybody to allege that what he drew out was the first £100, the trust money, and that he misappropriated it, and left his own £100 in the bag? It is obvious that he must have taken away that which he had a right to take away, his own £100. What difference does it make if, instead of being in a bag, he deposits it with his banker, and then pays in other money of his own, and draws out some money for his own purposes? Could he say that he had actually drawn out anything but his own money? His money was there, and he had a right to draw it out, and why should the natural act of simply drawing out the money be attributed to anything except his ownership of money which was at the bankers.'

The above dictum was qualified by the decision of Joyce J in *Re Oatway* [1903] 2 Ch 356. In cases such as *Re Hallett's Estate*, the rule, that the trustee is deemed to draw on his own funds first so that any balance left in the account belongs to the trust, works well if there is sufficient left in the account to meet the claim of the trust. But this may not always be so, as *Re Oatway* illustrates. In that case Oatway paid £3,000 of trust money into his bank account which contained substantial funds. He then purchased shares for £2,137 and afterwards dissipated all of the balance in the account, and died insolvent. His executors claimed that the shares belonged to his estate as he had more than enough of his own money in the account to purchase them at the time, so that under *Re Hallett's Estate* he must have used his own money first. Joyce J rejected this saying:

> '... in order to determine to whom any remaining balance or any investment that may have been paid for out of the account ought to be deemed to belong, the trustee must be debited with all sums that have been withdrawn and applied to his own use so as to be no longer recoverable ...'

The trust fund had a charge over the whole mixed fund and anything purchased, using it until such time as the trust funds were restored in full. The shares Oatway purchased were never free from this charge. This emphasises the inherent bias of the courts to permit tracing by the claimants if at all possible.

Another difficulty which may arise in tracing into a fund mixed by the trustee is that the trustee may have dissipated nearly all of the fund and then paid further sums into it. The question arises whether the trust has a claim on those further sums. For example, if X, a trustee, paid £10,000 of trust money into his bank account which was empty at the time and dissipated £8,000 leaving a balance of £2,000 but then paid in £10,000 of his own money, the issue is whether the trust can claim £10,000 or only the £2,000 left before the last £10,000 was paid in. In *Roscoe* v *Winder* [1915] 1 Ch 62 this point arose and Sargent J held that tracing was only available for the lowest intermediate balance, the £2,000. This is because tracing may only be applied to the extent that trust funds can still be shown to be in the account. The rule is designed to take account of the interests of ordinary creditors in such instances where the trustee will invariably be insolvent. The only way the later payments could be traced is if the trustee showed an intention that they should be repayments of the trust money. More importantly, it is evident that this 'intention' is not presumed, rather it must be shown on the facts of each case.

Innocent volunteer mixes trust funds

If an innocent volunteer is given trust money by the trustee and he mixes it with his own moneys in, say, his bank account, there will be a right to trace but it will be subject to a number of qualifications. The position of the innocent volunteer, and the volunteer with notice, in such circumstances was considered by Lord Parker in *Sinclair* v *Brougham* who said:

> 'Suppose ... property is acquired by means of money, part of which belongs to one owner and part to another, the purchaser being in a fiduciary relationship to both. Clearly each owner has an equal equity. Each is entitled to a charge on the property for his own money, and neither can claim priority over the other. It follows that their charges must rank pari passu according to their respective amounts ... Suppose, ... the fiduciary agent parts with the money to a third party who cannot plead purchase for value without notice, and that the third party invests it with money of his own in the purchase of property. If the third party had notice that the money was held in a fiduciary capacity, he would be in exactly the same position as the fiduciary agent, and could not, therefore, assert any interest in the property until the money misapplied had been refunded. But, if he had no such notice this would not be the case.'

An innocent volunteer ranks pari passu with those who claim part of the mixed fund which he mixed. This point was further amplified by the Court of Appeal in *Re Diplock* where it was said in the judgment of the court:

> 'It would be inequitable for the volunteer to claim priority for the reason that he is a volunteer: it would be equally inequitable for the true owner of the money to claim priority over the volunteer for the reason that the volunteer is innocent and cannot be said to act unconscionably if he claims equal treatment for himself. The mutual recognition of one another's rights is what equity insists upon as a condition of giving relief.'

The mixing of trust funds with his own by an innocent volunteer in an active banking account calls for special consideration. If, for example, a trustee wrongly gives A, an innocent volunteer, £10,000 of trust money, which he puts into his bank account already containing £5,000, and he then applies £6,000 in the purchase of shares and £6,000 in living expenses, the issue arises as to how the balance of £3,000 in the account should be dealt with. If the pari passu principle were followed this would suggest that A and those tracing would rank pari passu as to their respective amounts. But, the rule in *Devaynes* v *Noble: Clayton's Case* (1816) 1 Mer 572 has been applied here: see *Re Stenning* [1895] 2 Ch 433. Under this rule – the first in, first out rule – withdrawals out from the account are deemed to have been made in the order of payment in. In the example, as A's £5,000 was already in the account this was used up, so the balance of £3,000 goes to those who are tracing. The application of the rule in such circumstances has been criticised since it is a rule of commercial convenience which was not formulated with this kind of claim in mind. The rule does not apply as between trustee and beneficiary as it could give the trustee a prior claim to which he is not entitled. Similarly the rule does not apply where the funds are mixed in accordance with express, or implied, terms which conflict with the rule's operation: see *Vaughan* v *Barlow Clowes International*

Ltd [1992] 4 All ER 22. However, it can be applied in cases where the trustee mixes trust money with that of the innocent volunteer.

Trustee mixes funds belonging to two or more trusts

A trustee may hold the office of trustee in two or more trusts or he may be a trustee of a trust and hold another fiduciary position, for example, a directorship. In the circumstances he might mix the funds he holds in each of these fiduciary positions in breach of trust. This occurred in *Re Hallett's Estate*, where Hallett, a solicitor, was one of the trustees of a marriage settlement for the benefit of his wife and children, and of a settlement for the benefit of a Mrs Cotterill. Hallett paid moneys from both settlements into his private bank account where he had funds of his own and drew on the account, and on occasions added further moneys to the account. He died insolvent and the issue arose as to how the moneys in the account should be dealt with. The Court of Appeal held that Hallett should be presumed to have drawn on his own money first in the account so that the balance, being sufficient to cover the claims of the settlements, should be deemed to belong to them. There was no need to consider tracing further, as Fry J had at first instance, on the basis that *Devaynes* v *Noble*: *Clayton's Case* applied. But, if Hallett had left insufficent funds in the account to meet the claims of both trusts, then *Clayton's Case* would have been applied in the manner already explained above.

In some cases the trust funds being traced may have been applied unmixed in a manner resulting in substantial profits. For example, the trustee may have used trust funds he misappropriated to buy shares which have doubled in value, or an innocent volunteer may have done likewise. In the case of the trustee, the position must be that as the funds were misappropriated in breach of trust, he holds them and any accretions on constructive trusts for the beneficial owners, who could recover them. Any other conclusion would enable the trustee to profit from breach of fiduciary duty: see *Boardman* v *Phipps* [1967] 2 AC 46. The dicta of Fox LJ in *O'Sullivan* v *Management Agency* [1985] 3 All ER 351 suggest that if the trustee acted with complete honesty, then the court might allow him a share of the profits. The position of an innocent volunteer who makes profits out of an unmixed fund seems to be that he is only obliged to give recognition to the claim of the beneficial owner and not to give him precedence: see *Re Diplock*. It seems that the innocent volunteer would only be obliged to return the sum he received and not the profit; any other result would make him a fiduciary, which *Re Diplock* stresses he is not. To oblige him to account for the profit would be to give those tracing an undeserved windfall made by his efforts and skill. Any claim against the innocent volunteer will be subject to the issue as to whether it is equitable to permit tracing at all: see section 21.5.

A more difficult problem arises where the trustee or innocent volunteer mixes the trust funds with his own funds and applies the mixture in the purchase of, say, shares which increase in value and produce substantial dividends. In the case of the trustee, it is submitted that he should disgorge the whole profit, if he acted dishonestly or otherwise in breach of trust. But, in other cases it seems that part of the profit proportionate to the original claim of the beneficial owner will be subject to the charge. There are some dicta in *Re Tilley's Will Trusts* [1967] Ch 1179 which support this view, and this approach was applied by the Australian High Court in *Scott* v *Scott* (1963) 109 CLR 649. For example, if a trustee gave £10,000 to A, an innocent volunteer, who used it together with £10,000 of his own to buy £20,000 of shares, and the shares produced dividends of £5,000 and were sold for £30,000, it seems the profits would have to be divided equally between A and those tracing the £10,000 trust money. However, it is also arguable on the basis of the dicta in *Re Diplock* that A should have nothing more than a duty to account for the £10,000 and not the profits, these being the result of his skill and effort.

The following are examples of the application of the principles considered above to given situations:

1. T mixes £1,000 of trust money with £1,000 of his own money in his bank account. He withdraws £750 to buy a car and £750 to pay for his summer holidays, leaving £500 in the account.

   Re Hallett suggests that he must have drawn his own money out first so that any money remaining in the account belongs to the trust. *Sinclair* v *Brougham* also suggests that the trust could claim the £500 remaining in the account on the ground that the trustee could not assert any claim to the fund or the assets purchased out of it until the trust charge has been satisfied. *Re Hallett* suggests the trust has a charge, on the assets purchased, to recover its £1,000. No tracing would be possible against the money spent on the holiday – this has been dissipated. Tracing is, however, possible against the car.

2. T mixes £1,000 belonging to Trust A and £1,000 belonging to Trust B in his bank account in the following way:

Date		Payment in
January	1987	£1,000 trustee's money in account
March	1987	£1,000 Trust A money paid in
May	1987	£1,000 trustee's money paid in
July	1987	£1,000 Trust B money paid in

   Withdrawals are made from the account as follows:

February	1987	£ 500 to pay for holiday
April	1987	£ 500 to purchase camera
August	1987	£1,000 to purchase shares
September	1987	£ 800 to purchase furniture

   Re Hallett suggests that A and B will have a charge on the account, and anything purchased out of it, to recover their money. *Sinclair* v *Brougham* suggests that A and B will rank pari passu in respect of this charge. *Re Hallett* will be applied as between the trustee, on the one hand, and A and B on the other; but as between A and B only, *Devaynes* v *Noble: Clayton's Case* will apply. Under *Re Hallett* A and B can claim that T has withdrawn all of his funds from the account, so that the balance in the account belongs to them.

As regards the balance of £1,200 in the account, the claim between A and B to it is dealt with by *Clayton's Case*; 'first in first out'. On this basis £800 of A's money was withdrawn from the account, not £1,000, because *Clayton's Case* is not applied as between a trustee and beneficiary. Hence the £1,200 is divided, £1,000 to B and £200 to A.

A has a claim for a further £800 and has a charge on the assets purchased out of the mixed fund. This would cover the camera, the shares, and the furniture, since the fund was mixed at the time they were purchased. If the camera had been purchased in February rather than April then it would not be subject to the charge as it would not at the time have been purchased from a mixed fund. If the shares had produced profits, it would follow from *Re Tilley's WT* that the profit should be divided proportionately between A and B and the trustee. If the trustee had earmarked the shares purchased as investments for, say, A, then A would not need to trace. B would still be able to claim £1,000 from the moneys in the account, as suggested above.

The application of trust funds by an innocent volunteer in a number of particular ways gives rise to the question as to whether it is traceable. These include:

Improvement of assets

If the trust funds are used by the innocent volunteer to improve an asset, for example, repairing a house or building an extension, then the issue arises whether the money is traceable. The point was considered in *Re Diplock* and the judgment in that case suggests much depends on the nature of the improvement. It would seem that money spent on labour only, resulting in improvements, would not be traceable; for example, where it was paid to have hedges clipped or windows cleaned or rubbish removed. In other cases, it seems that if the improvement does not bring any increase in the value of the property, it is not traceable because 'the money will have disappeared leaving no monetary trace behind'. Lord Greene MR referred to the case where the improvement made the house more convenient for the owner, but lowered its value for a purchaser. Examples might be aluminium double glazing in an 18th century period house or adaptations to a house for the benefit of an invalid owner. Apart from these difficulties, improvements and extensions seem to be traceable, but it may often be inequitable to permit tracing against them: see section 21.5.

Overdrafts

If an innocent volunteer pays trust funds into an overdrawn account, it seems that tracing will not be available. The Court of Appeal has recently held that equitable tracing is not possible through an overdrawn and therefore non-existent fund: *Bishopsgate Investment Management Ltd (In Liquidation)* v *Homan and Others* [1994] 3 WLR 1270.

Payment of debts

If a trustee or volunteer uses trust money to pay off debts it seems, according to *Re Diplock*, that there will be nothing to trace. Two examples of this arose in *Re Diplock*, where two charities received payments from the estate for the purpose of repaying loans, one unsecured, the other secured. In the latter, £6,000 was given to the Leaf Homoeopathic Hospital to pay off a bank loan secured on its property. On this Lord Greene MR said, 'We think that the effect of the payment to the bank was to extinguish the debt and the charge held by the bank ceased to exist.' The court refused to treat the case as one where subrogation would have been appropriate, so that the beneficial owner could have been subrogated to the position of the creditors. This does not cause any hardship because it is merely putting the trustee or volunteer in the position he was in before the debts were paid. There is some support in the Court of Appeal decision in *Boscawen* v *Bajwa* [1996] 1 WLR 328 for the remedy of subrogation being made available in the future, subject to a defence of change of position.

21.5 Tracing in equity: no inequitable results

Tracing in equity will not be allowed if it will produce inequitable results. This is so even if there is an initial fiduciary relationship and property in a traceable form. The reason for this being that tracing in equity is itself subject to general equitable considerations which, when appropriate, can prevent its operation. The nature of those against whom tracing is sought and the consequences upon them will be considered.

Tracing might be sought against the following:

1. Bona fide purchaser for value of the legal estate without notice. No tracing claim is available here; such a purchaser takes the property free from all equities: see *Re J Leslie Engineers Co Ltd* [1976] 2 All ER 85.
2. Purchaser with notice. Such a purchaser takes subject to equities of which he had notice so that he will be bound by any tracing claims of which he had notice: see *Re Diplock*.
3. Volunteer with notice. Tracing is available here as the volunteer takes subject to the equities.

4. Innocent volunteer. An innocent volunteer takes the trust funds or property gratuitously without notice that it has been given to him in breach of trust. The position of the innocent volunteer was considered in section 21.4 above and, as stated there, tracing is available against him, but he ranks pari passu with those who are tracing.

If the consequences of tracing are such that they would produce hardship or injustice to those against whom it is sought, then it will be refused. This arises particularly in the context of an innocent volunteer who takes without notice of the trusts. If he has used trust moneys received to alter or improve his property or has changed his position on the strength of the moneys received, it may be difficult or even impossible for him to go back to his old position. This was recognised by the Court of Appeal in *Re Diplock* in respect of improvements and alterations to property; a charge sought on the property might not produce an equitable result for three reasons:

1. The improvements might not have increased the value of the property, and it may even have depreciated as a result.
2. It would be difficult to decide what part of the improved property the charge should attach to. If the money was used to repair one building in a large complex or used only to repoint the brickwork on a building, the charge might not be fair to the innocent volunteer. In *Re Diplock* the Court of Appeal said:

'What, for the purposes of the inquiry, is to be treated as "the charity property"? Is it to be the whole of the land belonging to the charity? Or is it to be only that part of it which was altered or reconstructed or on which a building has been erected by means of Diplock money? If the latter, the result may well be that the property, both in its original state and as altered or improved, will, when taken in isolation, have little or no value. What would be the value of a building in the middle of Guy's Hospital without any means of access through other parts of the hospital property? If, on the other hand, the charge is to be on the whole of the charity land, it might well be thought an extravagant result if the Diplock estate, because Diplock money had been used in reconstruction on a corner of it, were to be entitled to a charge on the entirety.'

3. The innocent volunteer, as already stated, ranks pari passu with those who are tracing, and the charge and sale of property under it may put an unfair burden on him. As the Court of Appeal said in *Re Diplock*:

'The result of a declaration of charge is to disentangle trust money and enable it to be withdrawn in the shape of money from the complex in which it has become involved. This can only be done by sale under the charge. But the equitable owner of the trust money must in this process submit to equality of treatment with the innocent volunteer. The latter too, is entitled to disentangle his money and to withdraw it from the complex. Where the complex originates in money on both sides there is no difficulty and no inequity. Each is entitled to a charge. But if what the volunteer had contributed is not money but other property of his own such as land, what then? You cannot have a charge for land. You can, it is true, have a charge for the value of land, an entirely different thing. It is equitable to compel the innocent volunteer to take a charge merely for the value of the land when what he has contributed is the land itself? In other words, can equity, by the machinery of a charge, give to the innocent volunteer that which he has contributed so as to place him in a position comparable with that of the owner of the trust fund? In our opinion it cannot ...'

The case of an innocent volunteer using trust money to improve his assets should be distinguished from that in which he uses his own money and trust money to purchase a property. In this situation, tracing will be available according to *Re Diplock* because the charge imposed on the property in the hands of the innocent volunteer will not be forcing him to sell his property, but giving him back what he contributed to the purchase of the property. If the purchase took place many years before tracing began, it might be refused as causing hardship, but there seems to be no authority on this.

21.6 Personal remedy against recipient

If trust money has been wrongly paid by the trustee and it is not possible for the unpaid or underpaid beneficiary to sue the trustee personally – because he is, for example, insolvent and tracing is impossible because, for example, the assets have been dissipated – the question arises whether the beneficiary can sue those who were wrongly paid or over-paid for recovery of the money. This problem was considered by the House of Lords in *Ministry of Health* v *Simpson* [1951] AC 251, on appeal from *Re Diplock*. The availability of such a personal claim was affirmed but was specifically confined to the administration of estates. The claim was developed in relation to the administration of estates by the Court of Chancery to enable a creditor, legatee or next-of-kin to recover money wrongly paid. In *Re Diplock* it was used to enable the next-of-kin to sue the charities personally after other remedies had been exhausted. In *Harrison* v *Kirk* [1904] AC 1 it was used to enable an unpaid creditor to obtain a refund from the next-of-kin and legatees. Lord Davey said of the remedy in *Harrison* v *Kirk*:

'... the Court of Chancery, in order to do justice and avoid the evil of allowing one man to retain what is really and legally applicable to the payment of another man, devised a remedy by which, ... it has allowed the creditor to recover back what has been paid to the beneficiaries or the next-of-kin who derive title from the deceased testator or intestate.'

Two requirements must be satisfied if the personal remedy against a recipient for a refund is to apply:

1. There must have been a wrong payment by the personal representative. The wrong payment may be in the form of a distribution to a recipient who had no right to anything at all or in the form of an overpayment: see *Re Diplock*.
2. All other remedies against the personal representative must have been exhausted so that the claim is limited to what cannot be recovered by a claim in personam

against the personal representative or, if used, by tracing: see *Ministry of Health* v *Simpson*.

The personal representative cannot use this remedy to claim a refund from a recipient to whom he distributed assets: see *Orr* v *Kaines* (1750) 2 Ves Sen 194. There appears to be one exception to this, namely, where the personal representative had no notice of a claim when he made distribution and afterwards learns of such a claim, for example an unpaid debt, and is obliged to pay: see *Nelthrop* v *Hill* (1669) 1 Cas in Ch 135.

As a personal remedy against a recipient is probably not available in trust cases, as opposed to administration of estates, it would seem that if a beneficiary under a trust finds that a personal action against the trustee, or tracing, are fruitless, his only course of action is to see if he can hold the recipient liable as a constructive trustee. As a stranger to the trust he might be liable as a constructive trustee. In *Westdeutsche Landesbank Girozentrale* v *Islington London Borough Council* [1996] 2 All ER 961 Lord Browne-Wilkinson stated three principles relevant to the imposition of a constructive trust:

1. A constructive trust is imposed because of unconscionable conduct.
2. A person cannot be a trustee if ignorant of the facts alleged to affect his conscience.
3. There must be identifiable trust property, the only apparent exception to this rule being where a constructive trust is imposed on a person who *dishonestly* (emphasis added) assists in a breach of trust.

22

Future Interests: The Rules against Perpetuities and Accumulations

22.1 Introduction

22.2 Vested and contingent interests

22.3 The rule against perpetuities

22.4 The common law rule against perpetuities

22.5 Modifications to the common law rule before 1964

22.6 Gifts which follow void gifts

22.7 Determinable and conditional interests

22.8 Perpetuities and Accumulations Act 1964

22.9 Powers

22.10 Exceptions to the perpetuity rule

22.11 The rule against accumulations

22.12 Revision summary

22.13 Worked examples

22.14 Duration of trusts; rule against perpetual trusts

22.15 Reform

22.1 Introduction

Common law, essentially for reasons of public policy, has long reviled against arrangements which purport to create future interests which are not vested. Accordingly to prevent unacceptable restrictions or free alienation of property (put alternatively, to ensure that property is generally capable of being freely dealt with or disposed of) the courts have developed a series of rules (albeit complex) to determine whether or not an arrangement which does attempt to create a future interest, which is not vested, is valid.

These common law rules, unfortunately, often lead to ridiculous outcomes resulting in statutory reform initially by the LPA 1925 and, more substantially, by the Perpetuities and Accumulations Act 1964. Both the common law rules and statutory reform are detailed in this chapter. However, before these are outlined certain key phrases (as have been, unavoidably, used in this introductory paragraph) are noted as follows:

Interests in possession and future interests

An interest in possession gives an immediate right to the enjoyment of the property. A future interest gives a right of enjoyment at some time in the future, this being conditional either on some requirement which has yet to be fulfilled, or requiring the identification of the person to take the benefit.

Future interests (as a general rule) take the form of one of the following two categories:

Interest in reversion
This is that part of the grantor's interest not disposed of by the grant and which will revert back to him or his successors when the estates which have been created come to an end.

Interest in remainder
This is that part of the grantor's interest that is disposed of by the grant, provided it is postponed to an interest in possession created at the same time. The future interest must be held by someone other than the original grantor, or his successors, and the name is derived from the fact that possession will remain away from the original grantor.

The grant by X, a fee simple owner, to A for life, remainder to B for life, remainder to C in tail.

This creates:

1. One interest in possession: A's life interest.
2. Two interests in remainder: B's life interest, C's fee tail.
3. One interest in reversion: X's fee simple.

The rule against perpetuities applies only to interests in remainder. This is because interests in reversion are always vested.

22.2 Vested and contingent interests

Interests in remainder can be either vested or contingent. An interest is vested when the grantee of the interest is certain that he will be entitled to the interest at some time in the future, as soon as the interests prior to his own have determined. An interest is contingent if the grantee cannot say with certainty whether or not he will be so entitled.

The time at which it must be decided whether a grant is vested or contingent is the date at which the grant takes effect:

1. If by will: the date of the testator's death.
2. If inter vivos: the date of the grant.

Note that the word vested does not mean that the grantee is entitled in possession; a future interest can be vested. The test to be adopted is to ascertain whether the owner is absolutely entitled at the present time to assume possession whenever it may fall vacant.

Vested interests

A contingent future interest becomes vested in interest (whether or not in possession) when three conditions are satisfied:

1. The identity of the beneficiary or beneficiaries are known.
2. All conditions attached to the grant must have been complied with.
3. The respective shares of the beneficiaries are known.

Contingent interests

An interest is contingent if any of the three conditions is not satisfied, and it will stay contingent until all the conditions are satisfied. Megarry and Wade explain this in *Law of Real Property* at p231: 'A contingent interest is one which will give no right at all unless or until some future event happens.' It is vital to understand the distinction between vested and contingent interests, as the rule against perpetuities (see sections 22.3 and 22.4) applies only to contingent interests.

Examples of vested and contingent interests

1. 'Gift by will to A for life, remainder to B.'
   At testator's death A and B are alive.
   B's interest in remainder is vested as all three conditions are satisfied.
2. 'Gift by will to A for life, remainder to B when he reaches 21.'
   At testator's death A is alive and B is 14.
   B's interest in remainder is contingent: condition 2 is not satisfied as B has not reached 21. The gift to B will vest when he reaches 21.
3. 'Gift by will to A for life, remainder to all the children of A.'
   At testator's death A is alive with two children.
   The children's interest in remainder is contingent; A may have more children. Condition 1 is not satisfied; the identity of all possible children of A is

not known. Nor is condition 3 satisfied: the respective shares will depend on how many children A has. The gift will vest when A dies, as no more children can then be born to A. (However, see also the 'class closing rule' in *Andrews* v *Partington* (infra) which potentially affects this example.)

Importance of the distinction

1. If someone holds a vested interest then he cannot lose it. If he holds a contingent interest it is uncertain whether he will obtain the benefit from the property concerned. (Note: Section 31 Trustee Act 1925 and s175 LPA 1925 which, subject to their respective conditions, provide for a potential beneficiary to take the benefit of the intermediate income.)
2. If an interest is contingent it is subject to the rule against perpetuities but if it is vested it is not subject to the rule.

22.3 The rule against perpetuities

Before the Settled Land Act 1882, a landowner could ensure that land remained in the family by creating a long succession of future interests. These interests were not necessarily contingent, but often were, in order to provide for circumstances unknown to the settlor, for instance, whether his grandson would have two or three sons. In order to prevent land being tied up for generations, the rule against perpetuities was developed. The common law rule was settled by the beginning of the 19th century.

The aim of the rule was to allow a landowner to tie up land in contingent future interests so as to benefit his children and grandchildren, but no further. To achieve this, gifts had to vest within the lifetime of persons alive at the date the gift took effect. A man's children were normally alive at his death, but his grandchildren need not be. As donors frequently made it a condition of receipt of the interest that the grandchildren should reach 21, a period of 21 years was allowed in addition to the lifetime during which the gift had to vest.

The common law rule was very strictly interpreted by the courts, who applied pure logic rather than common sense. Many gifts failed because they might not vest within the period, even though it was highly likely that they would vest. The possibility of failure renders the gift void ab initio.

In response to these problems, the common law rules were supplemented by first the LPA 1925 and then by the Perpetuities and Accumulations Act 1964, which applies to gifts taking effect after 15 July 1964, which would fail at common law.

In applying the rule against perpetuities the following steps should be followed:

1. Determine which interests are interests in remainder.
2. Determine whether any interests in remainder are vested or contingent (see section 22.2).
3. Apply the common law rules to the contingent future interests.

4. If the gift fails at common law and it took effect after 15 July 1964, apply the PAA 1964 rules.

22.4 The common law rule against perpetuities

The rule is: the grant of a *contingent* interest is *void ab initio* at common law unless it is certain that the interest will *vest*, *if it vests at all*, within the perpetuity period which consists of *a life or lives in being* when the grant takes effect, plus 21 years. The italicised words and phrases are explained below.

Contingent
This means the gift is not vested, that is, one or more of the three requirements for a vested interest have not been met: the identity of the beneficiary or beneficiaries is not known; or a condition has not been fulfilled; or the respective shares of the beneficiaries are not known.

Void ab initio
The gift, if it fails at law, is void from the moment that it takes effect. The interest concerned will be held by trustees on trust for the residuary legatees (if it is a gift by will) or the original settlor (if it is an inter vivos gift).

Vest
A gift vests when all three requirements for a vested interest above become satisfied. It then ceases to be contingent.

If it vests at all
It is not necessary to show that the gift will actually vest. It must merely be shown that it is possible for it to vest within the period.

A life or lives in being
This means the lifetimes of persons alive at the date that the gift comes into effect.

Calculation of the perpetuity period
The period starts at the date the instrument takes effect, that is, the date of the testator's death if the gift is by will, or the date of the instrument if an inter vivos gift. The period stops after the lifetime or lifetimes of the life or lives in being plus 21 years.

Lives in being at common law
A life in being is the lifetime of anyone alive when the gift takes effect. It is necessary to know the date of death of lives in being, so it is obviously impractical to apply this wide definition. Lives in being are consequently limited to:

1. Lives in being expressly nominated by the testator; or if there are no nominated lives.
2. Lives in being relevant to whether or not the gift will vest – implied lives.

Nominated lives

It is common for a testator to nominate lives in being. There is no requirement that any of the nominated lives in being have any interest in the gift, so a donor can ensure a relatively lengthy perpetuity period by nominating a number of lives in being.

It is necessary for the persons administering the gift to be able to ascertain when the nominated lives die, so it is usual to select the descendants of a named monarch. The monarch should be fairly recent as otherwise it will not be possible to trace all his descendants.

In *Re Moore* [1901] 1 Ch 936, the testatrix nominated as lives in being all the persons alive at the date of her death. The gift was held void.

In *Re Villar* [1929] 1 Ch 243, a testatrix who died in 1926 nominated all the descendants of Queen Victoria (died 1903, having had 11 children) alive at the time of her death. There were then approximately 120 descendants, scattered all over Europe. It was held that the difficulty in ascertaining their dates of death was not sufficient to render the gift void. The valid clause read: 'ending at the expiration of 20 years from the day of the death of the last survivor of all the lineal descendants of her late Majesty Queen Victoria who shall be living at the time of my death'.

In *Re Leverhulme* [1943] 2 All ER 274, a 'Queen Victoria' clause was held valid, but it was suggested that no further use be made of Queen Victoria's descendants. Today it is normal to use the descendants of George V, or George VI. The lives must be human lives and not trees: see *Re Kelly* [1932] IR 255.

Example of nominated lives in being. 'The lives in being are all those lineal descendants of George VI alive at my death.' The testator died in September 1981. At that date there were ten lineal descendants of George VI alive, the youngest being a few weeks old. The perpetuity period runs from September 1981 until the death of the longest lived of those ten plus 21 years.

Implied lives

If there are no expressly nominated lives, the lives in being are the lives of persons who are concerned in the gift. In practice, it is only necessary to consider the lifetimes of persons who are relevant to whether the gift will vest.

EXAMPLES

1. 'Gift by will 'to my grandson, John.'
   The lives in being will be John and his parents, if they are alive when the gift takes effect.
2. 'Gift by will 'to all my grandchildren to attain 21.'

At the date of the testator's death, two of the children and two of his grandchildren are alive.

The lives in being are the two children and the two grandchildren.

The perpetuity period will run from the death of the testator until 21 years after the death of the last of the lives in being to die. Note that any grandchildren born after the testator's death will not be lives in being. The two children are lives in being because they are relevant to when the gift will vest. The gift must vest, if it vests at all, 21 years after the death of the last of the children, as it is only after those events that it is certain that no more grandchildren can be born, and that all the grandchildren will be 21.

In *Re Drummond* [1988] 1 WLR 234, a 1924 settlement directed property to be held for the settlor for life, thereafter to his daughters for life and thereafter as to each daughter's share, for such of the children or issue of that daughter as she should appoint, in default of appointment for her children equally at 21 or, if female, earlier marriage, and failing such children, for the settlor's daughters (if living) or their issue (taking their parent's share) equally at 21.

The Court of Appeal had to consider the destination of a share under this concluding limitation. The problem was to decide when to close the class of 'issue' in this final limitation. By a majority the Court of Appeal decided the appropriate time to close the class was on the death of the life tenant as the life in being. This reasoning was supported by the words introducing all the trusts subsequent to the daughter's life tenancy and was, in the words of Nourse LJ:

> '... the natural and convenient time for ascertaining the class of the issue of a deceased life tenant'.

The words referred to the date of the deaths of the objects of the gifts and the gift to the issue took effect as a gift to the issue then living.

As a result no interest might vest outside the perpetuity period and the share under the final limitation was, therefore, valid.

Application of the common law rule

The following steps should be gone through:

1. Is the gift vested or contingent; have all three conditions been complied with?
2. If contingent, when will it vest – when will all three conditions be complied with?
3. Is it absolutely certain that the gift must vest, if it vests at all, within the lifetimes of persons alive at the time the gift takes effect plus 21 years?

EXAMPLES:
1. 'Gift by will to A for life, remainder to A's first son to reach 21.'
   At date of testator's death, A is alive, a bachelor with no children.
   Apply steps:

A's gift is vested.

The gift to A's son is contingent.

His identity is unknown and he has not reached 21.

The gift to A's son will vest when he reaches 21. Note that A may never have a son. This does not matter. The test is whether any son that A might have would reach 21 within the period.

The life in being is A. Hence the perpetuity period is A's lifetime, which is extended to include the gestation period plus 21 years. Any son born to A must be born within A's lifetime and must reach 21 within 21 years of A's death.

Therefore, the gift will vest, if it vests at all, within the perpetuity period.

2. 'Gift by will to A for life, then to first of A's sons to be called to the Bar.'

On testator's death, A is alive with no children.

Apply steps:

A's interest is vested. His son's is not: his identity is not known and the condition (being called to the Bar) has not been fulfilled.

The 'event' on which the gift would vest (initially in interest, then in possession on the death of A) is when the first of A's sons is called to the Bar (ie the first son to be called, not the first of A).

The life in being is A. The perpetuity period is A's lifetime plus 21 years. The son must be born, at the latest, within nine months of A's death. But he may be called to the Bar more than 21 years after A's death.

Hence, the gift to A's son is void at common law.

Future parenthood at common law

At common law any possibility, however remote, that a gift may not vest within the period renders the gift void. The law is not concerned with the probability that the gift will vest, but the possibility that it might not. Consequently the possibility that one of the lives in being may have another child – who would not be a life in being, and who might qualify under the terms of the gift after the perpetuity period – must be taken into account. The fact that it is extremely unlikely, or physically impossible, for such a child to be born is ignored.

In *Jee* v *Audley* (1787) 1 Cox Eq Cas 324 a gift was held void because the court presumed that it was possible that a 70-year-old woman might have another child. Megarry and Wade comment at page 245:

> 'Even when it can be proved that the birth of further children is a physical impossibility, the rule at common law maintains the same stubborn disregard for the facts of life.'

EXAMPLE:

'Gift by will to all the grandchildren of A to reach 21.'

At the testator's death, A is a 64-year-old woman with two daughters and no grandchildren.

The lives in being are A and her two daughters.

At common law the gift fails, because the following sequence of events might occur.

1958: Testator dies.

1960: A has a daughter, B. B is not a life in being.

1967: A and her elder daughters are all killed in a car crash. The perpetuity period now has 21 years left to run. B is seven.

1987: B has a child, A's grandchild. This grandchild will not be 21 until 2008. The perpetuity period ran out in 1988.

Legal impossibility is not ignored at common law. In *Re Gaite's Will Trusts* [1949] 1 All ER 459, there was a gift by will to A for life and then to such of A's grandchildren living at the testator's death or born within five years thereof who should attain the age of 21 years.

At the testator's death, A was a 67-year-old widow with children. The remainder to A's grandchildren was contingent.

HELD:

1. It must be assumed that A could have more children, but they would not be lives in being because they would not be alive at the testator's death. Those children could have children (A's grandchildren) who would reach 21 more than 21 years after the death of A and those of her children alive at the testator's death. Therefore some of the beneficiaries under the will would fulfil the condition after the end of the perpetuity period.

2. The gift to the grandchildren was valid, because it was limited to grandchildren born within five years of the testator's death. To qualify, any grandchild of A would have to be born to A's hypothetical child before that child was five. This gift was held to be valid because at that time a five year old could not legally marry (this would contravene the Marriage Act 1969) and could not therefore bear a legitimate child. It was *not* because a five year old could be presumed to be physically incapable of bearing a child. This distinction is important as from 1 January 1970 there is effectively no legal distinction between illegitimate and legitimate children (s15 Family Law Reform Act 1969).

The possibility that a trustee might not fulfil his duties under the trust is also ignored: see *Re Atkin's Will Trusts* [1974] 1 WLR 761.

The result of the decisions on future parenthood is that a contingent gift will fail at common law if the beneficiaries are the grandchildren of anyone alive at the testator's death.

Unborn spouses

The possibility that a life in being might marry a spouse who was not born at the date of the testator's death may cause a gift to fail at common law.

EXAMPLE:

'Gift by will to my son A for life, remainder to his widow (if she survives him) for life, remainder to any of their children living at the death of the survivor.'

At the testator's death A is a bachelor. The life in being is thus A. A may marry a woman born after the death of the testator, so his potential wife cannot be treated as a life in being. This makes the gift to A's children void, as A's widow might survive for more than 21 years after the death of A, so that the gift to the children may not vest until after the perpetuity period.

Any gift to children to take effect on the death of the survivor of their parents will fail unless:

1. Both parents are alive at the testator's death.
2. The children to benefit are limited to the children of persons alive at the testator's death, by naming both parents, the children of A and B.

22.5 Modifications to the common law rule before 1964

There are three ways in which the harshness of the common law rule is modified so as to save gifts otherwise void:

Class closing under the rule in Andrews v Partington (1791) 3 Bro CC 401

The rules as to class closing apply only to class gifts. A class gift is a gift of property to all persons who come within some description, the property being divisible in shares varying according to the number of persons in the class.

Gifts of property to: 'all my children who attain 25'; 'all the nephews and nieces of my late husband'; 'A, B, C, D, and E if living'; are class gifts.

The perpetuity rule applies to class gifts in two ways:

1. The gift cannot vest until the size of the respective shares is known. If, at the date the gift comes into effect, it is possible that any class member could become entitled to a share after the end of the perpetuity period, the whole gift fails, and no member of the class can take any share.

EXAMPLE:

'Gift by will to A for life, and remainder to all A's grandchildren.'

If A is alive at the testator's death, the gift to the grandchildren will be void because A might have more children whose children might be born, and thus qualify for membership of the class of grandchildren, after the end of the perpetuity period.

2. If any member of the class might take a vested interest outside the perpetuity period, the whole gift fails, even though all the other members qualify inside the period.

EXAMPLE:
'Gift by will to A for life, then to all the children of A to attain 25.'
If A is alive at the testator's death, the gift to A's children is void, because a child might be born to A who might not reach 25 until after the end of the perpetuity period.

The rule in *Andrews* v *Partington* (1791) is a rule of convenience, allowing members of a class to become entitled to their share as soon as they become qualified. The rule states: a numerically uncertain class closes as soon as the first member becomes entitled to claim his share. The class is thereupon limited to potential members who are already born. Potential members born later are not entitled to any share.

As each member becomes entitled, he is given his share. If a potential member dies before qualifying, the shares of the remaining members of the class are adjusted.

The rule can save class gifts otherwise void for perpetuity only if one member of the class has qualified when the gift takes effect.

EXAMPLES:
1. 'Gift by will to A for life, remainder to all the grandchildren of A.'
   If A is alive at the testator's death, the gift will be saved by the rule in *Andrews* v *Partington* (1791), if any grandchildren have been born by the testator's death. The class will then be limited to those grandchildren already born who are all lives in being and whose shares must vest within the perpetuity period.
2. 'Gift by will to A for life, remainder to all the children of A to attain 25.'
   If A is alive at the testator's death, the gift to the children will be valid only if one of the children is already 25. The class is then limited to those of A's children already born.
   If there are four, aged 26, 24, 22 and 21, they will be entitled to a quarter share each. If one of the younger ones dies before the age of 25, the shares are adjusted to a third each.

Note that the gift in the above example could also be saved by age reduction. See below.

Age reduction under s163 LPA 1925

Gifts conditional on the beneficiary reaching an age greater than 21 are often void at common law.

EXAMPLE:
'To all the children of A to reach 25.'
This gift could be valid only if:

1. A was dead at the time the gift took effect so that no more children could be born; or
2. A was alive, but one of A's children was already 25 so that the class could be limited to lives in being.

If A is alive, and no child has reached 25, the gift will fail at common law.

Section 163 LPA 1925 allows the age of 21 to be substituted for the excessive age provided:

1. The gift came into effect after 1925 and before 15 July 1964.
2. The gift would otherwise be void.
3. The excess is in the age of a beneficiary or class of beneficiaries.
   In this example, the age of 21 can be substituted for 25 if the gift would otherwise fail.

Alternative contingencies

Where the vesting of a gift is dependent upon the occurrence of one or the other of two events, the strict common law rules are relaxed.

If the gift is 'to A if X happens or if Y happens' and event X must occur within the perpetuity period, but event Y may occur outside the period, then by the strict common law rules, the gift is void.

But in these circumstances the 'wait and see' principle of the 1964 Act (see below) is applied at common law. It is not necessary to decide whether the gift is valid when it comes into effect; the trustees can wait and see which of the two alternative events happens. If the valid event happens, the gift is valid, if not, the gift is void.

In *Re Curryer's Will Trusts* [1938] Ch 952 there was a gift by will to the testator's grandchildren to take effect on the death of the last surviving child of the testator or on the death of the last surviving widow or widower of the testator's children, whichever happened later.

The gift to the grandchildren would be valid if it took effect on the death of the last surviving child of the testator. The alternative contingency is void because of the possibility of an unborn spouse: see section 22.4.

It was held that the trustees could wait and see if all the widows and widowers did in fact die before the last surviving child.

In order for the 'wait and see' exception to apply, the alternative contingencies must be expressly stated in the instrument or will.

In *Proctor* v *Bishop of Bath and Wells* (1794) 2 Hy Bl 358 property was left by will to the first son of A to become a clergyman or if A had no sons, to B.

Both A and B were alive at the date of the testator's death. B claimed the property on the death of A.

HELD: The gift over to B in fact depended on two alternative contingencies – either A had no sons, or none of his sons became a clergyman. As the alternatives were not expressed, the wait and see exception did not apply, and the gift over to B was void, as it was dependent upon a prior void gift: see section 22.6.

22.6 Gifts which follow void gifts

Gifts which follow void gifts are divided into three categories:

Vested gifts

A vested gift following a void gift is valid.

EXAMPLE:
'Gift for life to first son of A to marry, remainder to B in fee simple.'

If A is alive when the gift comes into effect, the gift to A's son is void, for perpetuity. B's gift is vested, and can take effect in possession at once. B is entitled to the fee simple.

Contingent but independent gifts

A contingent gift that follows a void gift is valid providing it is independent of the prior void gift.

EXAMPLE:
'Gift for life to first son of A to marry, remainder in fee simple to B when he attains 21.'

If A is alive at the date of the gift, the gift to A's son is void. If B is under 21, the gift to B is contingent. But the gift to B is contingent upon B reaching 21, not upon A's son marrying. B will be entitled on A's death.

Hence the gift to B is valid, and he will be entitled to the fee simple as soon as he reaches 21.

Contingent and dependent gifts

A contingent gift that follows a void gift and is dependent upon it, is itself void ab initio.

EXAMPLE:
'Gift for life to the first son of A to marry, but if no son of A marries, to B in fee simple when he attains 21.'

If A is alive, the gift to A's son is void. If B is an infant, the gift to B is contingent. But, B's gift is also dependent upon A's gift. B is entitled only if both he reaches 21 and A does not marry.

B's gift is thus void.

The gift over in *Proctor* v *Bishop of Bath and Wells* (above) was contingent and dependent and hence void.

22.7 Determinable and conditional interests

Determinable interests

Neither a determinable fee simple nor a possibility of reverter are subject to the rule against perpetuities at common law. But see section 22.8.

Conditional interests

Conditions precedent
These are subject to the perpetuity rule at common law. A gift to 'A provided he survives B' is subject to the rule and will be void if B could die outside the perpetuity period.

Conditions subsequent
The grant of a conditional interest involves both the grant of a conditional fee simple and the creation of a right of re-entry. The conditional fee simple is not affected by the rule. But the right of re-entry is void if it could take effect outside the perpetuity period. The conditional fee simple is converted into an absolute interest if the right of re-entry is void.

EXAMPLE:
Gift of fee simple in possession to testator's grandchildren provided that no grandchild marries outside the Jewish faith.

The provision might not take effect until after the perpetuity period and is void: the grandchildren are absolutely entitled: see *Re Pratt's Settlement Trusts* [1943] Ch 356.

22.8 Perpetuities and Accumulations Act 1964

The PAA 1964 applies to gifts coming into effect after 15 July 1964 that are void at common law. The common law rules are applied first. The PAA 1964 modifies the common law rules.

Section 1: the perpetuity period

A period of 80 years or less may be substituted for the normal perpetuity period in the instrument creating the gift.

Section 2: future parenthood

Where a gift would be void at common law because of the possibility of future parenthood, it may be valid under the PAA 1964.

Section 2(1)(a) provides that for the purposes of the rule it shall be presumed that women are capable of having a child only between the ages of 12 and 55, and men's capacity is limited to the age of 14 or over.

Any presumption arising in the case of a living person under s2(1)(a) may be rebutted and it would be possible to give evidence of actual capacity: s2(1)(b). These presumptions only arise in any legal proceedings.

Section 3: wait and see

Under the common law the general rule was that it must be clear when the instrument took effect that the interest could not vest outside the perpetuity period. There was no wait and see facility. Where a gift would be void apart from the provisions of s3, s4 (age reduction, class closing) and s5 (the unborn spouse), then s3 allows the trustees to wait and see if the gift does in fact vest within the perpetuity period. Under s3 the interest is to be treated as valid until it is clear that it cannot vest within the period.

EXAMPLES:
1. 'Gift to A (a man), for life, remainder to those of A's grandchildren to reach 21.'
   If A is alive at the date of the gift, the gift to the grandchildren is void at common law. Under the Act, it is possible to wait and see whether the gift will in fact vest. This will be known when A dies. If he had no more children after the testator's death, the gift will vest, as the grandchildren's parents are lives in being see below. If A did have more children, then any potential grandchildren, as yet unborn at A's death, can be excluded from the class s4(4), see below.
2. 'Gift to the first son of A to be called to the Bar.'
   If A is alive when the gift is made, it is void at common law. Under the Act, the trustees can wait and see whether any son of A does become a barrister within the perpetuity period.

Sections 3(4) and 3(5): lives in being

When the 'wait and see' provisions of this Act (see above) are to be applied, then the perpetuity period must be calculated with reference to statutory classes of lives in being, unless the donor has nominated a fixed period of 80 years or less. These classes are (s3(5)):

1. The person by whom the disposition was made – the donor.
2. A person to whom or in whose favour the disposition was made, that is to say, in the case of a disposition to a class of persons, any members or potential member of that class – the donees; in the case of an individual disposition to a person taking only on certain conditions being satisfied, any person as to whom some of the conditions are satisfied and the remainder may in time be satisfied – the donee; in the case of a special power of appointment exercisable in favour of members of a class, any member or potential member of the class – the donee;

the first two provisions equally apply to special powers of appointment – the donee; a person on whom any power, option or right is conferred – the donee.

3. A person having a child or grandchild who qualifies as a statutory life or would, if subsequently born, so qualify – the donee's parents and grandparents.

4. Any person on the failure or determination of whose prior interest the disposition is limited to take effect – the owner of a prior interest. If any of these categories is too numerous for determination it may be disregarded.

The lives in being under the Act do not differ, in practical terms, from lives in being implied at law, although the Act is wider.

Section 3(5) does not apply unless the 'wait and see' provisions are applied. Where the gift was made before 1964, or is valid at common law, a royal lives clause can be used.

Section 4(1): age reduction

1. Where a gift would be void because it is limited to persons attaining an age of more than 21, then the age may be reduced to that which will allow the gift to be valid, so long as the reduced age is not less than 21. This provision differs from s163 LPA 1925 in that the reduction need not be to 21.

   EXAMPLE:
   'To all the grandchildren of A to attain 30. A is alive, with no children.'
   The wait and see provisions are applied until A's death. There are three grandchildren aged 2, 4 and 6. Section 4(1) can then be applied, reducing the qualifying age to 23, the age which will allow the gift to vest within the perpetuity period, that is, 21 years from A's death.

2. Section 163 LPA 1925 is repealed for gifts made after 15 July 1964.

Sections 4(3) and 4(4): class reduction

1. Class reduction under the Act operates in a similar, but more straightforward, fashion to the rule in *Andrews* v *Partington* (1791).

2. Under s4(3), persons can be excluded from the class of potential beneficiaries where their inclusion would prevent the age reduction provisions from operating to save the gift.

   EXAMPLE:
   In the example above, age reduction to 23 will not save the gift, if any of A's children are still capable of having children. Section 4(3) can be used to exclude any potential unborn grandchildren from the class of beneficiaries.

3. Section 4(4) allows the exclusion of members from the class of beneficiaries where their inclusion would cause the gift to fail for remoteness, and age reduction is not appropriate.

EXAMPLE:
'To all the children of A who marry.'
If, at the end of the perpetuity period, any of A's children are not married, they can be excluded from the class, leaving only the married children as beneficiaries.

Section 5: unborn spouses

Section 5 prevents the possibility of an unborn spouse from causing a gift to fail. The wait and see provisions are applied first, and if it becomes apparent that an unborn spouse will survive the perpetuity period, the gift can then be treated as though it was to take effect immediately before the end of the period.

EXAMPLE:
'To A for life, remainder to his widow (if she survives him), remainder to any of their children living at the death of the survivor.'
A is a bachelor, who does marry a woman who was born after the death of the testator, who survives A.
The trustees should wait until the end of the perpetuity period, and if A's widow is still alive, the gift to the children can be saved by treating the gift to the children as taking effect immediately before the end of 21 years after the death of A, rather than upon the death of A's widow.

Section 6: gifts following void gifts

Where the Act applies, no gift is itself void only because it is dependent upon a prior gift which is void for remoteness. Each distinct gift must stand or fall by itself, and the perpetuity period must be applied to each in isolation.
This removes the complications of the common law rules: see section 22.6. Section 6 operates as soon as the gift is made, and the wait and see provisions do not have to be applied.

EXAMPLE:
'Gift for life to the first son of A to marry, but if no son of A marries, to B in fee simple when he reaches 21.'
A is alive and B is under 21. Section 6 allows the gift to B to be valid ab initio. There is no need to wait and see if any son of A does marry within the perpetuity period.

Section 9: options relating to land

The Act makes one important change in the common law rules on options. At common law all options, except an option to renew a lease, are subject to the normal period of a life (or lives) in being plus 21 years.
Under the Act, options are divided into two classes:

Options for a lessee, contained in a lease, to purchase the freehold or a superior tenancy

These options are not subject to the perpetuity rule, provided that the option ceases to be exercisable not later than one year after the end of the lease and it is exercisable only by the lessee or by his successors in title.

All other options

These are subject to a perpetuity period of 21 years, and no longer. The wait and see principle applies. The owner of an option must use it within 21 years of its grant, after which time the option is void.

In all cases, the perpetuity rule applies to options being enforced against successors in title. Prior to 1964 the perpetuity rule did not apply to the original parties to an option. Section 10 of the 1964 Act changes the common law rule in respect of instruments taking effect after 15 July 1964. As a result the perpetuity rule now applies to options to purchase both between the original parties and successors in title.

Section 12: determinable and conditional interests

The Act changes the common law rules for grants made after 15 July 1964 by making determinable interests subject to the perpetuity rule, so that the common law distinction between determinable and conditional interests no longer exists.

22.9 Powers

Powers, because they are concerned with the disposition of property, come within the perpetuity rule. The application of the rule depends on the type of power.

General powers

1. Must be exercisable within the perpetuity period.
2. Need not be exercised within the perpetuity period.
3. When exercised the interest must vest within the perpetuity period reckoned from the date of its exercise – a second perpetuity period.

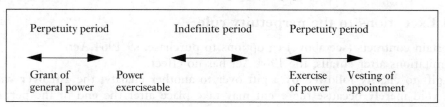

General testamentary powers

1. Must be exercisable within the perpetuity period.
2. Must be exercised within the perpetuity period.
3. When exercised the interest must vest within the perpetuity period reckoned from the date of its exercise – a second perpetuity period.

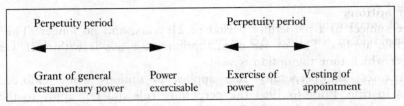

Special powers

1. Must be exercisable within the perpetuity period.
2. Must be exercised within the perpetuity period.
3. The interest appointed must vest within the original perpetuity period.

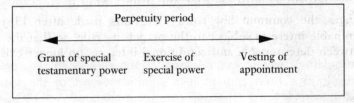

If a power cannot be exercised beyond the perpetuity period it is valid, even though an invalid appointment may be made under it.

For powers granted after 15 July 1964 the 'wait and see' provisions of the 1964 Act apply. The Act also does not recognise any type of hybrid power except a general testamentary power, treating all powers as special unless:

1. It is expressed by the instrument creating it to be exercisable by one person only.
2. The donee of the power, being of full age and capacity, can exercise it to transfer the whole appointable interest to himself unconditionally.

22.10 Exceptions to the perpetuity rule

1. Certain contracts (see above) eg options to purchase: s9 1964 Act.
2. Limitations after entails; the 1964 Act has no effect.
3. A gift to charity followed by a gift over to another charity; the gift over will not be void merely because the event may take place after the end of the perpetuity period.
4. Restrictive covenants.

5. Forfeiture clauses in leases by which the tenant agrees that if at any time the terms of the lease are broken the landlord may re-enter and bring the lease to an end.
6. Mortgages – does not apply to the postponement of a mortgagor's right to redeem: *Knightsbridge Estates Trusts Ltd* v *Byrne* [1939] Ch 441.
7. Resulting trusts – these were not subject to common law but are now subject to the 1964 Act.
8. Right of survivorship in joint tenancy.
9. Section 11(1) of the 1964 Act exempts all powers and remedies for enforcing rentcharges.

See Megarry and Wade in *Law of Property* at p295:

> 'The general effect of the exemptions is to enable rights which are merely ancillary to other valid interests to be exercised outside the perpetuity period.'

22.11 The rule against accumulations

An accumulation is a direction to add income from a fund to the capital rather than distributing it. Originally accumulations were subject only to the rule against perpetuities, but at the end of the 18th century a celebrated case caused a change in the law. The case, *Thellusson* v *Woodford* (1799) 11 Ves 112, showed that a long period of accumulation, which was valid under the rule against perpetuities, could theoretically result in a fund containing a significant part of the national wealth. Parliament hastily intervened by passing the Accumulations Act 1800, often said to be one of the worst-drafted Acts on the statute book.

The present law is contained in the Law of Property Act 1925 ss164–166 as amended, for instruments taking effect after 15 July 1964, by s13(1) Perpetuities and Accumulations Act 1964.

The statutory periods

Income can only be accumulated for one of the following periods:

s164 LPA 1925
{
The life of the settlor or settlors.
Twenty-one years from the death of the settlor.
The minority or respective minorities of any persons living or en ventre sa mere at the death of the settlor.
The minority or respective minorities only of any person or persons who, under the limitations of the settlement would, if of full age, be entitled to the income directed to be accumulated.
}

$$
\left\{
\begin{array}{l}
\text{PLUS} \\
\text{Twenty-one years from the date of the settlement.} \\
\text{The duration of the minority or respective} \\
\text{minorities of any person or persons in being} \\
\text{at the date of the settlement.}
\end{array}
\right.
$$

s13(1)
PAA
1964

Purchase of land

Where the accumulation is directed for the purpose of purchasing land only the fourth period may be selected: s160(1) LPA 1925. The choice of period is a matter of construction of the instrument directing accumulation.

Excessive accumulation

1. If the accumulation period may possibly exceed the perpetuity period, the direction to accumulate is totally void. The 1964 Act has not affected this rule.
2. If the accumulation period cannot exceed the perpetuity period but exceeds the relevant accumulation period, the direction to accumulate is good for the relevant accumulation period and only the excess is void.
3. If a direction to accumulate is wholly or partially void, the income for the void period passes to the person or persons who would have been entitled if no direction to accumulate had been made. There is no acceleration of subsequent interests.

The rule in *Saunders* v *Vautier* (1841) 4 Beav 115 enables a beneficiary of full age who has an absolute, vested and indefeasible interest in property to terminate any accumulation and require that the property be vested in him.

Exceptions to the rule against accumulations: s164(1) LPA 1925

1. Accumulation for the payment of the debts of any grantor, settlor, testator or other person.
2. Accumulation to raise portions for children.
3. Accumulation of the produce from timber or wood.

TOPIC	BEFORE 16 JULY 1964 COMMON LAW OR LPA 1925	AFTER 15 JULY 1964 PERPETUITIES AND ACCUMULATIONS ACT 1964
1. Perpetuity period	Lives in being – no restriction as to number selected	s1 – Add a fixed period not exceeding 80 years
2. Possibility of vesting	Applied rigidly – any remote chance then void – 'fertile octogenarians': *Jee* v *Audley* (1787)	s2 – Male under 14 and female under 12 or over 55 presumed incapable of having children
3. 'Wait and see' rule	No general wait and see rule – significant date was the moment of vesting	s3 – An interest is to be treated as valid until it is clear that it cannot vest within the period
4. Age contingencies	Fail if contingent on beneficiary attaining an age greater than 21: s163 LPA 1925 substituted 21 as the relevant age	s4(1) – (repealed s163 LPA 1925). Substitutes the age nearest to that specified which will save it from being void for remoteness (no longer reduced to 21)
5. Class gifts	Composition of class and share of each member of the class must be known within perpetuity period – gift is wholly valid or wholly void. But – closing of classes – if uncertainty as to numbers, class will close as soon as first member becomes entitled: *Andrews* v *Partington* (1791)	s4(3) and 4(4) – Member whose interest can vest only outside the period and not saved by reducing the age is excluded from the gift – and gift in favour of the rest of the class is valid
6. Subsequent interests	A limitation which follows a void limitation and is dependent on it is void, even though it must vest during the perpetuity period	s6 – No longer fails because 'ulterior to and dependent upon' a void gift – now each gift stands or falls by itself and perpetuity rules applied to each in isolation
7. Accumulations	Rule applies to directions to accumulate income – the income could be accumulated for some period as property could be made inalienable – that is for the perpetuity period: *Thellusson* v *Woodford* (1799) then see Accumulations Act 1800, then ss164–166 LPA 1925	ss164–166 LPA 1925; s13 of 1964 Act. Now a total of six possible accumulation periods, comprising life, or 21 years or minority: see Megarry and Wade: 'In determining the appropriate period, the starting point is to ascertain which of the periods the testator or settlor seemingly had in mind.'

22.12 Revision summary

One of the problems with this area of law is the collecting of the material into some cohesive whole for revision purposes. The following is suggested as a method of revision based on the normal style of question which invites the candidate to consider the law before and after the Perpetuities and Accumulations Act 1964 became effective.

22.13 Worked examples

Q Jack died in 1960 leaving the following bequests in his will:

1. I leave Blackacre to the first son of my old friend Graham to become a barrister or, if no such son becomes a barrister or, if he has no son, to my nephew Robert.

2. I leave Whiteacre to my daughter Vivianne for life, and then to such of her children as attain the age of 21 and to such of her grandchildren who shall attain the age of 21 born to any of her children who shall die before reaching 21. At Jack's death Vivianne was aged 60, with two children and no grandchildren.

    a) Advise on the validity of these dispositions.

    b) Would your answer be different if Jack had died in 1970?

A 1. a) If Graham is dead the gift to the son is valid because all Graham's sons must be lives in being and if any of them are to become barristers they must do so in their own lifetimes. The gift over to Robert, who is a life in being, must therefore also be valid.

    If Graham is alive he could have another son, born after Jack's death, who is not a life in being, and that son could be the first to become a barrister more than 21 years after the death of all the lives in being. That gift is therefore void at common law. The gift to Robert is expressed to depend on two alternative contingencies – that Graham will have sons but none of them will become barristers; that Graham will have no sons.

    The first of these contingencies is too remote but the second is valid as it will be known whether that occurs at the death of Graham, a life in being. When the gift depends on express alternative contingencies the common law allows one to 'wait and see'. If it is the valid contingency which occurs the gift to Robert is valid; if the other then Robert's gift is void: *Re Curryer's Will Trusts* (1938).

1. b) If Graham is dead the gift is valid at common law so the 1964 Act does not apply.

    If Graham is alive, the 'wait and see' provisions of s3 should be applied. The statutory lives in being will be Graham and his wife, Graham's parents and his wife's parents and any sons of Graham alive at Jack's death. The gift over to Robert is in itself valid and is not void merely because it is dependent on s6.

2. a) This is a class gift. The gift to the children would be valid but the gift to the grandchildren invalidates the whole gift, because Vivianne could have another child which could die leaving a child who could attain 21 more than 21 years

after the death of all the lives in being. The common law takes no account of the fact that Vivianne, being aged 60, is most unlikely to have another child. The gift might be saved, however, by the rule in *Andrews* v *Partington* (1791), if at least one child has attained 21. In that case the class will close, with the children alive at Jack's death as potential beneficiaries.

2. b)The fertility presumptions of s2 of the PAA 1964 apply, so Vivianne can be presumed to be incapable of having another child. This means that all the children she can possibly have are lives in being, and any children they might have must attain the age of 21 within 21 years from the death of the lives in being, so the gift is valid.

Q Under a bequest in the will of a testator who died in 1964, £10,000 was given to trustees with instructions that the sum was to be placed on deposit and left untouched until the first of the testator's grandsons to do so reached the age of 25; the total was then to be paid to that grandson. The trustees tell you that the oldest grandson is now aged 18 and ask your advice.

A The gift to the grandson would be void for perpetuity at common law, but as the gift takes effect after 1925 it can be saved by reducing the age of vesting to 21 under s163 LPA 1925.

The direction to leave the money untouched is a direction to accumulate. The relevant period of accumulation must be 21 years from the death of the testator, because there were no grandsons alive at the date of his death, nor is anyone entitled under his will to the income directed to be accumulated. This period has now (in 1985) run out. The direction to accumulate is basically valid because it does not infringe the rule against perpetuities, but the period directed is too long. The trustees will have been obliged to stop the accumulation on the 21st anniversary of the testator's death. The gift to the grandson is not, however, accelerated and will only vest at 21. In the meantime the income goes into residue, or if there was no residuary provision in the will, it goes as on intestacy.

22.14 Duration of trusts; rule against perpetual trusts

Note that a further very important rule, closely related to the rule against perpetuities, is the rule against perpetual trusts. A trust, other than a charitable trust, must not be such that it causes property to be inalienable for a period longer than the perpetuity period. It appears, although the matter is not entirely free from controversy, that the 80 year period, per the PAA 1964, cannot be chosen as the perpetuity period for purpose trusts. For further discussion see Chapter 9, section 9.5 and Chapter 10, section 10.2.

22.15 Reform

The Law Commission has recently published its Consultation Paper No 133 entitled 'The Rules Against Perpetuities and Excessive Accumulations'.

The Consultation Paper provides an invaluable resumé of the current law and criticisms. The latter can best be summarised as follows:

1. Complexity.
2. Uncertainty.
3. Inconsistency.
4. Interference with commercial contracts.
5. Potential harshness.
6. Lack of adaptability.
7. Expense.

Options for reform, as perceived by the Law Commission, are presented in the following format:

Perpetuities

1. To do nothing (rejected).
2. Abolition.
3. Replacement with a new rule; for example, one limiting the duration of trusts, or alternatively one giving the courts a wide discretion to vary dispositions. (Again this option was rejected as, potentially, causing more problems than would be solved.)
4. Retaining but reforming the rule.

The Law Commission's Paper identified (ii) and (iv) as the only real options available but does not, at this stage, rule in favour of any one. However, the Law Commission does favour the argument that any change should, subject to vested interests being protected, be retrospective.

Accumulations

1. To do nothing (again rejected).
2. Abolition.
3. Retaining but reforming the rule.

Again the Paper identified (ii) and (iii) as the only real options but does not rule in favour of either one of them. Similarly, subject to vested interests being protected, the change should be retrospective.

Comments and proposals on this Consultation Paper are requested by 30 June 1994, and definite proposals are expected to be presented within the following year.

23

Election

23.1 Introduction

23.2 Conditions for election

23.3 Method of election

23.4 When does election arise?

23.1 Introduction

Election is based on the presumed intention that if there are two gifts or purported gifts in the same instrument, one being a gift of the donor's property to X and the other being a gift of X's property to Y, then the gift to X will only take effect if X elects that the gift to Y (of X's property) shall take effect (*Noys* v *Mordaunt* (1706) 2 Vern 581).

Election applies to both deeds and wills: see *Birmingham* v *Kirwan* (1805). It is intended to overcome the difficulties which arise when a testator either makes a mistake as to what he owns when drawing up his will or deliberately disposes of another's property. A basic case of election would be:

T gives X £10,000 under his will and in the same will gives Blackacre to Y.

X in fact owns Blackacre.

In the above example X will be called upon to elect, that is to choose between the two gifts, he is not permitted to take both. In *Birmingham* v *Kirwan* (1805) it was said by Lord Redesdale that the doctrine was based on the general rule, 'that a person cannot accept and reject the same instrument'. Two courses are open to X, he can either:

1. Take under the instrument, that is, accept the £10,000 give to him by the donor and permit Y to receive his property, Blackacre.
2. Take against the instrument, refusing the scheme of the will and keeping his own property, Blackacre. In this case Y will be compensated for his disappointment in not receiving Blackacre out of the £10,000 X would otherwise have taken.

Election is said to be based on the presumed intention of the donor, that the testator only intended X to have one or other of the benefits and not both. This is doubtful, as in *Cooper* v *Cooper* (1874) LR 7 HL 53 Lord Cairns said that the rule

337

was based not on any expressed or presumed intention but on the coincidence of gifts in the same instrument. The true position is probably that stated by Buckley J in *Re Mengel's WT* [1962] 2 All ER 490:

> 'It is a doctrine by which equity fastens on the conscience of the person who is put to his election and refuses to allow him to take the benefit of a disposition in the will, the validity of which is not in question, except in certain conditions.'

23.2 Conditions for election

This intention must appear on the face of the will itself: see *Pickersgill* v *Rodger* (1876) 5 Ch D 163. It would not be sufficient if the testator did not refer to the property concerned in an unambiguous manner. If T leaves £10,000 to X and in the same will leaves X's property Blackacre to Y, election will arise as the property Blackacre has been clearly identified. But, if T had simply referred to 'my farm' this would be insufficient. Where property is held by several persons either as joint tenants or tenants in common in equity, mistakes are often made as to ownership. If one joint tenant or tenant in common purports to dispose of the whole property by his will, election will arise: see *Padbury* v *Clarke* and *Re Gordon's WT* (below).

T must give away some of his own property

If a testator purports to dispose of somebody else's property by his will, without more, the disposition is ineffective. The will of T which disposes of X's house Whiteacre and contains nothing more is ineffective. A testator is no more at liberty to give away the property of other people by his will than he is to do so inter vivos. Election only arises where T has given away X's property by his will and in the same will has given X some of his own property.

In *Bristowe* v *Warde* (1794) 2 Ves 336 a father had a power of appointment over stock in favour of his children who were also entitled in default of appointment. The property would pass to some of the children whatever happened. The father appointed some of the stock to non-objects of the power but he did not give his children anything from his own property as compensation.

HELD: No case of election arose. The children were entitled to keep what had been appointed to them and also they could claim in default of a proper appointment the property improperly appointed to non-objects.

The property which is not T's must be alienable

Election presupposes that the person called upon to elect can make a choice. If he is not in a position to choose no election arises: see *Re Lord Chesham* (1886); *Re Gordon's WT* (1978) (below).

In *Re Lord Chesham* (1886) 31 Ch D 466 T left certain chattels to his younger sons and the residue of his estate to his eldest son. The chattels were subject to a settlement of which the eldest son was the life tenant. The two younger sons claimed that the eldest son was called upon to elect.

HELD: As the eldest son had only a limited interest in the chattels under the settlement he was not called upon to elect. He could take the residue and retain his interest in the chattels.

In *Re Dicey* [1957] Ch 145 it was argued that property should not only be alienable for a case of election to arise but also that the person called upon to elect must be able to fulfil all the terms of the will precisely if he elects in favour of it. The Court of Appeal rejected this argument and Romer LJ illustrated the point using the following example:

> 'A testator gives Blackacre or the proceeds of sale to A. Blackacre in fact belongs to B, C and D as joint tenants and the testator gives legacies to each of these persons. Each of them has a separate and individual right and obligation to elect for or against the will notwithstanding that the gift to A can only take full effect according to the terms if B, C and D all elect in favour of the will. In other words a class is not exempted from the principle of election merely because each can contribute only a part of the total subject-matter of the gift which the testator has purported to effect.'

The property which T is disposing of must belong to the person called upon to elect independently of T's will

There is no election except between a gift under the will and a claim dehors the will. Thus election would not arise between two clauses in the same will: *Wollaston* v *King* (1869). If T specifically devises Blackacre to X, and then gives all his residuary realty 'including Blackacre' to Y, and all his residuary personalty to X, there is no election. Some doubt has been cast on this rule and it was not followed in *Re Macartney* [1918] 1 Ch 300. However, *Wollaston* v *King* is generally regarded as authoritative on the point.

In *Wollaston* v *King* (1869) LR 8 Eq 165 under a marriage settlement T had a special power of appointment in favour of the children of her marriage. The children were to take in default of appointment. By her will T appointed part of the fund to her son for life with remainder to her three daughters. The son was given a general power of appointment in that part of the fund appointed to him for life. The daughters were given other benefits by T's will. The son exercised the power of appointment given to him but his appointments were void for perpetuity. As a result the property appointed by him was caught by the residuary appointment to the daughters. The son argued that the daughters were called upon to elect between the property which fell to them as a result of his void appointment and the other benefits they received under T's will.

HELD: There was no case of election. The daughters took the property which fell to them as a result of the son's void appointment under the terms of T's will and not under the gift in default of appointment in the marriage settlement. Their rights arose wholly under the will and the rule as to election was not to be applied as between one clause in a will and another clause in the same will.

Election must be tested as at death

The conditions raising a case of election must be applied to the state of affairs existing at the testator's death: see *Re Coole* [1920] 2 Ch 536; *Re Edwards* [1958] Ch 168. An intention to dispose of property by will which does not belong to the testator at his death does not necessarily give rise to election.

In *Re Edwards* [1958] Ch 168 by her will T left a house in Hounslow and the residue of her estate to be divided between seven relatives. After making the will T made a gift inter vivos of the house to one of the seven relatives, a Mrs W. The question arose whether Mrs W was put to election.

HELD: There was no case for election because the transfer of the house to Mrs W adeemed the devise by will. When the will came into operation on T's death there was no gift of the house. By making the inter vivos gift T had shown that the gift by will was no longer to operate.

As election is tested at the date of death a derivative claim made through someone who could not be called upon to elect will not bring about a case of election.

In *Grissell* v *Swinhoe* (1869) LR 7 Eq 291 a fund was held for the benefit of T and X in equal shares. By his will T bequeathed the whole fund, half of it to X's husband and half of it to Y. X died after T and by her will her husband became entitled to all her property. The question arose whether X's husband was called upon to elect.

HELD: He need not elect between the quarter of the fund T had effectively bequeathed to him and X's half share as the latter was not his when T died. X's husband was accordingly entitled to three quarters of the fund.

23.3 Method of election

Where all the conditions required to raise a case of election have been fulfilled, the person called upon to elect has the choice of electing with the will or electing against it. Each of these alternatives shall be considered on the basis of the following example:

T leaves £10,000 to X under his will and in the same will leaves Blackacre to Y. X in fact owns Blackacre.

Election with the will

X takes the £10,000. He thereby allows his property Blackacre to be treated as if it belonged to the testator's estate: *Douglas* v *Douglas* (1871) 12 Eq 617. This means that Blackacre becomes subject to all the incidents on T's death, such as debts: see *Re Williams* [1915] 1 Ch 450.

Election against the will

If X chooses this course he will keep Blackacre. In such circumstances the benefit he would have received must be used to compensate Y so far as possible: see *Rich* v *Cockell* (1804). To determine the amount of compensation payable to Y a valuation will have to be made of Blackacre, and this must be the value at the date of T's death: see *Re Hancock* [1905] 1 Ch 16. If Blackacre was valued at, say, £20,000, Y would only receive £10,000 compensation. The only fund which is available to compensate him is the £10,000 legacy and he can never receive more than this: see *Douglas* v *Douglas* (1871). If Blackacre was valued at only £8,000 then Y would only be entitled to receive compensation to this extent. The other £2,000 of the £10,000 legacy would go to X.

If, in the above example, X died before he had elected, much would depend on how he left his estate. In *Cooper* v *Cooper* (1874) it was held that if he left his property in such a manner that it was possible for a beneficiary under his will to elect, then that beneficiary must step into X's shoes and elect. If X's assets devolve so that no one person can elect in his place it is as if X had elected against the will: see *Pickersgill* v *Rodger* (1876).

EXAMPLE:

T leaves £10,000 to X and Blackacre to Y. X owns Blackacre.

If X died before electing leaving all his estate to Z, Z would have to elect in X's place.

If X died leaving all his realty to A and all his personalty to B, then neither of those two could elect. The position is as if X had elected against the will to keep Blackacre.

If X had elected before his death then in all cases the election would be binding on the beneficiaries of X's estate.

Election will normally take place in an express form, for example where the person electing gives written notice of his intentions to T's executors. However, it can be implied. Receiving rents or income from property prima facie indicates an election to take it: see *Giddings* v *Giddings* (1827) 3 Russ 241. Before a party can be held bound by an implied election, five requisites must be satisfied. (*Sweetman* v *Sweetman* (1868) IR 2 Eq 141; per Chatterton V-C):

1. The party must have a knowledge of his right; he must know that the property T has attempted to give to another person was not T's property and it would on T's death become his independently of T's will.
2. The party must know as a matter of fact that T had no power to give the property which he purported to devise and that it belongs to him not by virtue of T's will but by an earlier title.

3. The party must know the relative values of the properties between which he is called upon to elect.
4. The party must know as a matter of fact, and not as a rule of law, that the rule of election exists.
5. The court must be satisfied that he made a deliberate choice.

23.4 When does election arise?

Where T makes a mistake about the property he owns

If T has only a limited interest in property he may make a will which disposes of more than his interest in the property. If he devises 'my freehold house Blackacre' to Y and £10,000 to X and X is in fact the freeholder, election would arise. T's mistake may have arisen because he thought he had a greater interest in the property. He may only be:

1. A lessee.
2. A statutory tenant.
3. A licensee.
4. A squatter.

Where T is a joint tenant or a tenant in common

If T was entitled to a share in property under either a joint tenancy or a tenancy in common he may have, in error, disposed of more than his share in the property. In such an instance if he gives the surviving joint tenants or tenants in common some of his own property by will, they will be called upon to elect.

Joint tenancy
T and X are joint tenants of Blackacre. On T's death the effect on the joint tenancy is that X, by right of survivorship, takes the whole interest in Blackacre. This occurs automatically by operation of law. If T left Blackacre to Y and a £10,000 legacy to X, X would be called upon to elect: see *Re Dicey* (1957) per Romer LJ (above).

In *Re Gordon's WT* [1978] 2 All ER 969 by her will T left her son some furniture and a legacy of £1,000 and devised a house – of which she and her son were joint tenants and which became his on her death by right of survivorship – on trust for sale for her son for life 'on protective trusts', with remainder to her son's two daughters. The son sold the house and it was argued that he had thereby elected against the will.

HELD: A joint tenant could be put to his election if his interest in that property subject to the joint tenancy was disposed of by a will which also conferred benefits upon him. No election arose in the present case as the life interest given to the son under the will was not available to compensate should he elect against the will, as he was incapable of alienating it under s33 TA 1925.

Tenancy in common

Where there is a tenancy in common each tenant in common has a separate share in the property which he can freely dispose of by his will. Sometimes a tenant in common may dispose of the whole interest in the property by his will.

EXAMPLE:

T, A and B are tenants in common in Blackacre. Each has a one-third share in the property. By his will T leaves Blackacre to C and a legacy of £10,000 to B.

B will be called upon to elect between his one-third share in Blackacre and the £10,000 legacy. If he elects with the will he will take the legacy and C will become a tenant in common with A, holding T's one-third share received by the will and B's one-third share received by election. If B elects against the will to keep his one-third, then A, B and C will be tenants in common of Blackacre.

A will not have to elect in this example as he has not received any benefits under T's will.

In *Padbury* v *Clarke* (1850) 2 Macq & G 298 T was entitled to a half-share in a freehold property as a tenant in common. By his will T devised the whole interest in the property to a third party and also gave the owner of the other half share a legacy.

HELD: As there was a clear intention on the part of T to dispose of the whole freehold, the owner of the other half-share had to elect.

Where T republishes or revises his will

If T makes a will devising Blackacre to X and £10,000 to Y and subsequently sells or gives Blackacre to Y but dies without changing his will, there is no election, as the gift to X in the will is adeemed: see *Re Edwards* (1958) (above). Neither will there be election if T has contracted to sell Blackacre to Y at the date of his death but has not conveyed the property to him, because the doctrine of conversion applies to make T trustee of Blackacre for Y from the date of the contract: see *Re Edwards* per Jenkins LJ. However, if T republishes or revives his will matters would be very different.

Republication

This arises where T executes a codicil to his will. The general rule is that a duly executed codicil containing some reference to the will republishes it: see *Re Harvey* [1947] Ch 285. Republication can also occur if the will is re-executed with the proper formalities: see *Dunn* v *Dunn* (1866) LR 1 P & D 277. A republished will is read as if it were made on the day of republication. The effect on an adeemed gift in the will would be that republication brings about a case of election. For example, if T in *Re Edwards* had republished her will it would be as if she had made a new will on the day of republication purporting to give away a property which was no longer hers.

Revival

A will which has been revoked may be revived by re-execution in compliance with s9 Wills Act 1837. A revived will may well have the effect of bringing about a case of election in similar circumstances to republication if it is not carefully reviewed before revival.

Where T exercises a power of appointment in favour of a non-object

A power of appointment may be conferred on a person either by a will or by deed giving that person the right to give the money or property subject to the power to certain persons. The person with such a power is referred to as the donee of the power. If the power permits him to appoint the property to anyone, including himself, it is a general power. But, if the power can only be exercised in favour of a limited class of objects, it is called a special power. In the case of the exercise of special powers election may arise.

EXAMPLE:

£10,000 to T to appoint among such of X's children as he in his absolute discretion thinks fit and in default to X's children in equal shares.

X had four children, A, B, C and D. By his will T exercises the power in favour to E, a non-object, giving him £5,000. In this gift T has used the power incorrectly. In effect he has given property which would pass to the persons entitled in default – A, B, C and D. Without more the appointment to E would be ineffective and the gift in default would operate on the whole £10,000. If T by his will gave his own property to all or any of A, B, C or D and exercised the power of appointment in favour of E in the same will, then election would arise: see *Bristowe* v *Warde* (1794) (above).

It is to be noted that election only arises here to require the persons entitled in default to elect if the appropriate circumstances occur. If in the example the gift in default were to A only, then only A would have to elect. The other objects of the power would only have a right to property given to them in the exercise of the special power and in no other circumstances: see *Re Neave* [1938] Ch 793.

24

Conversion and Reconversion

24.1 Introduction

24.2 Cases where conversion operates

24.3 Failure of conversion

24.4 Reconversion

24.1 Introduction

This equitable doctrine is based on the maxim that 'Equity regards that as done which ought to be done.' It governs the occasions when equity will treat realty as if it were converted into personalty and vice versa. It is also related to the maxim that 'Equity looks at the intent rather than the form' in that here equity is looking at rights and interests as they should be and not as they are in fact, and therefore at law.

The doctrine is intended to prevent unfairness to beneficiaries under trusts where the trustees prejudicially postpone sales and purchases of land. If S settled £100,000 on trustees with a direction to buy land and hold it 'on trust for B absolutely' and B died before the purchase of land is made, the rights of those entitled to B's estate ought not to depend on the precise moment at which the duty to convert is carried out. There is a notional conversion as soon as the trust becomes operative with the result that the £100,000 goes to those entitled to B's realty.

Conversion operates within a particular sphere and is closely connected with land law. It can convert personalty into realty (equity viewing money as land), or convert realty into personalty (equity viewing land as money).

24.2 Cases where conversion operates

Conversion is deemed to take place in six main situations:

Contract for sale and purchase of land

It is well settled that the moment there is a valid contract for the sale of land the vendor becomes in equity a trustee for the purchaser of the land sold, and the

345

beneficial ownership passes to the purchaser: *Lysaght* v *Edwards* (1876) 2 Ch D 499. In the eyes of equity the purchaser becomes the owner of the land and the vendor the owner of the money.

The key factor in deciding if conversion applies to a contract for the sale of land is whether the court would be prepared to grant specific performance of the contract: see *Holroyd* v *Marshall* (1862) 10 HL Cas 101. The purchaser will not be regarded as the owner in equity if specific performance is not available due to defects in the vendor's title: see *Re Thomas* (1886), or to a misrepresentation or a mistake.

Should either the vendor or purchaser die before completion of the contract then their personal representatives will be obliged to carry the contract through to completion. In the vendor's case the proceeds of sale will probably go to his residuary legatees and, in the case of the purchaser, the land will go to his residuary devisees provided he is willing to pay the money himself: see s35 AEA 1925 and *Re Birmingham* [1959] Ch 523.

Options to purchase land

An option to purchase does not of itself constitute a contract but an equitable interest vests in the grantee as soon as the option is granted rather than on its exercise when a contract comes into existence: see *Beesly* v *Hallwood Estates* [1961] Ch 105. As the option gives the grantee the right to take away the land it is considered as giving him an interest in the land: see *London and South West Rail Co* v *Gomm* (1882) 20 Ch D 562.

Where a contract has granted an option to purchase conversion takes place when the option is actually exercised and not when it is granted: *Re Isaacs* [1894] 3 Ch 506.

Because conversion only takes place when the option is exercised an option to purchase land can have a dramatic effect on the dispositions in the will of the owner of the land subject to the option. For example, if T makes a will leaving all his realty to X and all his personalty to Y and grants A an option to purchase Blackacre within six months from the date of his death, until A exercises the option Blackacre is considered as part of X's inheritance. But, when A exercises the option Blackacre becomes part of Y's inheritance. This is known as the rule in *Lawes* v *Bennett* (1785) 1 Cox 167. The rule is considered to be unsatisfactory in that it applies the doctorine of conversion in a situation where there is no necessity for it.

In *Lawes* v *Bennett* (1785) 1 Cox 167 a leased a farm to B for seven years in 1758. The lease gave B an option to purchase the fee simple of the farm for £3,000 at any time within the last four years of the lease – at any time between 1761 and 1765. B assigned the lease together with the option to C. In 1763 A died leaving a will by which he left all his realty to D and all his personalty to D and E equally. C exercised the option after A's death and D conveyed the farm to him. The question arose whether the purchase money should be considered as part of A's real or personal estate.

HELD: The purchase money on being paid over became part of A's personal estate and should accordingly be divided equally between D and E. The fact that C had an option to purchase did not make the case any different from a contract to sell real estate.

There has been a tendency to restrict the application of the doctrine in *Lawes* v *Bennett* and the court will exclude it if the evidence permits. Prima facie, *Lawes* v *Bennett* applies whether the option is granted before or after the will is made. It has, however, been held to be excluded in the following circumstances:

1. Where T grants A an option to buy Blackacre before making his will in which he specifically devises Blackacre to X.

   Weeding v *Weeding* (1861) 1 J & H 424 per Page-Wood V-C:

   'When you find that in a will, made after a contract giving an option to purchase, the testator, knowing of the existence of the contract, devises the specific property which is the subject of the contract without referring in any way to the contract ... then it is considered that there is sufficient indication of an intention to pass that property, or to give the devisee all the interest, whatever it may be, that the testator had in it.'

   EXAMPLE:

   T grants A an option to purchase Blackacre for £10,000 in 1980, the option to be exercised at any time within six months after T's death. In 1981 T makes a will specifically devising Blackacre to X. X will take Blackacre or the proceeds of sale. *Lawes* v *Bennett* will not apply.

2. Where a will containing a specific devise of Blackacre to X is republished at a date after the grant of the option.

   In *Emuss* v *Smith* (1851) 2 De G & Sm 722 T made a will specifically devising a certain estate to X. Afterwards he granted A an option to purchase the estate specifically devised. After the grant of the option T executed a codicil to his will which republished it. After T's death A exercised the option. The question arose whether the devisee was entitled to the proceeds of sale.

   HELD: The republication of a will by a codicil had the effect of excluding *Lawes* v *Bennett* when the gift in the will was specific.

3. Where the will and option are executed on the same day but it is uncertain which came first.

   In *Re Pyle* [1895] 1 Ch 724 by will land was specifically devised to X. A later codicil confirmed the will and on the same day a lease of the land which included an option to purchase was granted to Y. The option was exercised after the testator's death.

   HELD: The specific devisee X took the proceeds of sale. The facts showed an intention not to be bound by the principle in *Lawes* v *Bennett*.

4. Where the claim is not one to realty or personalty under a will.

   In *Edwards* v *West* (1878) 7 Ch D 858 a landlord granted his tenant an option to purchase the freehold for a fixed sum. Under the lease the landlord covenanted to insure the premises. The premises were burned down and the landlord received the insurance money. The tenant then exercised the option and claimed the insurance money.

HELD: The claim to receive the insurance money must fail as the rule in *Lawes* v *Bennett* was not applicable in such a case.

Once an option to purchase has been exercised the conversion takes place at that point. The fact that the purchase is not completed does not cause a reconversion: see *Re Blake* [1917] 1 Ch 18. Otherwise, much uncertainty would result.

Rents and profits received from the land between the date of the owner's death and the exercise of the option belong to the person claiming the deceased's realty. In *Re Isaacs* [1894] 3 Ch 506 Isaacs granted a lease coupled with an option to purchase within six months of his death. Isaacs died intestate and the lessee exercised the option.

HELD: The purchase money passed to the next-of-kin, not the heir at law; pending the exercise of the option the rents and profits from the land should pass to the persons entitled to it until conversion.

The principle in *Lawes* v *Bennett* has been extended to cover an option to purchase shares.

In *Re Carrington* [1932] 1 Ch 1 a testator specifically bequeathed shares to A. Subsequently, he granted an option to X to purchase those shares which was duly exercised within the period agreed, one month after the testator's death.

HELD: There was a conversion from shares to money. The bequest of shares to A had adeemed.

This decision has been criticised because conversion is a doctrine governing the devolution of realty and personalty and it was not intended to govern the devolution of different types of personalty. The case can possibly be supported on the ground that it was primarily concerned with ademption rather than conversion.

Land held on statutory trusts for sale

Under the 1925 legislation the doctrine of conversion had been extended by the imposition of statutory trusts for sale in certain situations. The most important cases of these were:

1. Under ss34–36 LPA 1925, where two or more persons become entitled to land as beneficial joint tenants or tenants in common, their interests, in the eyes of equity, lay in the proceeds of sale of the property rather than in the property itself.
2. Under s33 AEA 1925, if a person died intestate all his property was held on trust for sale.

Some cases decided shortly after the introduction of the property legislation in 1925 illustrate the effect of the doctrine of conversion in this context.

In *Re Kempthorne* [1930] 1 Ch 268 a testator made a will in 1911 but died in 1928, entitled to an undivided share in freehold property. He gave all his freehold and copyright property to R and all his leasehold and personal estate to P. There was no codicil indicating any intention on the testator's part to pass the property after the statutory conversion in 1925.

HELD:

1. Under s35 and Schedule 1 Part IV LPA 1925, as from 1 January 1926 the freehold was held on trust for sale since it was an undivided share.
2. The testator's interest was on that day statutorily converted into personalty under s28(3) LPA 1925, a provision which is of general application. In consequence it passed under the general gift of personal property to P.
3. The effect would have been the same if the will had been made after the Act came into force.

In *Re Newman* [1930] 2 Ch 409 by a will made in 1922 a testator who was entitled to an undivided freehold devised 'all my moiety or equal half part, or share and all my other share in the said freehold premises to my brother'. The testator died in 1929 without having altered or confirmed the will.

HELD: The devise had been adeemed by the imposition of the statutory trust for sale which converted the property to personalty:

1. The testator had used language that could only be construed as a devise of real estate. The conversion effected by the statutory trust adeemed the devise because there is nothing left for it to operate upon.
2. If the testator had used language wide enough to carry any interest in the property, whether it be in law real or personal property, then the statutory conversion would have been immaterial.

According to the Trusts of Land and Appointment of Trustees Act 1996, the doctrine of conversion is abolished in relation to trusts for sale of land. The doctrine survives, however, in relation to specifically enforceable contracts for the sale of freehold land, discussed above. The transitional provisions for pre-commencement statutory trusts for sale are detailed in the amendments contained in Sch 2.

An express trust for sale

Where there is an imperative direction by a testator or settlor to trustees either to sell or purchase realty, with a beneficiary able to insist on the conversion, then the property is treated as converted from the moment the will or trust instrument becomes effective, though the trustees may have a discretionary power to postpone sale or purchase: see *Fletcher* v *Ashburner* (1779) 1 Bro CC 479.

If the conversion is optional, that is, a mere power of sale or purchase has been conferred, there is no immediate conversion. The property is considered to be realty or personalty according to the actual condition in which it is found. For example, a settlor gives £10,000 to trustees coupled with a discretion to buy land or good securities to be held on trust for his daughter. She dies after the settlor but before the purchase of the land. The result is that the £10,000 goes to the daughter's next-of-kin, not the heir, since the money is not converted until the land is bought: see *Curling* v *May* (1734) 3 Atk 255.

A trust for sale or purchase may only be exercisable at the request of or with the consent of a beneficiary such as the life tenant. If the purpose is to make sure there is a conversion, then such a conversion is effective from the date of the instrument embodying the trust, but if the purpose is merely to give the beneficiary a discretion as to whether there shall be a sale or not, there is no conversion until the actual sale.

Partnership land

Under s22 Partnership Act 1890 it is provided that unless a contrary intention appears, land which becomes partnership property is treated as personal not real estate as between the partners themselves, their representatives after death, and those persons entitled to the property of the deceased partner. The reason for this is that on dissolution of the partnership the land will have to be sold and the proceeds apportioned among the partners.

Order of the court

The court may order a sale of realty in which two or more persons are interested. If one dies before the sale occurs his interest will be regarded as being in personalty, not realty, the conversion being effected at the date of the court order. It is immaterial that the sale was ordered for some particular purpose which will not exhaust the whole of the proceeds, for example, payment of costs.

This general provision may be affected by statutory provisions. For example, the s107 Mental Health Act 1959 preserves the right of persons interested in the mental patient's property. Real property disposed of is still to be treated as realty. Conversely, personalty used to buy realty is still to be personalty if the judge so directs.

24.3 Failure of conversion

The purpose for which conversion was directed may fail in whole or in part. If one or all of the beneficiaries under a will predecease the testator the question arises, who should receive the lapsed shares?

If the objects for whom conversion was directed fail completely before the time when conversion is appointed to take place, then there will be no conversion at all. If T directs the residue of his real estate to be held on trust for sale for X and Y and both predecease the testator, then conversion does not arise at all.

Where there is a partial failure of conversion, different rules apply to cases where conversion was directed in a deed and cases where it was directed by will.

Deeds
Where conversion is directed by deed and there is partial failure the property reverts to the settlor and those claiming under him in its converted form to the extent of the failure. For example, a deed may create a trust for sale of land with A and B entitled equally to the proceeds. If A dies before the deed becomes operative the settlor gets back half of the sale proceeds. If he is dead the proceeds go to his residuary legatee. If a trust to purchase realty had been created the residuary devisee could claim the money directed to be invested in realty by the settlor: see *Clarke* v *Franklin* (1858) 4 K & J 257.

Wills – conversion of realty to personalty
Where by will a testator directs that certain lands be held on trust for sale, and the proceeds divided equally between A and B, A's share would lapse should he predecease the testator. In this case A's share would pass to the residuary devisee under the will since the direction to convert was only for the purposes of the gift to A and B and has failed to the extent of A's share: see *Ackroyd* v *Smithson* (1780) 1 Bro CC 503. Although A's share passes to the residuary devisee, it passes to him in its converted form as there is still a duty to convert for B and this duty necessarily applies to the whole property. Should the residuary devisee die before he receives A's lapsed share then it would pass as part of his personal estate and not as realty. This is because the persons claiming R's realty are volunteers who are unable to insist on a reconversion to realty: see *Smith* v *Claxton* (1820) 4 Madd 484.

Will – conversion of personalty to realty
In these circumstances if the direction to convert fails either in whole or in part then the residuary legatee will take the interest which has failed: see *Cogan* v *Stephens* (1835) 1 Bear 482. However, it is not clear whether the residuary legatee should take the interest in its converted form, as realty. In *Re Richardson* [1892] 1 Ch 379 Chitty J thought that he would, but some dicta of the Court of Appeal in *Curtis* v *Wormald* (1878) 10 Ch D 172 suggest that he will take it as he finds it.

24.4 Reconversion

Reconversion is a notional further step by which an earlier conversion which has in theory taken place is reversed so that in the eyes of equity the property reverts to its original state. The principle is based on the maxim that equity will do nothing in vain. Situations where reconversion arises are as follows:

By act of the parties

If a testator devised realty on trust for sale for the benefit of A absolutely, from the moment of the testator's death A has an interest in the proceeds of sale of the property – a conversion has taken place. However, A may elect to receive the property in its unconverted form, thus dispensing with the necessity of a sale. In such instances the court will not compel a sale.

Harcourt v *Seymour* (1851) 2 Sin NS 12 per Lord Cranworth:

> 'Where, by a settlement land has been agreed to be converted into money, or money to be converted into land, a character is imposed on it until somebody entitled to take it in either form chooses to elect that, instead of its being converted into money, or instead of its being converted into land, it shall remain in the form in which it is actually found. There can be no doubt that this is the law; and the only question in each particular case is whether there have been acts sufficient to enable the court to say that the party has so determined.'

Slight acts will be sufficient to raise the inference that there has been reconversion, such as retaining land which is directed to be sold, or receiving the capital directed to be invested in land but not the income.

Where the property is 'at home'

This is the situation where the whole legal interest and the whole equitable interest vest in the same person. In such circumstances the need for conversion will probably have passed and no one could enforce the trust for conversion.

In *Re Cooke* [1948] Ch 212 the legal estate in a freehold dwellinghouse was vested in a husband and wife on a statutory trust for sale for themselves as joint tenants in equity. On the husband's death his share in the house passed automatically to the wife and she became the absolute owner of the property both in law and in equity. When the wife died subsequently the question arose whether it passed as part of her real estate or under a bequest of 'my personal estate'.

HELD: There was a reconversion on the death of the husband. The wife could not be trustee for herself alone, there being no separation of the legal and equitable interests. The property was realty in the wife's hands and it passed to her residuary devisees accordingly.

Undivided shares

A person entitled to an undivided share in land, which under the provision of the LPA 1925 is subject to a trust for sale, can elect to reconvert his share with the consent of the other beneficiaries who are of full age and as between themselves entitled to the whole trust fund: see *Saunders* v *Vautier* (1841). Where only one of several beneficiaries under a trust wishes to reconvert, whether he can do so depends on whether conversion is from realty to personalty or vice versa.

Conversion of land into money.

If reconversion is to take place here all those entitled must elect to reconvert otherwise the conversion will not go ahead. The reason why unanimity is required among the beneficiaries was explained by Cozens-Hardy MR in *Re Marshall* [1914] 1 Ch 192 at 199:

> '... where real estate is devised on trust for sale and to divide the proceeds of sale between A, B, C and D – some of the shares being settled and some of them not – A has no right to say "Transfer to me my undivided fourth of the real estate, because I would rather have it as real estate than personal estate". The court has said long ago that it is not right because it is a matter of notoriety, of which the court will take judicial notice, that an undivided share of real estate never fetches quite its proper proportion of the proceeds of sale of the entire estate; therefore, to allow one undivided share to be elected to be taken as real estate by one of the beneficiaries would be detrimental to the other beneficiaries.'

Conversion of money into land.

Where money is to be laid out in the purchase of land then one of the beneficiaries may elect to reconvert irrespective of the wishes of the others: see *Seeley* v *Jago* (1717). This is because the other beneficiaries are not prejudiced and may still go ahead and invest their shares in land.

Remaindermen

In some circumstances a remainderman can elect to take property in its unconverted form but this is subject to the rule that no such election can prejudice prior interests. If land was directed to be held on trust for sale 'for A for life, remainder to B', B cannot elect to take the property as realty so as to prevent A insisting on a sale. However, B may elect to the extent that his interest is absolute, for example, 'to A and C in equal shares for life, remainder to B'. Should C predecease B then B can elect to reconvert C's share which he now owns absolutely: see *Re Sturt* [1922] 1 Ch 416.

Minority

A minor cannot ordinarily elect. However, if the matter cannot wait until he attains his majority, the court may direct an inquiry as to whether it will be for his benefit to reconvert. It may then either elect for him or sanction his election: see *Robinson* v *Robinson* (1854) 19 Bear 494.

Mental patients

The Court of Protection has jurisdiction to elect on their behalf but will only reconvert if it is for the patient's benefit: s101 Mental Health Act 1959.

25

Satisfaction and Ademption

25.1 Introduction

25.2 Satisfaction of debts by legacies

25.3 Satisfaction of debts by inter vivos payments

25.4 Satisfaction of portions by legacies/ademption of legacies by portions

25.5 Satisfaction of legacies by legacies

25.1 Introduction

Satisfaction is based on the maxim 'Equity imputes an intention to fulfil an obligation.' It was described by Lord Romilly in *Chichester* v *Coventry* (1867) LR 2 HL 71 as 'the donation of a thing with the intention that it be taken either wholly or in part extinguishment of some prior claim of the donee'.

Satisfaction is closely related to performance. In satisfaction the court is concerned to see if something agreed to be done is satisfied by something different which is done. In performance the court is concerned to see if an act done can be taken as a step towards performing an act which the performer has covenanted to do.

Satisfaction operates in three main areas. These are:

1. Satisfaction of debts by legacies.
2. Satisfaction of debts by inter vivos payments.
3. Satisfaction of portions by legacies.

Each of these is dealt with below.

Ademption is a form of satisfaction which operates in one case, namely, ademption of legacies by portions. It is in fact the reverse of satisfaction of portions by legacies. It should be distinguished from ademption of legacies through failure for some reason such as uncertainty or lapse. This is a matter for books on wills and succession.

25.2 Satisfaction of debts by legacies

In *Talbot* v *Duke of Shrewsbury* (1714) Prec Ch 394 Trevor MR said:

> 'If one being indebted to another in a sum of money, does by his will give him as great, or greater sum of money than the debt amounts to without taking any notice at all of the debt, that this shall nevertheless be in satisfaction of the debt, so as that he shall not have both the debt and the legacy.'

EXAMPLE:
A owes B £500 and dies leaving the debt unpaid but leaving B a legacy of £500. Equity will presume that the legacy was given in satisfaction of the debt, and if the legatee chooses to receive the legacy he thereby admits that he no longer can enforce the debt.

Satisfaction of debts by legacies is disliked by the courts. In *Thynne* v *Earl of Glengall* (1848) 2 HLC 131 Lord Cottenham LC said: 'Equity leans against legacies being taken in satisfaction of debt.' As a result a large number of restrictions have been imposed so as to prevent satisfaction operating.

Restrictions imposed are as follows:

1. The legacy must be equal to or greater in value than the debt owed: *Gee* v *Liddell* (1866) 35 Bear 621. It will not operate pro tanto: *Crichton* v *Crichton* [1895] 2 Ch 583.
2. The legacy must be as beneficial to the credit to the debt. If the legacy is of uncertain value, for example, a gift of residue, *Barrett* v *Beckford* (1750) 1 Ves Sen 519; or of a different character or nature than the debt, for example, land for personalty, *Eastwood* v *Vinke* (1731) 2 P Wms 613; or a contingent gift for an immediate debt, *Haynes* v *Mico* (1781); or an unsecured gift for a secured debt, *Re Van Den Bergh's WT* [1948] 1 All ER 935, there is no satisfaction.
3. No satisfaction will arise if the will was made before the debt was incurred. The testator could have no intention of satisfaction in such cases: *Cranmer's Case* (1702) 2 Salk 508.
4. No satisfaction will arise where there is a direction in the will to pay debts or to pay debts and legacies. In *Re Manners* (1949) Evershed MR said:

> 'It seems tolerably clear that a direction for payment either of debts and legacies or of debts simpliciter is treated as being, whether or not artificially – and I do not think it is particularly artificial – something which prima facie takes the case altogether out of the rule.'

Satisfaction applies to ordinary debts here and it does not matter whether the creditor is the testator's child or wife: *Atkinson* v *Littlewood* (1874) LR 18 Eq 595.

25.3 Satisfaction of debts by inter vivos payments

Where a debt is owed by a parent to a child then it is presumed to be satisfied by a subsequent payment from parent to child of a sum equal to or greater than the debt, for example, on marriage. In *Wood* v *Briant* (1742) 2 Atk 521 Lord Hardwicke said:

> 'There are very few cases where a father will not be presumed to have paid the debt he owes to a daughter, when, in his lifetime, he gives her in marriage a greater sum than he owed her.'

It is unclear if this form of satisfaction applies to cases other than parent and child. In *Drewe* v *Bidgood* (1825) 2 Sm & St 424 it was presumed that satisfaction could apply between brother and sister, though it was held not to on the facts.

25.4 Satisfaction of portions by legacies/ademption of legacies by portions

These rules are closely related. Satisfaction of portions by legacies takes place where a father or someone in loco parentis to a child covenants to give his child a portion. Subsequently the father makes a will leaving his child a gift. If at the father's death the portion is unpaid the legacy will be deemed to be in satisfaction of it. Ademption of legacies by portions will occur where the will is made first leaving the child a legacy and subsequently the father actually gives the child a portion.

These rules are sometimes described as the rules against double portions, and are generally designed to achieve equality among children of the same family. Equity leans in favour of satisfaction in this area. In *Thynne* v *Earl of Glengall* (1848) 2 HLC 131 a father covenanted to settle £100,000 on the trusts of a marriage settlement on the occasion of the marriage of his daughter. Subsequently he transferred stock to the trustees of the settlement and promised to transfer more to them on his death. On his death the father left a share of his residue on trust to two of the trustees of the marriage settlement. The trusts in the will were different from those in the marriage settlement. The question arose whether there was satisfaction.

HELD: The share of residue satisfied the covenant to settle notwithstanding the differences in the trusts.

Conditions for satisfaction

The donor must be the father of or in loco parentis to the child
A parent stands in loco parentis if he intends to undertake the parental duty of making financial provision for the child: see *Fowkes* v *Pascoe* (1875) 10 Ch App 343. A grandfather was held in loco parentis to an illegitimate grandchild on this basis in *Rogers* v *Soutten* (1839) and an uncle to a nephew in *Booker* v *Allen* (1831). A mother may in exceptional circumstances stand in loco parentis to her children if she

is providing for them herself and has assumed the duty of providing for them: see *Re Ashton* [1897] 2 Ch 574.

Portions

There must be a portion promised and a portion given by the will. For these purposes a portion is a gift made for the purpose of establishing the child in life or making permanent provision for him. Most gifts by will are treated as portions. In *Re Furness* [1901] 2 Ch 346 a £20,000 legacy to a daughter was treated as a portion; in *Thynne* v *Earl of Glengall* (1848) a gift of residue was held to be a portion, but gifts of specific chattels such as watches and jewellery are not portions. In *Re Tussaud's Estate* (1878) 9 Ch D 363 a diamond necklace to a daughter was not treated as a portion.

Inter vivos dispositions which count as portions include provision for a child by a marriage settlement: *Taylor* v *Taylor* (1875); payments of money or transfers of property to establish a child in business or a profession: *Taylor* v *Taylor*; or gifts of farming stock to a son to help him begin farming: *Re George's WT* [1949] Ch 154. Small inter vivos gifts such as birthday and Christmas presents will not normally count as portions (*Schofield* v *Heap* (1858) 27 Bear 93) nor will payments of money for a child's education or maintenance or by way of temporary assistance: see *Re Scott* [1903] 1 Ch 1.

In *Taylor* v *Taylor* (1875) LR 20 Eq 155 a father died intestate leaving two sons surviving him. The father had made certain payments to each of the sons during his lifetime and the question arose as to which payments should be taken into account as portions on intestacy. The payments included:

1. Money given to one son to become a clergyman.
2. An entry fee for the Middle Temple.
3. The price of a commission in the army.
4. A fee paid to a special pleader.
5. The price of an outfit on entering the army.
6. The price of an outfit and a passage for India.
7. Money to pay off debts.
8. Advances to finance mining operations in Wales.

HELD: 2, 3 and 8 were advancements but the remainder were not, as they were mere casual payments.

Satisfaction pro tanto

If the legacy is equal to or greater than the portion it is considered as being in complete satisfaction of it: see *Thynne* v *Earl of Glengall*. There can also be satisfaction pro tanto, as where the legacy is less than the portion promised. If T covenants to pay his son X £10,000 to set up a business and later in his will leaves X a £5,000 legacy without having fulfilled his obligation under the covenant, satisfaction will operate so that a further £5,000 only is payable on the covenant: see *Pym* v *Lockyer* (1841) 5 My & Cr 29.

Both portions must be provided by, and for, the same persons

The same person must covenant to give the portion and to eventually give the legacy and the same person must be promised the portion and given the legacy. The necessity for this rule is based on problems concerning marriage settlements where a father covenanted to give portions to his daughter and later gave money to his son-in-law. In some cases satisfaction has operated, as in *Nevin* v *Drysdale* (1867) LR 4 Eq 517, and in others it has not: see *Cooper* v *MacDonald* (1873) LR 16 Eq 258.

The principle must not be applied to benefit strangers

As the main purpose of satisfaction is to ensure equality among the donor's children, it must not be allowed to benefit strangers. For example, if a father gave his son A a portion £10,000 and later makes a will leaving his residuary estate to his sons A and B, and C also in equal shares, C being a complete stranger, then the rule cannot be allowed to benefit C. If the residue was worth £90,000 C would receive £30,000 and the advancement of £10,000 would only be taken into account as between A and B: see *Re Vaux* [1938] Ch 581.

Operation of the presumptions

Satisfaction of legacies by portions can only operate if the portion promised has not been paid. There can be no satisfaction if the portion has already been satisfied: see *Taylor* v *Cartwright* (1872) LR 14 Eq 167. Where this presumption operates the legatee/donee is not compelled to take either the legacy or the portion; he can elect to take whichever he chooses. This does not apply to ademption because the legacy is deemed to have failed and the only choice is to take the portion.

Rebutting the presumptions

Satisfaction and ademption depend on the intention of the donor/testator for their operation. If he makes express provision that such presumptions are not to operate they cannot be applied.

In *Chichester* v *Coventry* (1867) LR 2 HL 71 it was said that it would be much easier to rebut the presumption of satisfaction than the presumption of ademption. In the former, satisfaction, it is easy to suppose that the father may have made the legacy by way of additional provision to the portion, but in the latter, ademption, it could be supposed that he knew of his will and intended the later provision to be a substitute.

In the case of satisfaction differences in the limitations of the two provisions may rebut the presumption unless these differences are only slight. What is 'slight' is a question of fact in each case. In *Thynne* v *Earl of Glengall* the differences were considered slight where the limitations on a marriage settlement and the limitations on a will trust were different. Cases where the limitations were sufficient to rebut the presumption of advancement include *Chichester* v *Coventry* (1867) and *Re Tussaud's Estate* (1878).

In *Chichester* v *Coventry* (1867) LR 2 HL 71 a father covenanted to pay £10,000 to the trustees of his daughter's marriage settlement on trust for her husband for life with remainder to the wife for life with remainder to the children of the marriage as the wife should appoint. Later by his will, the father left half of his residue to the wife for life for her own separate use with remainder to such persons, including her husband, as she should appoint.

HELD: There was no satisfaction, the different words of limitation militated against such a conclusion.

In *Re Tussaud's Estate* (1878) 9 Ch D 363 CA under a marriage settlement a wife had a general power of appointment over the property with the consent of the trustees. In default of appointment the property was to be held on trust giving successive life interests to the husband and wife, remainder to the children of the marriage with an ultimate remainder to the husband absolutely. Under her father's will the wife was given a life interest in certain property with remainder to her children and ultimate remainders were given to the wife's brothers. The question arose whether the disposition by will was in satisfaction of the covenant to settle on the marriage settlement.

HELD: There was no satisfaction.

There may be satisfaction by a legacy where the legacy only affects some of those who were to benefit from the portion. Thus, in *Chichester* v *Coventry* (1867) Lord Romilly said:

> 'A provision by will may satisfy one part of a covenant without satisfying the other parts of it; for instance, that if a father, on the marriage of his daughter, should settle £10,000 on her for life, remainder to the children of the marriage, a bequest of £10,000 to that daughter would satisfy her life interest in the £10,000, but would not satisfy or touch the interests of the children.'

In *Re Blundell* [1906] 2 Ch D 222 a father covenanted to settle on a marriage settlement £5,500 for the wife (his daughter) for life then the husband for life and then the children of the marriage. Afterwards the father made a will leaving his daughter a share of residue absolutely which was worth much more than £5,500.

HELD: There was satisfaction of the wife's life interest under the settlement, but not of the interests of the other beneficiaries.

Differences in limitation do not affect the operation of ademption: see *Durham* v *Wharton* (1836) 10 Bli NS 526.

The presumptions will be rebutted in cases where the two provisions are not ejusdem generis: see *Re Jaques* [1903] 1 Ch 267. Money is not to be taken as in satisfaction of land and vice versa, nor is a legacy to be taken as adeemed by a gift of stock in trade, nor a contingent legacy as satisfaction for a vested portion.

25.5 Satisfaction of legacies by legacies

This is not really a case of equity applying the doctrine of satisfaction but instead, a case of equity adopting special rules of construction in wills. As it is frequently mentioned alongside the doctrine of satisfaction it will be discussed here.

Satisfaction of legacies by legacies is really a matter of deciding whether double legacies should be regarded as cumulative or substitutional.

Two legacies in same instrument

If two legacies are contained in the same will of the same value and are given to the same person, the presumption is that they are substitutional and the legatee can only take one of them: see *Garth* v *Meyrick* (1779). If, however, the legacies are of different value they will be considered as cumulative: see *Brennan* v *Moran* (1857).

Two legacies in different instruments

The presumption is that such legacies are cumulative: see *Hooley* v *Hatton* (1773). This is on the assumption that a testator intends each and every disposition which he makes to take effect, where these are not mutually inconsistent.

Legacies in different instruments given for the same motive

If a testator gives two legacies of the same amount by different instruments and expresses the same motive in each instrument for giving each legacy, the legacies are presumed to be substitutional. In *Benyon* v *Benyon* (1810) a testator gave £100 by his will and £100 by his codicil to B in each case for his trouble as executor. The legacies were held to be substitutional.

If the rules of construction raise the presumption that the legacies are cumulative, then parol evidence is not admissible to rebut this. If, on the other hand, it is presumed that the legacies are substitutional, parol evidence may be admitted in rebuttal.

26

Performance

26.1 Introduction

26.2 Covenant or statutory duty to purchase land

26.3 Covenant to leave personalty

26.1 Introduction

This equitable doctrine is based on the maxim 'Equity imputes an intention to fulfil an obligation.' It arises where a party covenants to do a certain act, such as purchase land to place in a marriage settlement, but fails to carry out that act. Should the same party do some other act which could be construed as a step towards performance of the covenant, for example buying land, then it will be treated as such. In short, the act of buying the land is treated as a notional performance of the covenant.

In *Sowden* v *Sowden* (1785) 1 Cox Eq 165 it was said by Kenyon MR:

'Where a man covenants to do an act, and he does an act which may be converted to a completion of this covenant, it shall be supposed that he meant to complete it.'

The doctrine is of limited application, but it operates in two main areas:

1. Where there is a covenant or a statutory duty to purchase and settle land and a purchase of land is made by the covenantor.
2. Where there is a covenant to leave personalty to X, and X in fact inherits property under the covenantor's will or intestacy.

26.2 Covenant or statutory duty to purchase land

Where a man has covenanted to purchase and settle land, or to convey and settle land, or to pay money to trustees to be used in the purchase of land, and has in the circumstances failed to carry out the obligation, but has subsequent to the covenants purchased land, the court will presume that the purchase was in performance or part performance of the covenant.

361

The leading case in support of this proposition is *Lechmere* v *Lady Lechmere* (1735) Cas t Talb 80. On the marriage of Lord and Lady Lechmere articles were entered into whereby Lord Lechmere covenanted to lay out, within a year of marriage and with the consent of his trustees, £30,000 in the purchase of freehold lands in fee simple in possession. These lands were to be settled for his use for life with remainders over to his sons. Lord Lechmere died intestate without issue and without having complied with his covenants. Under the doctrine of conversion the £30,000 was to be considered as realty and would therefore devolve on Lord Lechmere's heir-at-law. However, Lord Lechmere owned estates in fee simple at the time of his marriage and after marriage he purchased and contracted to purchase more estates, some in possession and some in reversion. The question arose whether these should be considered as being in performance of his covenant.

HELD: The purchase of and contracts to purchase the estates in possession should be regarded as having been in part performance of the covenant even if these were not purchased within a year of marriage or with the consent of the trustees. Their values would accordingly be subtracted from the £30,000. However, the estates purchased in reversion were not in performance of the covenant as the covenant specifically referred to 'estates in possession'.

The following points emerge from *Lechmere* v *Lady Lechmere*:

1. There can be performance pro tanto. The purchase of land the value of which is less than the land covenanted to be purchased and settled, is considered to be part performance of the covenant.
2. Land owned by the covenantor or purchased by him before the covenant was made cannot be taken in performance of a covenant which contemplates the purchase of land in the future.
3. If the covenantor purchases property entirely different in nature from that which he originally covenanted to purchase there is no performance.
4. The absence of the trustees' consent, if required under the covenant, will not prevent performance operating.

The effect of performance is that land is presumed purchased in performance of the covenant so that the beneficiaries are not dependent upon the trustees claiming against the covenantor for damages for breach of covenant. In place of such a claim they have the security of equitable remedies against the land itself as the covenant constitutes a specialty-debt, a useful right where the covenantor is insolvent or where the land has increased in value since the purchase or where any action on the covenant is statute-barred.

In some cases the covenant may create a lien on the land in favour of the beneficiaries. This depends on whether the covenant is general or specific. If it is general, to purchase land of a particular type, for example freehold land, a lien will be created on any such land purchased afterwards. However, if this land is later sold or mortgaged then performance cannot operate, as this shows that the covenantor did not intend performance: see *Deacon* v *Smith* (1746) 3 Atk 323. If the covenant is specific –

to settle specific property already belonging to him or to be acquired by him or even all his property – then an equitable lien will be created on the land as the court would order specific performance of the covenant: see *Pullan* v *Koe* [1913] 1 Ch 9.

26.3 Covenant to leave personalty

A man may covenant that his executors will pay X £1,000 or, that he will leave X £1,000 in his will. If the covenantor dies intestate, that is, without having made a will, and under his intestacy X becomes entitled to either a sum of £1,000 or some smaller sum, the money received will be treated as in performance or part performance of the covenant: see *Garthshore* v *Chalie* (1804) 10 Ves 1.

Performance may operate upon covenants to make legacies which are not fulfilled because the covenantor dies intestate, provided the beneficiary benefits from the covenantor's intestacy: see *Blandy* v *Widmore* (1716) 1 P Wms 323. It may also operate where the covenantor has covenanted to leave the beneficiary property after his death and there is provision for the beneficiary under the covenantor's will: see *Re Hall* [1918] 1 Ch 562.

In *Blandy* v *Widmore* (1716) 1 P Wms 323 a husband covenanted in a marriage settlement that if his wife should survive him he would leave her £620. The husband eventually died intestate without issue, survived by his wife. Under the Statute of Distribution the wife became entitled to a moiety of personal estate worth much more than £620. The question arose as to whether this distributive share was to be taken as being in performance of the covenant to leave £620.

HELD: Performance operated so as to extinguish the widow's rights under the covenant.

In *Re Hall* [1918] 1 Ch 562 a husband covenanted to leave his wife an annuity of £1,000 after his death. This was not done but he left her a life interest in his residuary estate under his will, the income from this being well over £1,000 per annum.

HELD: The husband intended the bequest of income to his wife to be in performance of his liability to her under the covenant.

A gift by will may be taken as in performance of a covenant to pay certain money to the beneficiary after the covenantor's death, as it was in *Re Hall*. Where the covenant is one to pay money it will not be performed by a specific bequest of chattels (see *Devese* v *Pontet* (1785) 1 Cox Eq Cas 188), nor will it be performed by a legacy which is payable at a date later than the covenant debt: see *Haynes* v *Mico* (1781) 1 Bro CC 129.

There can be no performance once a breach of the covenant has occurred. In *Oliver* v *Brickland* (1732) a husband covenanted to pay his wife money within two years of their marriage. He died intestate more than two years later and his wife inherited most of his estate under his intestacy. It was held that there was no performance, as the covenant had been breached before the husband's death.

27

Equitable Remedies

27.1 Introduction

Prior to the Judicature Acts of 1873 and 1875 the courts of common law and the courts of equity existed as separate institutions, each administering its own system of law according to its own tenets, neither able nor willing to utilise the procedures and remedies of the other. A common law remedy was available if there had been an infringement of a legal right, and the relief it afforded was usually that of damages supported by a writ of, for example, fieri facias. The grant of an equitable remedy required proof that there had been the infringement of a right and the plaintiff had further to establish that the issue was one in which equity should give relief. Whereas the common law awarded damages, enforceable by writ, equitable remedies were only awarded where damages were considered inappropriate or inadequate. The basic effect of the Judicature Acts was to fuse the administration of law and equity, by transferring the jurisdiction of their superior courts to the Supreme Court of Judicature. The Supreme Court could now give effect on legal and equitable rights and remedies by virtue of ss24 and 25 Judicature Act 1873. Today s49 Supreme Court Act 1981 confers the right to administer equitable remedies on all courts exercising jurisdiction in civil cases. Section 49(1) states:

'Every court exercising jurisdiction in England and Wales in any civil cause or matter shall continue to administer law and equity on the basis that, wherever there is any conflict or variance between the rules of equity and the rules of common law with reference to the same matter, the rules of equity shall prevail.'

Section 49(2) states:

'Every such court shall give effect as hitherto to all equitable estates, titles, rights, reliefs, defences and counterclaims, and to all equitable duties and liabilities ... '

There are certain principles which govern the availability of equitable remedies:

1. Equitable remedies are discretionary whereas at common law remedies are available as of right. The successful plaintiff at common law is entitled to damages, and a means of enforcing judgment, even where such judgment would appear unfair to the other party. In equity the courts may exercise their discretion and refuse a remedy if, for example, the behaviour of the plaintiff is questionable: 'He who comes to equity must come with clean hands'; or severe hardship would be caused to the defendant; or if the plaintiff has delayed unreasonably in bringing his action: 'Delay defeats equity.' See *Tinsley* v *Milligan* [1993] 3 WLR 126, in which the House of Lords held that a claim based on an equitable interest can succeed so long as the claimant, albeit not wholly 'innocent', is not required to plead or rely on an illegality.

2. The use of the discretion is determined by settled equitable principles; it is not used in an arbitrary fashion. The courts will draw on a body of principles known as the maxims of equity. Thus the maxim 'He who comes to equity must do equity' may result in a plaintiff being refused relief, due to the nature of his own conduct. In *Duchess of Argyll* v *Duke of Argyll* [1967] Ch 302 the plaintiff was refused an injunction to restrain the publication of her ex-husband's account of the intimate details of their married life, due to the fact that it was her subsequent immorality that led to the termination of the marriage.

3. Generally, equitable remedies are only available if there is no adequate common law remedy:

'The court gives specific performance instead of damages, only when it can by that means do more perfect and complete justice' per Lord Selborne LC in *Wilson* v *Northampton and Banbury Junction Railway Co* (1874) 9 Ch App 275 at 284.

The common law remedy of damages will usually be an adequate remedy in contracts for the sale of goods, since the buyer could go back to the market and obtain similar goods elsewhere, unless the goods in the contract are unique or possess a particular intrinsic value which renders them irreplaceable.

4. A court will not grant an equitable remedy unless it can ensure execution of the remedy.

27.2 Specific performance

Definition

A decree of specific performance is an order of the court compelling a person to perform an obligation existing under either a contract or a trust. It 'presupposes an executory as distinct from an executed agreement, something remaining to be done, such as the execution of a deed or a conveyance in order to put the parties in the position relative to each other in which by preliminary agreement they were intended to be placed' per Lord Selborne LC in *Wolverhampton and Walsall Railway Co v London and North Western Railway Co* (1873) LR 16 Eq 433 at 439.

Nature of the remedy

It will only be granted if the common law remedy is inadequate. Damages are only available at common law for an actual breach of contract; equity does not require such a breach.

In *Marks* v *Lilley* [1959] 2 All ER 647 specific performance was awarded of a contract for the sale of land, despite the fact that the agreed completion date had passed, and that no notice had been served making time of the essence of the contract.

Equity may take a more flexible view of the circumstances than the common law. If one of the parties to a contract has given a misdescription which is not of fundamental importance the common law would not allow him a remedy, whereas a decree of specific performance, with compensation, may be awarded by equity.

Conversely, if the common law remedy of damages would give a remedy that is as good as actual performance of the contract, then equity will not interfere.

The remedy is not available as of right, it is of a discretionary nature. However, it should be remembered that this discretion is not of an arbitrary nature but is determined in the light of a carefully formulated set of maxims.

> '(It) must be exercised according to fixed and settled rules; you cannot exercise a discretion by merely considering what, as between the parties, would be fair to be done, what one person may consider fair, another person may consider unfair; you must have some settled rule and principle upon which to determine how that discretion is to be exercised' per Romilly MR in *Haywood* v *Cape* (1858) 25 Beav 140.

Accordingly matters such as delay in seeking a remedy and the conduct of the plaintiff may have a serious bearing on the court's final decision as to whether or not to award a decree of specific performance.

By the Chancery Amendment Act 1858 (Lord Cairns' Act) the Court of Chancery was given power to award damages in addition to, or in lieu of, an injunction or a decree of specific performance. This is now effectively re-enacted in s50 Supreme Court Act 1981; see *Kennaway* v *Thompson* [1980] 3 All ER 329.

The decree of specific performance is issued against an individual defendant and a refusal to comply with its requirements is ultimately subject to the criminal sanctions of contempt of court.

The decree is not available against the Crown, although the plaintiff may seek a declaratory order of rights: s21 Crown Proceedings Act 1947.

Enforceable contracts

Contracts involving land or the grant of a lease

Due to the unique qualities that each parcel of land possesses it is rare for an award of damages alone to be considered adequate. Specific performance, with or without compensation, will be the appropriate remedy

Such contracts are specifically enforceable by both parties, vendor and purchaser. Since a purchaser can obtain specific performance on the contract he is considered in equity as already being the owner of the land, following the equitable maxim 'Equity regards that as done which ought to be done.' Once the contract has been made the purchaser may secure the land from the estate of the vendor, even if the vendor becomes insolvent.

As a corollary of the above, the vendor is similarly considered as owning the price. If he has conveyed the land to the purchaser, but is yet to be paid, he is in possession of an equitable lien on the land for the price.

Not only are contracts for estates in land and interests in land specifically enforceable, so too are contractual licences: see *Verrall* v *Great Yarmouth Borough Council* [1981] QB 202. The Conservative council of Great Yarmouth agreed to hire out Wellington Pier to the National Front. Prior to the performance of the contract the control of the council passed to Labour who then, for political motives, tried to repudiate the contract. It was held by the Court of Appeal that specific performance was available.

Finally it should be noted that specific performance may be awarded even where the land in question is situated abroad. In *Penn* v *Lord Baltimore* (1750) 1 Ves Sen; (1558–1774) All ER Rep 99 specific performance of an English agreement concerning boundaries between Pennsylvania and Maryland was decreed, despite the lack of jurisdiction to enforce this remedy in rem. The seeming futility of such an action derived from the principle that the remedy is 'in personam' (concerning the person) and not 'in rem' (concerning the property). This view has been supported more recently in *Richardson West and Partners (Inverness) Ltd* v *Dick* [1969] 1 All ER 289; affd [1969] 2 Ch 424 CA where specific performance was decreed with respect to a contract for the sale of land against a defendant who was within the jurisdiction of the court.

Contracts concerning personal property

Specific performance only lies in cases where the chattels are unique, or possess a particular intrinsic value of their own, such as a racehorse or the sale of stones from the dismantled Westminster Bridge: see *Thorn* v *Public Works Commissioners* (1863) 32 Beav 490.

Similar considerations apply to stocks and shares that cannot be purchased on the International Stock Exchange, the Unlisted Securities Market or 'over the counter' shares: see *Duncuft* v *Allbrecht* (1841) 12 Sim 189. Specific performance will not be granted in respect of government stock since this is usually obtainable on the open market.

Section 52 Sale of Goods Act 1979 empowers the courts to order specific performance wherever the goods are specific or ascertained. The decree has been granted when goods are in short supply. Obviously if goods are available elsewhere the buyer should obtain them elsewhere and sue for damages. Conversely, if the buyer refuses delivery of the goods the seller should sell them elsewhere and then sue the original purchaser for damages.

It should be remembered that there is a duty on the plaintiff, whether he be buyer or seller, to mitigate his damages. Although specific performance may be obtained by summary process it still tends to impede the normal process of trade and therefore a subsequent action for damages would appear to be a more appropriate remedy – a legal attitude not supported in other member states of the European Community.

Employment

It will be seen below that generally employment contracts cannot be specifically enforceable against employees since:

1. Section 16 Trade Union and Labour Relations Act 1974 provides that no court shall compel an employee to work or to attend at a place of work via making of an order for specific performance.
2. They are contracts of personal service.

Two cases should be highlighted as exceptions, if only because of their unusual nature.

In *Hill* v *C A Parsons Ltd* [1972] Ch 305 a non-unionised employee had been dismissed due to pressure on the employer from the trade union attempting to impose a 'closed shop'. Specific performance was granted, re-employing the worker, since the Industrial Relations Act 1971 (since repealed) was due to come into force within a few weeks and this would then afford the employee greater rights. The court allowed a 'breathing space' to enable the employee's statutory remedies to catch up with the circumstances of the particular case.

In *Iranis* v *Southampton and South West Hampshire Health Authority* [1985] IRLR 203 the employee, a part-time ophthalmologist, was dismissed due to conflict with a consultant, not due to dissatisfaction on the part of the employer. The decree of specific performance was granted to ensure that correct disciplinary procedures were instituted by the Health Authority, not to ensure confirmed employment at all costs.

Contracts not specifically enforceable

Voluntary contracts

The dictum of Lord Hardwicke in *Penn* v *Lord Baltimore* (above) that 'the court never decrees specifically without a consideration' applies even if the contract was made under seal. This is the source of the equitable maxim 'Equity will not assist a volunteer.'

Contracts relating to personal property

As was stated in Chapter 26, section 26.2 above, unless the goods are unique or of particular significance to the buyer the courts would consider the award of damages a more satisfactory course of action.

However, s52 Sale of Goods Act 1979 does give the courts a discretion whether or not to allow specific performance for 'specific or unascertained goods'. 'Specific' means, per s61(1), goods as agreed upon at the time the sale is made. 'Ascertained' means goods agreed upon, after the contract of sale is made, in accordance with the express terms of the contract.

Contracts requiring constant supervision

In *Ryan* v *Mutual Tontine Westminster Chambers Association* [1983] 1 Ch 116 the Court of Appeal decided that it would be incorrect to award specific performance if this resulted in the need for a court to exercise constant supervision over a defendant in the performance of continuous acts, such as contracts to construct railways, or contracts to appoint a porter to carry out specified duties. But see *Posner* v *Scott-Lewis* [1986] 3 All ER 513.

However, building contracts deserve special consideration. Specific performance will not be granted as a general rule but may be granted if:

1. The building work is clearly defined in the contract.
2. The defendant is in possession of the land, and the plaintiff is, in consequence, unable to appoint and employ another builder.
3. The plaintiff's interest in the contract is of such a nature that an award of damages would represent inadequate compensation: see *Wolverhampton Corp* v *Emmons* [1901] 1 KB 515. The plaintiff corporation, in order to effect a street improvement programme, sold a plot of land adjoining a street to the defendant. The defendant agreed only to erect buildings in accordance with the specifications and plans, but failed to do so. In accordance with the above criteria specific performance was awarded.

Contracts for personal work/service

Equity refuses to enforce contracts of employment or contracts involving personal service, possibly due to the problems of supervision, and also because of the undesirability of doing so, on the grounds of public policy: 'the courts are bound to be jealous, lest they should turn contracts of employment into contracts of slavery' per Fry LJ in *Francesco* v *Barnum* (1890) 45 Ch D 430.

Many would assert that damages is a more appropriate remedy. The views of Megarry J in *C H Giles & Co Ltd* v *Morris* [1972] 1 All ER 960 at 969 probably represent the most plausible reason:

> 'If a singer contracts to sing there could no doubt be proceedings for committal if, ordered to sing, the singer remained obviously dumb. But if the singer sang flat, or too sharp, or too fast, or too slowly ... the threat of committal would reveal itself as a most unsatisfactory weapon: for who could say whether the imperfections of the performance were natural or self induced?'

The cases of *Hill* v *C A Parsons & Co Ltd* (1972) (above) and *Iranis* v *Southampton & South West Hampshire Health Authority* (1985) (above) are sound testament to reading too much into the unusual solutions that the courts are sometimes forced to provide for problems engendered by unusual cases.

Contracts lacking mutuality
Personal incapacity, the nature of the contract or other factors may mean that one party to the contract will be able to enforce the agreement but the other party cannot. In such cases the contract is not mutually binding, and, according to the principle of mutuality, will not be enforced by specific performance. In *Flight* v *Boland* (1882) 4 Russ 298 an infant sought a decree of specific performance for the sale of land. Since the court would not have enforced his payment of the purchase price, because of his infancy, specific performance was refused.

'The exception tries the rule' and, unfortunately, s40(1) Law of Property Act was a very trying exception to the refusal of specific performance, in cases where the contract lacks mutuality. It provided:

> 'No action may be brought upon any contract for the sale or other disposition of land or any interest in land unless the agreement upon such an action is brought, or some memorandum or note thereof, is in writing, and signed by the party to be charged or by some other person thereunto by him lawfully authorised.'

One party may have signed a memorandum, so entitling the other to a decree of specific performance, whereas the party who has not signed the memorandum would not have a decree of specific performance enforced against his failure to observe the contract. For repeal and replacement of s40 LPA 1925 as from 27 September 1989 see below.

Contracts tainted with immorality or illegality
'Ex turpi causa non oritur actio' (no action arises from a base or illegal cause).

Contracts capable of part performance only
'A contract cannot be specifically performed in part: it must be wholly performed, or not at all, and a part of the contract may be of such a nature as to vitiate the whole' per Romilly MR in *Ford* v *Stuart* (1852) 15 Beav 493 at 501.

If a contract contained two terms that are inextricably linked, the first being, for example, unenforceable by specific performance since it is a contract of a personal nature, the second being capable of enforcement by specific performance if it stood on its own, then according to Romilly MR's dictum neither part will be enforceable as they stand or fall together. This is exemplified by the case of *Brett* v *East India & London Shipping Co Ltd* (1864) 2 Hem & M 404. The agreement comprised two terms, firstly to employ the plaintiff as his broker, secondly to advertise that fact. Since specific performance is unavailable for contracts of personal service this also prevented the advertising condition from being enforced.

This rule can be displaced if, on a point of construction, the two items can be shown to be two separate or divisible contracts. In that case the contract for advertising in *Brett* would have been enforceable.

Contracts to lend or advance money
The very nature of this contract would indicate that damages would normally be considered an adequate remedy. Specific performance can be obtained:

1. On a contract to create a mortgage – an agreement to give security for money actually advanced.
2. In the exceptional circumstances wherein the contract involves payment of money to a third party: see *Beswick* v *Beswick* [1968] AC 58.

Contracts for arbitration
A contract to refer a dispute to arbitration cannot be enforced: see *South Wales Railway Co* v *Wythes* (1854) 5 De GM & G 880.

Specific performance of an arbitration award can be granted 'because the award supposes an agreement between the parties, and contains no more than the terms of that agreement ascertained by a third person' per Lord Eldon in *Wood* v *Griffith* (1818) 1 Swans 43 at 54.

Partnership agreements
Generally the courts will not award specific performance of an agreement to perform and carry on a partnership. Partners may be forced to execute a deed incorporating variation of the terms of the partnership from their original agreement if there has been adequate evidence of part performance.

Contracts to leave property by will
If a person agrees, for consideration, to bequeath property to another by will, and this does not occur, the court can order the conveyance of the property to the promisee: see *Synge* v *Synge* [1894] 1 QB 466. But this will not apply where the covenant or covenantor is merely the donee of a testamentary power of appointment: see *Re Parkin* [1892] 3 Ch 510.

Contracts for the transfer of goodwill

If the contract for sale of goodwill is not connected with business premises it is not enforceable by specific performance.

Unfair behaviour by the parties and use of the court's discretion

Generally the courts may exercise their discretion and refuse to grant a decree of specific performance if it can be demonstrated that the party seeking performance has behaved in an unfair manner towards the other:

Mistake

To constitute a valid defence the mistake must be of a fundamental nature that strikes at the root of the contract:

In *Mailins* v *Freeman* (1837) 2 Keen 25 specific performance was refused against a purchaser whose agent mistakenly bid for the wrong property at an auction. Since the mistake was of a fundamental nature, and was not the fault of the purchaser, specific performance was refused.

In *Webster* v *Cecil* (1861) 30 Beav 32 a slip of the pen led to the defendant offering to sell for £1,250 instead of £2,250. Since he had already refused an offer of £2,000 as being too low it was obvious to the plaintiff what the error was. Specific performance was refused. This does not mean that any person may allege mistake due to mere carelessness or sloppy bargaining, since if such actions were allowed it would open the floodgates to claims that would otherwise be excluded due to fraud or perjury.

Misdescription

Difficulties arise if the contract is not totally defective but merely imperfect. This usually occurs if there has been a mistake either of title to land or its acreage. The law differentiates between substantial and slight misdescription, a question of fact in each case. If the misdescription is substantial the purchaser may rescind the contract or obtain specific performance combined with an abatement of the purchase money as compensation: see *Mortlock* v *Buller* (1804) 10 Ves 292. If, on the other hand, the misdescription is slight in a contract for sale of land specific performance may be obtained by the vendor along with reciprocal compensation for the purchaser.

It should be noted that all these rules may be displaced by a fraudulent or wilful misdescription on the part of the vendor.

Misrepresentation

Fraudulent or innocent misrepresentation is a good defence to a claim for specific performance, if the defendant has been misled by the misrepresentation.

Default by the plaintiff

If the plaintiff has caused or is causing the problem through his unwillingness to perform all the terms of the contract, or has failed adequately to perform an essential part of that contract, specific performance may be refused.

Incomplete or uncertain contracts

If the contract has not included all the terms agreed upon, for instance, has failed to specify the price, or has not defined essential terms with sufficient exactitude, thus rendering a particular term vague and meaningless, the courts may refuse specific performance.

Hardship and want of fairness

Despite the fact that fraud, mistake, misrepresentation and other vitiating factors are not present the court may refuse specific performance if to grant it would be unfair, or a source of undue hardship to the defendant.

Questions of fairness or hardship are normally decided in relation to circumstances existing at the time the contract was entered into, not with reference to subsequent events. In exceptional cases subsequent changes in circumstances, that would inflict on the defendant a 'hardship amounting to injustice' were specific performance to be decreed, may result in its being refused performance: see *Patel* v *Ali* [1984] 1 All ER 978.

The court must consider all the surrounding circumstances such as the consideration offered, lack of age, weakness of mind, illiteracy, lack of proper advice and financial distress. However, lack of financial ability is not in itself considered a sufficient ground for refusal of specific performance. *Hope* v *Walters* [1900] 1 Ch 257 provides a good example of when the defence holds good. In this case the court refused to 'thrust down the throat of an innocent buyer the obligation of becoming the landlord of a brothel' (per Lindley MR at 258).

Laches and time clauses

Generally equity considers that time is not of the essence in a contract. This is now a rule of law by virtue of s41 Law of Property Act 1925 which states:

> 'Stipulations in a contract as to time or otherwise, which, according to the rules of equity are not deemed to have become the essence of the contract are also construed and have effect in law in accordance with the same rules.'

The parties to the contract are free to vary the position by negotiation. Indeed one party may force time to become an important issue in a contract by serving the appropriate notice at the correct time.

In the absence of express agreement, or notice, the courts may consider time to be of the essence after considering the full circumstances of the contract, for example, if property was needed for immediate residence.

Even if time is not of the essence delay in performance or delay in bringing proceedings may defeat a claim for specific performance under the equitable doctrine of 'delay defeats equity'. In *Eads* v *Williams* (1854) 4 De GM & G 674 three and a half years' delay defeated a claim for specific performance.

Absence of writing and acts of part performance

Before the coming into operation of s2 Law of Property (Miscellaneous Provisions) Act 1989, contracts involving the sale of land required written evidence in the form of a notice or memorandum: see s40(1) Law of Property Act 1925 (above). Absence of such writing was a good defence to a claim for specific performance if:

1. The defendant specifically pleaded the statute.
2. The defendant's plea was not a direct consequence of his fraud.

Notwithstanding s40(1), if the defendant had acquiesced or connived in the plaintiff's performance of his part of the contract he was barred from pleading lack of written evidence by the equitable doctrine of 'part performance'. Indeed this rule was specifically embodied in s40(2) Law of Property Act 1925. In order to plead part performance, and thus obtain a decree of specific performance, the plaintiff had to show, inter alia, that:

1. His act of part performance unequivocally referred to the existence of the contract – his conduct was explicable by no other reason apart from the existence of a contract: see *Maddison* v *Alderson* (1883) 8 App Cas 467.
2. The acts relied upon were acts of real performance, not merely acts preparatory to performance, such as obtaining a valuation of the property. Note that the mere payment of money, unaccompanied by a real performance, may now amount to a sufficient act of part performance: see *Steadman* v *Steadman* [1976] AC 536.

The position is now governed by the Law of Property (Miscellaneous Provisions) Act 1989 which has repealed s40 Law of Property Act 1925; see s4 and Schedule 2 of the 1989 Act.

Section 2 of the 1989 Act supersedes s40 LPA 1925 in respect of relevant dispositions made on or after 27 September 1989. Section 2 of the 1989 Act provides that a contract for the sale or other disposition of an interest in land – with certain exceptions, see subs (5) – must be in writing, not merely evidenced in writing, and signed by or on behalf of each party to the contract. For provisions covering the extent to which contractual terms may be incorporated by reference to other documents and for exchange of contracts see subss (2) and (3) respectively, and works on land law.

It is now clear that the doctrine of part performance no longer applies to contracts covered by s2 Law of Property (Miscellaneous Provisions) Act 1989. This was, indeed, the intention of Law Commissioners who considered that no injustice would arise as a result of this change since adequate alternative remedies exist, for example, estoppel: see Law Commission Report No 164.

Vendor's defective title

If the purchaser can prove that the vendor's title is bad, doubtful or contains undisclosed restrictive covenants, specific performance may be denied. However, if the faulty title can be cured prior to the purchaser repudiating the contract a claim for specific performance may be available to the vendor.

27.3 Injunction

Meaning and nature

Definition
An injunction is an order of the court directing a person or persons to refrain from doing or continuing some particular act or thing complained of, or less often, to do some particular act or thing.

Nature
Certain general principles pertain to the granting of an injunction, most of which were also consistent points in the nature of a decree of specific performance, namely:

1. In granting an injunction the 'court acts in personam and will not suffer anyone within its reach to do what is contrary to the notions of equity, merely because the act to be done may be in point of locality beyond its jurisdiction' per Cranworth LC in *Carron Iron Co* v *Maclaran* (1855) 5 HL Cas 416 at 436.
2. The granting of an injunction is discretionary, but it is not conferred according to 'the caprice of the judge, but according to sufficient legal reasons or on settled legal principles' per Jessel MR in *Day* v *Brownrigg* (1878) 10 Ch D 294.
3. An injunction will be refused if damages are considered to be an adequate remedy, but in *Elliott* v *Islington Borough Council* (1990) The Times 6 July the Court of Appeal held that damages in lieu of an injunction should not be awarded where this would, in effect, be depriving an individual of specific private rights.
4. Refusal to obey an injunction may result in the criminal penalty of contempt of court, with the risk of a fine and/or imprisonment.

Classification of injunctions

A prohibitory or restrictive injunction is an order directed to a person to refrain from the commission, continuation or repetition of a wrongful act. This form of remedy represents the original form of injunction.

A mandatory injunction restrains the continuation of act or omission by directing a person to perform a positive act.

There would appear to be a distinct similarity between a mandatory injunction and a decree of specific performance. However, one cannot get around the restrictive class of contracts for which specific performance does not lie merely by seeking an order for an injunction. It was held in *Powell Duffryn Steam Co* v *Taff Vale Railway Co* (1874) 9 Ch App 331 that such an order will not be granted if it requires the continuous employment of people. (Compare *Ryan* v *Mutual Tontine Westminster Chambers Association* [on specific performance] above). Note that in *Jakeman* v *South West Thames Regional Health Authority* (1989) The Independent 1 December, it was held that the court would not generally grant a mandatory injunction in industrial dispute cases.

A perpetual injunction is granted after the rights have been established in an ordinary action between parties in which they have both been given a full hearing. It is intended to represent a final settlement of the dispute in order to save the plaintiff from having to bring a series of actions as his rights are occasionally and intermittently infringed by the defendant.

In this sense the word 'perpetual' does not mean that the injunction will remain in force for all time. A perpetual injunction may be granted to prevent the infringement of a reasonable restraint of trade that the parties had agreed, by a clause in a contract, would last for, say, five years.

Certain issues should be considered before a perpetual injunction is granted or refused:

1. If damages are a suitable alternative remedy an injunction will be refused.
2. This form of injunction is only available if the injury will be of a continuing nature.
3. Although the award is discretionary care should be taken in considering the rights of the parties and all the surrounding circumstances including the rights and interests of other people who may be affected by the injunction. See the recent decision in *Guinness Peat Aviation (Belgium) NV* v *Hispania Lineas Aereas SA* [1992] 1 Lloyd's Rep 190.

Kindersley V-C observed in *Wood* v *Sutcliffe* (1851) 2 Sim NS 163 at 165 that the contract must 'have regard not only to the dry strict rights of the plaintiff and defendant, but also to the surrounding circumstances, to the rights and interests of other persons which may be more or less involved'.

The 'surrounding circumstances' may include whether the injury has ceased or is of a temporary nature; the damage complained of is so slight as not to warrant an injunction; the injunction would be ineffectual if granted; there are better remedies available.

1. Normally delay will not defeat a perpetual injunction unless the plaintiff, knowing all the details of the wrong committed, has delayed unreasonably in bringing his action.
2. The behaviour of the parties is obviously important: 'He who comes to equity must come with clean hands.'
3. If third party rights would be injured by the injunction the grant may be refused: see *Maythorn* v *Palmer* (1864) 11 LT 261. In this case the defendant agreed a valid covenant not to enter into employment, valid as the law then stood. He then went to work for a third party who was unaware of the

restriction. The first employer was refused an injunction, primarily on the ground of what it would do to the third party who was not a party to the action.

4. The plaintiff must have an interest in the subject-matter. In *Day* v *Brownrigg* (1878) 10 Ch D 294 the plaintiff, who lived at Ashford Lodge, was refused an injunction to restrain his neighbour from renaming his house (Ashford Villa) Ashford Lodge. Despite the inconvenience the confusion of names could cause there is no right of property in the name of a house.

5. The High Court or Court of Appeal may, by s50 Supreme Court Act 1981, award damages in addition to or in substitution for an injunction if the damage is slight, the injury is capable of being quantified in money terms, or the grant of an injunction would be oppressive to the defendant.

An interlocutor's interim injunction is a temporary measure granted on interlocutory application. It is normally framed to maintain the status quo until a full trial of the dispute can be given, in other words this injunction is often used as a 'holding action'.

Sometimes it may be used to dispose of an issue effectively and expeditiously. For example, it has been employed to evict a trespasser who had no possible defence, but was merely trying to delay his eviction from the property for as long as he could: see *Manchester Corporation* v *Connolly* [1970] Ch 420.

Generally it will only be granted if notice has been given to the defendant, in order that he may prepare his defence sufficiently. In cases of genuine emergency it may be granted 'ex parte' – in the absence of the person who is likely to be affected by the injunction. In an ex parte application the plaintiff has a duty to make a full disclosure of all the material facts that would affect the court's decision as to whether or not to grant this type of injunction: see *Bank of Mellot* v *Nikpoor* (1983) 133 NLJ 513 CA.

Interlocutory injunctions will generally be of a prohibitory nature. However, circumstances may be such that they take the form of a mandatory order: see *Van Joel* v *Hornsey* [1895] 2 Ch 744, where the defendant deliberately avoided the plaintiff, knowing that he was about to be served with a writ, in order that he could hurriedly complete the building that represented the basis of the plaintiff's complaint.

Other factors relevant to the question of whether or not an interlocutory injunction will be granted are as follows:

1. 'He who comes to equity must come with clean hands.' A court may refuse the injunction if the plaintiff is himself in breach of the agreement at issue.

2. The balance of convenience: if the court is in doubt as to the consequences of the prospective granting of an interlocutory injunction the onus of proof is on the plaintiff to show that the refusal of the injunction would, on balance, cause greater inconvenience to him than it would to the defendant.

3. The damage that the plaintiff wishes to avert must be 'substantial and irreparable', for example the defendant property developer proposing to knock down a listed building in order to develop a new shopping complex.

4. The court should be satisfied that there is a distinct probability that the plaintiff will be given relief at the subsequent full trial of the issue: see *Preston* v *Luck* (1884) 27 Ch D 497.
5. The equitable doctrine of laches: 'Delay defeats equity'. If the plaintiff delays in bringing his action then, when surrounding circumstances are considered, the court may reasonably construe such delay as amounting to acquiescence in the defendant's acts. Once the plaintiff becomes aware that he has a right to commence an action he should do so speedily.
6. The grant of an interlocutory injunction is discretionary and dependent on the circumstances of the case.
7. The most important principle of all is the maintenance of the status quo, that the parties' current positions be preserved until the case can be heard in full.
8. In *American Cyanamid Co* v *Ethicon Ltd* [1975] AC 396 the House of Lords decided that there was no need for the plaintiff to establish a prima facie case. The courts should address themselves to whether there was an important point at issue, and the paramount consideration should be the 'balance of convenience'. If the balance of convenience did not clearly favour either party then the relative strengths of the parties should be considered. In no circumstances should the court attempt to act in a manner which would, in effect, be a full trial of the action.
9. However it is different if the granting of an injunction would effectively dispose of the matter: see *Cayne* v *Global Natural Resources plc* [1984] 1 All ER 225. The classic example is an interlocutory injunction that is granted days before the happening of its subject-matter event and before a full trial can take place. See *Cambridge Nutrition* v *BBC* [1990] 3 All ER 523 which concerned the plaintiffs' obtaining an injunction preventing a screening of a programme in the few days following prior to an EC report being published very shortly afterwards. In such circumstances the courts need to balance all the factors and determine the overall strengths of each party's case.

Although the common law rule is that an interim injunction will not lie against the Crown so as, in particular, to suspend the operation of legislation, this does not apply where what is in issue is a claim by a party that such legislation be suspended pending the testing of its validity under European Community Law before the European Court of Justice. The European Court of Justice ruled that if a national court in the European Community, dealing with a topic of Community law, concludes that the only bar to its granting interim relief is a rule of national law, that court is bound to set aside such national rule: see *R* v *Secretary of State for Transport, ex parte Factortame Ltd and Others* (1990) The Times 20 June.

The quia timet ('because he fears') injunction
This is awarded so as to restrain a threatened action where there has been, at that time, no actual infringement of the plaintiff's rights.

Since all injunctions are aimed at future conduct it is difficult, at first sight, to determine why this form of injunction should be categorised separately from the others. After all, perpetual and interlocutory injunctions may also be obtained for injury that is threatened, despite there being no immediate infringement of the plaintiff's rights.

A solution to this problem was offered by the House of Lords in *Redland Bricks Ltd* v *Morris* [1970] AC 652. Their lordships perceived two classes of case:

1. Where the defendant has, as yet, done no harm to the plaintiff, but the plaintiff is alleging that the defendant is threatening and intending to do works which will cause irreparable harm to his property. In these cases negative injunctions are normally sought.
2. Where the plaintiff has been fully recompensed in law and equity for damage he has suffered, but he alleges that the defendant's past actions may led to future causes of action – the action has occurred but the damage may not become apparent for some time.

The second category would appear to be more suitably dealt with by mandatory injunctions. The availability of quia timet injunctions should be restricted to cases falling within the first category.

'The plaintiff must show a strong case of probability that the apprehended mischief will, in fact, arise' per Chitty J in *Attorney-General* v *Manchester Corporation* [1893] 2 Ch 87 at 92. He must demonstrate that the intended or threatened act would be an inevitable violation of his rights.

The line of demarcation is often difficult to draw, so it may be useful to contrast two cases:

1. In *Goodhart* v *Hyatt* (1883) 25 Ch D 182 an injunction was granted because the 'strong probability' criterion was satisfied. The plaintiff had a right to repair water pipes that ran through the defendant's land. The defendant had intended to build a house over part of the pipes, thereby raising a strong probability that repairs would be extremely difficult and expensive.
2. In *Attorney-General* v *Manchester Corporation* (above), conversely, the court declined to grant an injunction restraining the building of a smallpox hospital on the ground that the danger to the health of the surrounding community was a mere possibility, the likelihood of which had not been established to the court's satisfaction.

Apart from the 'strong probability' requirement the court must also be satisfied that:

1. Damages would not be an adequate remedy if such injury were actually to occur.
2. The cost to the defendant of preventing the continuance or recurrence of the wrongful act has been taken into account.
3. The defendant is absolutely aware of what he must do.

An ex parte injunction

This injunction is used in times of extreme urgency. Because of the need for a speedy decision the court will not have an opportunity of hearing the defendant's case.

Due to the apparently one-sided nature of the evidence given and received the court should only grant ex parte injunctions when immediate intervention is required in the interests of justice, or when the interests of the applicant so demand: *Bolivinter Oil SA* v *Chase Manhattan Bank* (1983) The Times 10 December.

Use of injunctions in particular types of cases

To restrain a breach of contract

There may appear to be no clear division between the use of a decree of specific performance and an injunction. Injunctions may be used to restrain a breach of a contractual term that is negative in substance, where the defendant has undertaken not to perform a particular act. In such instances the award of an injunction would appear to have the same effect as a decree of specific performance. Quaere: Is an order to refrain from not doing a particular act the same as a decree to do something?

The terms of a contract may be negative or affirmative, or partly one and partly the other. The general rule is that specific performance is the true remedy for enforcing an affirmative term, whereas an injunction is appropriate to enforce a negative term.

1. Purely negative contractual terms. Where a perpetual injunction is sought to restrain a threatened breach of a negative term, generally the court has no discretion to exercise.

   'If parties for valuable consideration, with their eyes open, contract that a particular thing shall not be done, all the court of equity has to do is to say, by way of injunction, that which the parties have already said by way of covenant, that the thing shall not be done; and in such case the injunction does nothing more than give the sanction of the process of the court to that which already is the contract between the parties. It is not a question of the balance of convenience or inconvenience, or of the amount of damage or injury - it is the specific performance by the court of that negative bargain which the parties have made, with their eyes open, between themselves' per Lord Cairns in *Doherty* v *Allman* (1878) 3 App Cas 709 at 720.

   The effect of delay, acquiescence and other surrounding circumstances may be taken into consideration.

   If the injunction sought is a mandatory injunction the court may have a limited discretion, even if this proves to be of little value.

2. Part negative and part positive contractual terms. If a contract contains both negative and positive terms the general rule is that the courts may enforce the negative stipulations by injunction even though they may not enforce the positive

stipulations by specific performance. A term must be negative in both substance and form if it is to be enforced, since an injunction will not be granted if it is little more than an indirect method of compelling specific performance in circumstances where that remedy could not be obtained directly, for instance, in contracts of personal service.

In *Rely-A-Bell Burglar and Fire Alarm Co Ltd* v *Eisler* [1926] Ch 609 the court refused to grant an injunction against an employee whose contract had stipulated that he would not enter into any other employment during the course of his employment with Rely-A-Bell. The defendant was confronted with a Hobson's choice of observing the contractual obligation or facing permanent unemployment, and to ban the defendant from working elsewhere would have been tantamount to ordering him to perform the contract with Rely-A-Bell. For a recent example see *Lansing Linde* v *Kerr* [1991] 1 WLR 251.

In *Warner Bros Pictures Inc* v *Nelson* [1937] 1 KB 209 the defendant film actress, Bette Davis, agreed not to work in that capacity for any other person during the period of her contract. The court granted the injunction, since she was still able to seek employment in other capacities, and it was of little import that the work would be less rewarding to her. Nonetheless the court refused to extend the injunction to restrain her from engaging in any other occupation since this would be enforcing a decree of specific performance by indirect means: see also *Page One Records Ltd* v *Britton* [1968] 1 WLR 157.

Injunctions to restrain legal proceedings
If proceedings are pending in the Supreme Court they cannot be restrained by injunction.

Property rights and torts
Injunction may be used to prevent threatened or apprehended harm in a whole series of tortious and proprietorial actions:

Trespass. The threatened tort of trespass may be prevented by injunction: see *Kelsen* v *Imperial Tobacco Co Ltd* [1957] 2 QB 334, which concerned the removal of an advertising hoarding, bearing the legend 'Players Please', that jutted from the defendant's property into the air-space above the plaintiff's property by several inches.

Nuisance. If the tort is a private nuisance, which is not of a trivial nature, and the plaintiff cannot be adequately compensated by damages, then the occupier of the property which suffers damage or apprehended harm may seek an injunction: see *Rugby Joint Water Board* v *Walters* [1967] Ch 397, in which an injunction was granted to restrain the owner of riparian rights from extracting water from a river for extraordinary purposes.

If the tortious act alleged is a public nuisance, it is usual for the Attorney-General, by relator action, to seek an injunction. A private individual may seek such an injunction if he can show that he has suffered particular damage: *Attorney-General* v *PYA Quarries Ltd* [1957] 2 QB 169.

Easements. An easement is a right to use another's land for specific and limited purposes. A neighbour may seek an injunction to prevent the defendant from commencing, or continuing, digging operations on that defendant's land if such operations are likely to weaken or undermine the foundations of the neighbour's property (the easement of support).

Restrictive covenants. A restrictive covenant is an agreement between owners of properties, whereby one of the parties agrees to limit the types of use to which he may put his property. An owner may agree not to use his land for industrial or commercial building, or he may agree not to build on that property at all. In such a case equity may grant an injunction if the terms of the covenant are negative in substance, if it is of benefit to the land, and if the party claiming the benefit of the restrictive covenant has retained that land to which the benefit attaches. This is enforceable under the rule in *Tulk* v *Moxhay* (1848) 2 Ph 744.

Waste. There is a duty on the tenant for life or tenant for a term of years, as the case may be, not to damage the interests of the reversioner – the person entitled to the estate at the end of the tenancy – by any positive and injurious acts. Such actions will constitute 'waste'. Not all forms of waste may be restrained by injunctions, so it is important to differentiate the varying forms.

Permissive waste. The tenant omits to do something, for example he allows buildings on the estate to fall into disrepair. An injunction will not be allowed in such circumstances.

Ameliorative waste. The tenant alters the nature of the property in such a manner as actually to improve the quality of the property. For example a tenant may convert a disused barn into profitable 'holiday lets'. Again, this form of waste is not restrainable by injunction.

Voluntary waste. The tenant performs some positive or injurious act which adversely affects the reversioner's interests. An example is cutting down and not replacing timber on the estate. Such actions are restrainable by injunction unless the terms of the lease or settlement exempt him from such liability.

Equitable waste. If the tenant attempts an act of wanton and malicious destruction, which would not otherwise constitute a cause for action at law, due to the circumstances of the case, then an injunction may be granted.

Trespass, nuisance, easements, restrictive covenants and waste possess a common element in that they may exclusively or partially refer to actions involving land, or an interest in land. The following actions do not specifically relate to land:

Libel. Prior to the Common Law Procedure Act 1854 equity possessed no jurisdiction on cases of libel. This Act and the Judicature Act of 1873 empowered the High Court to grant injunctions to restrain publication of libels, whether affecting character, trade or property.

The grant of an interlocutory injunction will be permissible where the possibility of repetition is clearly established, or where the matter complained of is so patently defamatory 'that a jury's verdict to the contrary would be set aside as being unreasonable': *Quartz Hill Consolidated Gold Mining Co* v *Beall* (1882) 20 Ch D 501.

Assaults. The courts have a right to grant an injunction in cases of threatened and continuing assaults: *Egan* v *Egan* [1975] Ch 218, where a mother obtained an injunction to restrain her son from continually assaulting her.

Economic torts. If a person, deliberately and without just cause or excuse, interferes with the trade or business of another, and does so by unlawful means, then he will be acting unlawfully, and an injunction may be granted to restrain him: see *Acrow (Automation) Ltd* v *Rex Chain Belt Inc* [1971] 3 All ER 1175 CA.

Breaches of confidence
The grant of an injunction may be ordered to prevent an employee, ex-employee or trader from disclosing trade secrets such as lists of customers: *Anton Piller KG* v *Manufacturing Processes Ltd* [1976] Ch 55; and secret processes: *Cranleigh Precision Engineering Ltd* v *Bryant* [1964] 3 All ER 289.

An injunction may be granted to prevent other forms of confidential relationship being broken, such as a solicitor disclosing client's confidentialities: *Robb* v *Green* [1895] 2 QB 315 CA; publication by a cabinet minister of discussions during cabinet meetings: *Attorney-General* v *Jonathan Cape Ltd* [1976] QB 752 (the 'Crossman Diaries'); or publication, for profit, of notes taken at an oral lecture: *Abernathy* v *Hutchinson* (1825) 1 H & TW 28.

All such breaches are potentially restrainable by injunction. An injunction may be granted not only against the divulger of the information, but also against the person who knowingly obtains the information.

Note that an injunction may, in certain situations, be granted to restrain the use of privileged information mistakenly disclosed in the process of 'discovery': see *Derby & Co Ltd and Others* v *Weldon and Others (No 8)* [1991] 1 WLR 73.

Public rights
It has already been stated that the Attorney-General has a right, through the relator procedure, to restrain acts that would constitute a public nuisance. For instance, he may seek an injunction to restrain publication of material detrimental to the public interest: *Distillers Co* v *Times Newspapers Ltd* [1975] QB 613 (the Thalidomide Case); and breach of a negative statutory duty where the statutory penalty is inadequate: see *Attorney-General* v *Sharp* [1931] 1 Ch 121.

In *Gouriet* v *Post Office Engineering Union* [1978] AC 435 at 500 Lord Diplock considered that the use of the injunction should be confined to statutes whose objects are to promote the health, safety or welfare of the public, and to particular cases, under such statutes, either where the prescribed penalty for the summary offence has proved to be insufficient to deter the offender from continued and repetitive breaches, or where the defendant's disobedience to a statutory prohibition may cause grave and irreparable harm. An example of the former is a case where a bus proprietor failed to obtain the necessary public transport licence, being content to pay a series of inconsequential fines: see *Attorney-General* v *Sharp* (1931) (above).

The fact that the defendant's actions may appear, in other circumstances, to be too trivial to warrant an injunction may have little bearing on the outcome of the hearing, since the overriding concern is to discourage wilful and persistent disobedience of the law. In *Attorney-General* v *Harris* [1961] 1 QB 74 an injunction was granted to prevent the continuance of sale of flowers from a stall erected outside a cemetery, contrary to the provisions of the Manchester Police Regulations Act 1844. Sellers LJ at p91 considered that the question of triviality ignores 'the effect on the administration of, and respect for, the law if the defendants continue in the future on the same lines as in the past, to laugh at the law, and say they are immune from its restraints so long as they pay recurringly a small price for their immunity'. Here, the two defendants had been prosecuted nearly 250 times before, merely receiving small fines each time.

Local authorities also have certain powers to initiate proceedings without the Attorney-General's intervention. These powers are derived from a series of statutory enactments such as the Public Health Act 1936 and the Local Government Act 1972: see *Stoke on Trent City Council* v *B & Q (Retail) Ltd* [1984] 2 All ER 332 HL.

It should be noted that the exercise of these statutory powers by local authorities may be subject to judicial review.

Companies and unincorporated associations

An injunction may be granted against a company to, for example:

1. Prevent the advertising of a petition for winding up.
2. Force company meetings to be called.
3. Prevent the passing of a resolution that may defraud the minority shareholders/members.

A single member may seek the intervention of the court, despite the wishes of the majority shareholders and the directors, if the alleged action is ultra vires the company's memorandum of association: see *Mosley* v *Koffyfontein Mines Ltd* [1911] 1 Ch 73.

Members of trade unions and other associations, such as clubs and professional bodies, may be granted an injunction to restrain their irregular expulsion from that body if it can be shown that:

1. The expulsion was not authorised by the rules: see *Lee* v *Showmen's Guild of Great Britain* [1952] 2 QB 329.
2. The expulsion did not adhere to the rules of natural justice: see *Lawlor* v *Union of Post Office Workers* [1965] Ch 712.
3. The proceedings were conducted in an irregular manner: see *Young* v *Ladies Imperial Club* [1920] 2 KB 523.
4. There was malice or ill feeling in reaching the decision.

The courts are reluctant to grant an injunction unless the member's right to earn a living would be removed by his expulsion from that association – actors, for instance, would find it nearly impossible to engage in their profession unless they belonged to their union Equity – or unless it is necessary to protect a proprietary righ: see *Lee* v *Showmen's Guild* (above).

Patents, copyrights and trade marks
These are now protected by the appropriate statutory devices. Although patents and trade marks are directly enforceable by injunctions, an injunction may also lie for the infringement of a copyright, even if there is no actual proof of damage: see *Borthwick* v *Evening Post* (1888) 37 Ch D 449.

Breach of trust
Injunctions are granted to protect a purely equitable claim, not to assist a legal right. Injunctions may be granted, for example:

1. To prevent trustees from distributing an estate other than according to the terms of the trust instrument: see *Fox* v *Fox* (1870) LR 11 Eq 142.
2. To restrain an unnecessary mortgage of trust property: see *Rigall* v *Foster* (1853) 18 Jur 39.

Family matters
Injunctions may be available in divorce and matrimonial proceedings, even after the granting of a decree absolute: for example, to prevent one former spouse molesting the other. Generally the courts often consider that a better remedy for a spouse would be to leave the matrimonial home, rather than to seek an injunction.

The courts have been given wide powers by statute:

1. The Matrimonial Homes Act 1983 allows the court to exclude a spouse from the matrimonial home, even if that spouse is the owner or tenant.
2. The Domestic Violence and Matrimonial Proceedings Act 1976 confers similar powers on the County Court.

Other examples of cases where injunction may be sought are:

1. To restrain the marriage of an infant ward of court: see *Smith* v *Smith* (1745) 3 All ER 304.

2. To prohibit a child being taken out of the country: see *Harris* v *Harris* (1890) 63 LT 262.

Preventing the removal of assets – the Mareva injunction

This form of injunction derives its name from the case of *Mareva Compania Naviera SA* v *International Bulk Carriers SA* [1975] 2 Lloyd's Rep 509.

The essential purpose of this type of injunction is to prevent foreign parties from causing assets to be removed from the jurisdiction, in order to avoid the risk of having to satisfy any judgment which may be entered against them in pending proceedings in this country. 'Assets' in this context include cash, or any other property, in this country.

In *The Siskina* [1979] AC 210 the House of Lords considered that certain limitations should be imposed on the practice of granting such injunctions. As Lord Diplock observed:

'It is interlocutory, not final: it is ancillary to a substantive pecuniary claim for debt or damages: it is designed to prevent the judgment against a foreign defendant for a sum of money being a mere brutum fulmen.'

Note: 'Brutum fulmen' literally means 'spent thunderbolt'. The plaintiff has a good cause of action but has no way of enforcing a subsequent judgment order. Therefore he is ill advised to commence action since there would be little likelihood of his being able to obtain the defendant's assets.

An interlocutory injunction will be granted on ex parte application thus preventing the defendant from removing his assets until the pending action has been determined.

In *Third Chandris Shipping Corporation* v *Unimarine SA* [1979] 2 All ER 972 affd CA at 980, Lord Denning spelt out the basic guidelines that the courts and plaintiff should adhere to:

1. The plaintiff should make full and frank disclosure of all matters within his knowledge which are material to the judge's deliberations.
2. The plaintiff should give particulars of his claim against the defendant, stating the ground of his claim and the amount, and fairly stating the points made against it by the defendant.
3. The plaintiff should show that he has some grounds for believing that the defendant has assets within the jurisdiction, including 'goodwill' or a bank account, even one that is overdrawn.
4. The plaintiff should show that he has some grounds for believing that there is a risk of the assets being removed before the judgment order can be satisfied. This must be a 'good arguable case' involving 'a real risk' that the award would remain unsatisfied.
5. The plaintiffs must give an undertaking in damages, in case their claim fails, or the injunction is subsequently shown to be unjustifiable.

Three further guidelines have been added by subsequent cases:

1. With respect to any asset to which the order applies, but which has not been identified with precision, for example, an unidentified bank account, the plaintiffs may have to give an undertaking to pay reasonable costs in respect of the expenses that any third party incurs when determining whether the order applies to relevant assets in their possession or control: see *Searose Ltd* v *Seatrain (UK) Ltd* [1981] 1 WLR 894.
2. If the injunction involves the movement of shipping within a port the plaintiffs should give an undertaking to the port authorities to cover loss of income and administrative costs, bearing in mind that the injunction may allow the port authorities to move the vessel within jurisdiction, or out of jurisdiction, if in danger: see *Clipper Maritime Co Ltd* v *Mineral Import Export* [1981] 1 WLR 1262.
3. It is the duty of a litigant who has obtained a Mareva injunction to press on with the proceedings. If he does not wish to press on with his action, even temporarily, he should apply by his own motion to have that injunction discharged: see Court of Appeal's ruling in *Town and Country Building Society* v *Daisystar Ltd and Another* (1989) The Times 16 October.

It should be noted that the High Court's jurisdiction is derived from s37 Supreme Court Act 1981. Section 38 County Courts Act 1984 gives similar powers to the County Courts; see also s25 Civil Jurisdiction and Judgments Act 1982.

Further, *Practice Direction* [1994] 4 All ER 52 provides an invaluable guide to the practice and procedure for obtaining a Mareva injunction.

Order to permit inspection – Anton Piller orders

See *Anton Piller KG* v *Manufacturing Process Ltd* [1976] Ch 55. The High Court orders of this type are interlocutory, mandatory injunctions obtained ex parte, since the essence of such an order is surprise. The order is designed to prevent the defendant from concealing, removing or destroying vital evidence such as documents, or other moveable property, prior to an inter partes hearing of the pending action.

The order allows the plaintiff to enter the premises of the defendant and to look at and make copies of any documents or similar material.

Failure to comply with an Anton Piller order is punishable by contempt of court. Jurisdiction is based on s37 Supreme Court Act 1981.

Film makers, video and musical recording companies find this form of action potentially useful when determining whether there has been a violation of copyright by 'private' organisations who may make and sell unauthorised copies of their works: see *Universal City Studios Inc* v *Muktar* [1976] 1 WLR 568.

Such orders are rarely made, and will only be considered by the courts if there is no suitable alternative method of securing justice for the plaintiff. Certain limitations are placed on their use, namely:

1. The plaintiff must have an extremely strong prima facie case.
2. The actual or potential damage must be very serious for the plaintiff.
3. There must be clear and convincing evidence that the defendants have in their possession incriminating documents, or other property, and that there is a real possibility that they may destroy such items before a full inter partes hearing can be achieved.
4. The court must be satisfied that the plaintiff will be able to make good any damages which may subsequently be ordered against him, since this may be made conditional upon the granting of the order.
5. The plaintiff must make a full disclosure of all material facts known to him, however unimportant he considers them to be, since failure will result in automatic discharge of the order.

The decision in *Rank Film Distributors Ltd* v *Video Information Centre* [1982] AC 380 that a defendant would not be forced to divulge information which might incriminate him was overruled by s72 Supreme Court Act 1981. This Act also removed such immunity from the spouse or other associates of the defendant.

The order has been extended to cover such cases as matrimonial proceedings. In *Emmanuel* v *Emmanuel* [1982] 1 WLR 669 the order was extended to allow the representatives of a wife to enter her estranged husband's house in order to ascertain the true nature of his earnings, for the purpose of subsequent matrimonial proceedings. The decision in *Gidrxslme Shipping Co Ltd* v *Tantomar-Transportes Maritimos Lda (the 'Naftilos')* [1994] 4 All ER 507 has confirmed that the court can, if appropriate, order 'worldwide' disclosure ie make a worldwide Anton Piller order. Further, *Practice Direction* [1994] 4 All ER 52 provides an invaluable guide to the practice and procedure for obtaining an Anton Piller Order.

27.4 Rescission

Definition and nature

Definition
The right which a party has, in specific circumstances, to set aside the contract he has entered into, and be restored to his former position.

Nature

1. The remedy is discretionary.
2. Rescission depends on whether 'restitutio in integrum' (explained below) is possible.
3. Rescission is a purely equitable remedy, since it involves the taking of accounts (explained below) which is particular to equity alone.

4. Rescission must be differentiated from discharge of contract by breach. In the latter situation damages are recoverable, in the former damages may not be considered an appropriate remedy.
5. The right to rescind a contract may not be assigned to a third party.
6. If rescission is granted all property must be returned to the parties and accounts must be taken of profits and losses. In effect the person who rescinds the contract must be returned to the position he would have been in had the contract not been concluded.

Grounds upon which rescission may be granted

Fraudulent misrepresentation

Fraud has always been recognised by both common law and equity; it is the universal terminator of agreements. Fraud, for the purposes of rescission, bears the common law meaning – usually referred to as 'actual fraud' – the basis of the action being the tort of deceit. Lord Herschell provided the classic definition of fraud in *Derry* v *Peek* (1889) 14 App Cas 337 and this definition is still adhered to:

'A fraud is proved when it is shown that a false representation has been made knowingly, or without belief in its truth, or recklessly, careless of whether it be true or false.'

Corruption is not a necessary ingredient of the definition. All that is required is that the statement should have been made with the intention that it be acted on, and it must have actually been acted on by the other party.

Innocent misrepresentation

This form of representation is made by a party who believes in its truth, although such belief may lack reasonable grounds. The common law never recognised this right, unless the representation had been incorporated into the contract. Equity only regarded it as a defence to an action for specific performance, until the case of *Attwood* v *Small* (1838) 6 Cl & Fin 232, and even then it only received limited approval. However, since the Misrepresentation Act of 1967 rescission has been available whenever the misrepresentation has become a term of the contract.

Mere silence

It is a general rule that silence does not amount to a representation. It is the duty of the buyer to make his own enquiries as to what is of importance to him – caveat emptor. In contract law silence could amount to a misrepresentation leading to possible rescission if:

1. The concealment gives to the truth which is told the character of falsehood: see *Oakes* v *Turquand* (1867) LR 2 HL 325.
2. The contract is a contract of uberrimae fidei – contracts in which one party is obliged to inform the other of all material facts that are likely to effect the latter's

decision of whether or not to enter into the contract, or the terms upon which he will enter the contract. It is a contract affected by the principle of absolute disclosure. Examples of such contracts are: all forms of insurance contract, where duty of disclosure is on the proposer, and contracts affected by the uberrima fides principle, such as partnerships and family settlements.

Mistake

If mistake operates at all it renders a contract void ad initio. It is necessary to prove fundamental mistake in order to apply successfully for rescission.

Although the common law recognised common mistake between the parties as a ground for declaring the contract void, it has recently been decided that where both parties have contracted under a mutual mistake, contracting at cross purposes, and this mistake would not prejudice any third party rights, the court may order rescission. A unilateral mistake by the plaintiff, which is unknown to the defendant, does not entitle the plaintiff to rescission, irrespective of the possibility of rectification: see *Riverplate Property Ltd* v *Paul* [1957] Ch 133.

Constructive fraud

If a gift or benefit has been obtained by undue influence the contract may be rescinded in equity. Undue influence may be presumed in certain relationships, such as parent and child, guardian and ward, solicitor and client, fiance and fiancee, doctor and patient, priest and parishioner. Otherwise undue influence may be established on a point of evidence: see *Lloyds Bank* v *Bundy* [1975] QB 326 and *National Westminster Bank* v *Morgan* [1983] 3 All ER 85.

Examples of evidential proof would be the taking advantage of weakness, or frauds on a power.

Substantial misdescription

If there has been a material and substantial misdescription in a contract for the sale of land the purchaser of that land may have a right to rescind the contract.

Express contractual terms

The parties to a contract are always free to negotiate their own terms. This right includes the ability to specify that the contract may be rescinded if the specific events referred to in the contract actually occur.

Loss of right to rescind

Affirmation of the contract

The right to rescind a contract is lost if the contract is affirmed expressly or by implication.

Affirmation could take place where a party, fully aware of his right to rescind, still decides to take the benefits of the contract.

Acquiescence and lapse of time will also provide evidence of a decision to affirm the contract, particularly if the delay by the purchaser is so unreasonable that it may, in practice, be treated as evidence of a positive election to affirm the contract: 'It behoves a purchaser to verify or, as the case may be, to disprove the representation within a reasonable time, or else stand or fall by it' per Jenkins LJ in *Leaf* v *International Galleries* [1950] 2 KB 86, and see *Long* v *Lloyd* [1985] 2 All ER 402.

The courts will also take into consideration all the surrounding circumstances as provided for by equity, such as the presence or absence of fraud, and the nature of the contract: see *Leaf* v *International Galleries* (above) where the right to rescind was barred after five years, despite the fact that the plaintiff only became aware of his rights immediately prior to commencing the action.

When restitutio in integrum becomes impossible
If the parties cannot be restored to their original positions the right to rescind is lost. The monies paid and property transferred under the contract must be returnable. In the case of property it should be capable of being restored to its original condition. In certain circumstances there is a right to indemnity for liabilities necessarily incurred or created under the contract: see *Nitrate Co* v *Lagunas Syndicate* [1899] 2 Ch 392.

The courts are more concerned with restoring the defendant to his original position than stressing the return of the plaintiff to his pre-contractual situation. The courts will always consider, if the parties cannot be restored in statu quo ante, whether it may be more equitable to utilise specific performance with compensation.

Where third parties have acquired rights
If an innocent and bona fide third party acquires rights for a consideration the right to rescind will be lost.

Misrepresentation Act 1967
In any case giving rise to a right to rescind, due to innocent misrepresentation, the court may declare the contract as subsisting and award damages in lieu of rescission, if, in the opinion of the court, it would be equitable to do so, having regard to:

1. The nature of the misrepresentation.
2. The potential loss that might be caused if the contract were upheld.
3. The loss that would be caused to the other party if rescission were granted: see *Resolute Maritime Inc* v *Nippon Kaiji* [1983] 2 All ER 1.

27.5 Rectification of documents

Definition and nature

Definition

If a written document, as a result of a common mistake by both parties, does not accurately express an agreement between those parties, equity will be empowered to rectify the document.

Nature of remedy

'Rectification is concerned with contracts and documents, not with intentions. In order to get rectification it is necessary to show that the parties were in complete agreement upon the terms of their contract, but by an error wrote then down wrongly ... One looks at their outward acts, that is what they said and wrote to one another in coming to their agreement and then compares it with the document they have signed ... If you can predict with certainty what their contract was, that it is, by common mistake, wrongly expressed in the document, then you may rectify the document' per Denning in *Frederick E Rose (London) Ltd* v *William H Pim & Co Ltd* [1953] 2 QB 450 at 461.

Some points to note are:

1. The remedy is discretionary.
2. The remedy is intended to correct the document, not improve it.
3. Rectification applies merely to the document not, to the agreement itself.
4. The remedy may be applied to many kinds of documents such as conveyances of land, settlements, bills of exchange, life assurance or marine insurance policies, leases, but not to wills or a company's articles of association. Note also that rectification is not possible to relieve a company officer from liability under s349(4) Companies Act 1985, where he has signed a company cheque or other prescribed instrument on behalf of the company from which the company's name has been omitted or has not been correctly stated, and in respect of which the company itself fails to make payment: see *Blum* v *OCP Repartition SA* [1988] BCLC 170 (CA) and *Rafsanjan Pistachio Producers Co-operative* v *Reiss* [1990] BCLC 352. Presumably the same would apply to liability arising under s111 Companies Act 1989 with regard to charitable companies.
5. Rectification permits a document to be amended so as to reflect the agreement originally intended by the parties; it may be considered as a retrospective validation of the original transaction.

Essential requirements for a grant of rectification

1. A complete agreement must have existed.
2. There must be an instrument which purports to specify the intentions of the contracting parties.

3. The parties' true intentions must have continued unchanged until the execution of the instrument.
4. The mistake contained in the instrument must be a common mistake of fact. The burden of proving this point rests on the party requesting rectification. This party must produce clear evidence to that effect.
5. The fault to be rectified must only be literal.
6. There must be no other alternative remedy.

Grounds for refusal of rectification

1. An alternative suitable remedy.
2. 'Delay defeats equity' – laches.
3. Acquiescence.
4. A bone fide purchaser for value without notice has acquired the instrument, and rectification may prejudice his rights.
5. Where the mistake is unilateral, unless the other party is guilty of fraud, be it actual, constructive or equitable, or where one party believed the term to be included in the contract but the other party varied or omitted the term in the instrument, knowing that the first party believed it to be included in that instrument: see *Roberts & Co* v *Leicestershire County Council* [1961] Ch 555.

27.6 Delivery up and cancellation of documents

In some circumstances equity may be ready to order the delivery and cancellation of a void document, since it would be inequitable for the defendant to be allowed to remain in possession of a seemingly valid document which may be subsequently used against the plaintiff when, due to the passage of years, the plaintiff would find it difficult, if not impossible, to find evidence to rebut or invalidate the document, or such evidence as once existed is now inadmissible.

Where the document is invalid at law and the invalidity patently appears on the face of the document, delivery up will not be ordered since there would be no apparent risk of its being successfully used as evidence in a future action: see *Gray* v *Mathias* (1800) 5 Ves 286.

The remedy is discretionary. It is possible that it may only be used if neither of the parties is prejudiced thereby. 'He who seeks equity must do equity.' In *Lodge* v *National Union Investments Co Ltd* [1907] 1 Ch 300, the courts were willing to order delivery up of securities on a contract that was illegal and void under the then Moneylenders Act of 1900 on the terms that the borrower should repay such money borrowed as remained outstanding. However, due to the particular circumstances of this case it cannot be considered as having established any wide general principle that is applicable to all moneylending cases that appear before the courts: see *Kasumu* v *Baba Egbe* [1956] AC 539.

Many kinds of documents may be ordered to be delivered up: negotiable instruments, forged documents, guarantees obtained by misrepresentation, policies of insurance and documents which 'form a cloud upon the title to land': see *Bromley* v *Holland* (1802) 7 Ves 3; *Hayward* v *Dinsdale* (1810) 17 Ves 111.

27.7 Receivers

Introduction

A receiver may be appointed either to preserve property which is in danger, or to enable a person to obtain the benefit of his rights over property, or to obtain payment of his debts where legal remedies are inadequate.

A receiver appointed without any other additional functions is only empowered to bring the operations of a business to a conclusion and to realise its trading assets – he is not a manager.

Methods of appointment

Appointment of a receiver out of court

1. A receiver may be appointed by debenture holders; his rights depend upon the document creating his powers. His primary duty, subject to specific statutory duties, is owed to those debenture holders. He is not bound by contracts to which the company (in which he is acting as receiver) is a party.

   Note: Under the Insolvency Act 1986 debenture holders have a right to appoint an 'administrative receiver' to procure the repayment of the monies owed to them by a company. The debenture holders, in such a case, may block the appointment of an administrator, whose function it is to revitalise the company.

2. A receiver is prima facie an agent for those who have made the appointment. His appointers may contract with the company to which he is attached that he shall be the agent of that company. This has the effect of making the company liable for the receiver's acts or defaults.

3. A receiver appointed out of court is entitled to remuneration or, if there is no such provision, to a claim on a quantum meruit basis.

Receiver appointed by the court

1. He is an officer of the court, therefore interference with the exercise of his duties is punishable by contempt of court.
2. He is personally liable for his acts.
3. The court may appoint two or more receivers to act jointly.
4. He is entitled to remuneration from the proceeds of the assets he has collected in.

Cases in which a receiver may be appointed by a court

Where 'the property is as it were in medio, in the enjoyment of no one, the court can hardly do wrong in taking possession. It is the common interest of all parties that the court should prevent a scramble': see *Owen* v *Homan* (1853) 4 HL Cas 997 at 1032.

As against executors and trustees

Where an executor or trustee is misapplying or mismanaging the assets.

Pending the grant of probate or letters of administration

Between vendors and purchasers

This can be in actions for specific performance or rescission. Particularly to preserve property, for example, to keep the mine working, the farm cultivated or, as in *Munns* v *Isle of Wight Railway Co* (1870) 5 Ch App 414, at the request of an unpaid vendor, in order to protect his lien against the purchaser who is in possession.

Creditors

Cummins v *Perkins* [1899] 1 Ch 16: if a creditor has a right to payment out of a particular fund he can obtain the equitable protection of a receiver to prevent that fund being dissipated.

Companies

Where the security of the company is in jeopardy, for example, where interest or repayment of principal is in arrears, or where a floating charge has crystallised into a fixed charge as the result of a winding up order.

Partnerships

To sell the business and realise assets when the partnership is obviously at an end.

Mortgages

At the request of the legal mortgagee, and at the request of an equitable mortgagee if the security is in jeopardy so long as there is no prior incumbrancer in possession: see *Berny* v *Sewell* (1820) 1 Jac & W 647.

Examples of other cases

1. Pending reference to arbitration.
2. Pending litigation in a foreign court.
3. For a mental patient: s99 Mental Health Act 1983.
4. Where a charity's affairs are in disarray.
5. Owner of a chattel is suing for its return by a bailee.

Equitable execution

The court may appoint a receiver in all cases in which it appears just and convenient so to do: s37 Supreme Court Act 1981. But no such appointment will be made if the assets are not available to be so taken in execution of law: for example, a debtor's future earnings, a patent which is not producing any profits: see *Edwards & Co* v *Picard* [1909] 2 KB 903 CA.

27.8 Account

Definition

The order is granted so that sums due to one party from the other, concerning specific types of transactions, may be impartially investigated.

Situations in which an account may be ordered

1. Principal against agent.
2. Mutual accounts, unless extremely simple.
3. Where the accounts are complicated.
4. Waste, where an injunction is sought, and waste had already been committed, and, in any case, equitable waste.
5. As an incidental to an injunction, but not for anything other than infringement of patent rights: see *Price's Patent Candle Co* v *Bauwens Patent Candle Co* [1958] 4 K & J 727.

Actions for account cannot be brought after the expiration of any time limit under the Act applicable to the claim which is the basis of the duty to account: s23 Limitation Act 1980.

Settled accounts

The plea may be sanctioned by the courts if the parties have agreed the account for valuable consideration and so the case should not be re-examined.

For a fuller explanation of the principle see the statement of Romer J in *Anglo-American Asphalt Co* v *Crowley and Russell & Co* [1945] 2 All ER 324 at 331.

To constitute a settled account it need not be signed by the parties, nor need vouchers be delivered up, and, despite the associated problems of evidence, it appears that oral agreements may be proved.

Settled accounts may be re-opened in the following circumstances:

1. If there has been mistake or fraud. The burden of proof is on the plaintiff. New accounts may be taken, additional debts ('surcharge') allowed, or an improperly inserted credit may be removed ('falsify').

2. 'If the court finds a credit bargain extortionate it may reopen the credit agreement so as to do justice between the parties': s137(1) Consumer Credit Act 1974.

27.9 Perpetuation of testimony

RSC (Rules of the Supreme Court) Ord. 39 r15:

> 'Any person who would under the circumstances alleged by him to exist become entitled, upon the happening of any future event, to any honour, title, dignity, or office, or to any estate or interest in any real or personal property, the right or claim to which cannot be brought to trial by him before the happening of such event, may begin an action to perpetuate any testimony which may be material for establishing such right or claim.'

This allows a person who fears that his right to a possession may be questioned by some unknown party at a later date to seal up his evidence and present it to the court, which may examine it at a later date if his right to the possession is questioned. This 'concerned person' cannot bring his action immediately, as no other cause of action is available to trigger off the case, neither is any suitable remedy.

The evidence held by the court could be taken from any form of witness, and may only be used in the event of them dying before the apprehended court hearing. Such evidence has also been used if a witness is too ill to attend, is prevented by accident from so attending, or is incapable of travelling to, the hearing: see *Biddulph v Lord Camoys* (1855) 20 Beav 402.

27.10 Ne exeat regno

The writ of ne exeat regno allows an equitable creditor to have a debtor, who he believes is about to leave the realm, arrested and made to give security for the debt if:

1. The action is one for which the debtor would formerly have been liable to arrest at law.
2. A sound cause of action for £50 or more is proven.
3. There is 'probable cause' to believe the debtor would otherwise flee the country if not arrested.
4. The defendant's absence would prejudice the plaintiff's prosecution of his action.

Such an award is discretionary and the standard of proof demanded, due to the custodial nature of the action, is so high that it is no surprise that a writ of this nature has very rarely been issued.

28

Recent Cases

28.1 Resulting trusts, constructive trusts and tracing

28.2 'Strangers'

28.3 The 'fair and reasonable' cases

28.1 Resulting trusts, constructive trusts and tracing

Westdeutsche Landesbank Girozentrale v *Islington London Borough Council* [1996] 2 All ER 961 House of Lords (Lords Goff, Browne-Wilkinson, Slynn, Woolf and Lloyd)

Local authority's ultra vires contract – compound or simple interest payable? – whether money held on trust for bank

Facts

The local authority had entered into an interest rate swap agreement with the bank. In an unrelated case in January 1991 the House of Lords held that interest rate swap transactions were outside the powers of local authorities and void ab initio. The bank, therefore, brought an action to recover from the local authority £1,145,525.93 and interest. The issue before the House of Lords was whether the local authority was liable to pay compound interest from the date that the bank had made the payments. The equitable jurisdiction to award compound interest exists, as per Lord Brandon in *President of India* v *La Pintada Cia Navegacion SA* [1984] 2 All ER 773, 779:

'... in cases where money had been obtained and retained by fraud, or where it had been withheld or misapplied by a trustee or anyone else in a fiduciary position.'

The question as to whether the local authority had to pay compound or simple interest depended upon whether it held the money on trust for the bank.

Held

The local authority, as a recipient of money under a contract subsequently found to be void for mistake or as being ultra vires, did not hold the money under a trust. The claim for money had and received under an ultra vires contract was a personal, restitutionary action based on the total failure of consideration. It would not be appropriate (Lords Goff and Woolf dissenting) to develop the law and award compound interest on the ground that equity could act in aid of the common law. The bank was entitled only to simple interest.

Comment

This is a very important decision in equity and trusts with far-reaching implications. It contains an extensive review of the circumstances when resulting and constructive trusts may arise.

Resulting trusts

Lord Browne-Wilkinson cast considerable doubt on the classification of resulting trusts made by Megarry J in *Re Vandervell's Trusts (No 2)* [1974] Ch 269. Lord Browne-Wilkinson identified two sets of circumstances when a resulting trust arises:

1. Where A makes a voluntary payment to B or pays (wholly or in part) for the purchase of property which is vested either in B alone or in the joint names of A and B, there is a presumption that A did not intend to make a gift to B: the money or property is held on trust for A (if he is a sole provider of the money) or, in the case of a joint purchase by A and B, in shares proportionate to their contributions.
2. Where A transfers property to B on express trusts, but the trusts declared do not exhaust the whole beneficial interest.

He went on to say at p991:

'Megarry J in *Re Vandervell's Trusts (No 2)* suggests that a resulting trust of type [1] does not depend on intention but operates automatically. I am not convinced that this is right. If the settlor has expressly, or by necessary implication, abandoned any beneficial interest in the trust property, there is in my view no resulting trust: the undisposed of equitable interest vests in the Crown as bona vacantia: see *Re West Sussex Constabulary's Widows, Children and Benevolent (1930) Fund Trusts* [1970] 1 All ER 544; [1971] Ch 1.'

If this view is followed, it would seem that the circumstances when a resulting trust will arise will turn purely on intention and the only type of resulting trust is the presumed resulting trust. This may well have an influential effect in determining ownership in cases where there is a surplus when the trust has been fulfilled.

Constructive trusts

Lord Browne-Wilkinson suggested that, if the remedial constructive trust were introduced into English law, it might provide a suitable basis for developing proprietary restitutionary remedies.

There is considerable support in this decision for the view that an innocent volunteer who has received trust property is not a constructive trustee of that property. Lord Browne-Wilkinson stated three principles relevant to the imposition of a constructive trust:

1. A constructive trust is imposed because of unconscionable conduct.
2. A person cannot be a trustee if ignorant of the facts alleged to affect his conscience.
3. There must be identifiable trust property, the only apparent exception to this rule being where a constructive trust is imposed on a person who *dishonestly* (emphasis added) assists in a breach of trust.

He then went on to cite *Re Montagu's Settlement Trust* [1987] 2 WLR 1587 and *Re Diplock* [1948] Ch 465, concluding that innocent receipt of property by a third party subject to an existing equitable interest does not by itself make the third party a trustee. This also appears to affirm, albeit indirectly, the test of dishonesty required, according to the advice of the Privy Council in *Royal Brunei Airlines Sdn Bhd* v *Philip Tan Kok Ming* [1995] 3 All ER 97, in order to impose liability on a stranger who assists in a breach of trust.

Property obtained through unlawful conduct

The *Westdeutsche* case also authoritatively resolves that, in English law, property obtained by theft is subject to a constructive trust.

Tracing

Although it remains impossible to classify all the situations in which an initial fiduciary relationship might arise, two controversial decisions were reconsidered by the House of Lords. The lower courts had concluded that there was jurisdiction to award compound interest to the bank because they were bound by the House of Lords authority in *Sinclair* v *Brougham* [1914] AC 398 to the effect that a trust arises in cases where money has been made under a contract which is ultra vires and, therefore, void ab initio. The majority of the House of Lords in the *Westdeutsche* case, Lords Lloyd and Slynn concurring with the reasoning of Lord Browne-Wilkinson, departed from the decision in *Sinclair* v *Brougham*. Lord Browne-Wilkinson overruled the decision on two grounds:

1. He rejected the concept that the claim for monies had and received is based on implied contract. The common law restitutionary claim is based not on implied contract but on unjust enrichment.
2. He overruled the decision as to rights in rem. A claimant for restitution of monies paid under an ultra vires and, therefore, void contract has a personal action at law to recover the monies paid as on a total failure of consideration. He or she will not have an equitable proprietary claim which gives rights against third parties or property in insolvency, nor will there be a personal claim in equity, since the recipient is not a trustee.

As a result of the departure from *Sinclair* v *Brougham*, the local authority in the *Westdeutsche* case was neither a trustee of, nor in a fiduciary position in respect of the money which it had received from the bank, and according to the majority, in such circumstances, there was no jurisdiction to award compound interest.

The comments of Lord Browne-Wilkinson in respect of the decision of Goulding J in *Chase Manhattan Bank* v *Israel British Bank* [1981] Ch 105 must also cast considerable doubt on the underlying rationale of that case. Lord Browne-Wilkinson explained that Goulding J held that,

'where money was paid under a mistake, the receipt of such money *without more* constituted the recipient a trustee: ... the payer "retains an equitable property in it and the conscience of" [the recipient] is subjected to a fiduciary duty to respect his proprietary right'.

Lord Browne-Wilkinson went on to say at p997:

'... I cannot agree with this reasoning. First, it is based on a concept of retaining an equitable property right in money where, prior to the payment to the recipient bank, there was no existing equitable interest. Further, I cannot understand how the recipient's "conscience" can be affected at a time when he is not aware of any mistake.'

Although Lord Browne-Wilkinson rejected the reasoning of Goulding J, he considered *Chase Manhattan* to have been rightly decided on the basis that the defendant bank knew of the mistake made by the paying bank within two days of the receipt of the money and that the retention of the money after the recipient bank learned of the mistake gave rise to a constructive trust.

28.2 'Strangers'

Brinks Ltd v *Abu-Saleh and Others (No 3)* (1995) The Times 23 October Chancery Division (Rimer J)

Whether accessory to breach of trust had to be aware of breach

Facts
The case arose as a consequence of the Brinks bullion robbery at Heathrow in 1983. The breach of trust was by a security guard employed by Brinks. One of the defendants, Mrs Elcombe, had accompanied her husband on car trips from England and Zurich when he was laundering money by carrying £3 million cash for one of the convicted robbers, a Mr Parry. Counsel for Brinks argued that, as a direct result of *Royal Brunei Airlines Sdn Bhd* v *Philip Tan Kok Ming*, in order to fix Mrs Elcombe with liability in equity as an accessory, all that was required was to prove:

1. that she had rendered assistance in what, objectively assessed, was a dishonest transaction;
2. that the transaction involved a breach of trust.

Held
Rimer J held that both Mr and Mrs Elcombe believed the source of the money to be derived from Mr Parry's business empire and was the subject of a tax evasion

scheme. They did not know that the source of the money was the breach of trust by Anthony Black and Mrs Elcombe could not, therefore, be liable for dishonest assistance in a breach of trust.

Comment

Rimer J concluded, albeit obiter, that there was no foundation for the argument put by counsel for Brinks that an individual could be liable as an accessory to a breach of trust even though unaware of the breach of trust. He interpreted the *Royal Brunei Airlines* case as providing sound authority against the imposition of liability against an accessory who dealt with a trustee in ignorance that he was a trustee, or who knew that he was a trustee but had no reason to know or suspect that the transaction in which he was assisting was a breach of trust. This is undoubtedly a correct interpretation of the opinion of Lord Nicholls, who not only rejected the imposition of liability when a third party is wholly unaware of the existence of a trust, but also rejected the imposition of liability on an honest third party who procures or assists in a breach of trust of which he would have become aware had he exercised reasonable diligence. Despite Lord Nicholls' suggestion that the five levels of knowledge outlined in *Baden Delvaux* v *Société Generale* [1983] 1 WLR 509 were 'best forgotten', they were cited by counsel for Brinks and, unfortunately, appear destined to be relied upon in legal argument.

28.3 The 'fair and reasonable' cases

Drake v *Whipp* [1996] 1 FLR 826 Court of Appeal (Hirst and Peter Gibson LJJ and Forbes J)

Joint contribution to purchase of property – subsequent expenditure – evidence of common intention – resulting trusts

Facts

Mrs Drake and Mr Whipp had contributed directly towards the purchase price of a barn which they intended to convert into a home in which to live together. The property was in need of substantial conversion and when it was conveyed into Mr Whipp's sole name, a considerable amount of money had already been spent on the costs of conversion. Those costs were largely met by Mr Whipp. Mrs Drake provided 40.1 per cent of the initial purchase price and claimed a corresponding beneficial interest on the basis of a mathematical calculation of a resulting trust in her favour which excluded the subsequent contribution of Mr Whipp to the enhancement of the property. The judge refused to exclude Mr Whipp's contribution and awarded Mrs Drake a beneficial share of 19.4 per cent, amounting to £43,650, and it was against his finding on resulting trust principles that Mrs Drake appealed.

Held

In delivering the judgment of the Court of Appeal, Peter Gibson LJ concluded that once there was evidence of common intention to share property, a situation as in the first category in *Lloyd's Bank plc* v *Rosset* [1990] 2 WLR 867, resulting trust principles were thereby displaced. There was clear evidence that the parties intended to share the property beneficially but no evidence of an agreement as to what their respective shares should be. Peter Gibson LJ noted that it was open to Mrs Drake to argue at the trial for a constructive trust and for a 50 per cent share but that she had opted to rely on a resulting trust and a 40.1 per cent share, and he took into account the parties' entire course of conduct. Mrs Drake was awarded a third share of the property, amounting to £75,000, by way of a common intention constructive trust.

Comment

The exclusion of resulting trust principles on the basis of express agreement to share the property beneficially is controversial and highly debatable on the facts of the case. There is no intimation in *Lloyd's Bank plc* v *Rosset* that the categories are mutually exclusive, and *Drake* v *Whipp* is inconsistent with earlier authorities such as *Re Densham* [1975] 3 All ER 727 where a claim under a resulting trust yielded a one-ninth share but a claim under a constructive trust yielded a half share. The case also highlights the scope for considerable judicial discretion in quantifying beneficial shares within the first category with the usual implication of inconsistency and unreliability. Peter Gibson LJ also welcomed the announcement that the Law Commission is to examine the property rights of home-sharers and the hope that reform occurs soon can only be re-iterated.

Index

405

Old Bailey Press

The Old Bailey Press integrated student library is planned and written to help you at every stage of your studies. Each of our range of Textbooks, Casebooks, Revision WorkBooks and Statutes are all designed to work together and are regularly revised and updated.

We are also able to offer you Suggested Solutions which provide you with past examination questions and solutions for most of the subject areas listed below.

You can buy Old Bailey Press books from your University Bookshop or your local Bookshop, or in case of difficulty, order direct using this form.

Here is the selection of modules covered by our series:

Administrative Law; Commercial Law; Company Law (no Single Paper 1997); Conflict of Laws (no Suggested Solutions Pack); Constitutional Law: The Machinery of Government; Obligations: Contract Law; Conveyancing (no Revision Workbook); Criminology (Sourcebook in place of a Casebook or Revision WorkBook); Criminal Law; English Legal System; Equity and Trusts; Law of The European Union; Evidence; Family Law; Jurisprudence: The Philosophy of Law (Sourcebook in place of a Casebook); Land: The Law of Real Property; Law of International Trade; Legal Skills and System (Textbook only); Public International Law; Revenue Law (no Casebook); Succession: The Law of Wills and Estates; Obligations: The Law of Tort.

Mail order prices:

Textbook £11.95

Casebook £9.95

Revision WorkBook £7.95

Statutes £9.95

Suggested Solutions Pack (1991–1995) £6.95

Single Paper 1996 £3.00

Single Paper 1997 £3.00

To complete your order, please fill in the form below:

Module	Books required	Quantity	Price	Cost
		Postage		
		TOTAL		

For Europe, add 15% postage and packing (£20 maximum).
For the rest of the world, add 40% for airmail.

ORDERING

By telephone to Mail Order at 020 7385 3377, with your credit card to hand.

By fax to 020 7381 3377 (giving your credit card details).

By post to:

Old Bailey Press, 200 Greyhound Road, London W14 9RY.

When ordering by post, please enclose full payment by cheque or banker's draft, or complete the credit card details below.

We aim to despatch your books within 3 working days of receiving your order.

Name

Address

Postcode   Telephone

Total value of order, including postage: £

I enclose a cheque/banker's draft for the above sum, or

charge my   ☐ Access/Mastercard   ☐ Visa   ☐ American Express
Card number

☐☐☐☐ ☐☐☐☐ ☐☐☐☐ ☐☐☐☐

Expiry date   ☐☐☐☐

Signature: ....Date: ....